"It's not a dream
if you believe it."

—Fernando Funger

ONI PRESS

AN ONI PRESS PUBLICATION

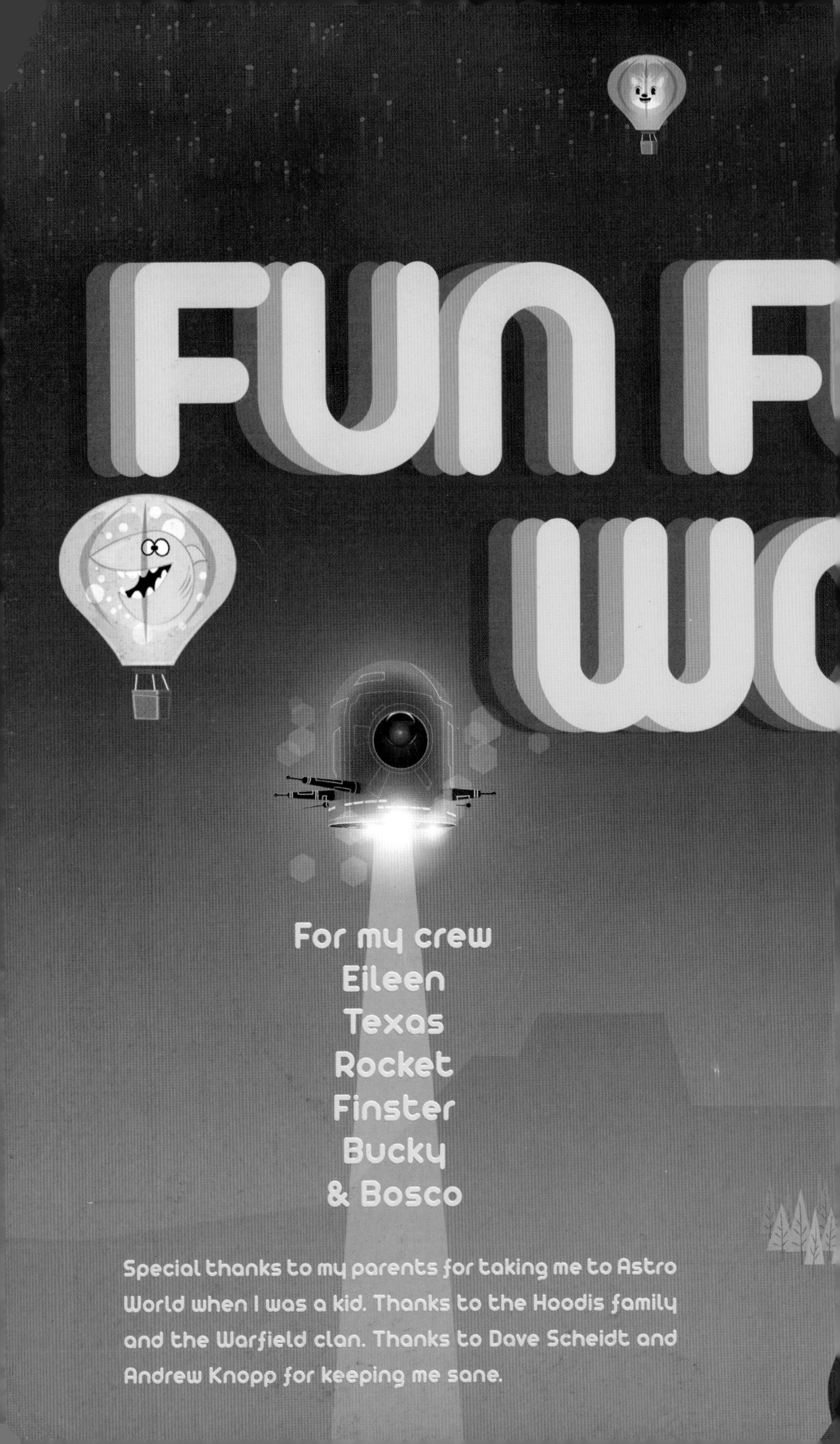
FUN

For my crew
Eileen
Texas
Rocket
Finster
Bucky
& Bosco

Special thanks to my parents for taking me to Astro World when I was a kid. Thanks to the Hoodis family and the Warfield clan. Thanks to Dave Scheidt and Andrew Knopp for keeping me sane.

WRITTEN AND ILLUSTRATED BY
yehudi mercado
with additional art assistance by sophia hoodis

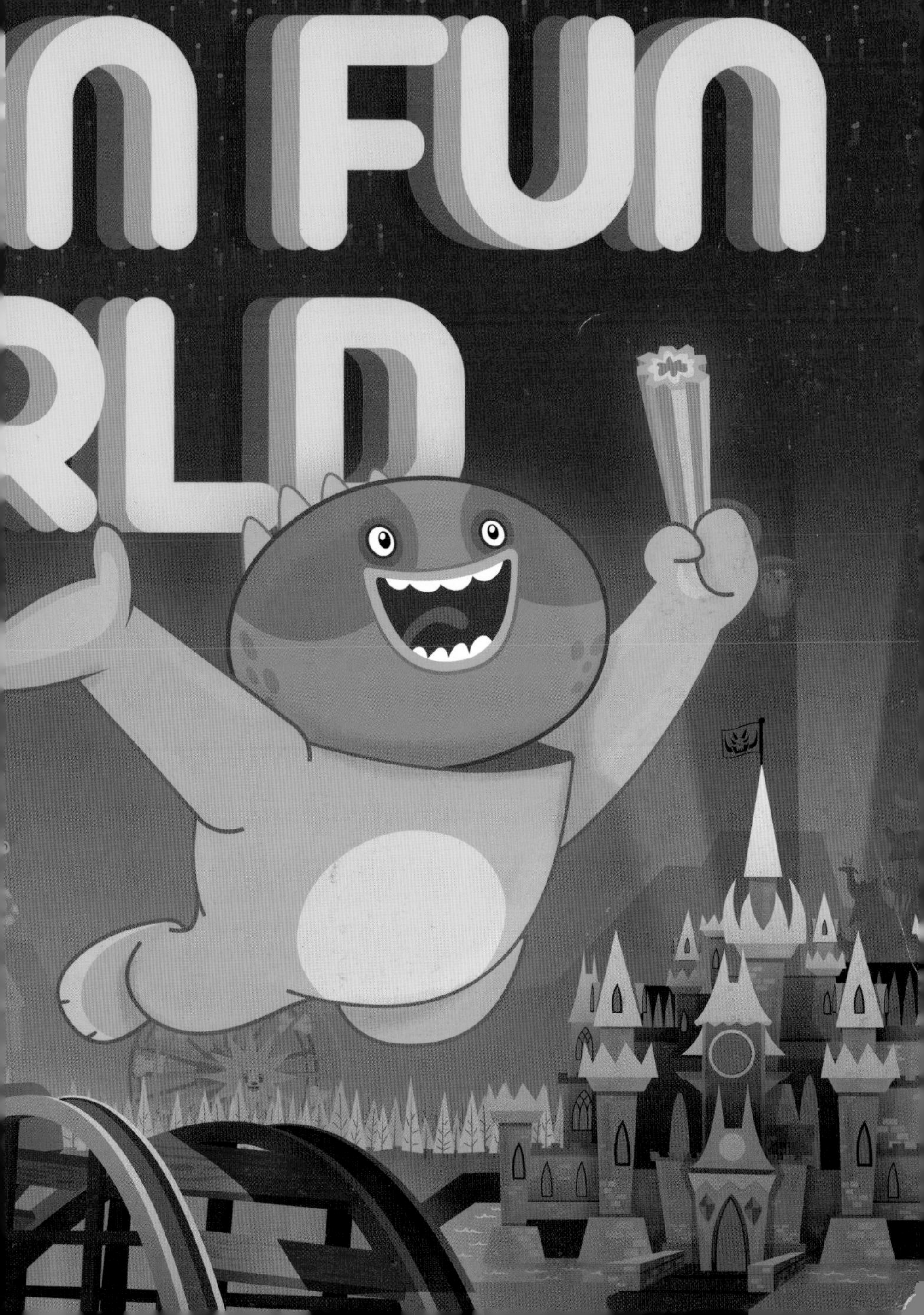
N FUN
RLD

DESIGNED BY Chad Beckerman and Sonja Synak
EDITED BY Andrea Colvin
ADDITIONAL EDITING ASSISTANCE BY Grace Bornhoft

PUBLISHED BY ONI PRESS, INC.

JAMES LUCAS JONES, PRESIDENT & PUBLISHER

SARAH GAYDOS, EDITOR IN CHIEF

CHARLIE CHU, E.V.P. OF CREATIVE & BUSINESS DEVELOPMENT

BRAD ROOKS, DIRECTOR OF OPERATIONS

AMBER O'NEILL, SPECIAL PROJECTS MANAGER

HARRIS FISH, EVENTS MANAGER

MARGOT WOOD, DIRECTOR OF MARKETING & SALES

JEREMY ATKINS, DIRECTOR OF BRAND COMMUNICATIONS

DEVIN FUNCHES, SALES & MARKETING MANAGER

TARA LEHMANN, MARKETING & PUBLICITY ASSOCIATE

TROY LOOK, DIRECTOR OF DESIGN & PRODUCTION

KATE Z. STONE, SENIOR GRAPHIC DESIGNER

SONJA SYNAK, GRAPHIC DESIGNER

HILARY THOMPSON, GRAPHIC DESIGNER

ANGIE KNOWLES, DIGITAL PREPRESS LEAD

SHAWNA GORE, SENIOR EDITOR

ROBIN HERRERA, SENIOR EDITOR

AMANDA MEADOWS, SENIOR EDITOR

JASMINE AMIRI, EDITOR

GRACE BORNHOFT, EDITOR

ZACK SOTO, EDITOR

STEVE ELLIS, DIRECTOR OF GAMES

BEN EISNER, GAME DEVELOPER

MICHELLE NGUYEN, EXECUTIVE ASSISTANT

JUNG LEE, LOGISTICS COORDINATOR

JOE NOZEMACK, PUBLISHER EMERITUS

onipress.com | lionforge.com
facebook.com/onipress | facebook.com/lionforge
twitter.com/onipress | twitter.com/lionforge
instagram.com/onipress | instagram.com/lionforge

supermercado.pizza

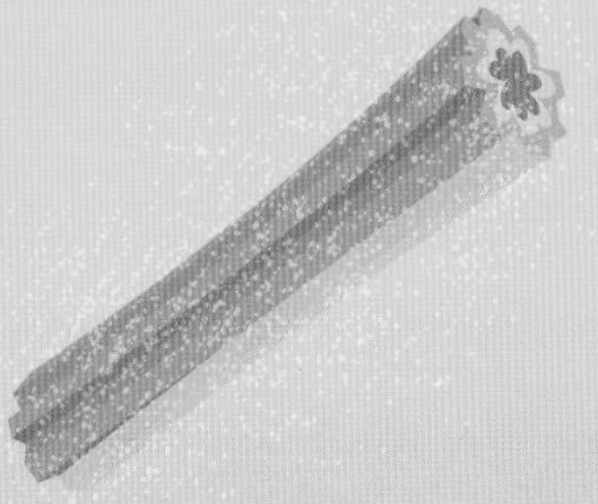

First Edition: April 2020

ISBN 978-1-62010-732-4
eISBN 978-1-62010-722-5
Variant ISBN: 978-1-62010-733-1

UN FUN WORLD, April 2020. Published by Oni-Lion Forge Publishing Group, LLC, 1319 SE Martin Luther
Jr. Blvd., Suite 240, Portland, OR 97214.

Printed in China.

Library of Congress Control Number: 2019945919

1 3 5 7 9 10 8 6 4 2

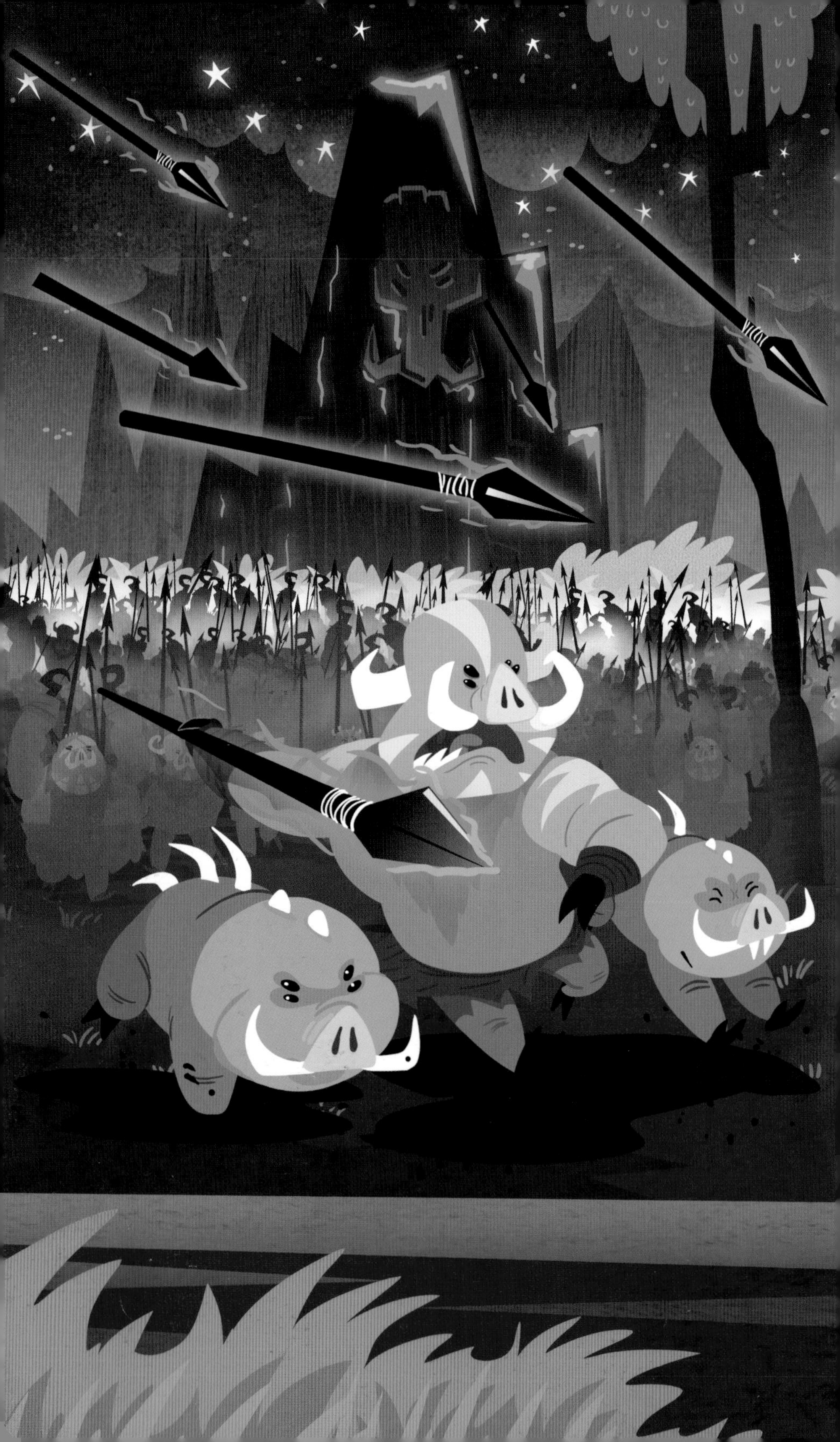

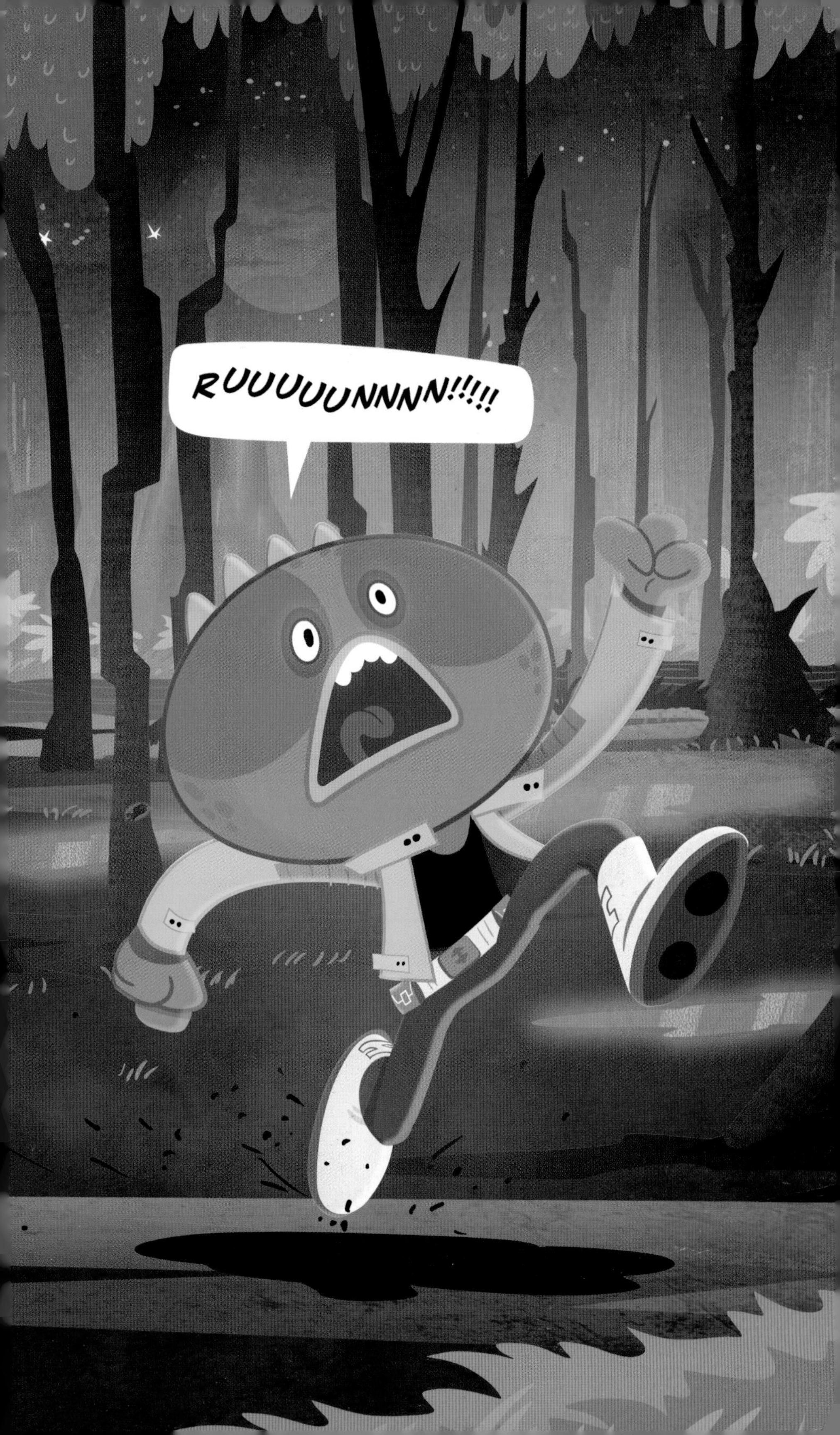
RUUUUUNNNN!!!!!

PLANET GARGLASH
WHY DO ALL OF OUR MISSIONS END WITH MINKY YELLING RUUUUUN?!?!?!
THIS IS GOING IN MY REPORT!
MINKY: CAPTAIN
ILLY: SCIENCE OFFICER
NOYTCH: COMMUNICATIONS OFFICER

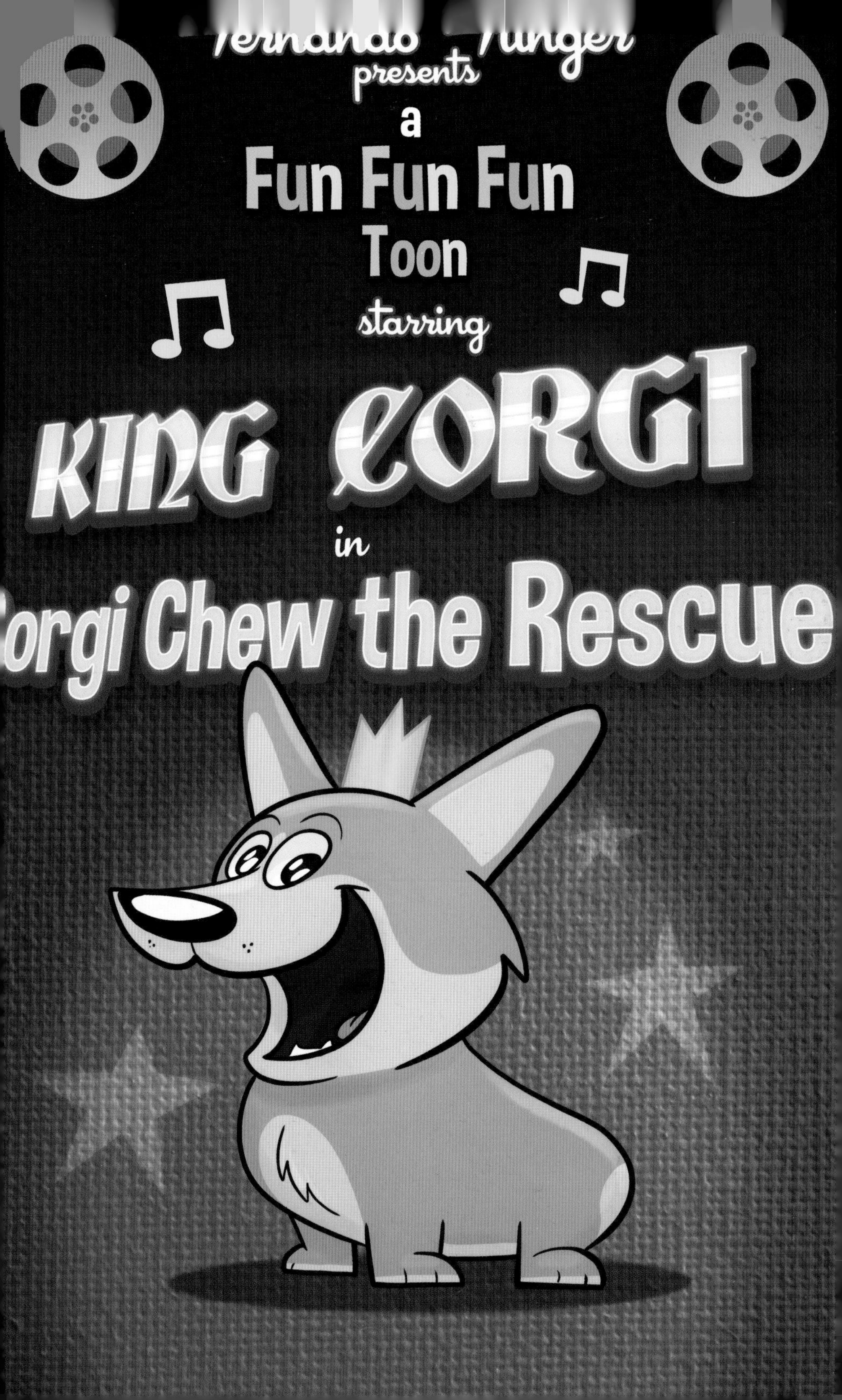
presents
a
Fun Fun Fun
Toon
starring
KING CORGI
in
orgi Chew the Rescue

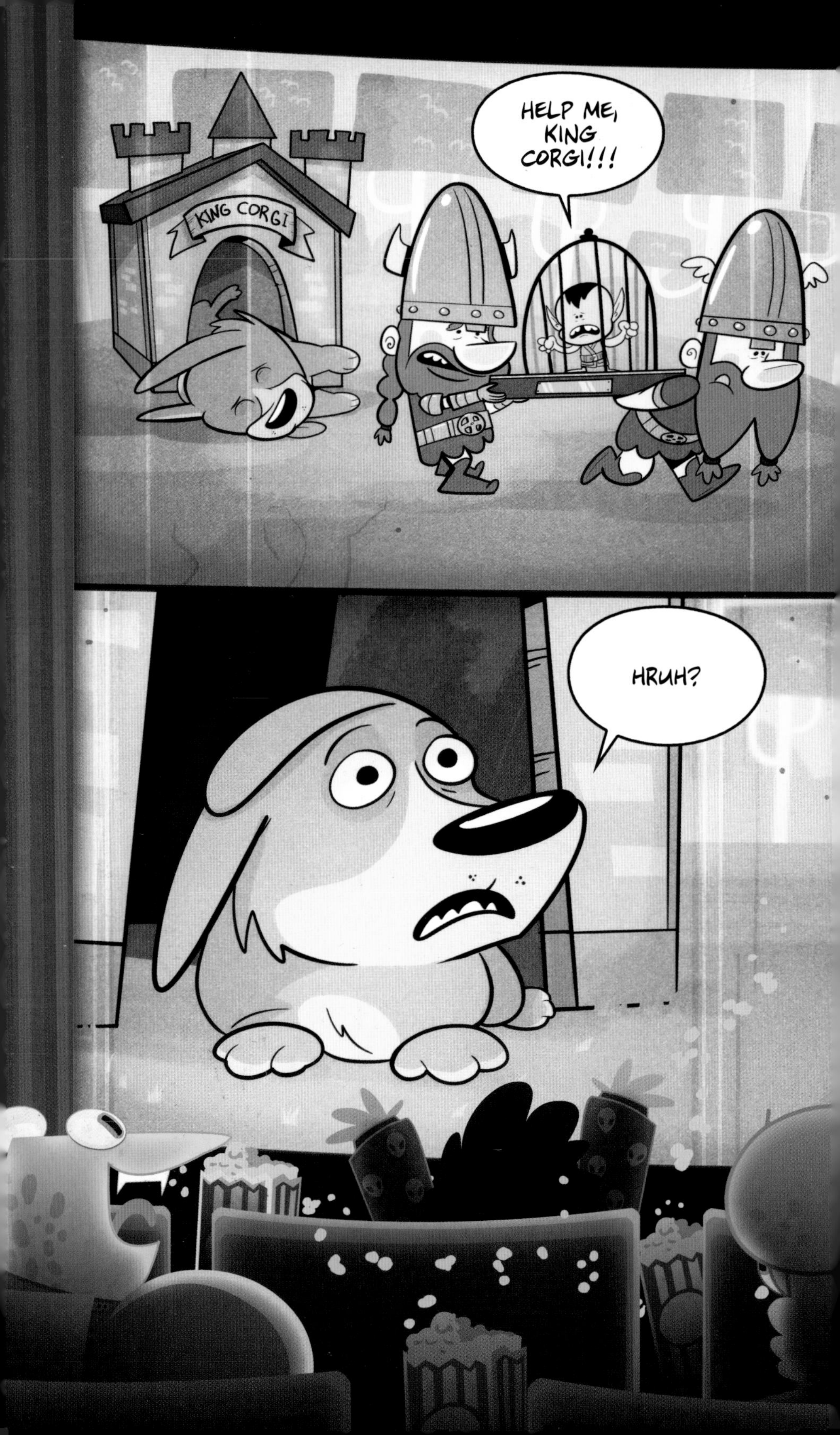
KING CORGI
HELP ME, KING CORGI!!!
HRUH?

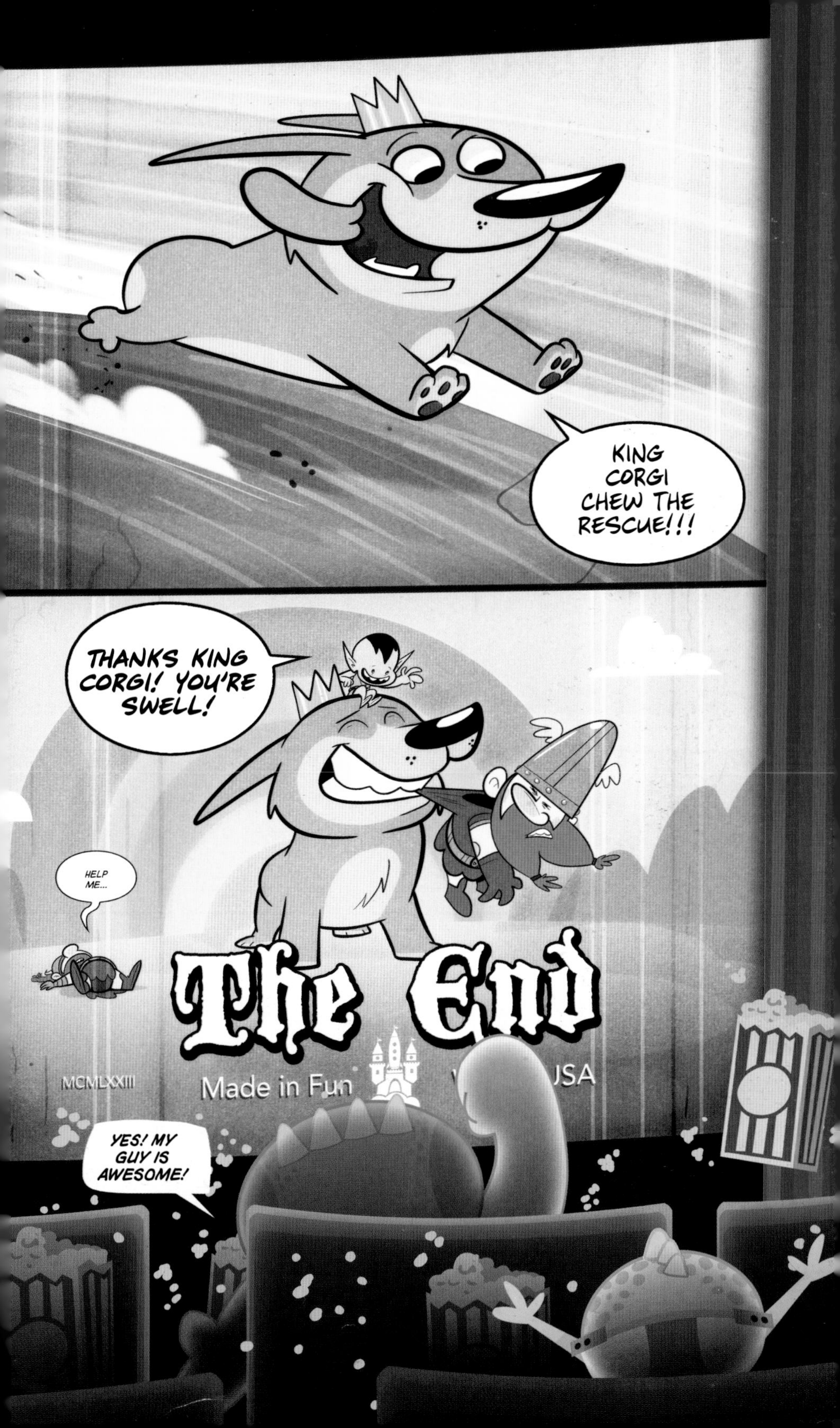
KING CORGI CHEW THE RESCUE!!!
THANKS KING CORGI! YOU'RE SWELL!
HELP ME...
The End
MCMLXXIII
Made in Fun
USA
YES! MY GUY IS AWESOME!

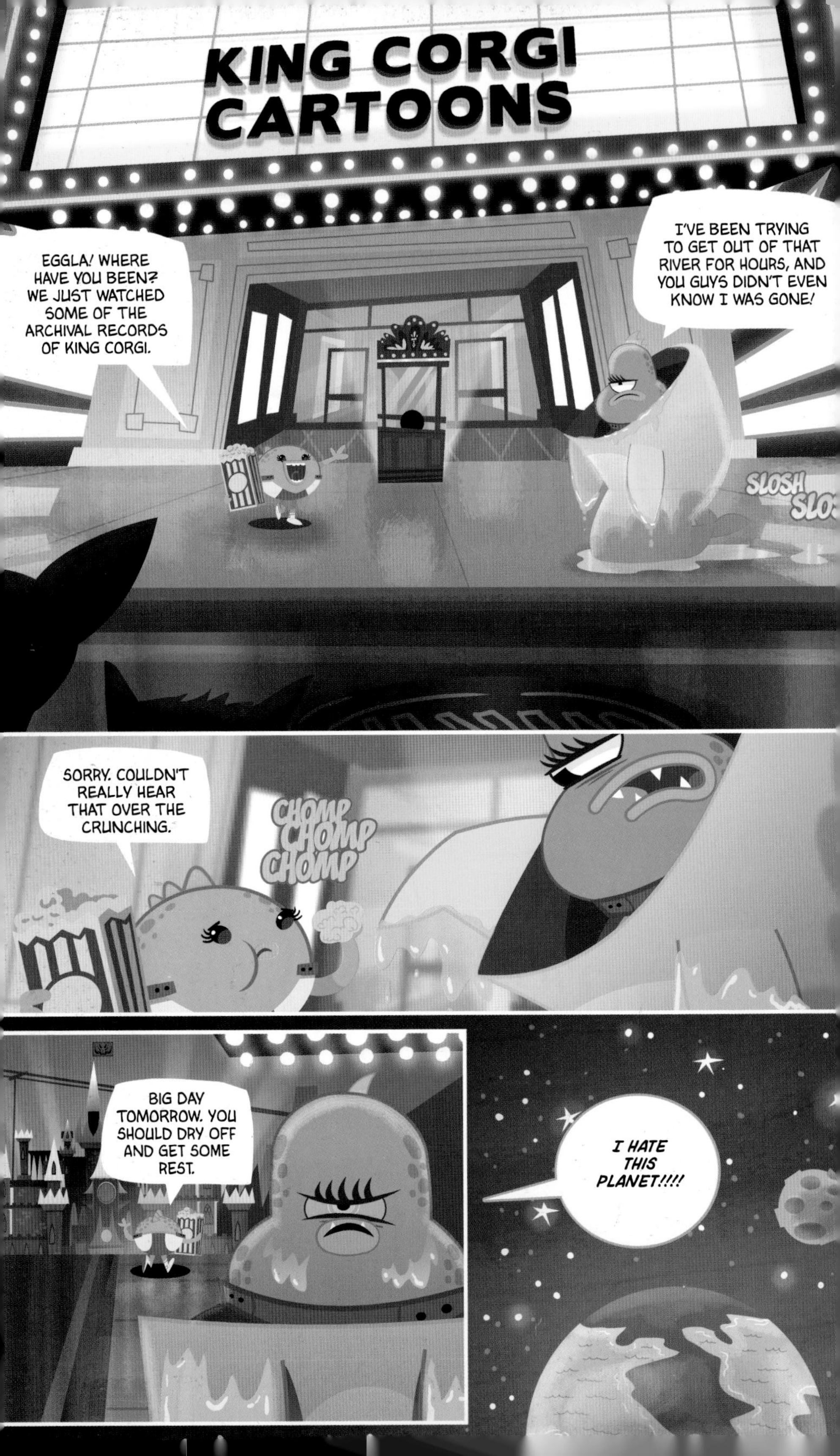
KING CORGI CARTOONS
EGGLA! WHERE HAVE YOU BEEN? WE JUST WATCHED SOME OF THE ARCHIVAL RECORDS OF KING CORGI.
I'VE BEEN TRYING TO GET OUT OF THAT RIVER FOR HOURS, AND YOU GUYS DIDN'T EVEN KNOW I WAS GONE!
SLOSH
SORRY. COULDN'T REALLY HEAR THAT OVER THE CRUNCHING.
CHOMP CHOMP CHOMP
BIG DAY TOMORROW. YOU SHOULD DRY OFF AND GET SOME REST.
I HATE THIS PLANET!!!!

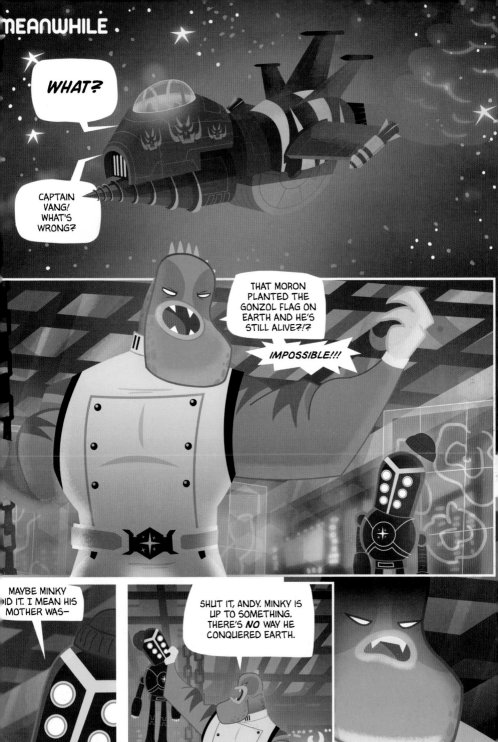

WHAT?

CAPTAIN VANG! WHAT'S WRONG?

THAT MORON PLANTED THE GONZOL FLAG ON EARTH AND HE'S STILL ALIVE?!?

IMPOSSIBLE!!!

MAYBE MINKY DID IT. I MEAN HIS MOTHER WAS—

SHUT IT, ANDY. MINKY IS UP TO SOMETHING. THERE'S NO WAY HE CONQUERED EARTH.

I NEED TO GET TO THE BOTTOM OF THIS.

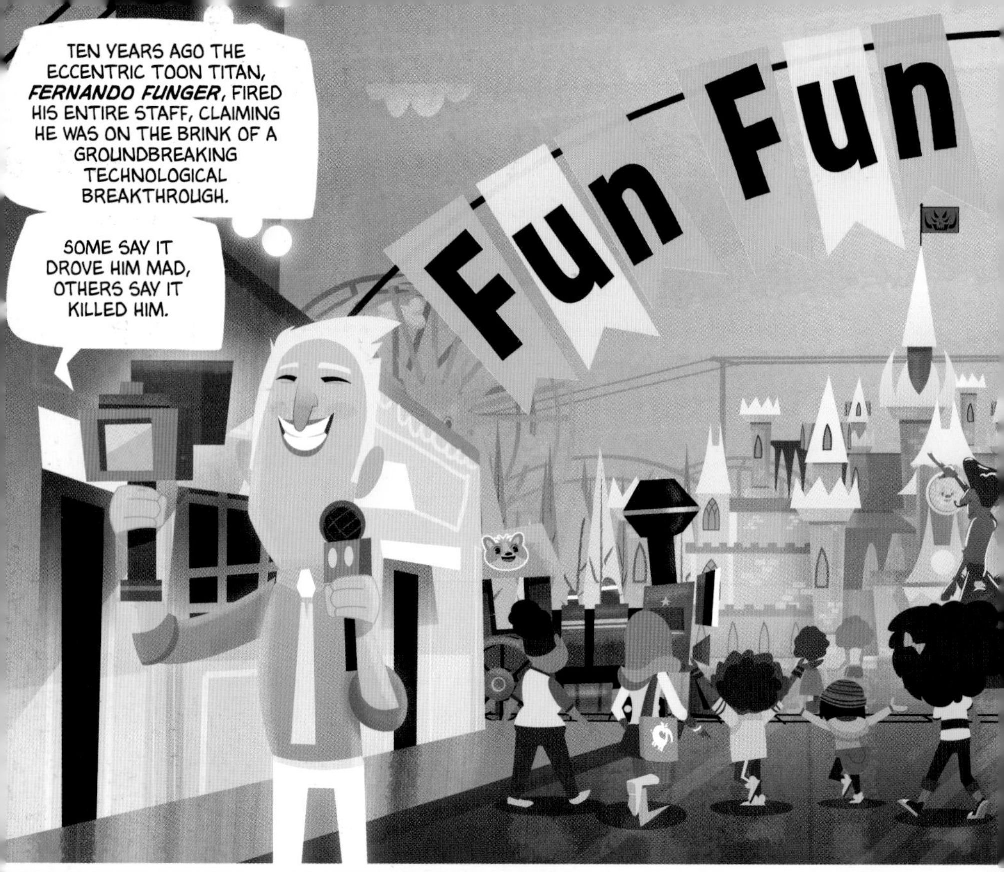
TEN YEARS AGO THE ECCENTRIC TOON TITAN, ***FERNANDO FUNGER***, FIRED HIS ENTIRE STAFF, CLAIMING HE WAS ON THE BRINK OF A GROUNDBREAKING TECHNOLOGICAL BREAKTHROUGH.
SOME SAY IT DROVE HIM MAD, OTHERS SAY IT KILLED HIM.
Fun Fun

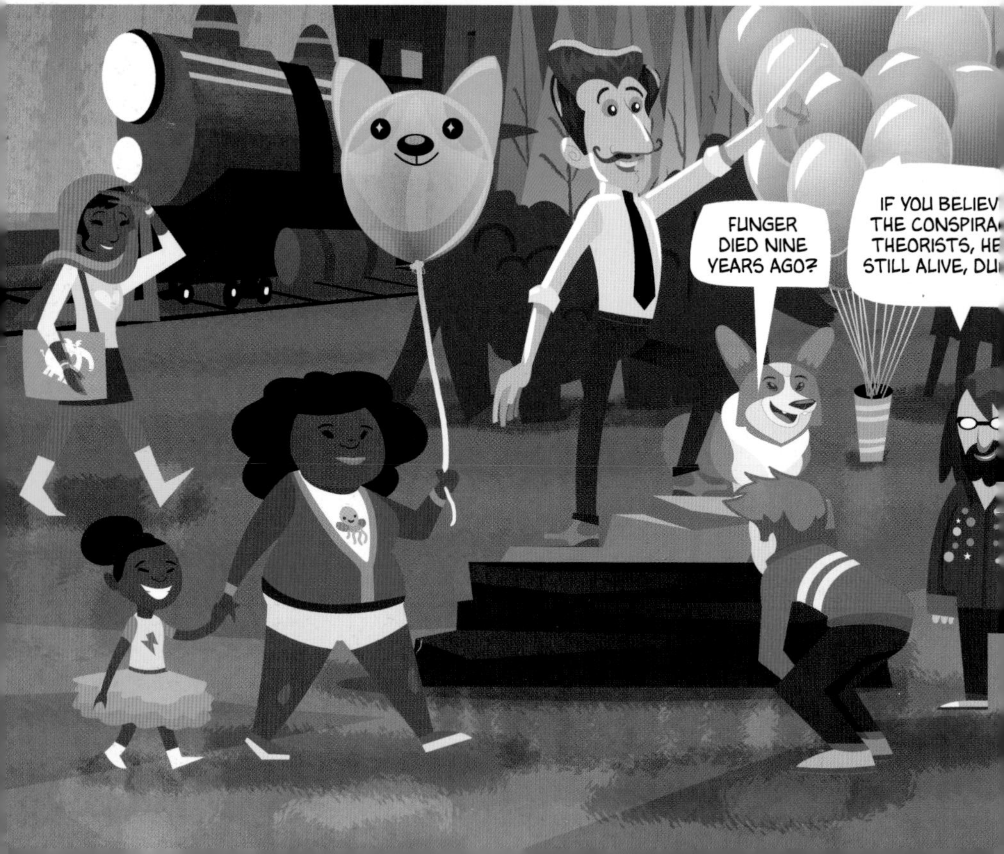
FUNGER DIED NINE YEARS AGO?
IF YOU BELIEV THE CONSPIRA THEORISTS, HE STILL ALIVE, DU

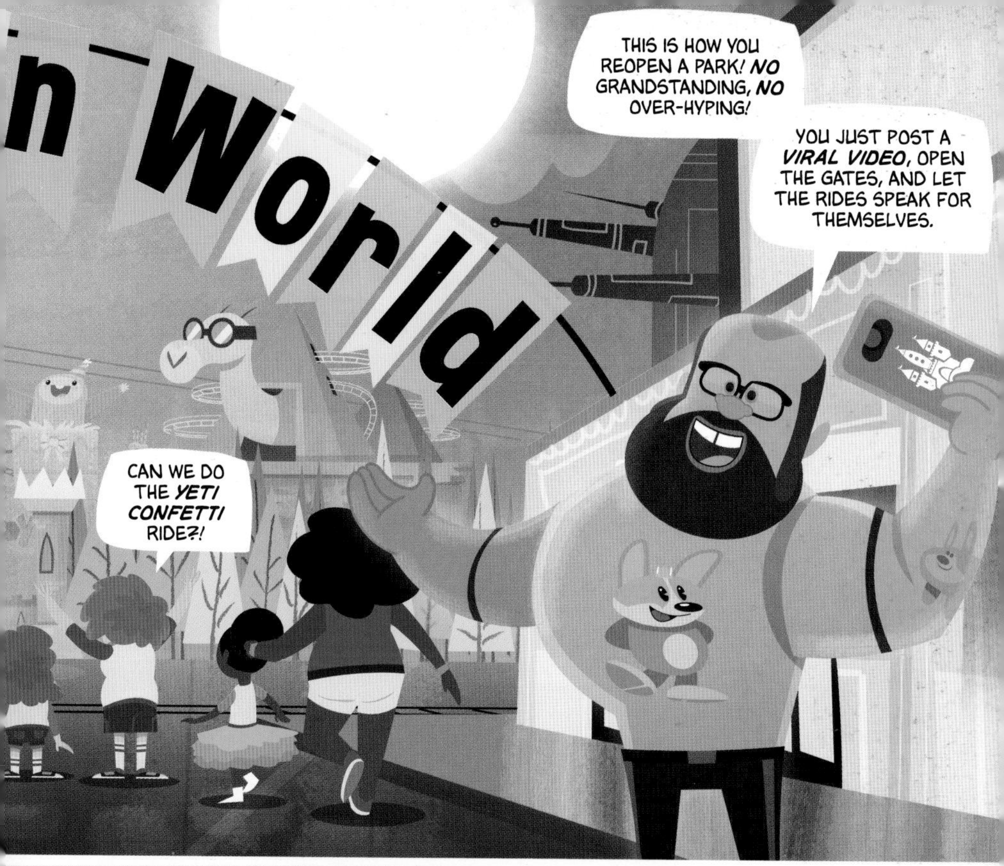
n World
THIS IS HOW YOU REOPEN A PARK! NO GRANDSTANDING, NO OVER-HYPING!
YOU JUST POST A VIRAL VIDEO, OPEN THE GATES, AND LET THE RIDES SPEAK FOR THEMSELVES.
CAN WE DO THE YETI CONFETTI RIDE?!

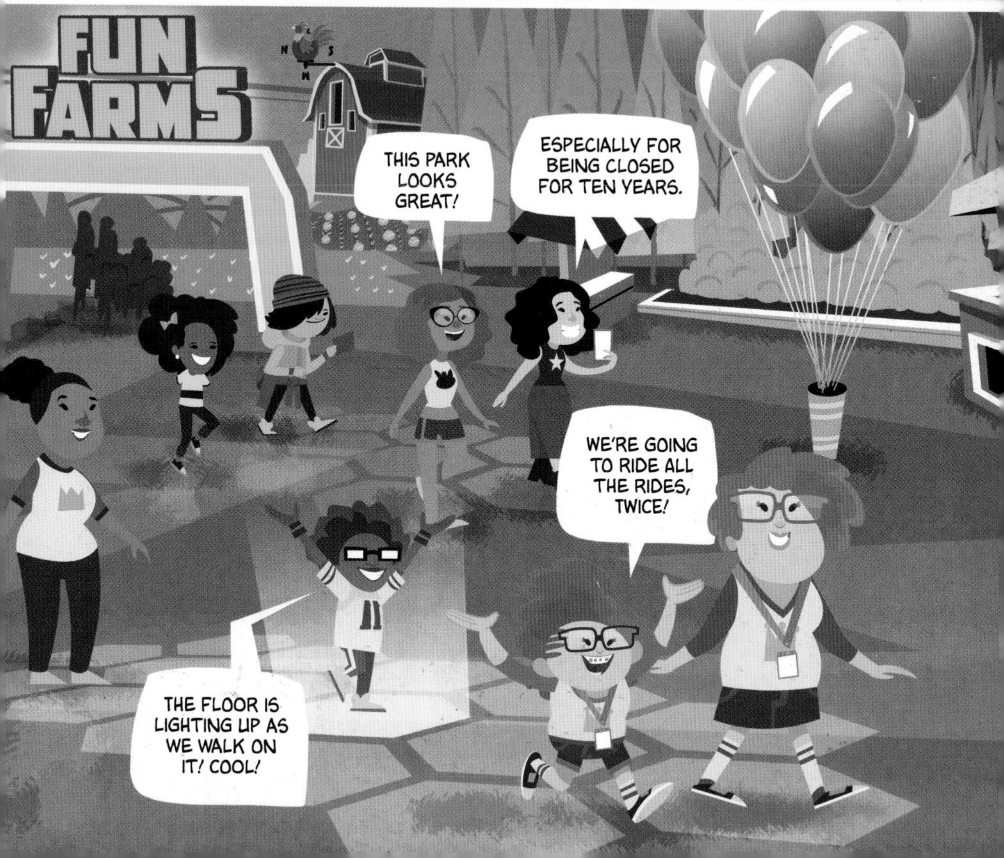
FUN FARMS
THIS PARK LOOKS GREAT!
ESPECIALLY FOR BEING CLOSED FOR TEN YEARS.
WE'RE GOING TO RIDE ALL THE RIDES, TWICE!
THE FLOOR IS LIGHTING UP AS WE WALK ON IT! COOL!

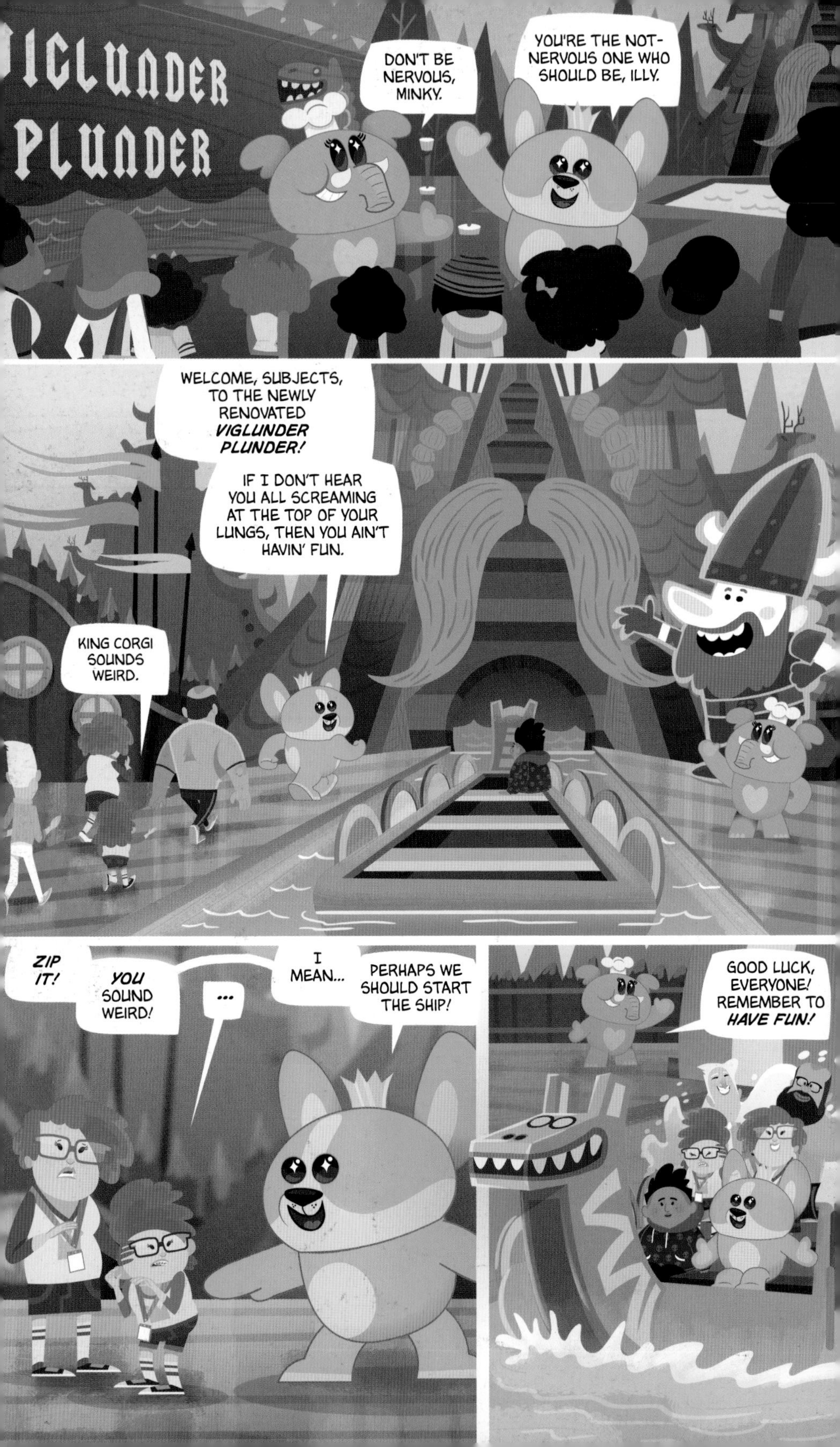
VIGLUNDER PLUNDER
DON'T BE NERVOUS, MINKY.
YOU'RE THE NOT-NERVOUS ONE WHO SHOULD BE, ILLY.
WELCOME, SUBJECTS, TO THE NEWLY RENOVATED *VIGLUNDER PLUNDER!*
IF I DON'T HEAR YOU ALL SCREAMING AT THE TOP OF YOUR LUNGS, THEN YOU AIN'T HAVIN' FUN.
KING CORGI SOUNDS WEIRD.
ZIP IT!
YOU SOUND WEIRD!
...
I MEAN...
PERHAPS WE SHOULD START THE SHIP!
GOOD LUCK, EVERYONE! REMEMBER TO *HAVE FUN!*

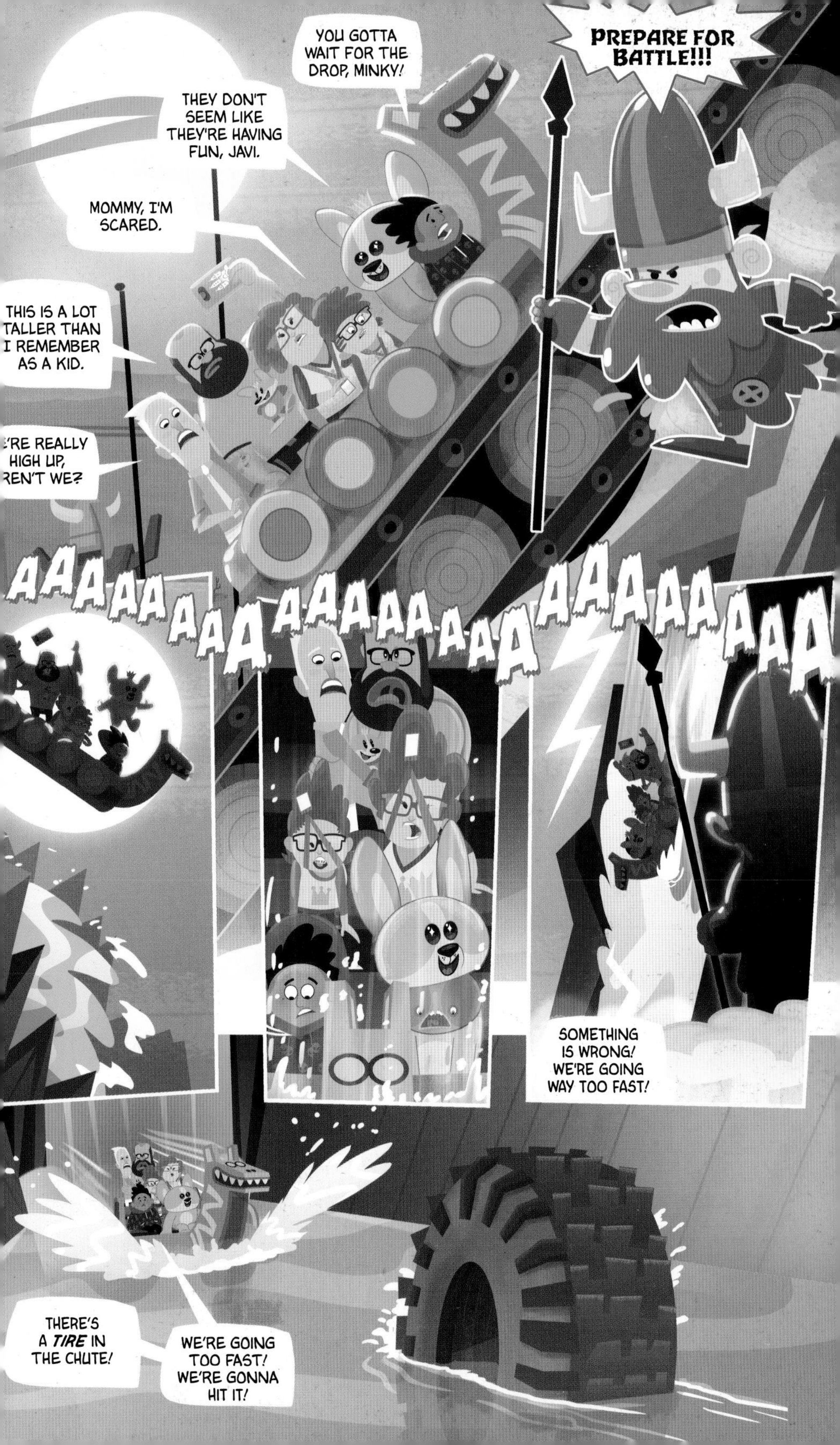
YOU GOTTA WAIT FOR THE DROP, MINKY!
PREPARE FOR BATTLE!!!
THEY DON'T SEEM LIKE THEY'RE HAVING FUN, JAVI.
MOMMY, I'M SCARED.
THIS IS A LOT TALLER THAN I REMEMBER AS A KID.
RE REALLY HIGH UP, REN'T WE?
AAAAAAAAAAAAAAAAAAAAAAAAAAAAAA
SOMETHING IS WRONG! WE'RE GOING WAY TOO FAST!
THERE'S A *TIRE* IN THE CHUTE!
WE'RE GOING TOO FAST! WE'RE GONNA HIT IT!

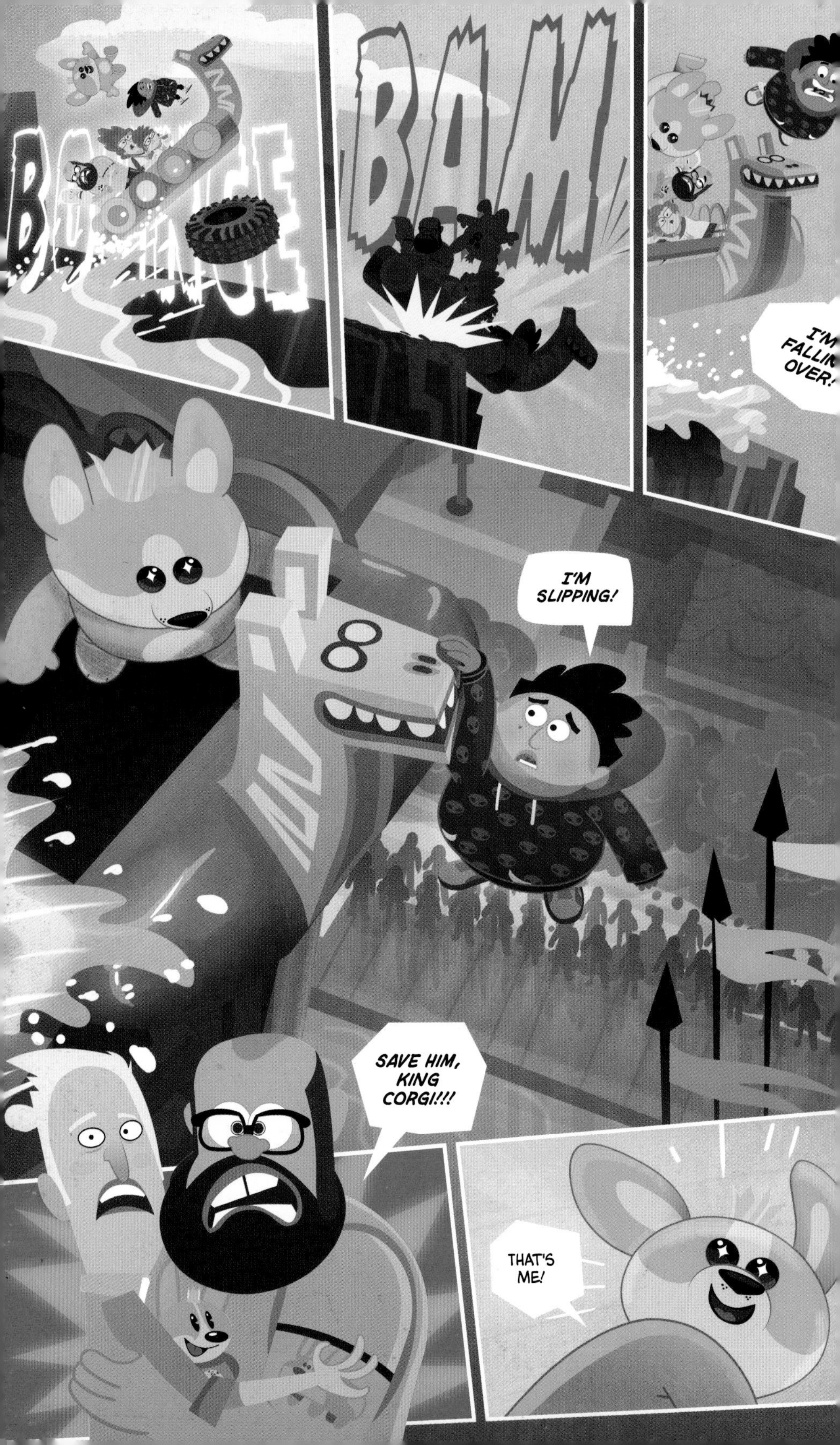
BAM
I'M FALLING OVER!
I'M SLIPPING!
SAVE HIM, KING CORGI!!!
THAT'S ME!

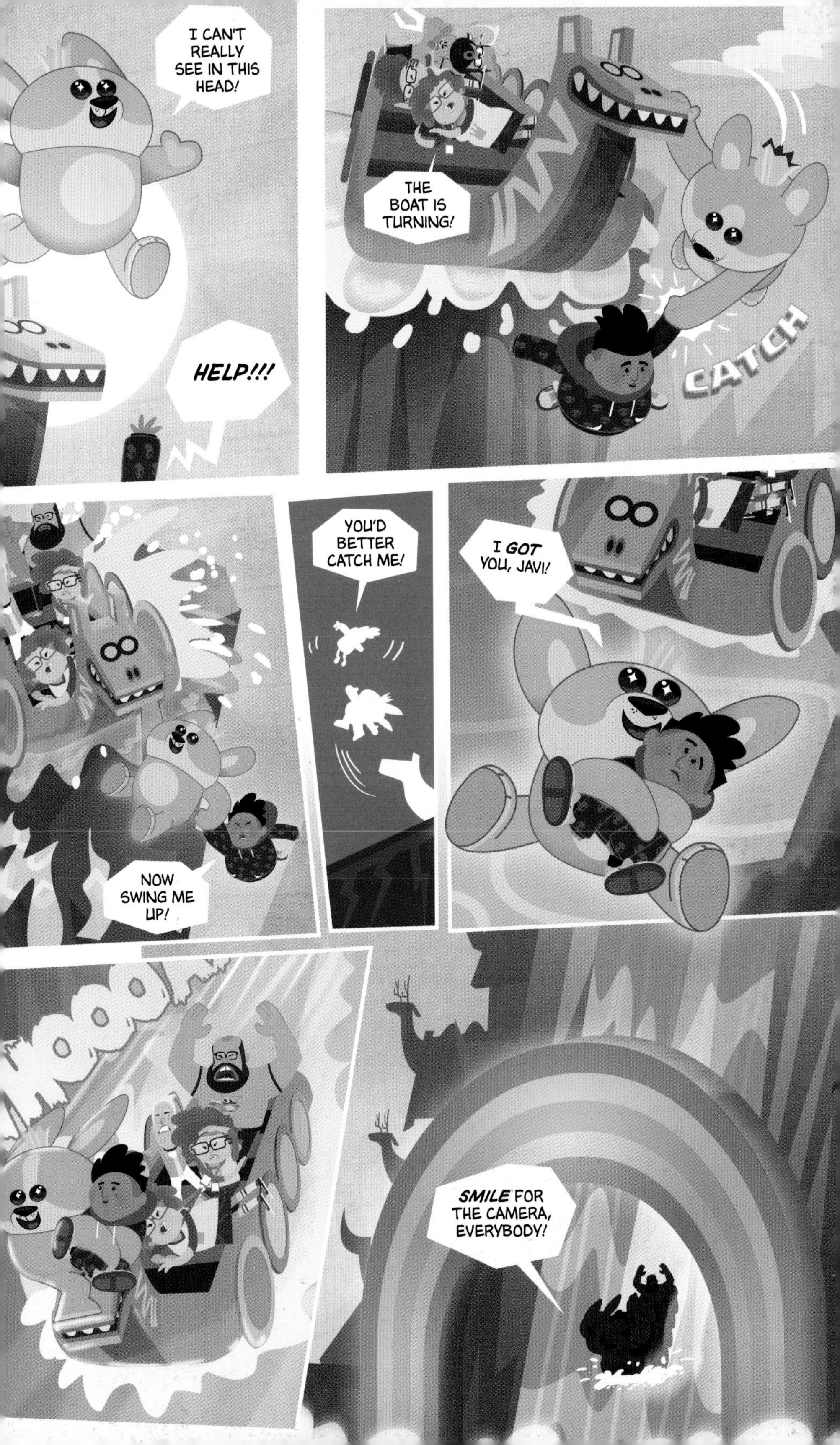
I CAN'T REALLY SEE IN THIS HEAD!
HELP!!!
THE BOAT IS TURNING!
CATCH
YOU'D BETTER CATCH ME!
NOW SWING ME UP!
I *GOT* YOU, JAVI!
SMILE FOR THE CAMERA, EVERYBODY!

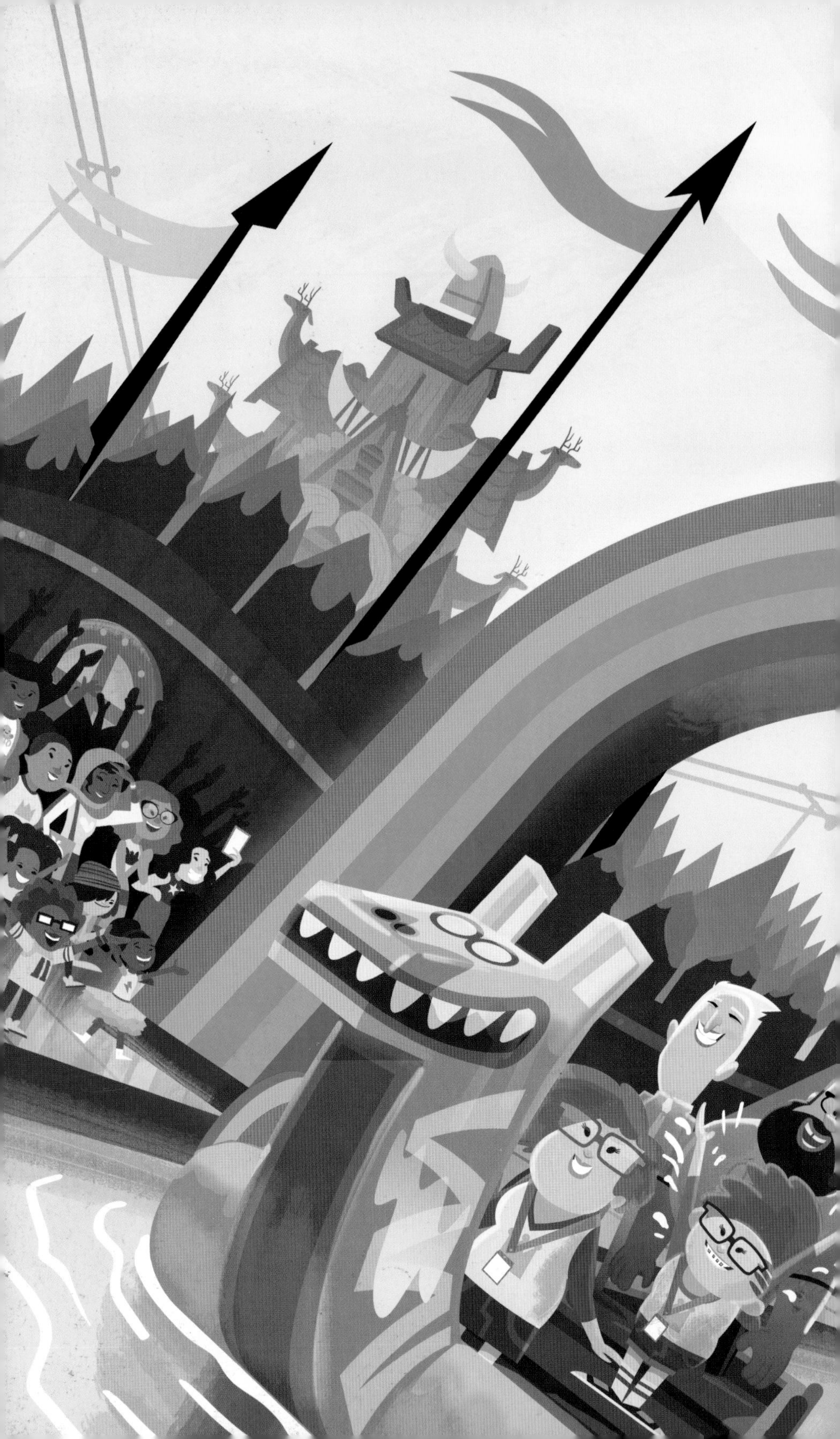

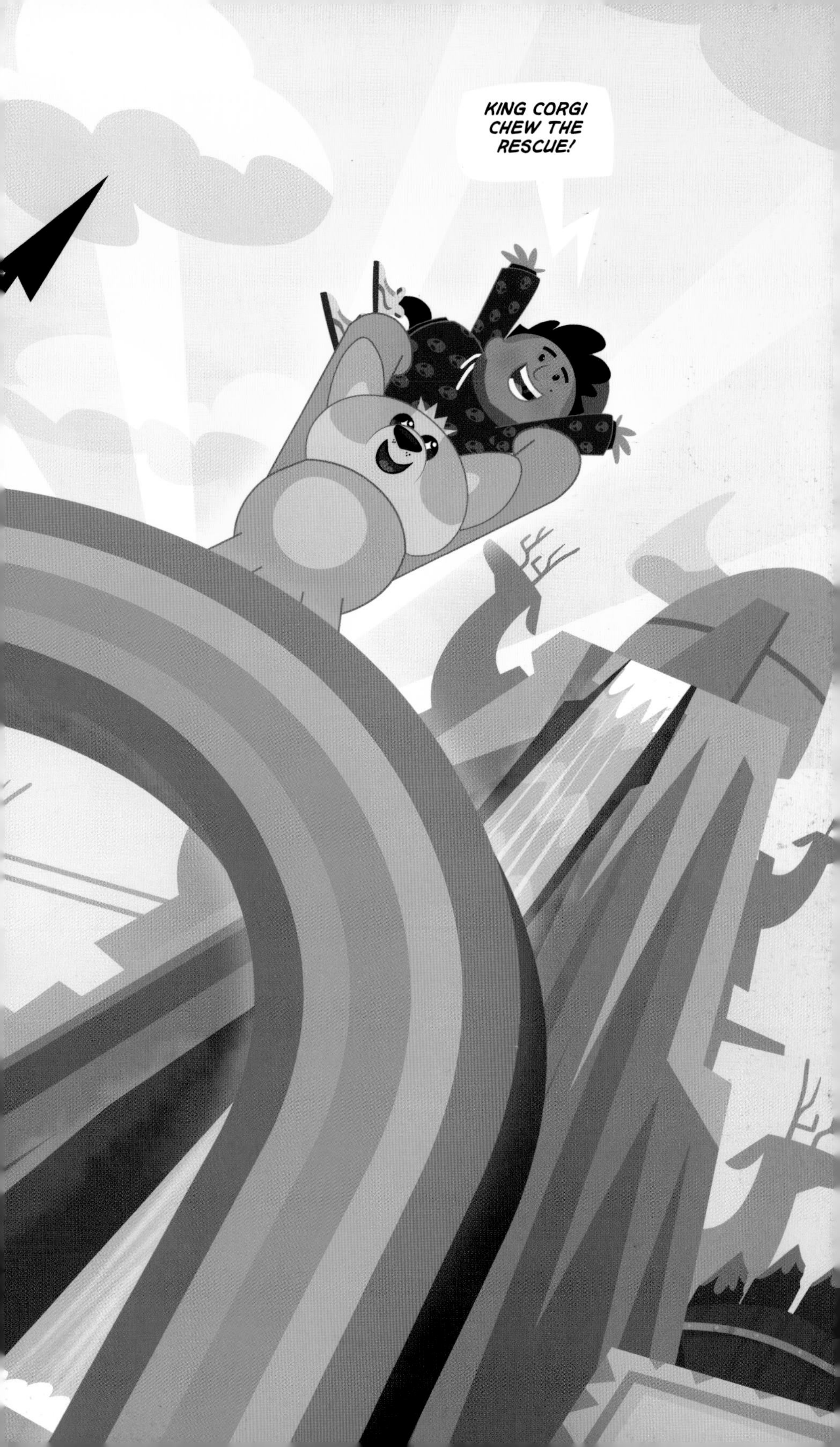
KING CORGI CHEW THE RESCUE!

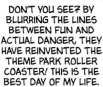

DON'T YOU SEE? BY BLURRING THE LINES BETWEEN FUN AND ACTUAL DANGER, THEY HAVE REINVENTED THE THEME PARK ROLLER COASTER! THIS IS THE BEST DAY OF MY LIFE.

THAT WAS INCREDIBLE!

I LOVE KING CORGI SO MUCH, MOMMY!

ME TOO, SWEETIE. ME TOO.

THANKS FOR COMING TO THE TEST RUN.

WE'LL LET YOU KNOW WHEN WE REOPEN!

WE HAVE A PROBLEM.

SOMEONE SABOTAGED THE TRANSPORT WITH THIS TIRE AND ALMOST KILLED THE CAPTAIN.

WHAT? THAT IS A BUMMER!

FLAHH VROO!

PERHAPS IF YOU LET ME DO A PROPER SECURITY SWEEP, THESE ACCIDENTS WOULDN'T HAPPEN.

???

GLA...

YOU TOTALLY TRIED TO HURT ME, DIDN'T YOU?

WHAT?

THAT WAS BASICALLY LIKE YOU CONFESSED, EGGLA.

THE WAY YOU SAID IT. ALL OMINOUS-LIKE. AND THE WAY YOU'VE BEEN ALL MOPEY THESE PAST COUPLE OF DAYS.

OU'RE THE ONLY NE NOT HAVING UN. CLEARLY IT WAS YOU. I MEAN, AM I CRAZY?

THE BLUUGS PICKED UP SOMETHING ON THEIR CAMERAS.

ALL THE BLUUGS HAVE CAMERAS NOW?

HOW DOES THE SECURITY OFFICER *NOT* KNOW THE BLUUGS ALL HAVE CAMERAS?

I WANT YOU TO ADMIT YOU DID IT!

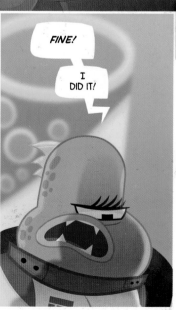

FINE!

I DID IT!

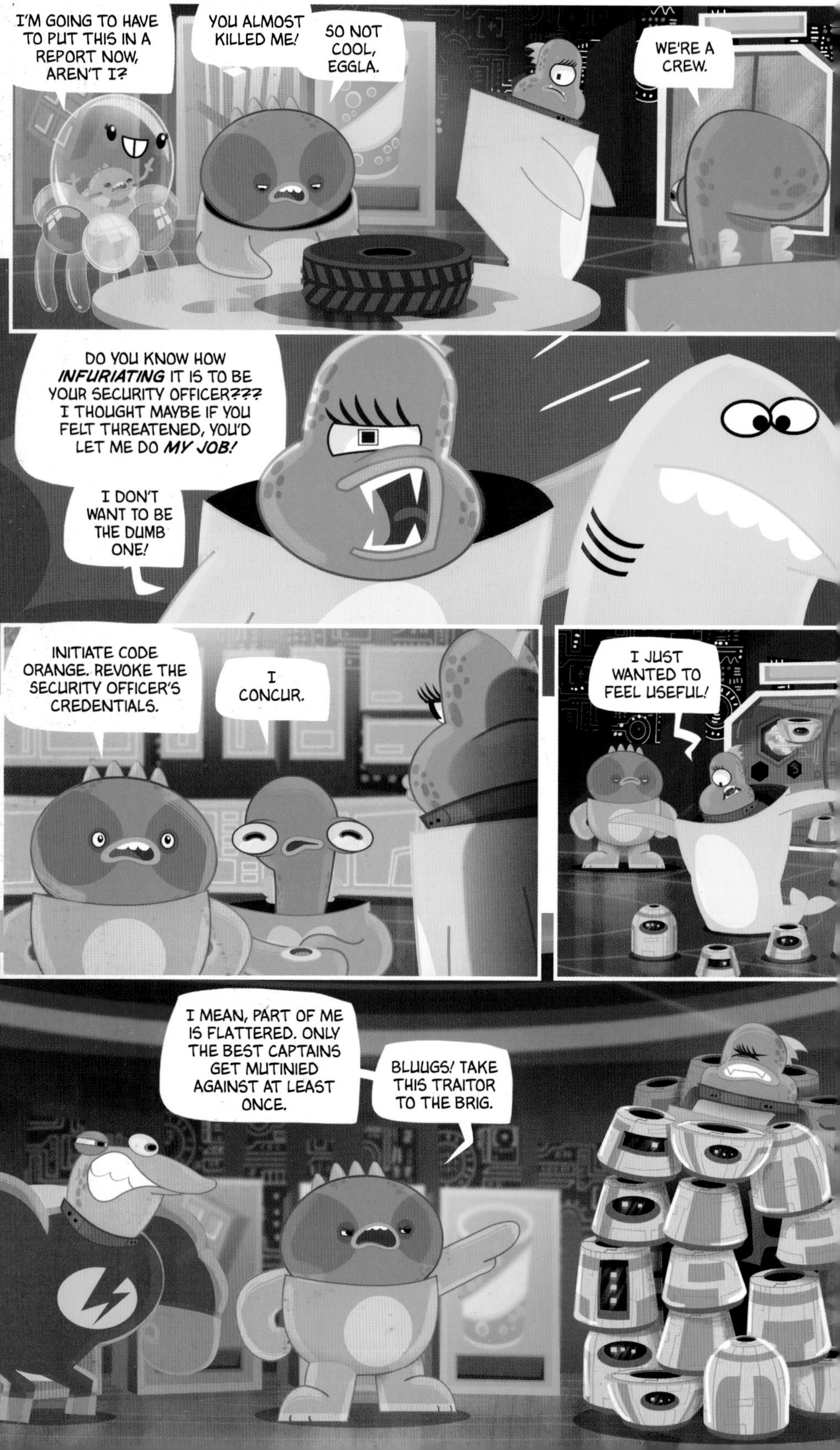

I'M GOING TO HAVE TO PUT THIS IN A REPORT NOW, AREN'T I?
YOU ALMOST KILLED ME!
SO NOT COOL, EGGLA.
WE'RE A CREW.
DO YOU KNOW HOW *INFURIATING* IT IS TO BE YOUR SECURITY OFFICER??? I THOUGHT MAYBE IF YOU FELT THREATENED, YOU'D LET ME DO *MY JOB!*
I DON'T WANT TO BE THE DUMB ONE!
INITIATE CODE ORANGE. REVOKE THE SECURITY OFFICER'S CREDENTIALS.
I CONCUR.
I JUST WANTED TO FEEL USEFUL!
I MEAN, PART OF ME IS FLATTERED. ONLY THE BEST CAPTAINS GET MUTINIED AGAINST AT LEAST ONCE.
BLUUGS! TAKE THIS TRAITOR TO THE BRIG.

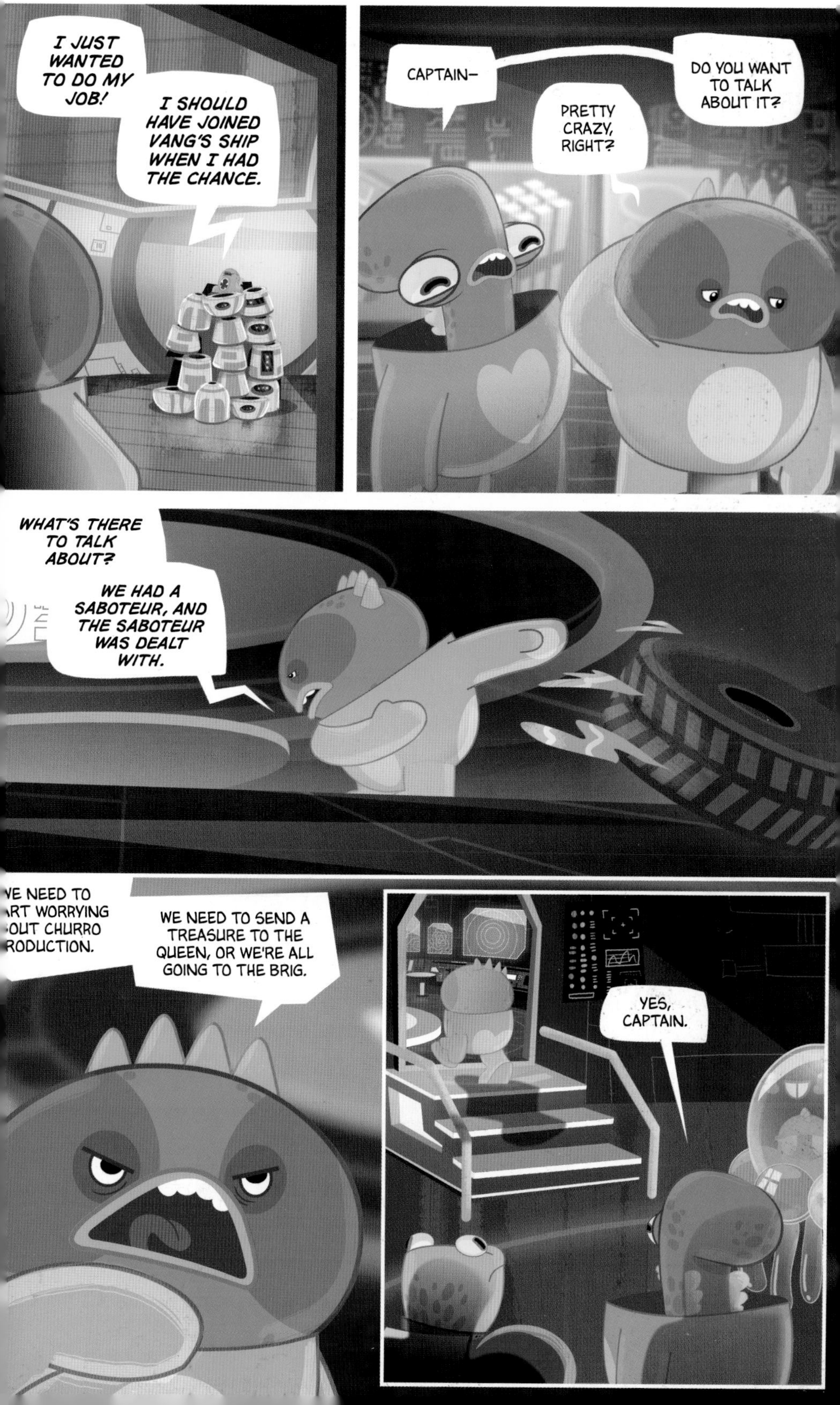
I JUST WANTED TO DO MY JOB!
I SHOULD HAVE JOINED VANG'S SHIP WHEN I HAD THE CHANCE.
CAPTAIN—
DO YOU WANT TO TALK ABOUT IT?
PRETTY CRAZY, RIGHT?
WHAT'S THERE TO TALK ABOUT?
WE HAD A SABOTEUR, AND THE SABOTEUR WAS DEALT WITH.
WE NEED TO SEND A TREASURE TO THE QUEEN, OR WE'RE ALL GOING TO THE BRIG.
YES, CAPTAIN.

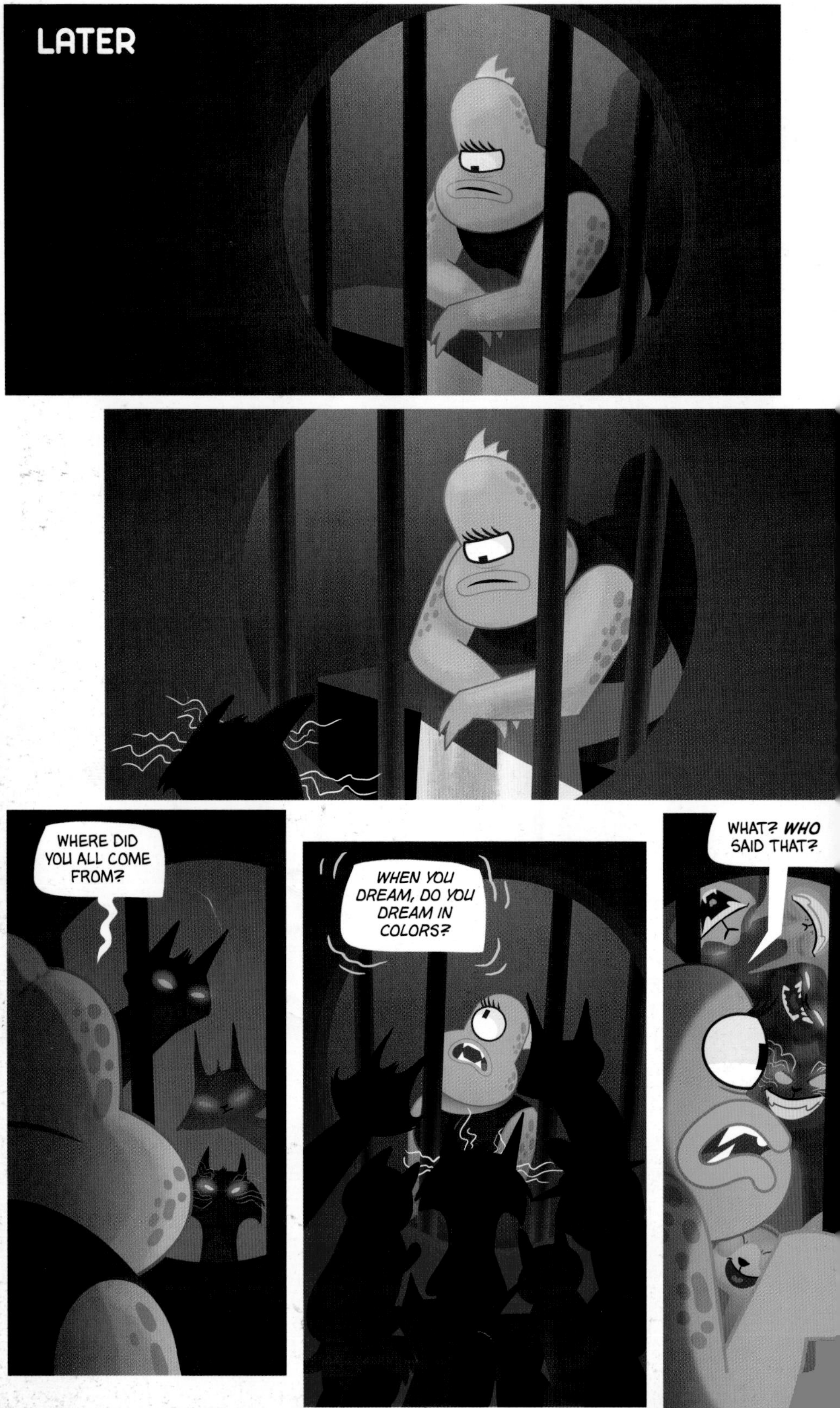
LATER
WHERE DID YOU ALL COME FROM?
WHEN YOU DREAM, DO YOU DREAM IN COLORS?
WHAT? WHO SAID THAT?

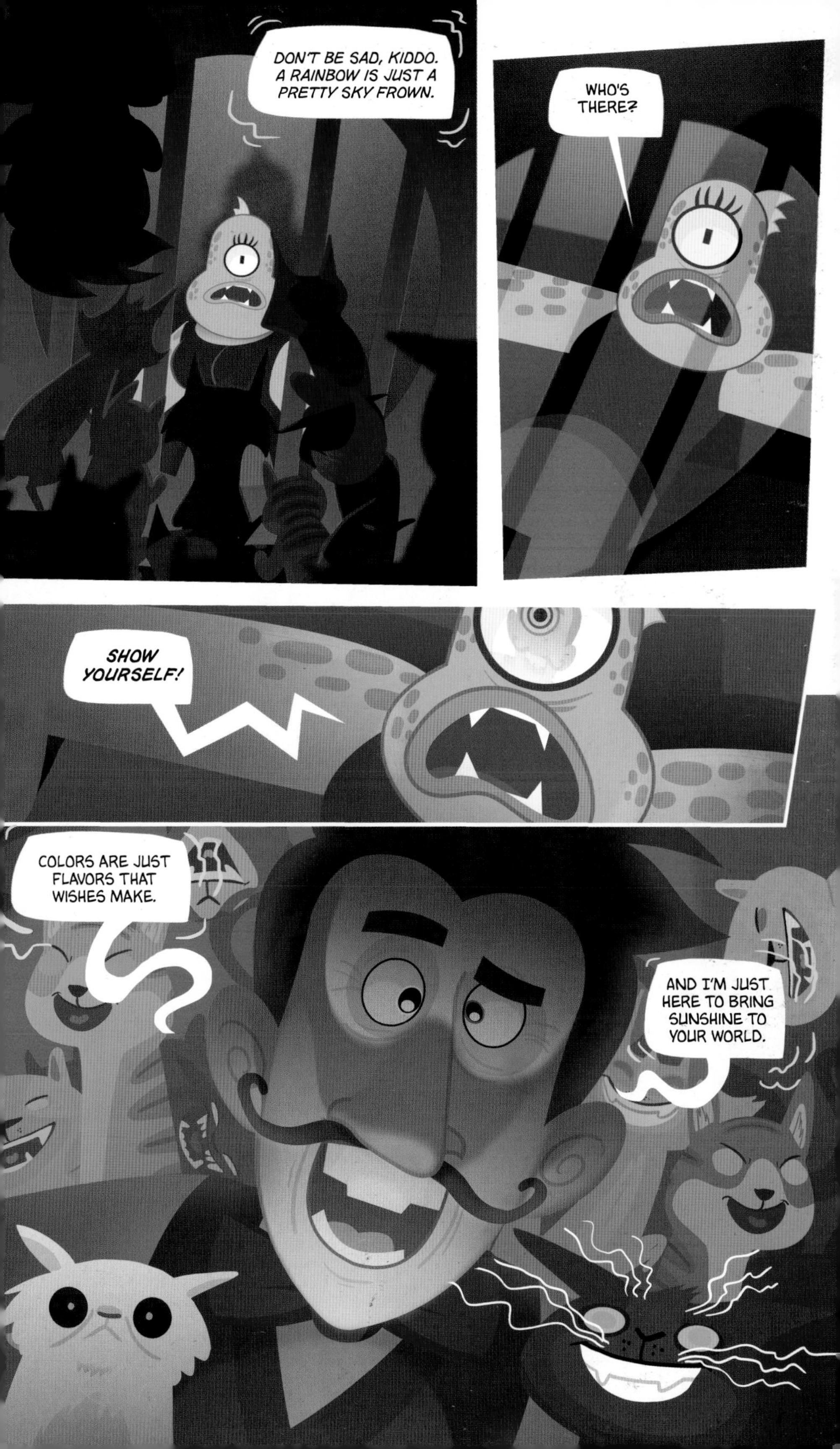
DON'T BE SAD, KIDDO. A RAINBOW IS JUST A PRETTY SKY FROWN.
WHO'S THERE?
SHOW YOURSELF!
COLORS ARE JUST FLAVORS THAT WISHES MAKE.
AND I'M JUST HERE TO BRING SUNSHINE TO YOUR WORLD.

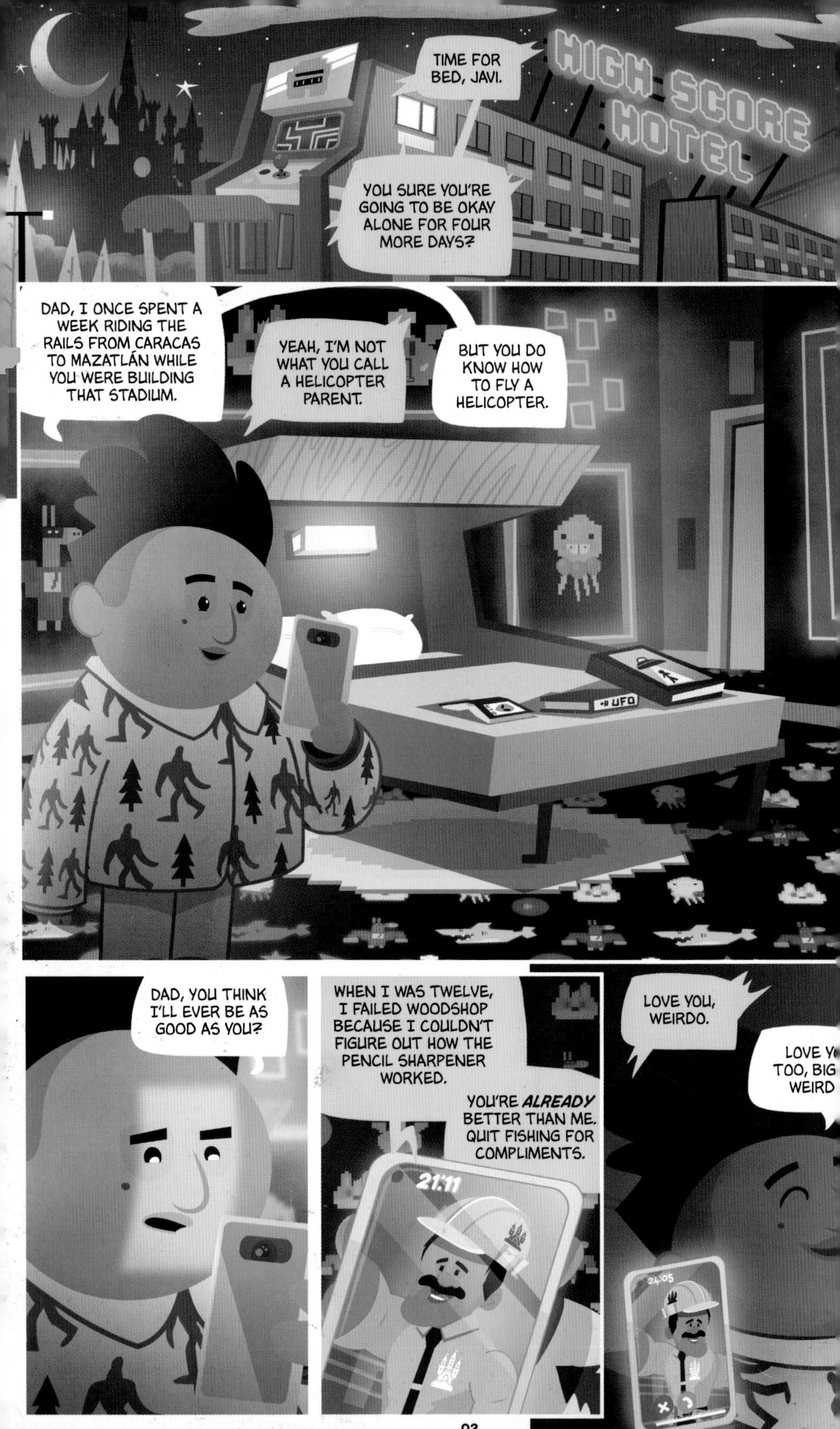
HIGH SCORE HOTEL
TIME FOR BED, JAVI.
YOU SURE YOU'RE GOING TO BE OKAY ALONE FOR FOUR MORE DAYS?
DAD, I ONCE SPENT A WEEK RIDING THE RAILS FROM CARACAS TO MAZATLÁN WHILE YOU WERE BUILDING THAT STADIUM.
YEAH, I'M NOT WHAT YOU CALL A HELICOPTER PARENT.
BUT YOU DO KNOW HOW TO FLY A HELICOPTER.
UFO
DAD, YOU THINK I'LL EVER BE AS GOOD AS YOU?
WHEN I WAS TWELVE, I FAILED WOODSHOP BECAUSE I COULDN'T FIGURE OUT HOW THE PENCIL SHARPENER WORKED.
YOU'RE *ALREADY* BETTER THAN ME. QUIT FISHING FOR COMPLIMENTS.
21:11
LOVE YOU, WEIRDO.
LOVE Y
TOO, BIG
WEIRD
24:05

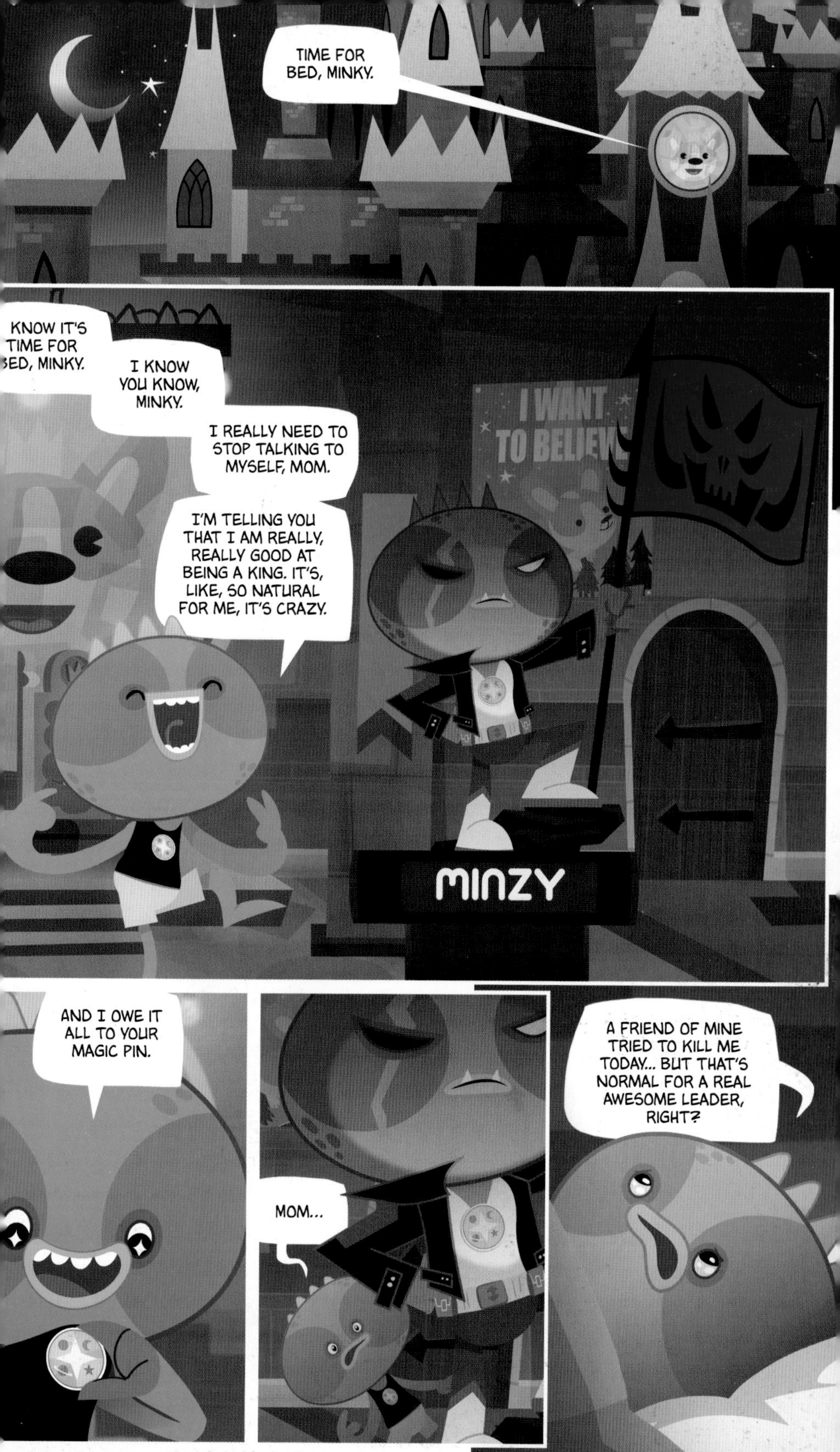
TIME FOR BED, MINKY.
KNOW IT'S TIME FOR BED, MINKY.
I KNOW YOU KNOW, MINKY.
I REALLY NEED TO STOP TALKING TO MYSELF, MOM.
I WANT TO BELIEV
I'M TELLING YOU THAT I AM REALLY, REALLY GOOD AT BEING A KING. IT'S, LIKE, SO NATURAL FOR ME, IT'S CRAZY.
MINZY
AND I OWE IT ALL TO YOUR MAGIC PIN.
MOM...
A FRIEND OF MINE TRIED TO KILL ME TODAY... BUT THAT'S NORMAL FOR A REAL AWESOME LEADER, RIGHT?

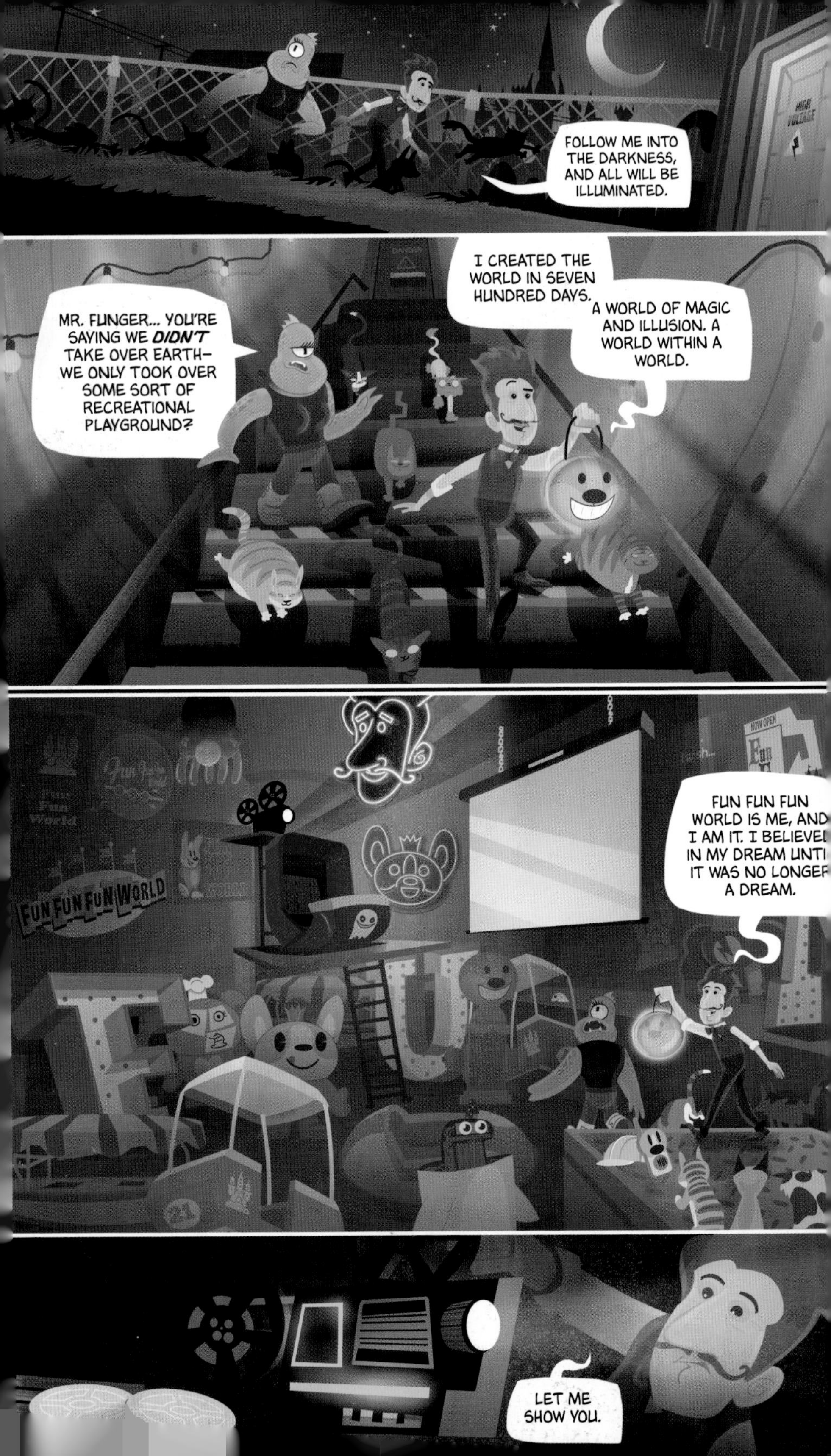
HIGH VOLTAGE
FOLLOW ME INTO THE DARKNESS, AND ALL WILL BE ILLUMINATED.
DANGER
MR. FUNGER... YOU'RE SAYING WE *DIDN'T* TAKE OVER EARTH— WE ONLY TOOK OVER SOME SORT OF RECREATIONAL PLAYGROUND?
I CREATED THE WORLD IN SEVEN HUNDRED DAYS.
A WORLD OF MAGIC AND ILLUSION. A WORLD WITHIN A WORLD.
FUN FUN FUN WORLD
NOW OPEN
FUN FUN FUN WORLD IS ME, AND I AM IT. I BELIEVED IN MY DREAM UNTIL IT WAS NO LONGER A DREAM.
21
LET ME SHOW YOU.

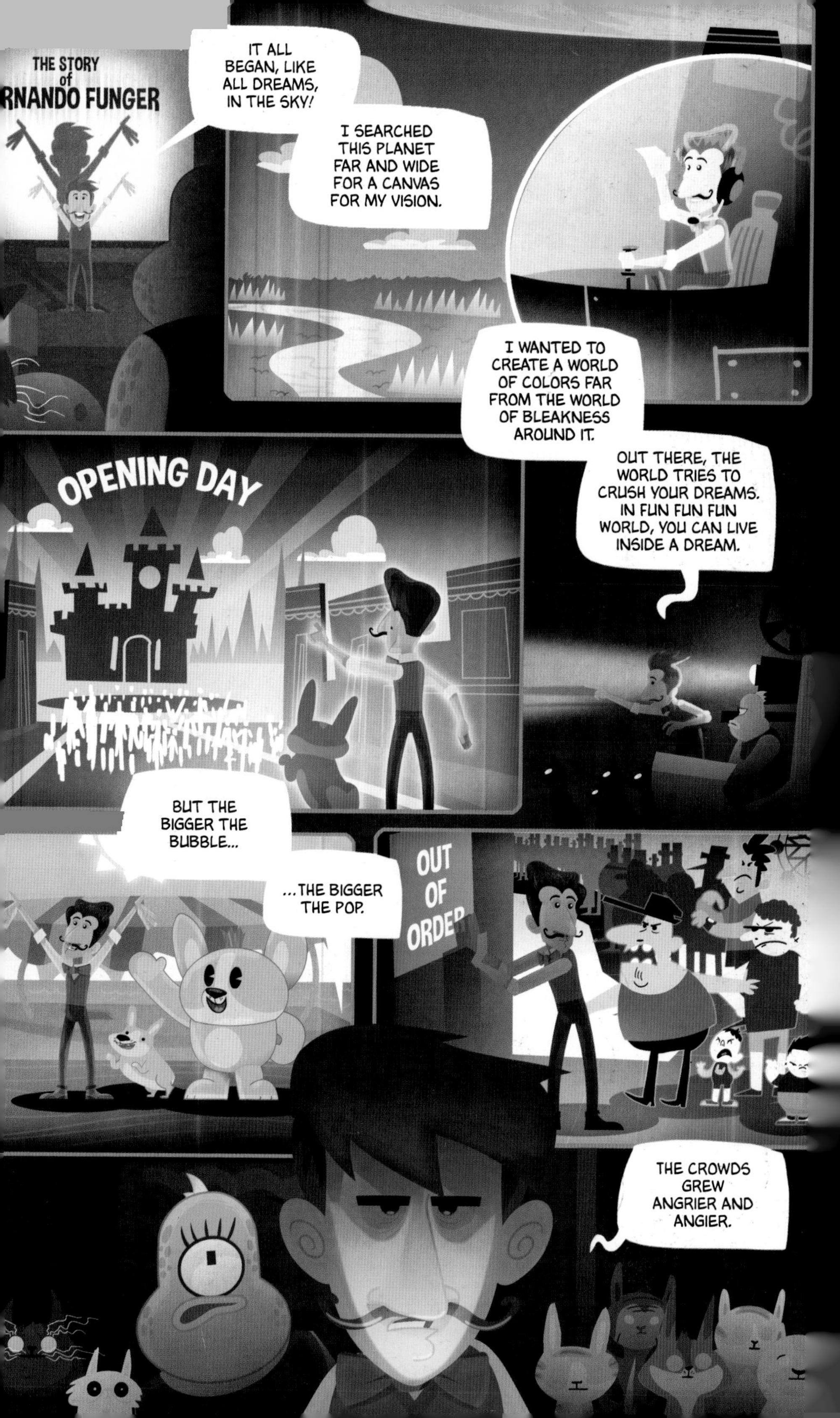
THE STORY of RNANDO FUNGER
IT ALL BEGAN, LIKE ALL DREAMS, IN THE SKY!
I SEARCHED THIS PLANET FAR AND WIDE FOR A CANVAS FOR MY VISION.
I WANTED TO CREATE A WORLD OF COLORS FAR FROM THE WORLD OF BLEAKNESS AROUND IT.
OPENING DAY
OUT THERE, THE WORLD TRIES TO CRUSH YOUR DREAMS. IN FUN FUN FUN WORLD, YOU CAN LIVE INSIDE A DREAM.
BUT THE BIGGER THE BUBBLE...
...THE BIGGER THE POP.
OUT OF ORDER
THE CROWDS GREW ANGRIER AND ANGIER.

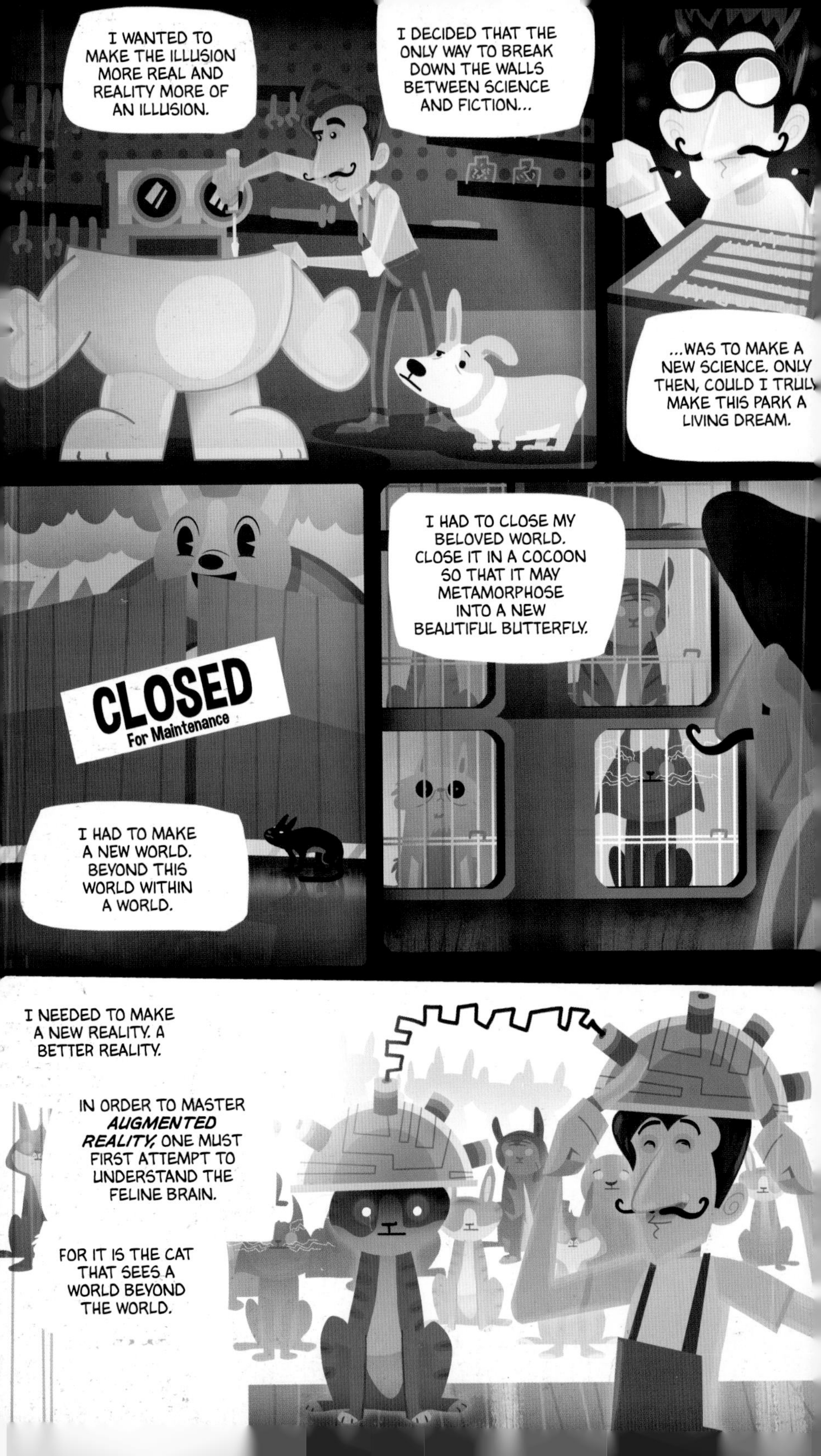
I WANTED TO MAKE THE ILLUSION MORE REAL AND REALITY MORE OF AN ILLUSION.
I DECIDED THAT THE ONLY WAY TO BREAK DOWN THE WALLS BETWEEN SCIENCE AND FICTION...
...WAS TO MAKE A NEW SCIENCE. ONLY THEN, COULD I TRULY MAKE THIS PARK A LIVING DREAM.
CLOSED
For Maintenance
I HAD TO MAKE A NEW WORLD. BEYOND THIS WORLD WITHIN A WORLD.
I HAD TO CLOSE MY BELOVED WORLD. CLOSE IT IN A COCOON SO THAT IT MAY METAMORPHOSE INTO A NEW BEAUTIFUL BUTTERFLY.
I NEEDED TO MAKE A NEW REALITY. A BETTER REALITY.
IN ORDER TO MASTER *AUGMENTED REALITY,* ONE MUST FIRST ATTEMPT TO UNDERSTAND THE FELINE BRAIN.
FOR IT IS THE CAT THAT SEES A WORLD BEYOND THE WORLD.

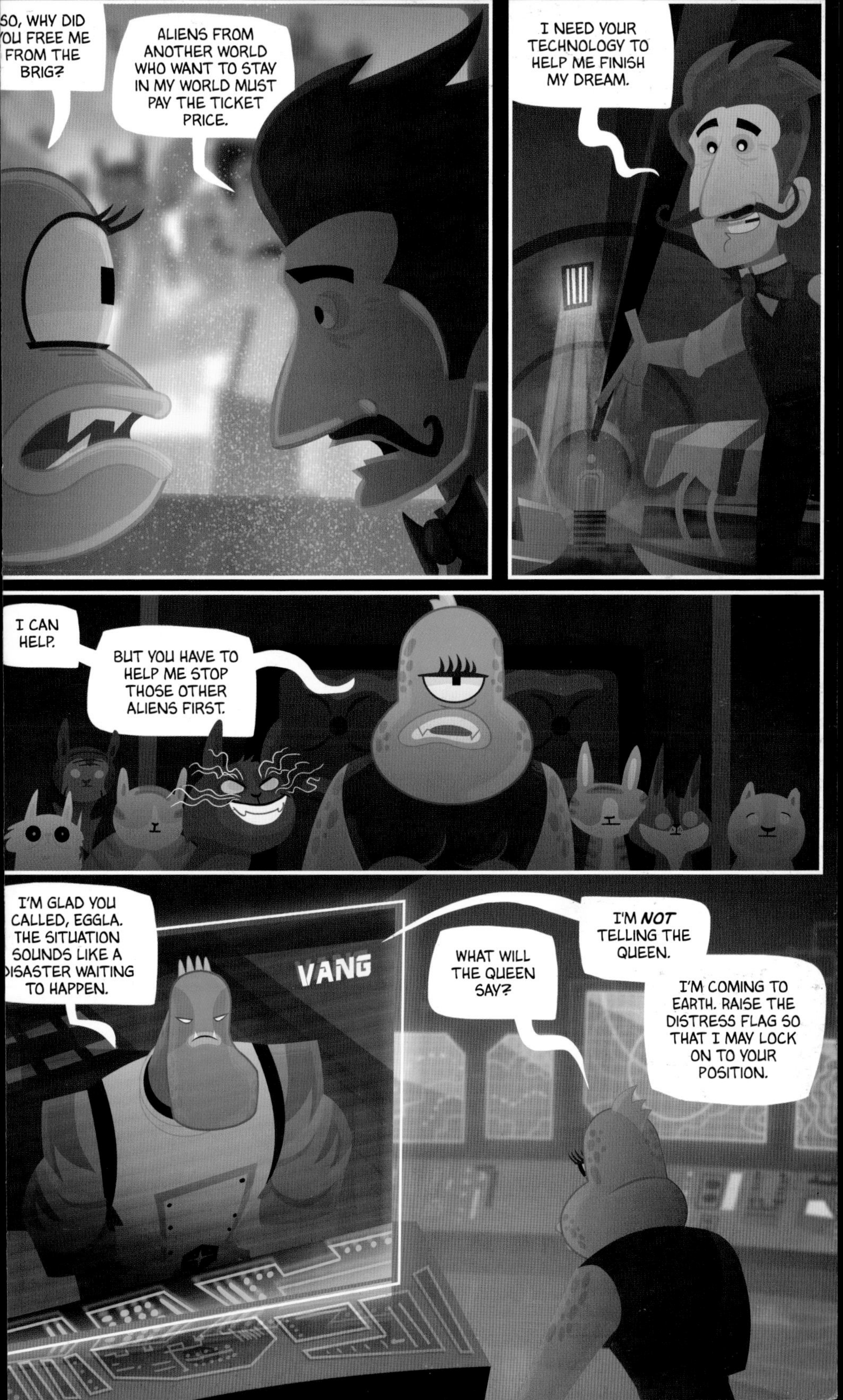
SO, WHY DID YOU FREE ME FROM THE BRIG?
ALIENS FROM ANOTHER WORLD WHO WANT TO STAY IN MY WORLD MUST PAY THE TICKET PRICE.
I NEED YOUR TECHNOLOGY TO HELP ME FINISH MY DREAM.
I CAN HELP.
BUT YOU HAVE TO HELP ME STOP THOSE OTHER ALIENS FIRST.
I'M GLAD YOU CALLED, EGGLA. THE SITUATION SOUNDS LIKE A DISASTER WAITING TO HAPPEN.
VANG
WHAT WILL THE QUEEN SAY?
I'M *NOT* TELLING THE QUEEN.
I'M COMING TO EARTH. RAISE THE DISTRESS FLAG SO THAT I MAY LOCK ON TO YOUR POSITION.

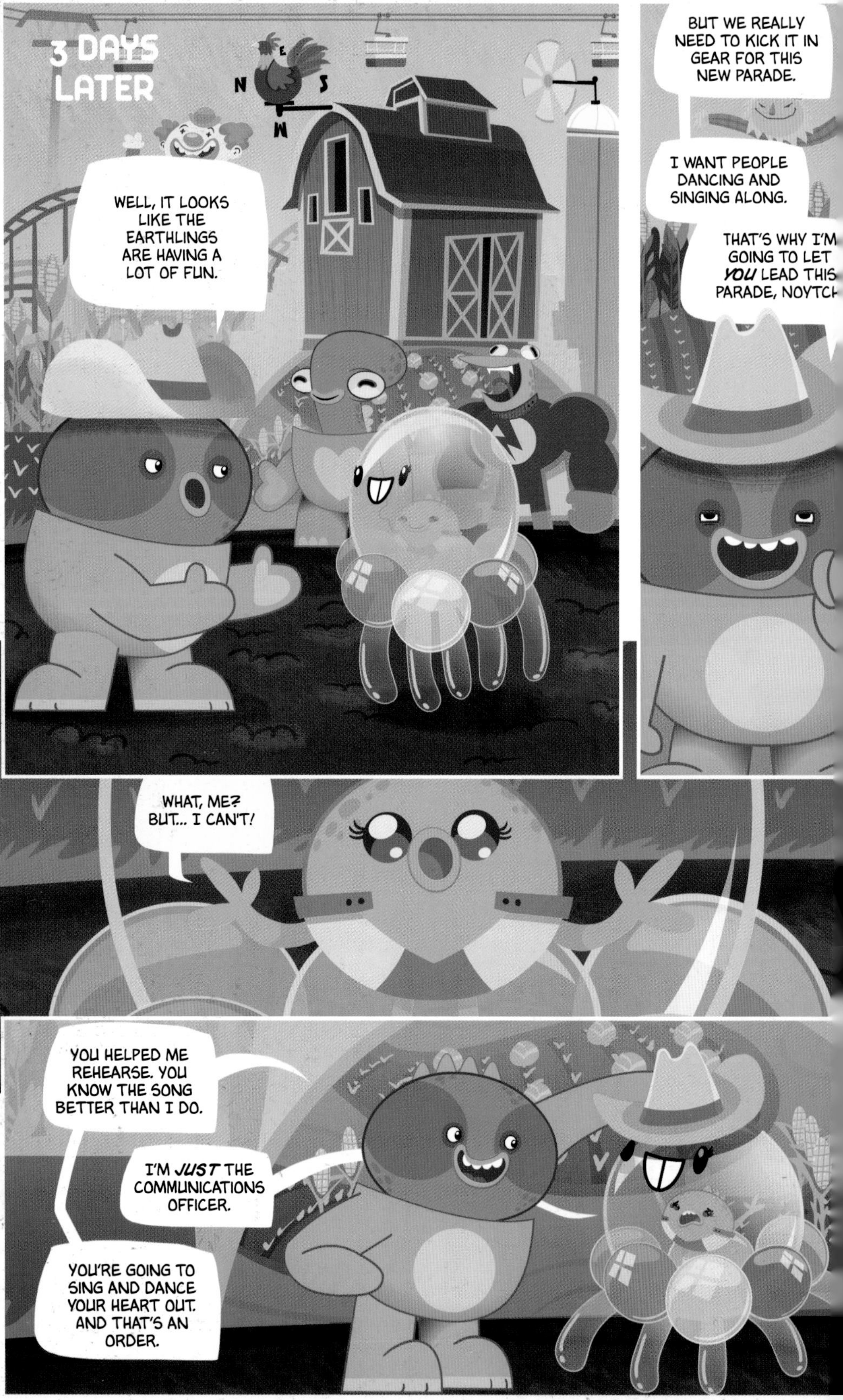
3 DAYS LATER
WELL, IT LOOKS LIKE THE EARTHLINGS ARE HAVING A LOT OF FUN.
BUT WE REALLY NEED TO KICK IT IN GEAR FOR THIS NEW PARADE.
I WANT PEOPLE DANCING AND SINGING ALONG.
THAT'S WHY I'M GOING TO LET *YOU* LEAD THIS PARADE, NOYTCH
WHAT, ME? BUT... I CAN'T!
YOU HELPED ME REHEARSE. YOU KNOW THE SONG BETTER THAN I DO.
I'M *JUST* THE COMMUNICATIONS OFFICER.
YOU'RE GOING TO SING AND DANCE YOUR HEART OUT. AND THAT'S AN ORDER.

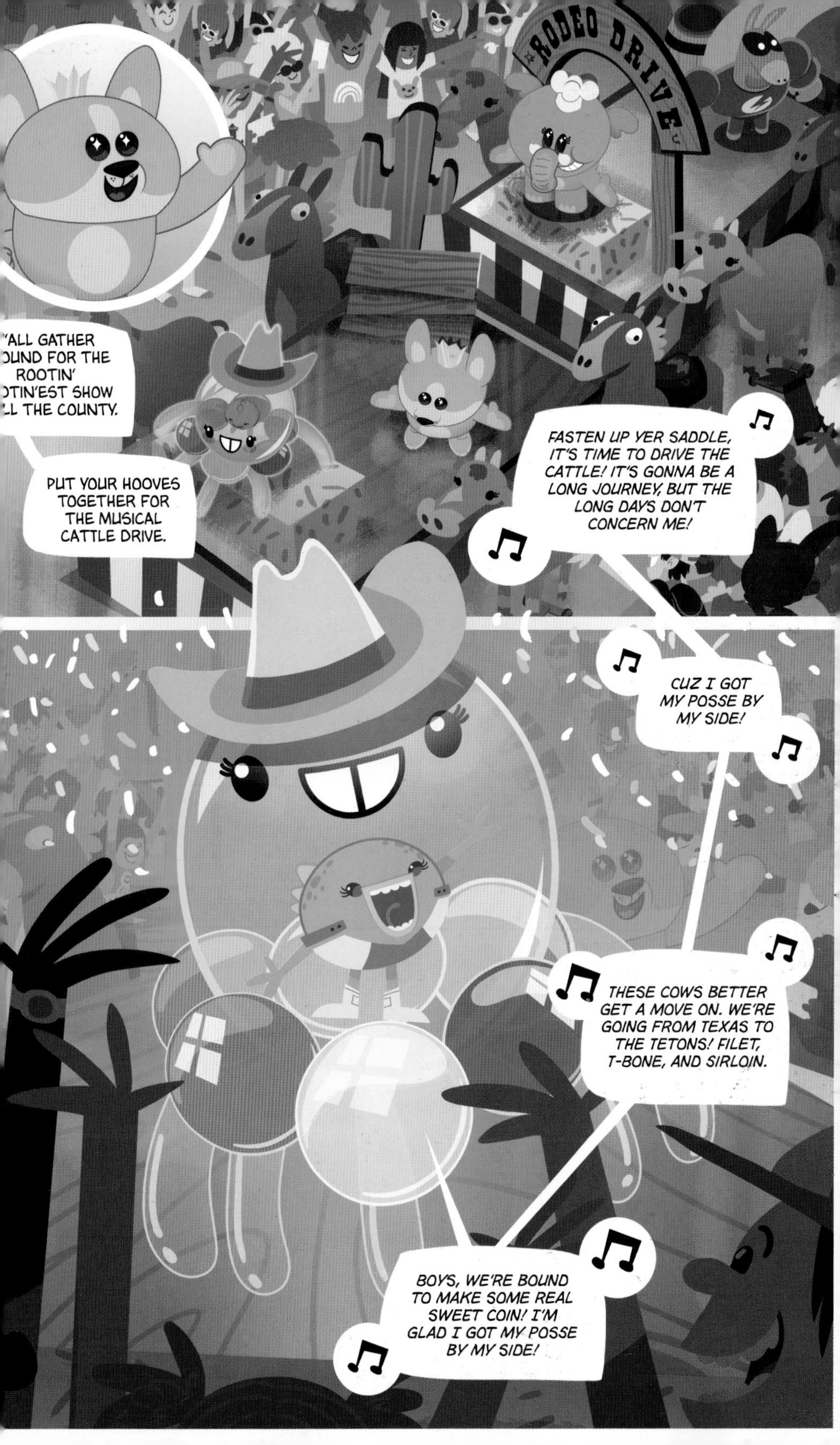

'ALL GATHER
OUND FOR THE
ROOTIN'
OTIN'EST SHOW
LL THE COUNTY.
PUT YOUR HOOVES TOGETHER FOR THE MUSICAL CATTLE DRIVE.
RODEO DRIVE
FASTEN UP YER SADDLE, IT'S TIME TO DRIVE THE CATTLE! IT'S GONNA BE A LONG JOURNEY, BUT THE LONG DAYS DON'T CONCERN ME!
CUZ I GOT MY POSSE BY MY SIDE!
THESE COWS BETTER GET A MOVE ON. WE'RE GOING FROM TEXAS TO THE TETONS! FILET, T-BONE, AND SIRLOIN.
BOYS, WE'RE BOUND TO MAKE SOME REAL SWEET COIN! I'M GLAD I GOT MY POSSE BY MY SIDE!

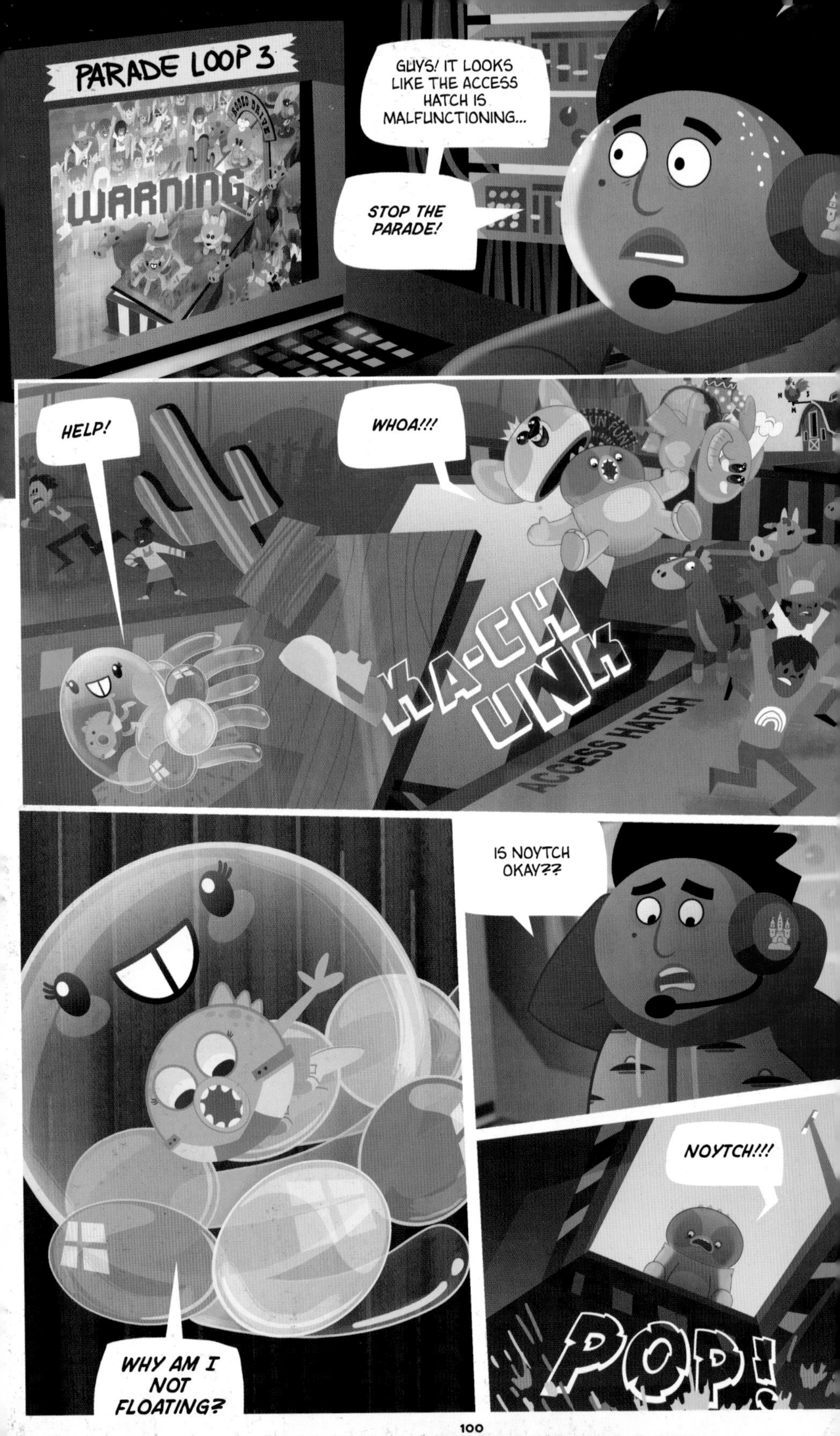

PARADE LOOP 3
WARNING
RODEO DRIVE
GUYS! IT LOOKS LIKE THE ACCESS HATCH IS MALFUNCTIONING...
STOP THE PARADE!
HELP!
WHOA!!!
KA-CH UNK
ACCESS HATCH
WHY AM I NOT FLOATING?
IS NOYTCH OKAY??
NOYTCH!!!
POP!

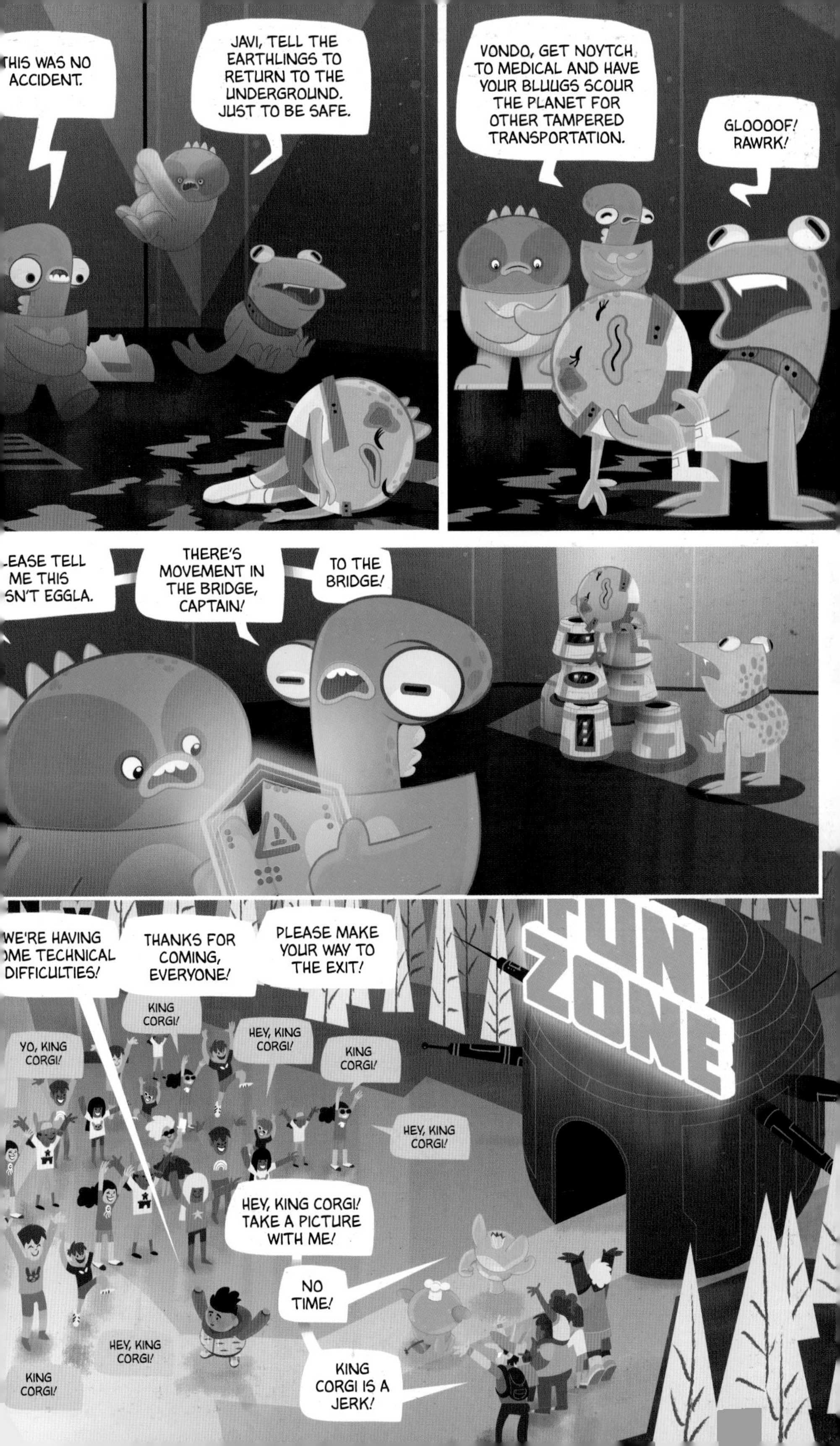
THIS WAS NO ACCIDENT.
JAVI, TELL THE EARTHLINGS TO RETURN TO THE UNDERGROUND. JUST TO BE SAFE.
VONDO, GET NOYTCH TO MEDICAL AND HAVE YOUR BLUUGS SCOUR THE PLANET FOR OTHER TAMPERED TRANSPORTATION.
GLOOOOF! RAWRK!
EASE TELL ME THIS SN'T EGGLA.
THERE'S MOVEMENT IN THE BRIDGE, CAPTAIN!
TO THE BRIDGE!
FUN ZONE
WE'RE HAVING OME TECHNICAL DIFFICULTIES!
THANKS FOR COMING, EVERYONE!
PLEASE MAKE YOUR WAY TO THE EXIT!
KING CORGI!
YO, KING CORGI!
HEY, KING CORGI!
KING CORGI!
HEY, KING CORGI!
HEY, KING CORGI! TAKE A PICTURE WITH ME!
NO TIME!
HEY, KING CORGI!
KING CORGI!
KING CORGI IS A JERK!

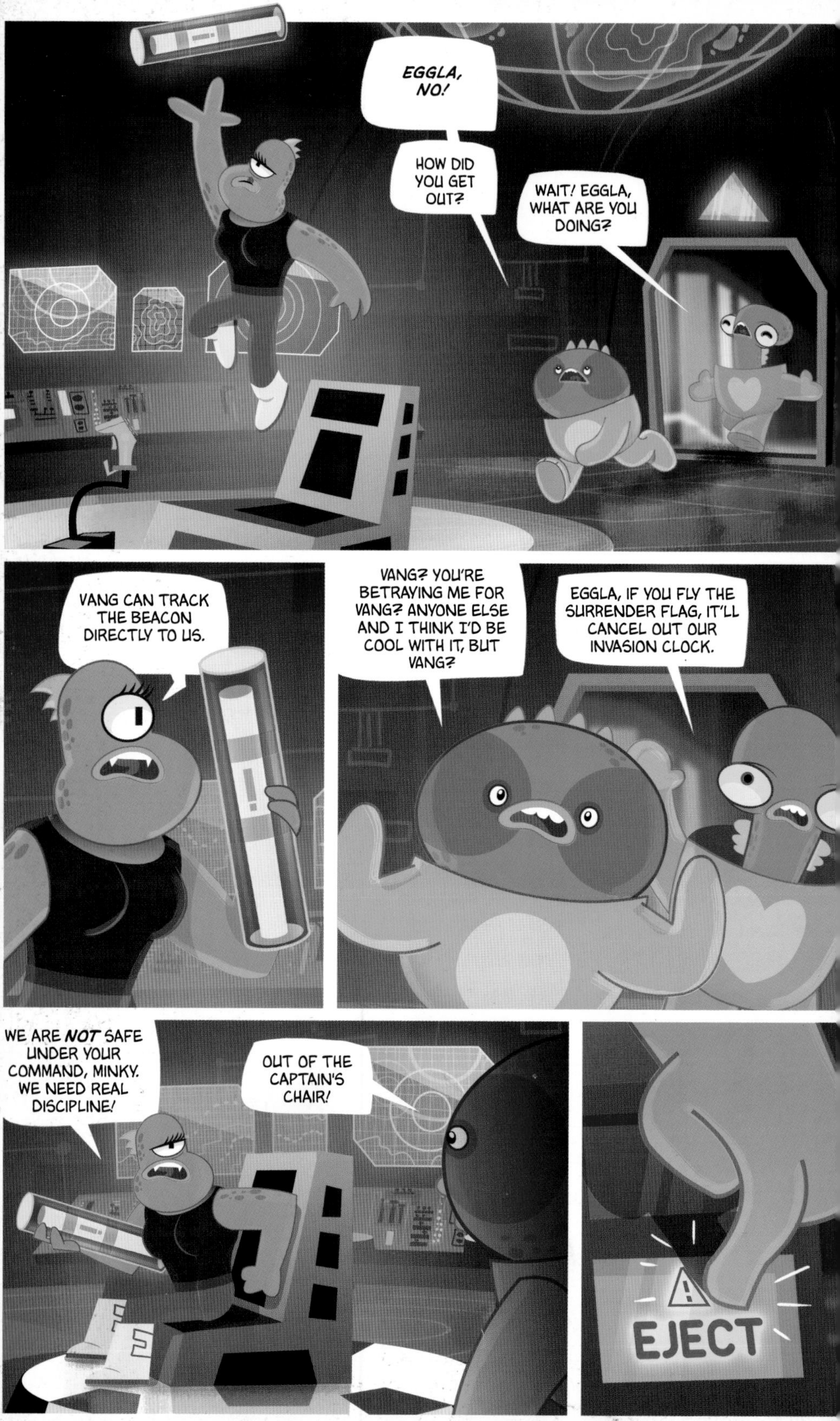
EGGLA, NO!
HOW DID YOU GET OUT?
WAIT! EGGLA, WHAT ARE YOU DOING?
VANG CAN TRACK THE BEACON DIRECTLY TO US.
VANG? YOU'RE BETRAYING ME FOR VANG? ANYONE ELSE AND I THINK I'D BE COOL WITH IT, BUT VANG?
EGGLA, IF YOU FLY THE SURRENDER FLAG, IT'LL CANCEL OUT OUR INVASION CLOCK.
WE ARE *NOT* SAFE UNDER YOUR COMMAND, MINKY. WE NEED REAL DISCIPLINE!
OUT OF THE CAPTAIN'S CHAIR!
EJECT

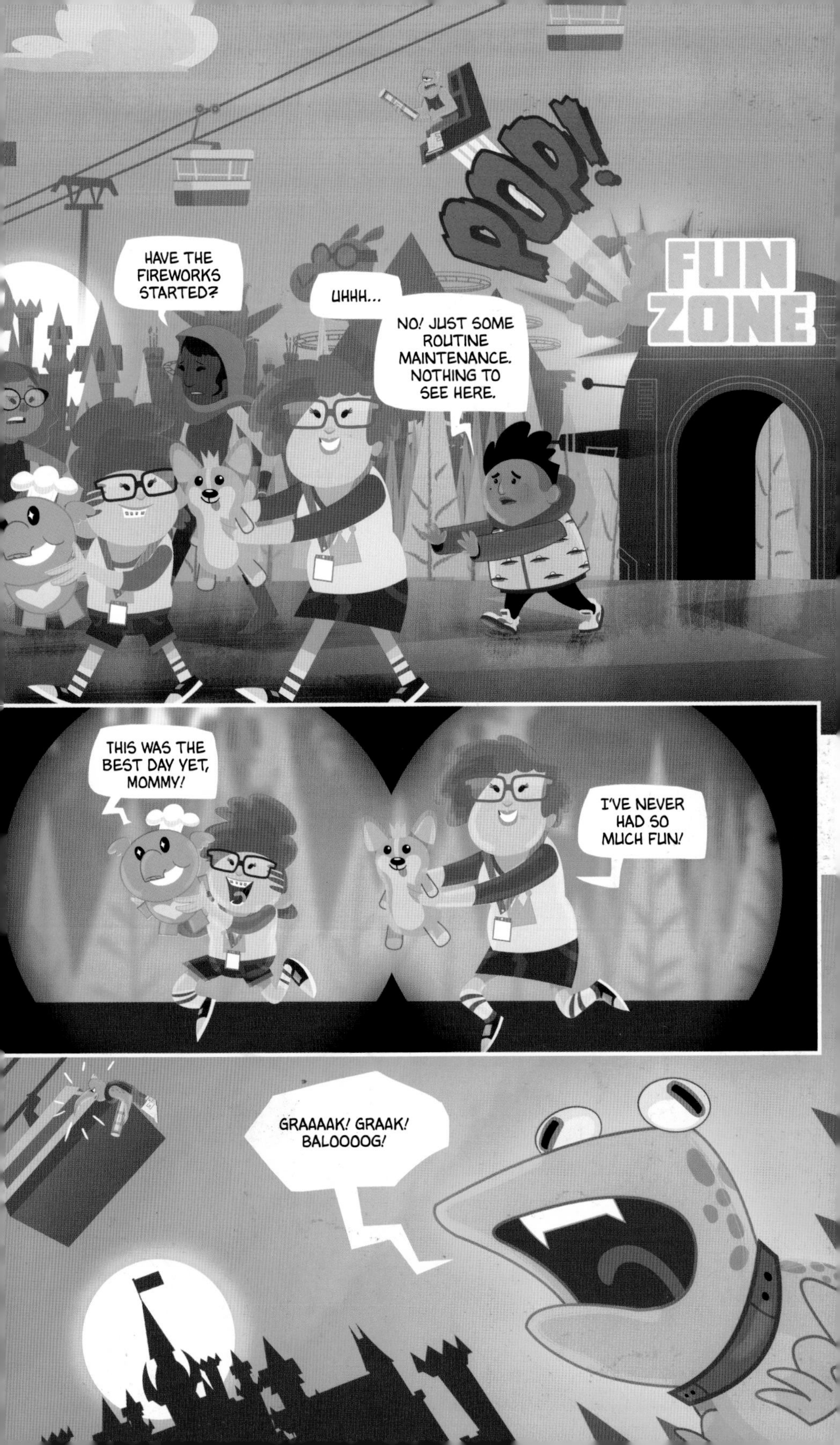
POP!
FUN ZONE
HAVE THE FIREWORKS STARTED?
UHHH...
NO! JUST SOME ROUTINE MAINTENANCE. NOTHING TO SEE HERE.
THIS WAS THE BEST DAY YET, MOMMY!
I'VE NEVER HAD SO MUCH FUN!
GRAAAAK! GRAAK! BALOOOOG!

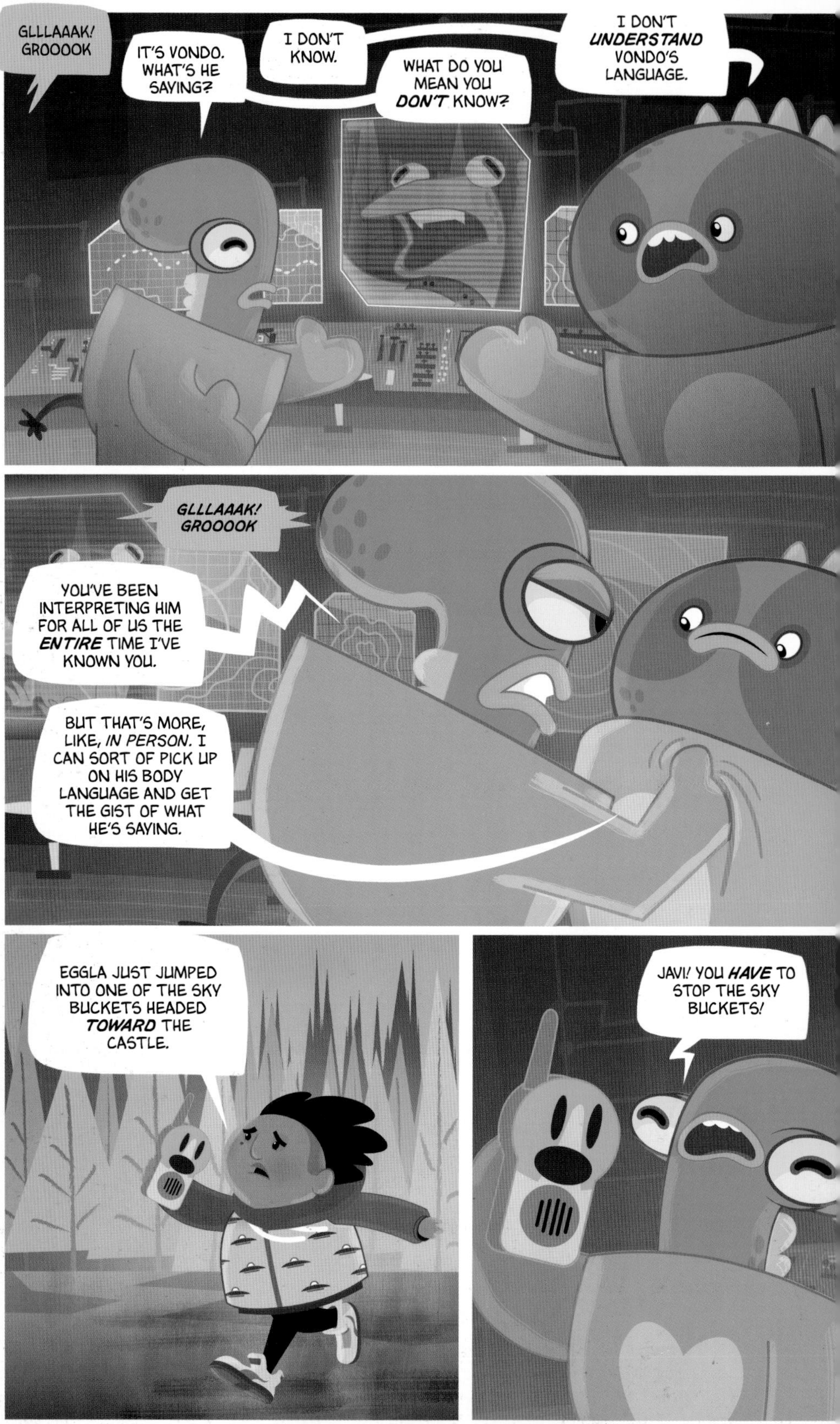
GLLLAAAK! GROOOOK
IT'S VONDO. WHAT'S HE SAYING?
I DON'T KNOW.
WHAT DO YOU MEAN YOU *DON'T* KNOW?
I DON'T *UNDERSTAND* VONDO'S LANGUAGE.
GLLLAAAK! GROOOOK
YOU'VE BEEN INTERPRETING HIM FOR ALL OF US THE *ENTIRE* TIME I'VE KNOWN YOU.
BUT THAT'S MORE, LIKE, *IN PERSON*. I CAN SORT OF PICK UP ON HIS BODY LANGUAGE AND GET THE GIST OF WHAT HE'S SAYING.
EGGLA JUST JUMPED INTO ONE OF THE SKY BUCKETS HEADED *TOWARD* THE CASTLE.
JAVI! YOU *HAVE* TO STOP THE SKY BUCKETS!

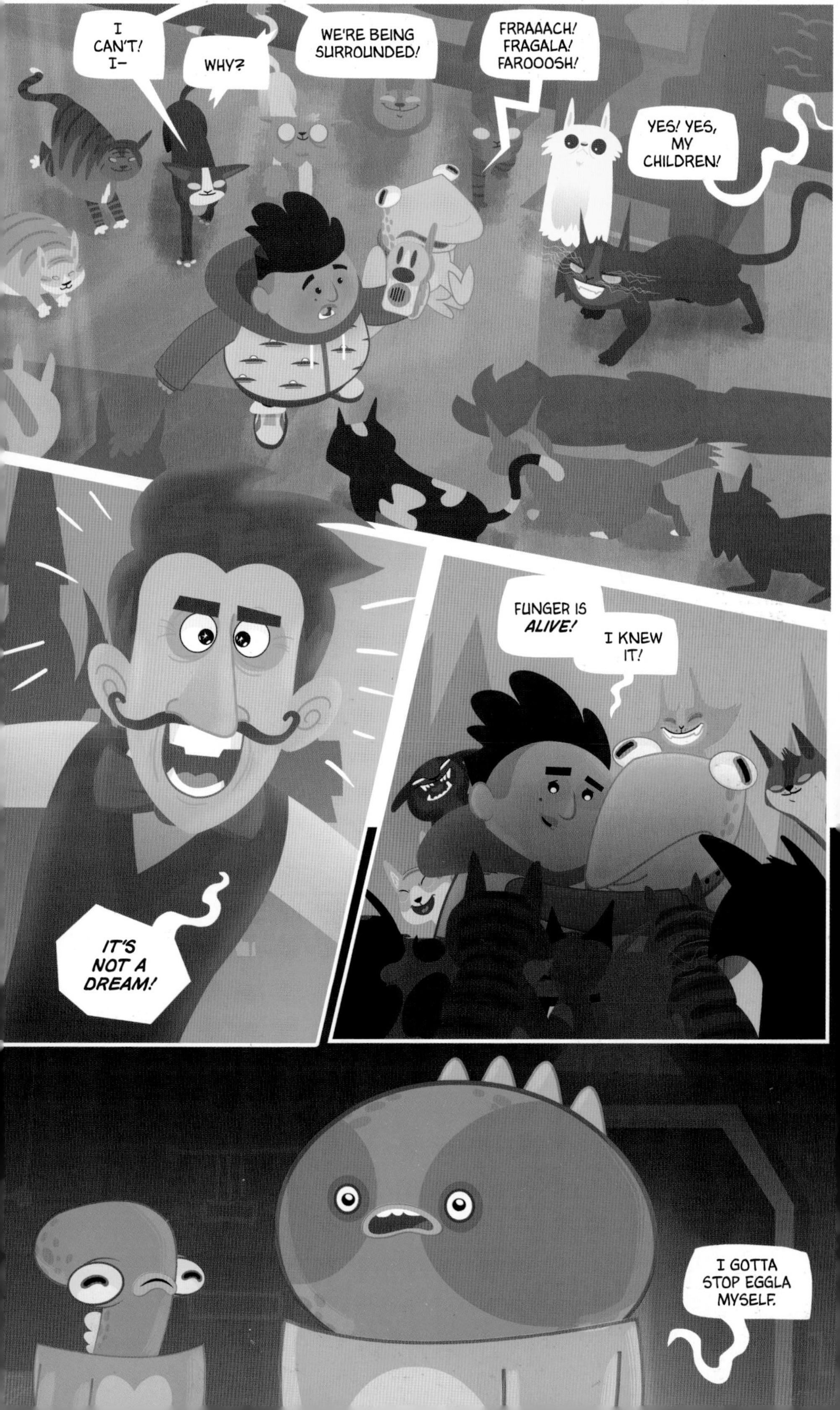
I CAN'T! I–
WHY?
WE'RE BEING SURROUNDED!
FRRAAACH! FRAGALA! FAROOOSH!
YES! YES, MY CHILDREN!
IT'S NOT A DREAM!
FUNGER IS ALIVE!
I KNEW IT!
I GOTTA STOP EGGLA MYSELF.

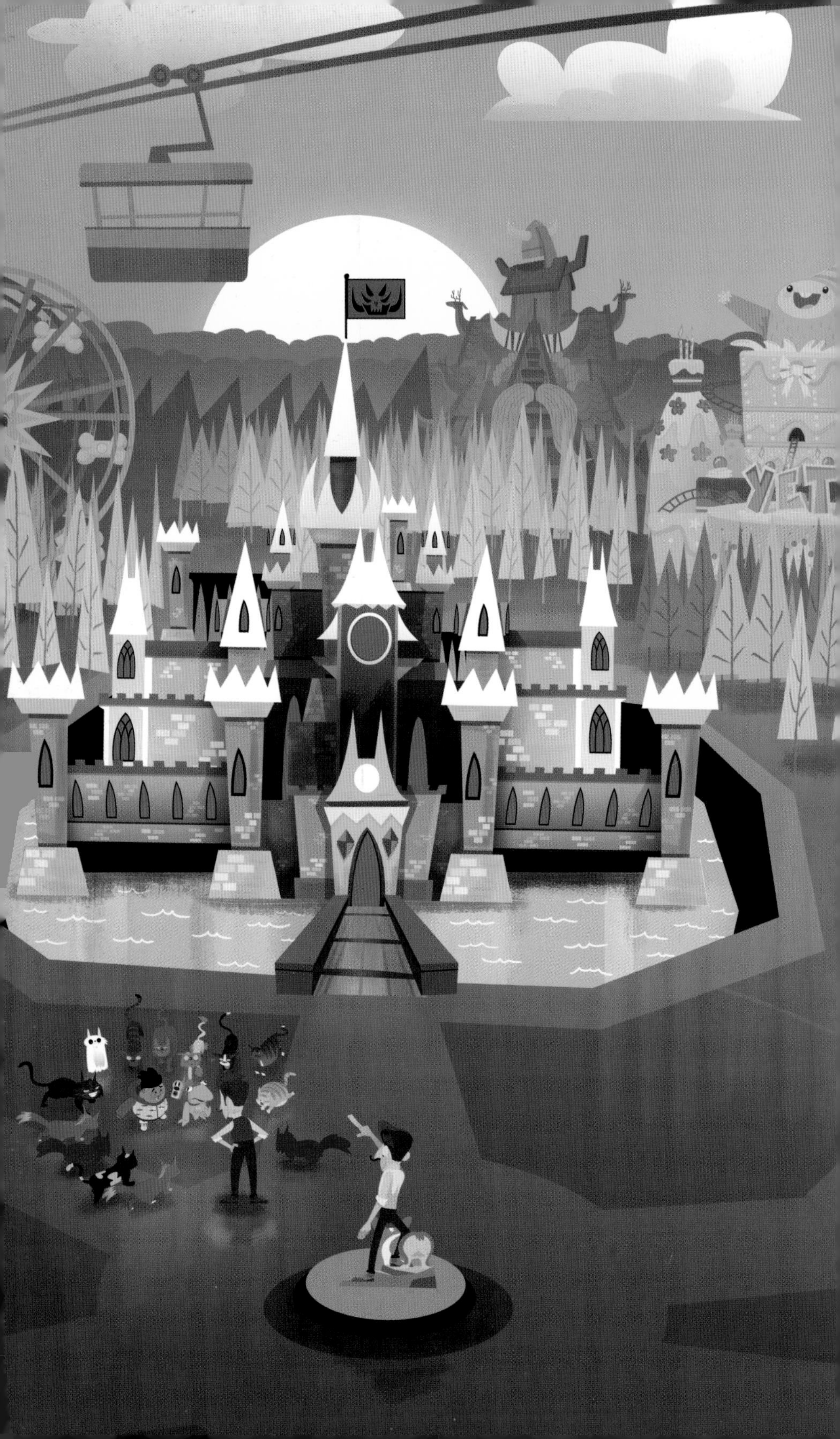

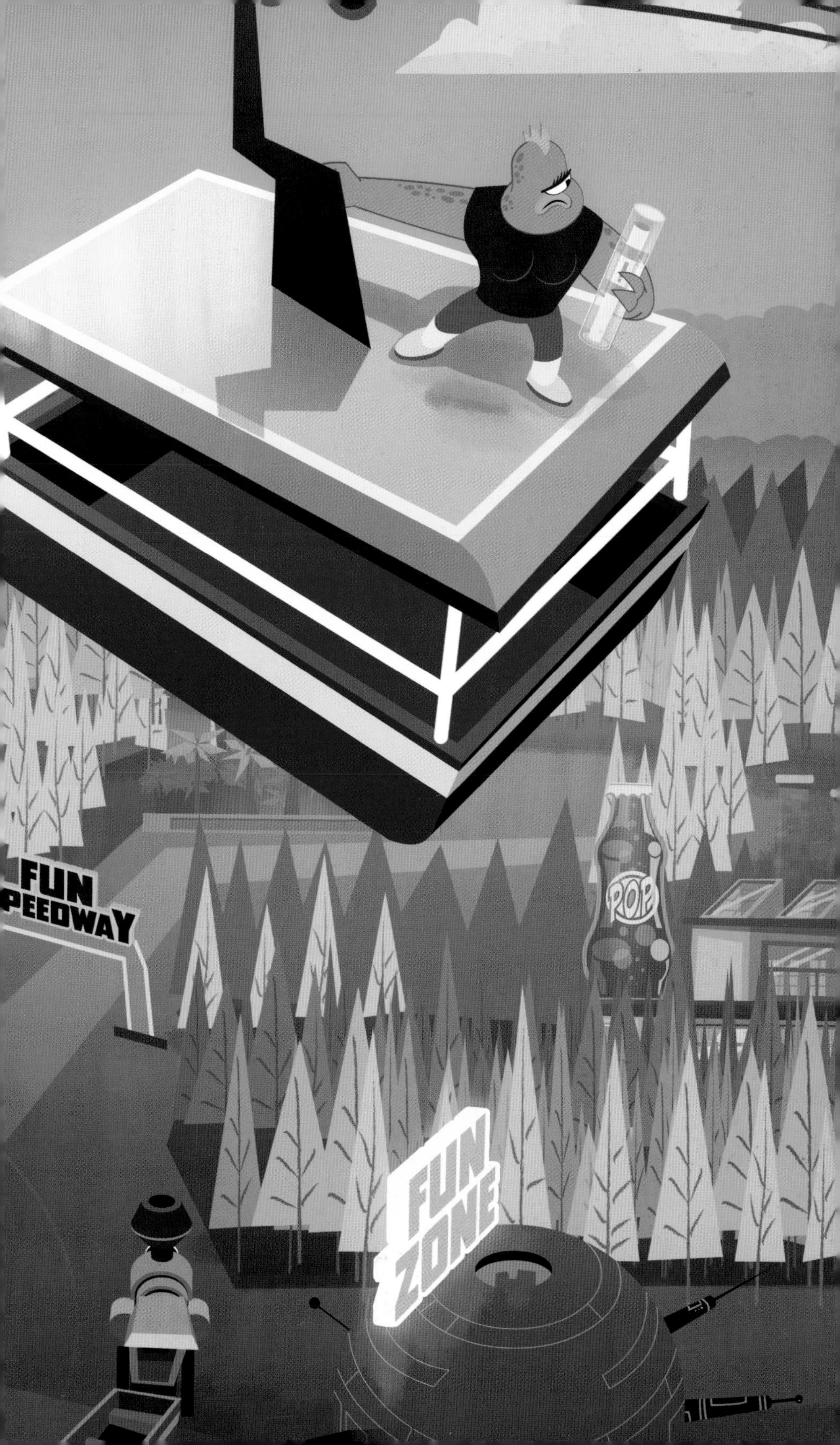
FUN
PEEDWAY
POP
FUN
ZONE

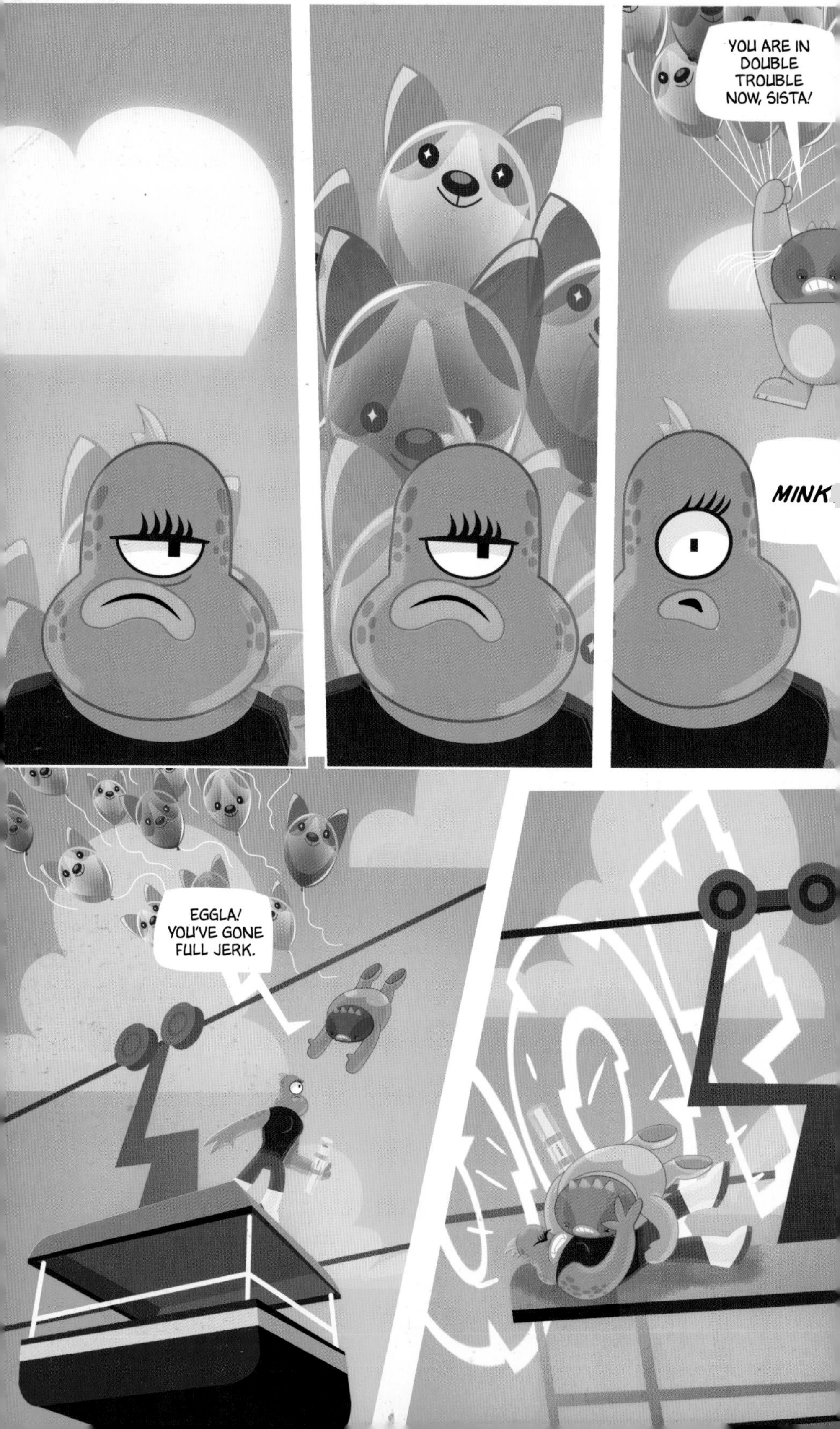
YOU ARE IN DOUBLE TROUBLE NOW, SISTA!
MINK
EGGLA! YOU'VE GONE FULL JERK.

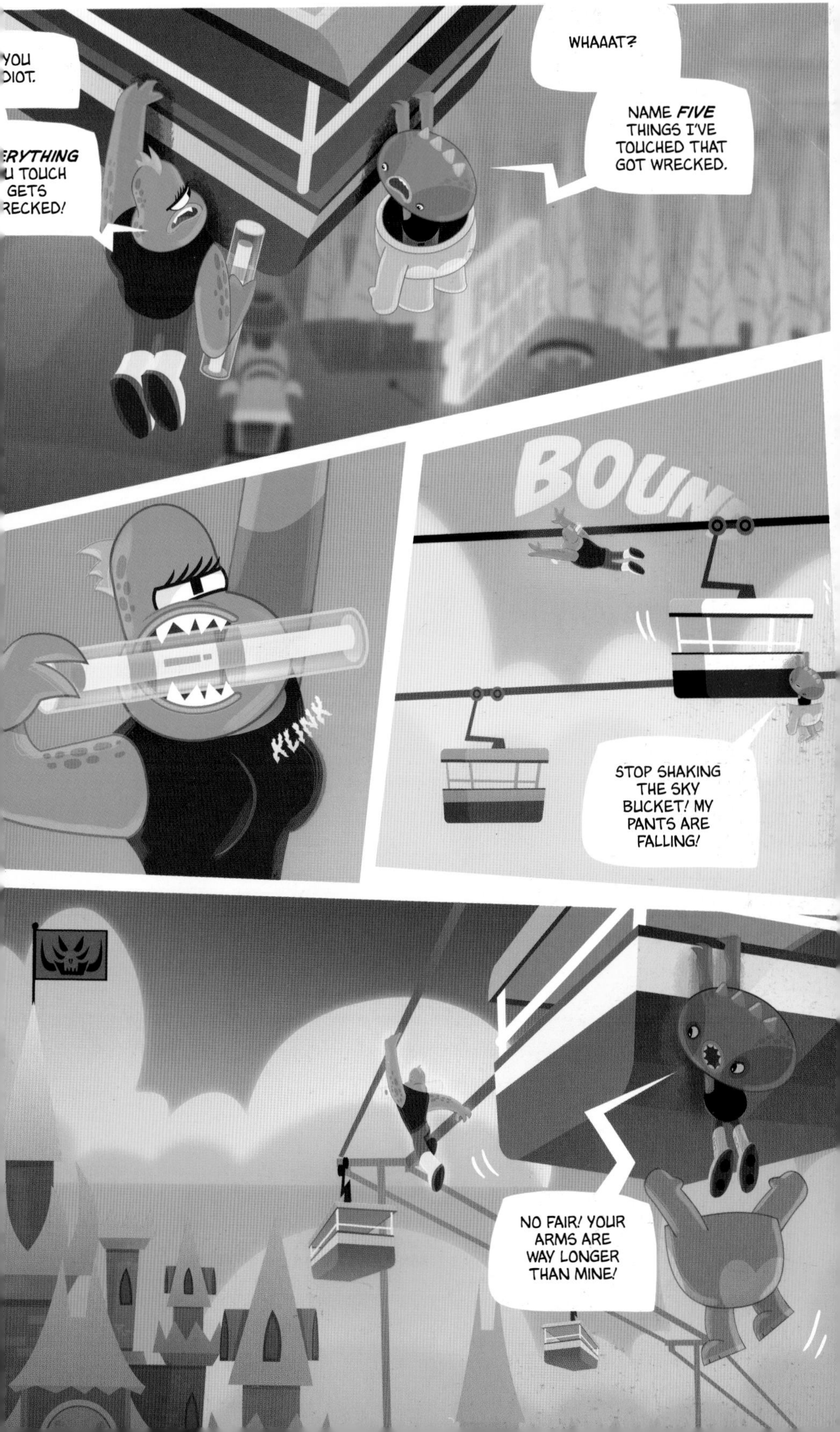
YOU
DIOT.
ERYTHING
U TOUCH
GETS
RECKED!
WHAAAT?
NAME *FIVE* THINGS I'VE TOUCHED THAT GOT WRECKED.
KLINK
BOUN
STOP SHAKING THE SKY BUCKET! MY PANTS ARE FALLING!
NO FAIR! YOUR ARMS ARE WAY LONGER THAN MINE!

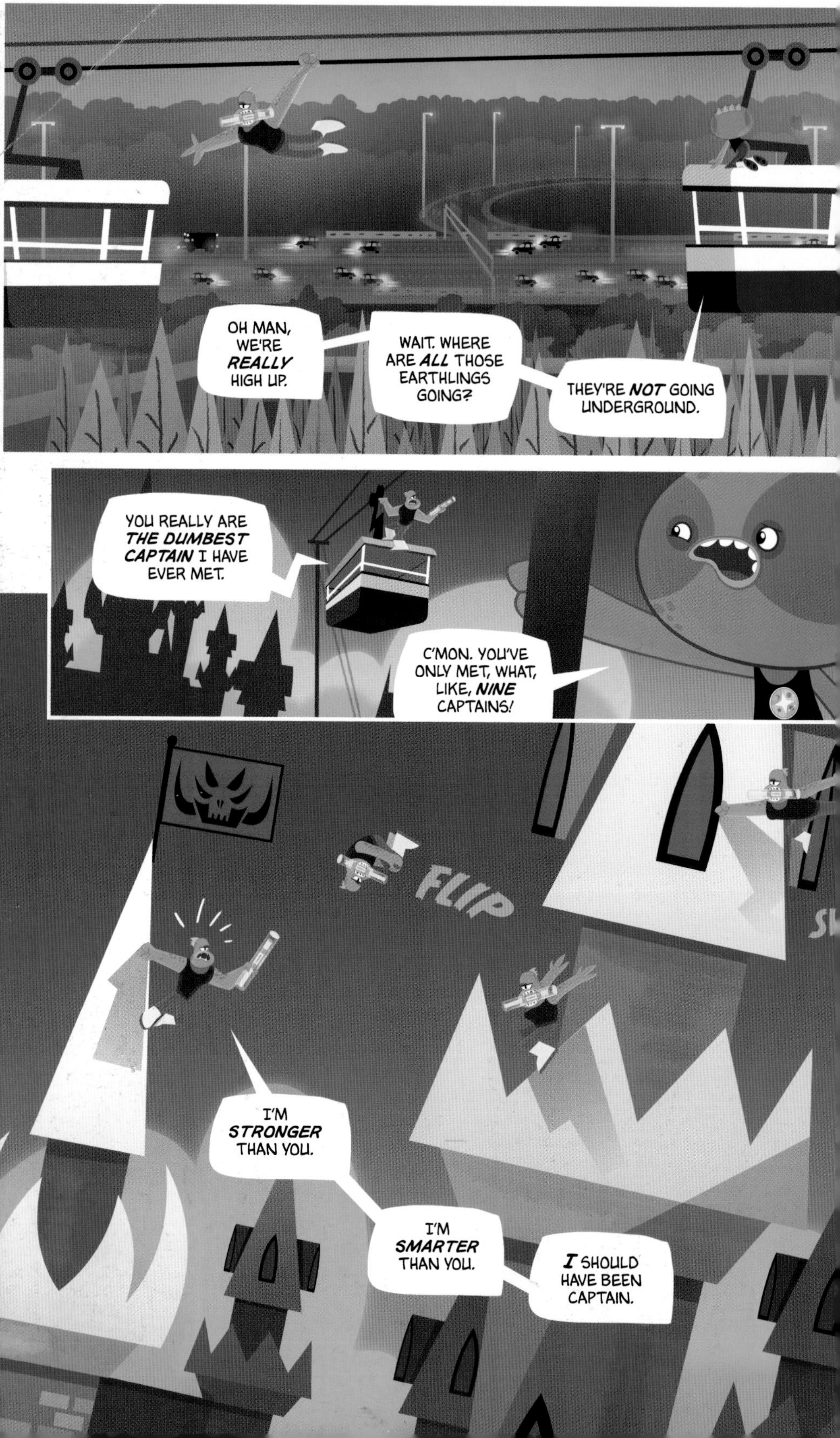
OH MAN, WE'RE *REALLY* HIGH UP.
WAIT. WHERE ARE *ALL* THOSE EARTHLINGS GOING?
THEY'RE *NOT* GOING UNDERGROUND.
YOU REALLY ARE *THE DUMBEST CAPTAIN* I HAVE EVER MET.
C'MON. YOU'VE ONLY MET, WHAT, LIKE, *NINE* CAPTAINS!
FLIP
I'M *STRONGER* THAN YOU.
I'M *SMARTER* THAN YOU.
I SHOULD HAVE BEEN CAPTAIN.

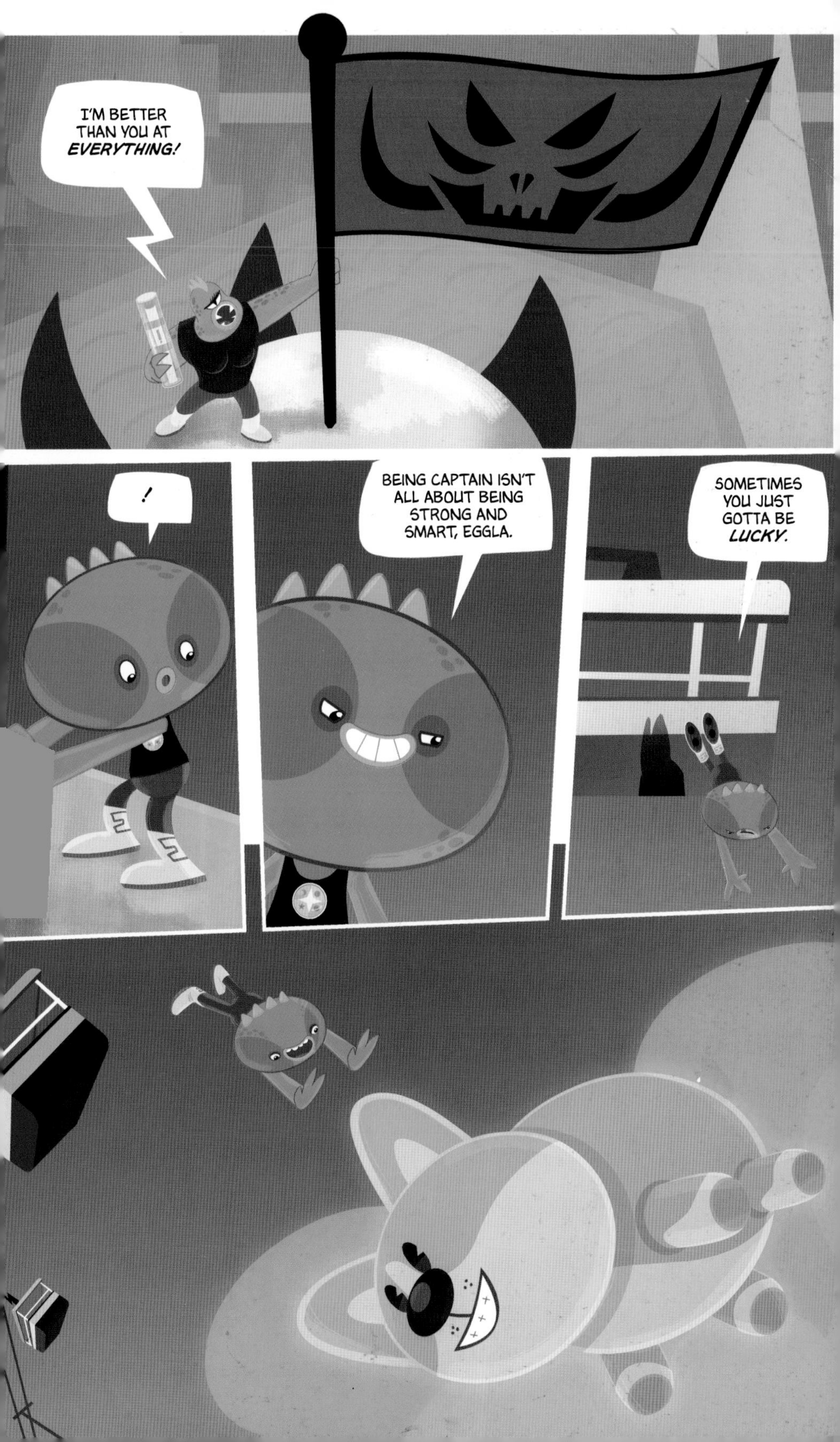
I'M BETTER THAN YOU AT EVERYTHING!
!
BEING CAPTAIN ISN'T ALL ABOUT BEING STRONG AND SMART, EGGLA.
SOMETIMES YOU JUST GOTTA BE LUCKY.

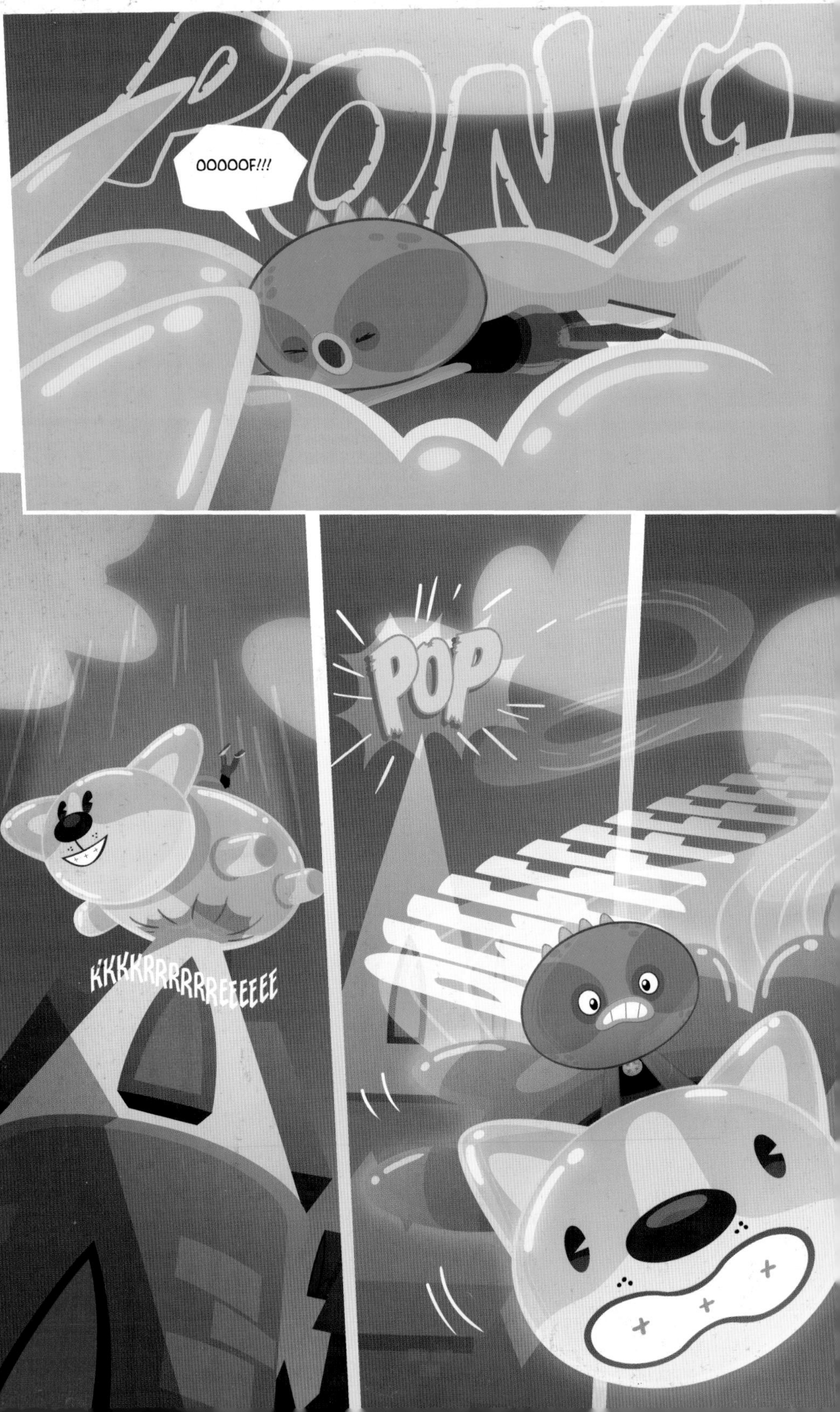
PONG
OOOOOF!!!
KKKKRRRRRREEEEEE
POP

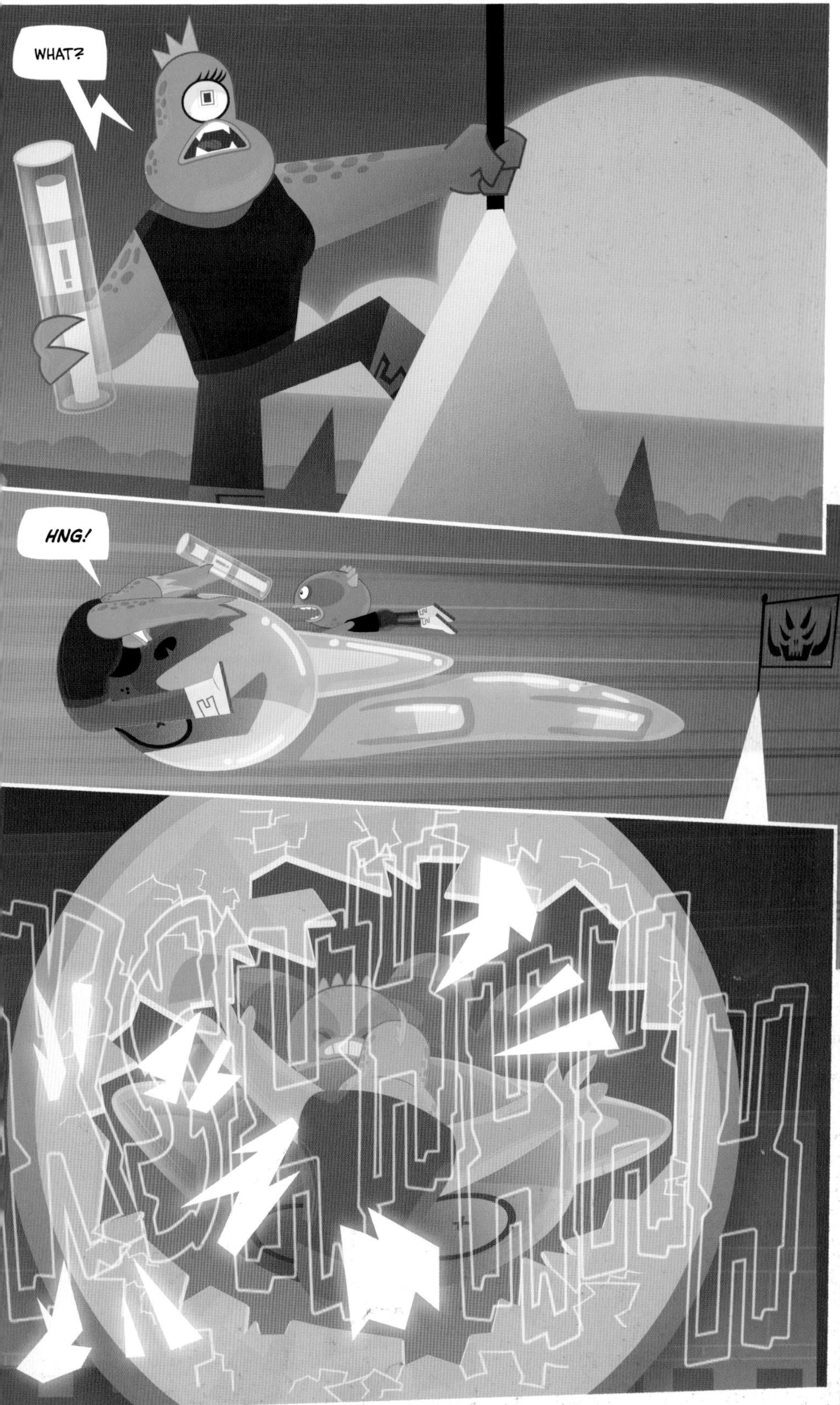
WHAT?
HNG!

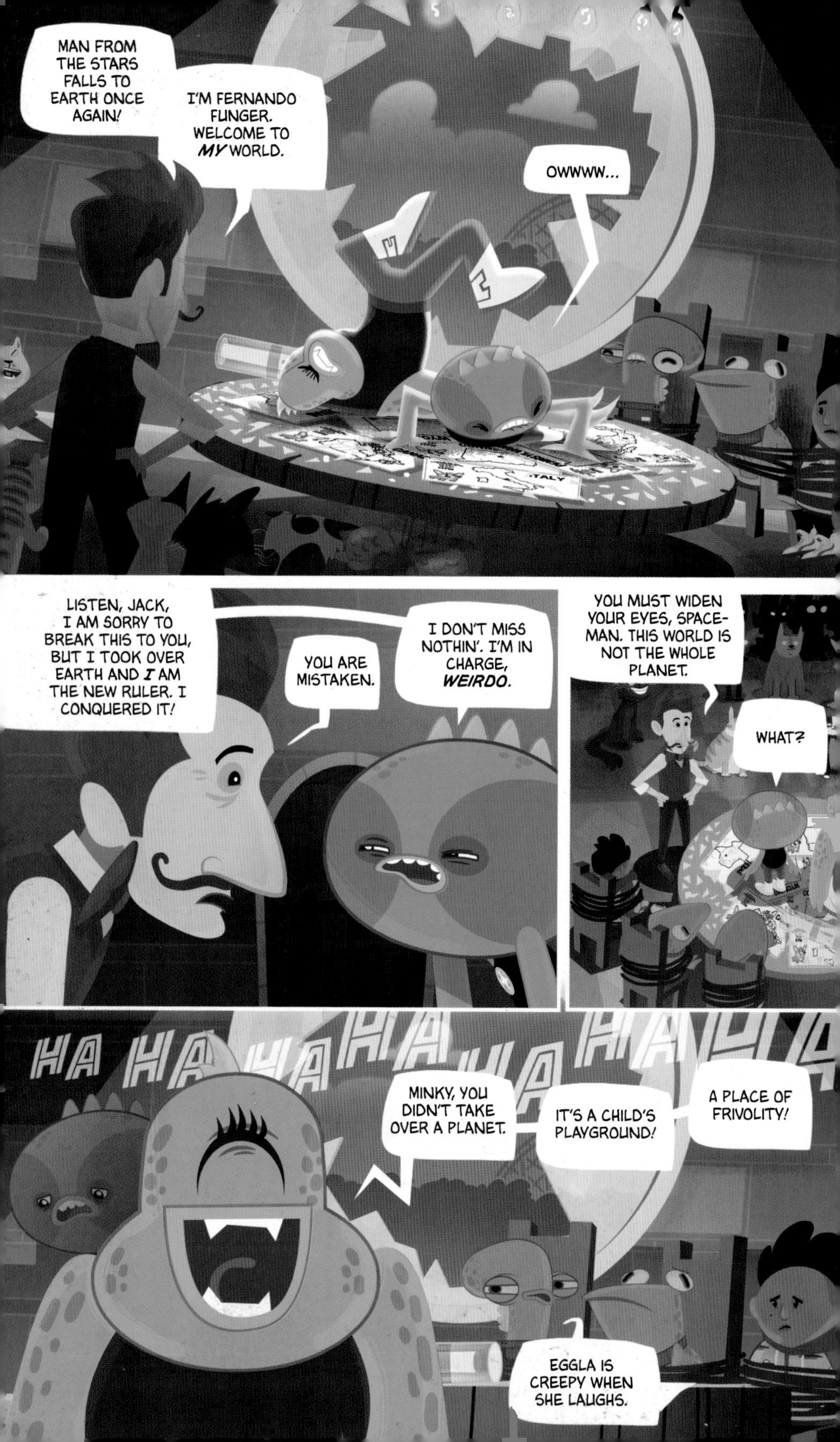
MAN FROM THE STARS FALLS TO EARTH ONCE AGAIN!
I'M FERNANDO FUNGER. WELCOME TO *MY* WORLD.
OWWWW...
ITALY
LISTEN, JACK, I AM SORRY TO BREAK THIS TO YOU, BUT I TOOK OVER EARTH AND *I* AM THE NEW RULER. I CONQUERED IT!
YOU ARE MISTAKEN.
I DON'T MISS NOTHIN'. I'M IN CHARGE, *WEIRDO.*
YOU MUST WIDEN YOUR EYES, SPACE-MAN. THIS WORLD IS NOT THE WHOLE PLANET.
WHAT?
HA HA HA HA HA HA HA HA HA HA
MINKY, YOU DIDN'T TAKE OVER A PLANET.
IT'S A CHILD'S PLAYGROUND!
A PLACE OF FRIVOLITY!
EGGLA IS CREEPY WHEN SHE LAUGHS.

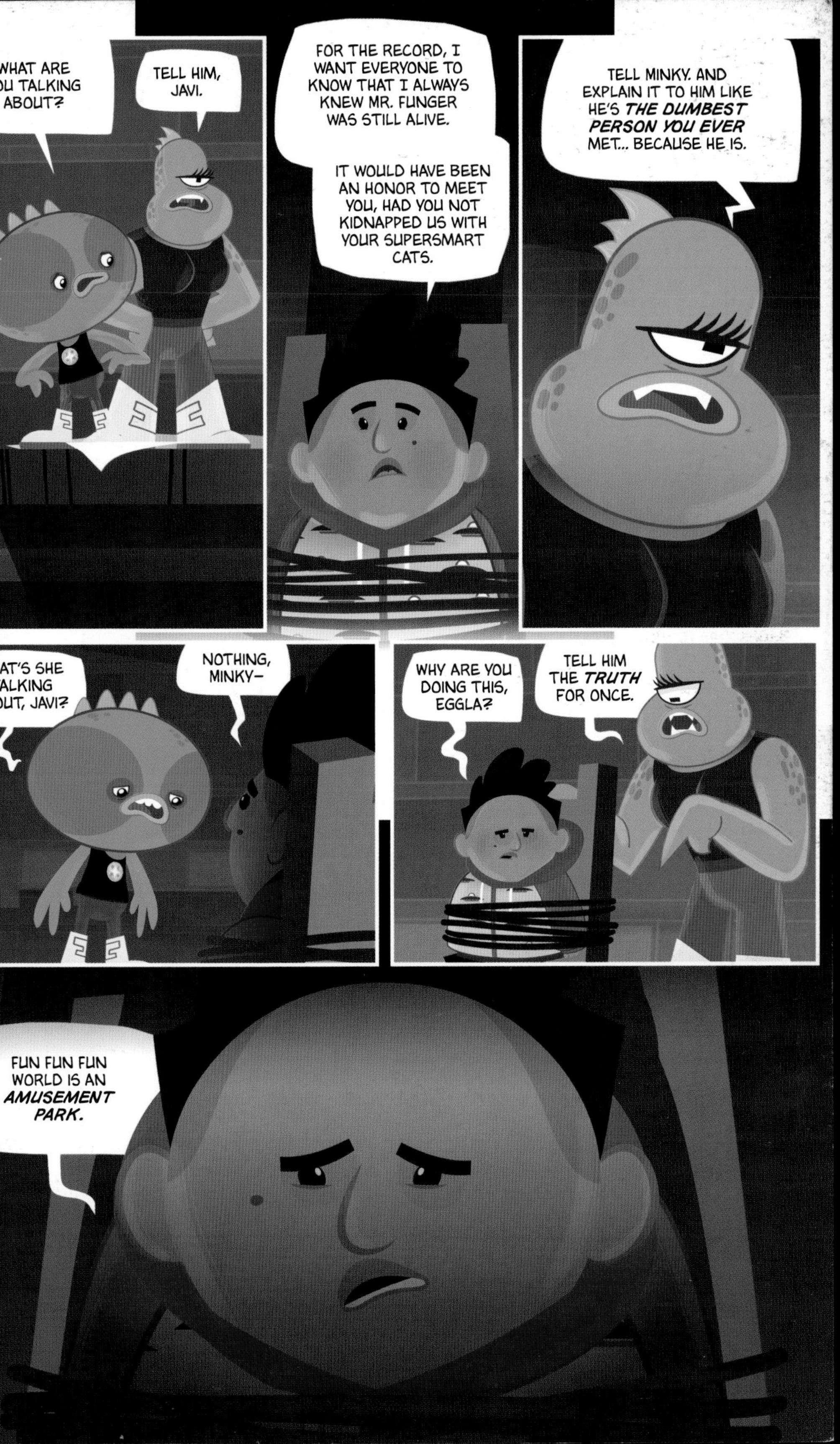
WHAT ARE OU TALKING ABOUT?
TELL HIM, JAVI.
FOR THE RECORD, I WANT EVERYONE TO KNOW THAT I ALWAYS KNEW MR. FUNGER WAS STILL ALIVE.
IT WOULD HAVE BEEN AN HONOR TO MEET YOU, HAD YOU NOT KIDNAPPED US WITH YOUR SUPERSMART CATS.
TELL MINKY. AND EXPLAIN IT TO HIM LIKE HE'S *THE DUMBEST PERSON YOU EVER* MET... BECAUSE HE IS.
AT'S SHE ALKING OUT, JAVI?
NOTHING, MINKY—
WHY ARE YOU DOING THIS, EGGLA?
TELL HIM THE *TRUTH* FOR ONCE.
FUN FUN FUN WORLD IS AN *AMUSEMENT PARK.*

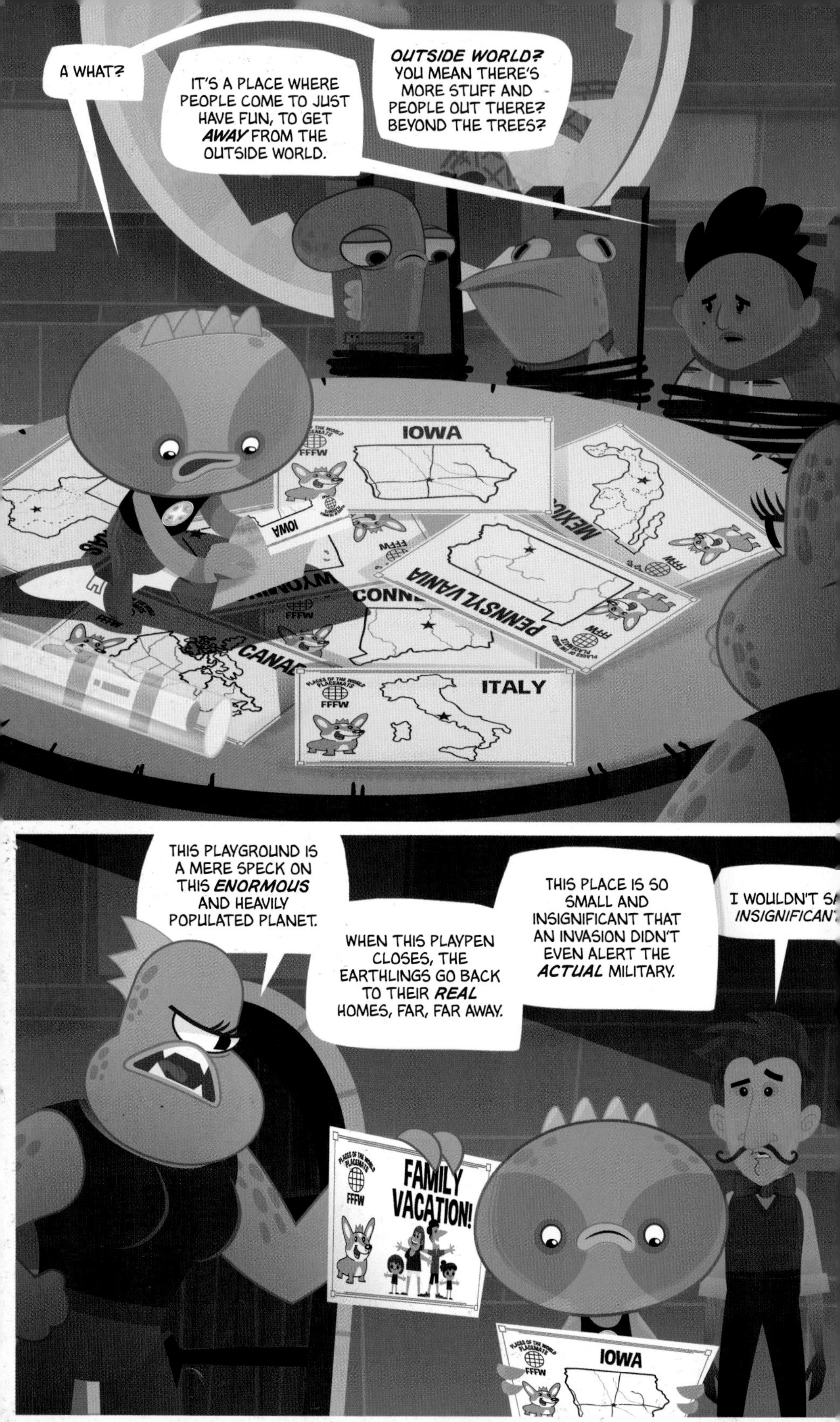
A WHAT?
IT'S A PLACE WHERE PEOPLE COME TO JUST HAVE FUN, TO GET *AWAY* FROM THE OUTSIDE WORLD.
OUTSIDE WORLD? YOU MEAN THERE'S MORE STUFF AND PEOPLE OUT THERE? BEYOND THE TREES?
IOWA
PENNSYLVANIA
ITALY
PLACES OF THE WORLD PLACEMATS
FFFW
THIS PLAYGROUND IS A MERE SPECK ON THIS *ENORMOUS* AND HEAVILY POPULATED PLANET.
WHEN THIS PLAYPEN CLOSES, THE EARTHLINGS GO BACK TO THEIR *REAL* HOMES, FAR, FAR AWAY.
THIS PLACE IS SO SMALL AND INSIGNIFICANT THAT AN INVASION DIDN'T EVEN ALERT THE *ACTUAL* MILITARY.
I WOULDN'T SA
INSIGNIFICAN
FAMILY VACATION!
IOWA

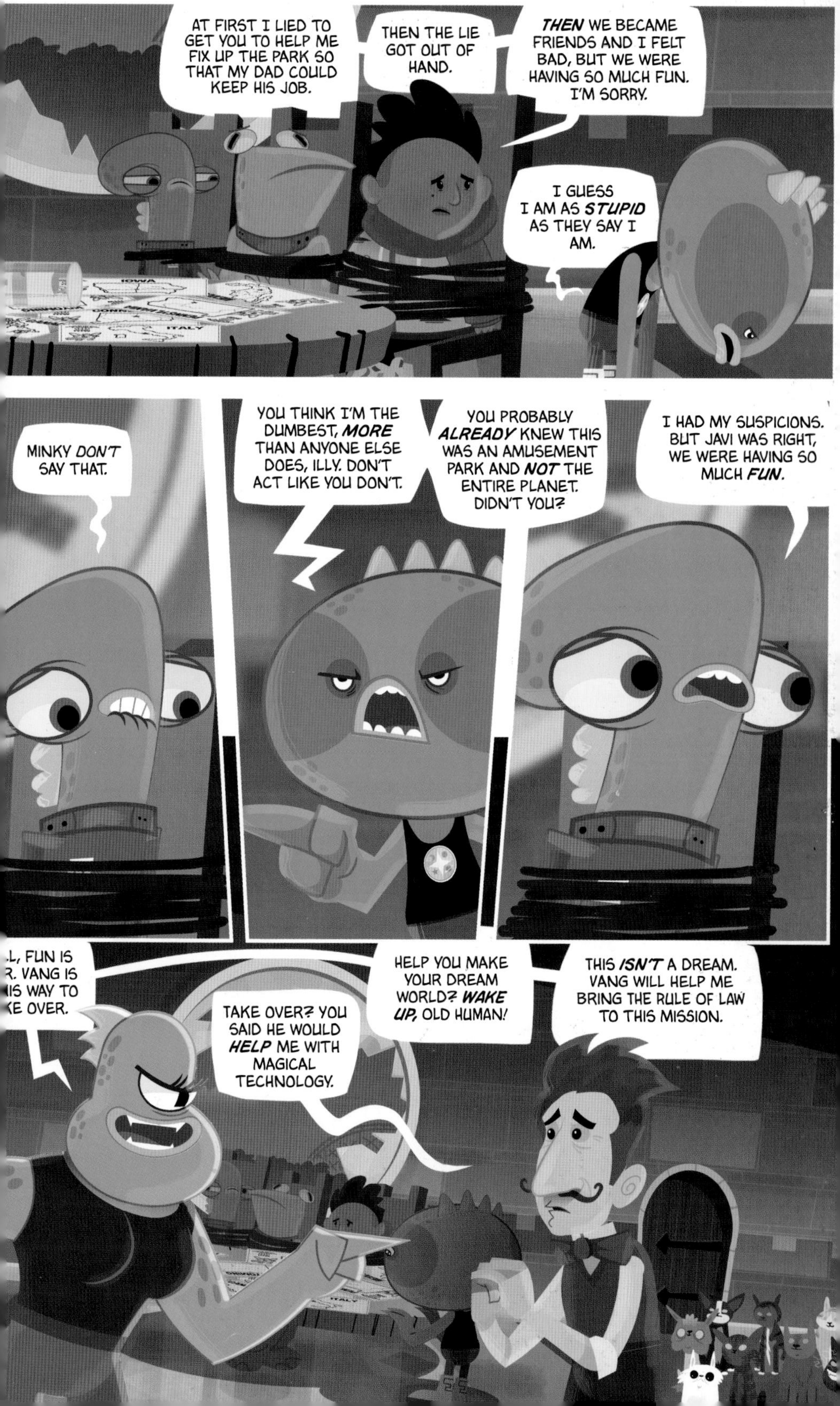

AT FIRST I LIED TO GET YOU TO HELP ME FIX UP THE PARK SO THAT MY DAD COULD KEEP HIS JOB.
THEN THE LIE GOT OUT OF HAND.
THEN WE BECAME FRIENDS AND I FELT BAD, BUT WE WERE HAVING SO MUCH FUN. I'M SORRY.
I GUESS I AM AS *STUPID* AS THEY SAY I AM.
IOWA
ITALY
MINKY *DON'T* SAY THAT.
YOU THINK I'M THE DUMBEST, *MORE* THAN ANYONE ELSE DOES, ILLY. DON'T ACT LIKE YOU DON'T.
YOU PROBABLY *ALREADY* KNEW THIS WAS AN AMUSEMENT PARK AND *NOT* THE ENTIRE PLANET. DIDN'T YOU?
I HAD MY SUSPICIONS. BUT JAVI WAS RIGHT, WE WERE HAVING SO MUCH *FUN*.
L, FUN IS R. VANG IS IS WAY TO KE OVER.
TAKE OVER? YOU SAID HE WOULD *HELP* ME WITH MAGICAL TECHNOLOGY.
HELP YOU MAKE YOUR DREAM WORLD? *WAKE UP,* OLD HUMAN!
THIS *ISN'T* A DREAM. VANG WILL HELP ME BRING THE RULE OF LAW TO THIS MISSION.

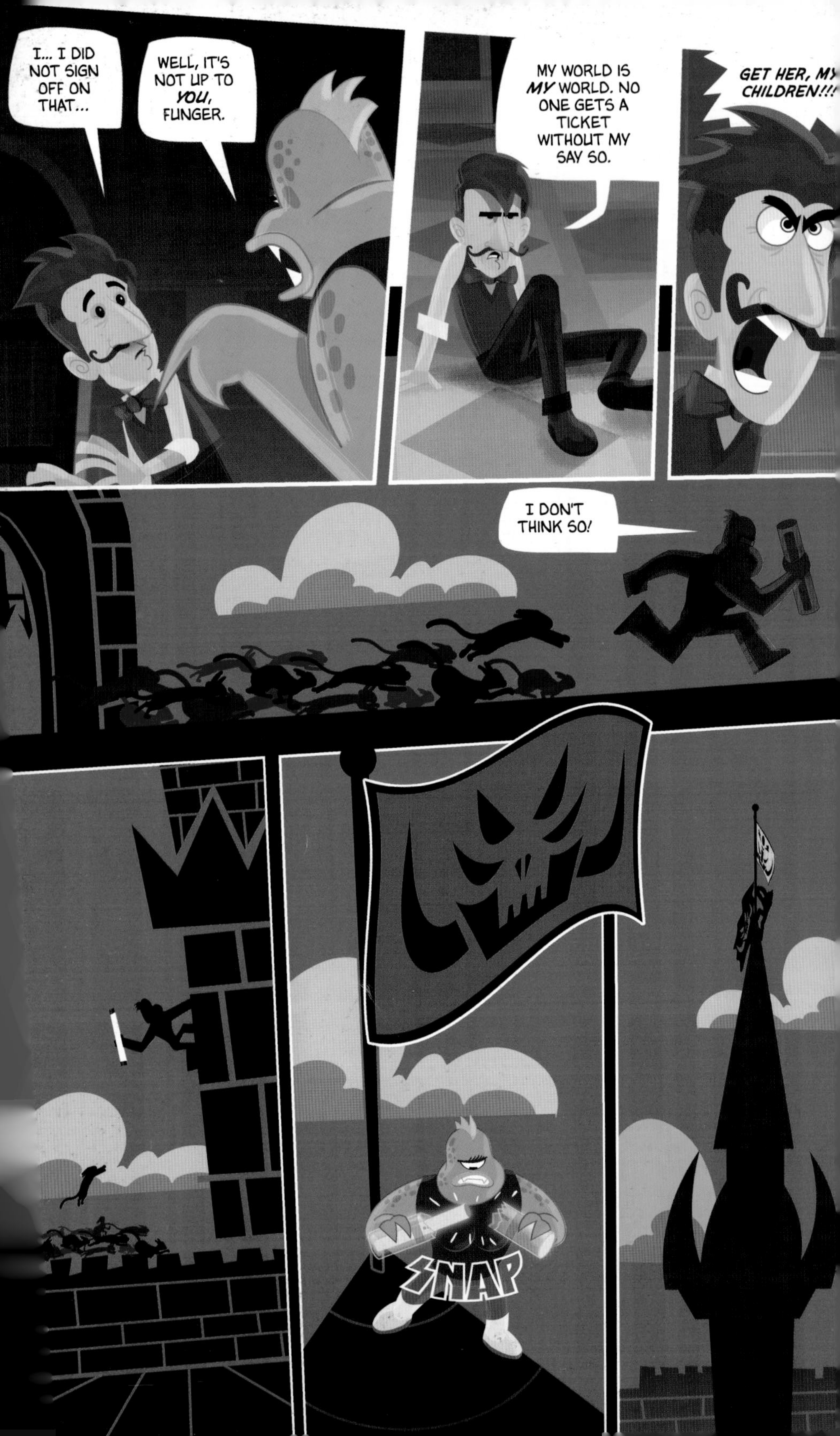
I... I DID NOT SIGN OFF ON THAT...
WELL, IT'S NOT UP TO *YOU*, FUNGER.
MY WORLD IS *MY* WORLD. NO ONE GETS A TICKET WITHOUT MY SAY SO.
GET HER, MY CHILDREN!!!
I DON'T THINK SO!
SNAP

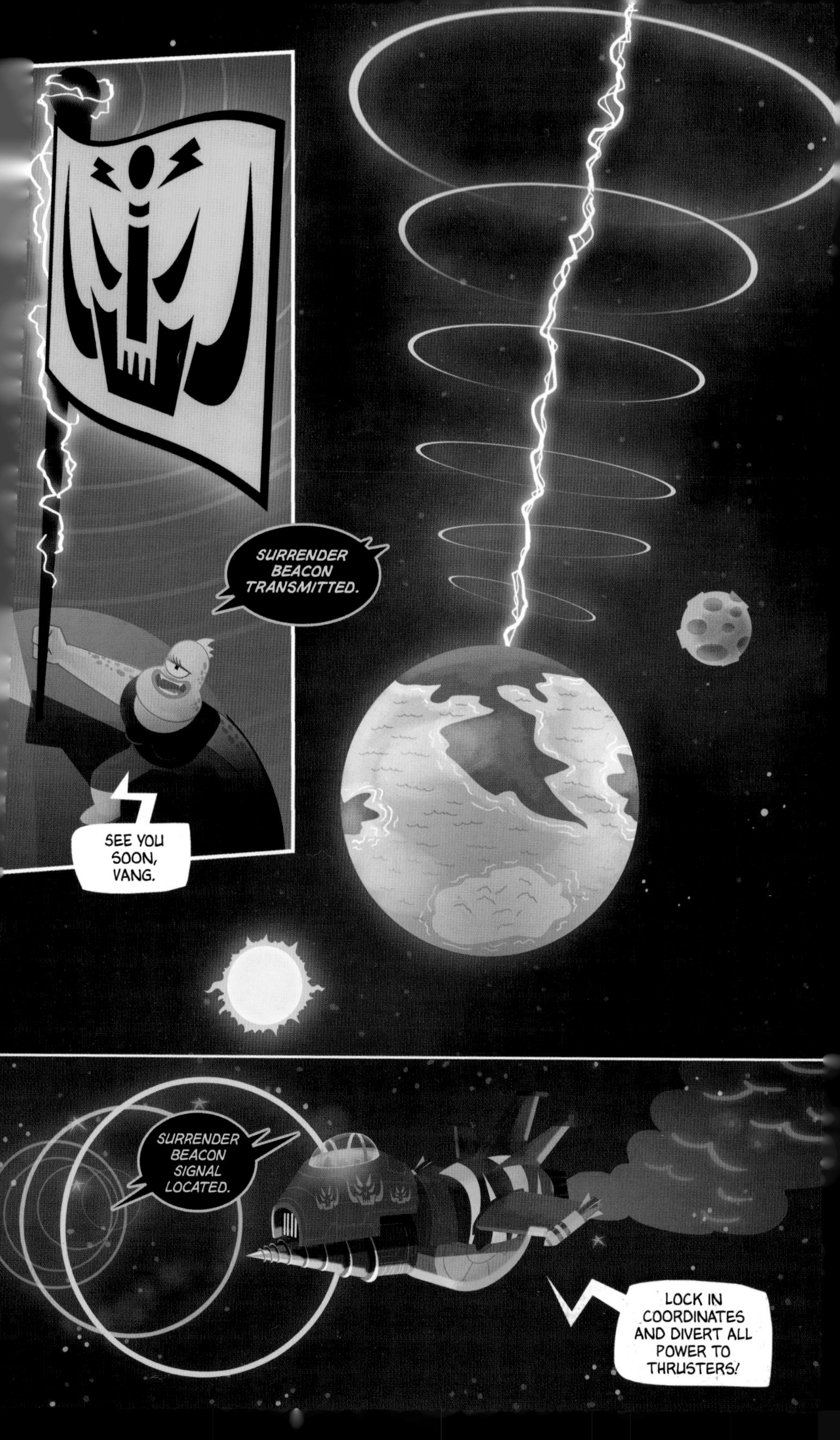
SURRENDER BEACON TRANSMITTED.
SEE YOU SOON, VANG.
SURRENDER BEACON SIGNAL LOCATED.
LOCK IN COORDINATES AND DIVERT ALL POWER TO THRUSTERS!

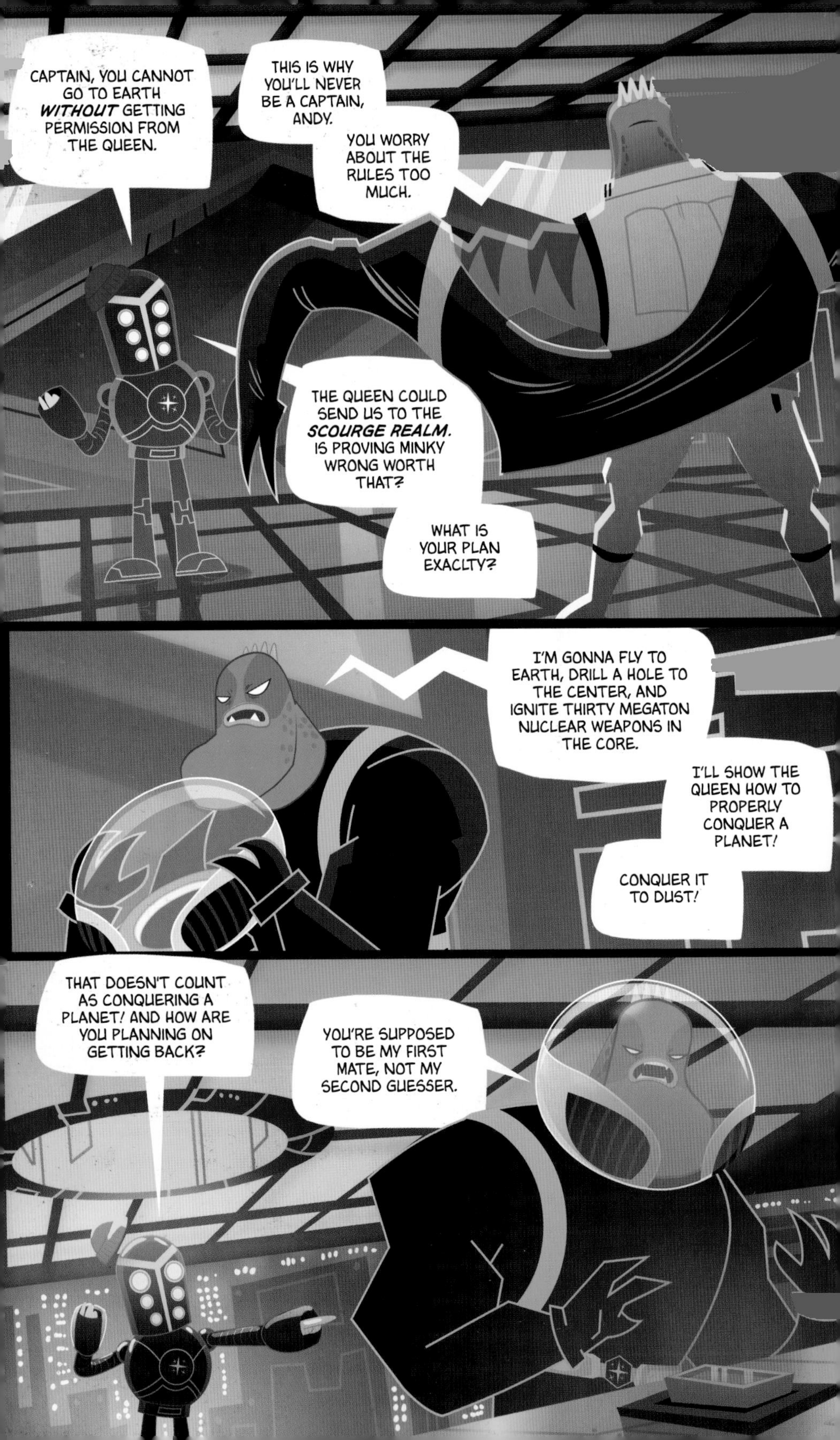
CAPTAIN, YOU CANNOT GO TO EARTH *WITHOUT* GETTING PERMISSION FROM THE QUEEN.
THIS IS WHY YOU'LL NEVER BE A CAPTAIN, ANDY.
YOU WORRY ABOUT THE RULES TOO MUCH.
THE QUEEN COULD SEND US TO THE *SCOURGE REALM.* IS PROVING MINKY WRONG WORTH THAT?
WHAT IS YOUR PLAN EXACLTY?
I'M GONNA FLY TO EARTH, DRILL A HOLE TO THE CENTER, AND IGNITE THIRTY MEGATON NUCLEAR WEAPONS IN THE CORE.
I'LL SHOW THE QUEEN HOW TO PROPERLY CONQUER A PLANET!
CONQUER IT TO DUST!
THAT DOESN'T COUNT AS CONQUERING A PLANET! AND HOW ARE YOU PLANNING ON GETTING BACK?
YOU'RE SUPPOSED TO BE MY FIRST MATE, NOT MY SECOND GUESSER.

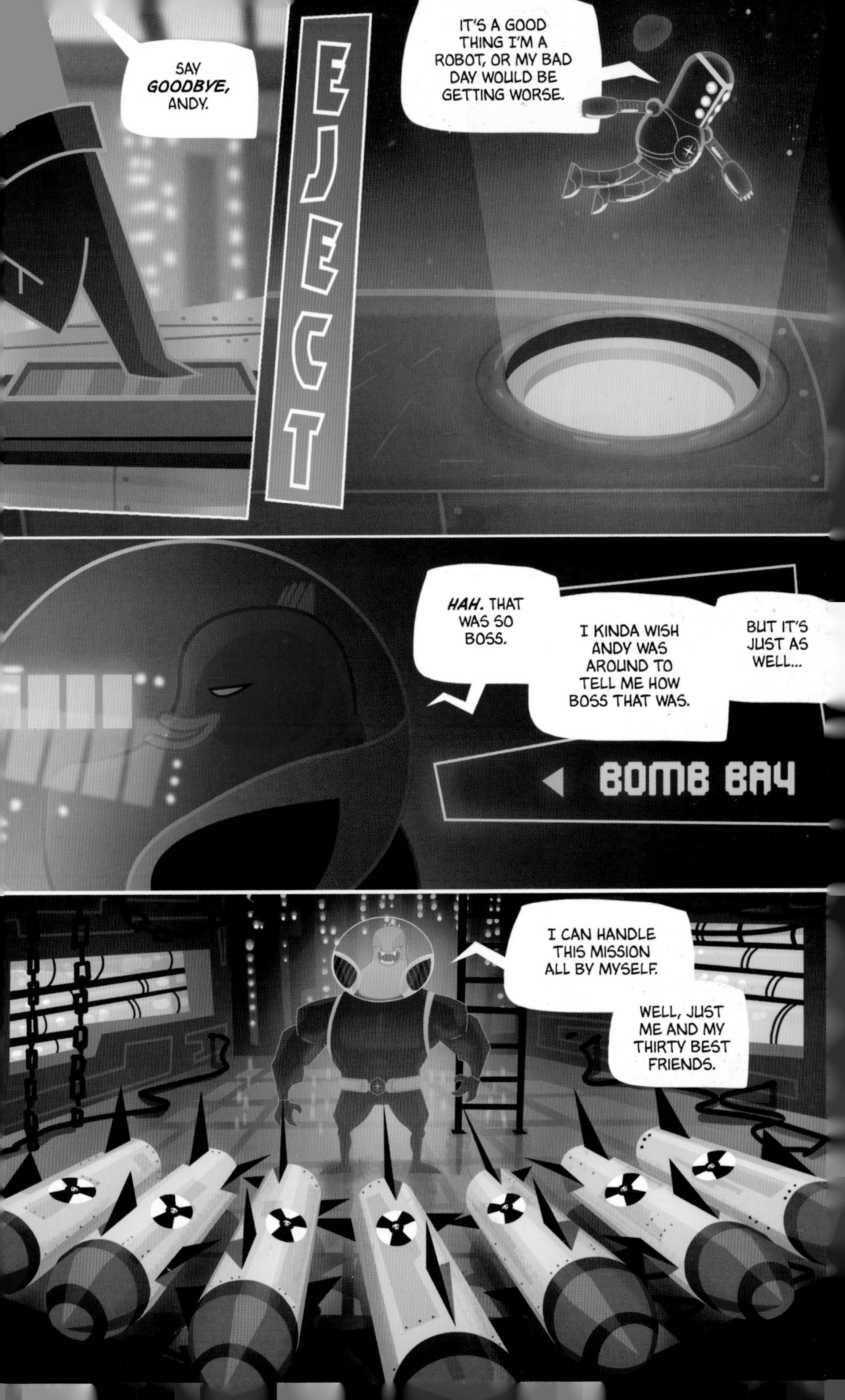
SAY *GOODBYE,* ANDY.
EJECT
IT'S A GOOD THING I'M A ROBOT, OR MY BAD DAY WOULD BE GETTING WORSE.
HAH. THAT WAS SO BOSS.
I KINDA WISH ANDY WAS AROUND TO TELL ME HOW BOSS THAT WAS.
BUT IT'S JUST AS WELL...
BOMB BAY
I CAN HANDLE THIS MISSION ALL BY MYSELF.
WELL, JUST ME AND MY THIRTY BEST FRIENDS.

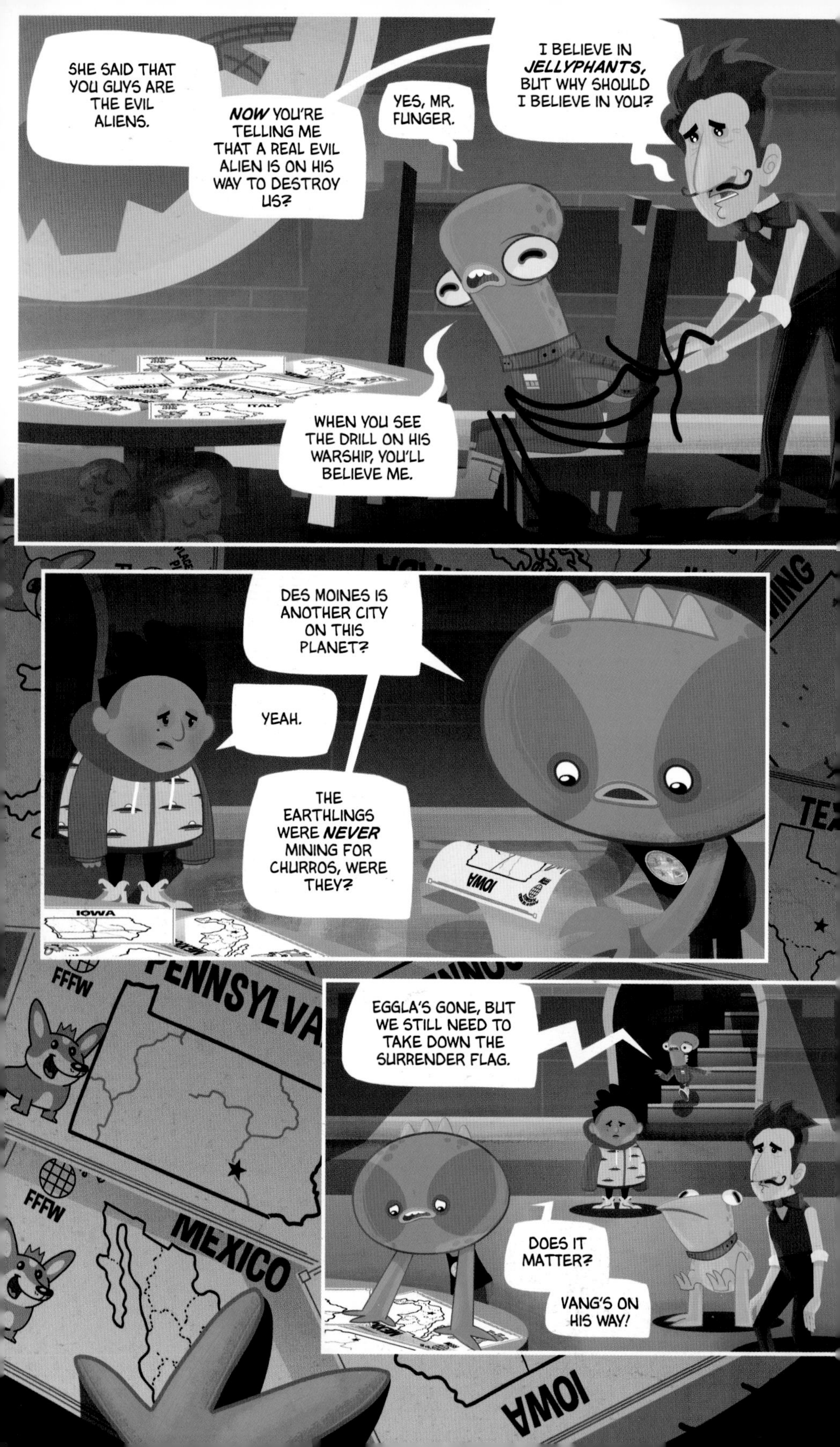
SHE SAID THAT YOU GUYS ARE THE EVIL ALIENS.
NOW YOU'RE TELLING ME THAT A REAL EVIL ALIEN IS ON HIS WAY TO DESTROY US?
YES, MR. FUNGER.
I BELIEVE IN *JELLYPHANTS,* BUT WHY SHOULD I BELIEVE IN YOU?
WHEN YOU SEE THE DRILL ON HIS WARSHIP, YOU'LL BELIEVE ME.
IOWA
ITALY
DES MOINES IS ANOTHER CITY ON THIS PLANET?
YEAH.
THE EARTHLINGS WERE *NEVER* MINING FOR CHURROS, WERE THEY?
IOWA
IOWA
PENNSYLVA
FFFW
FFFW
MEXICO
EGGLA'S GONE, BUT WE STILL NEED TO TAKE DOWN THE SURRENDER FLAG.
DOES IT MATTER?
VANG'S ON HIS WAY!
IOWA

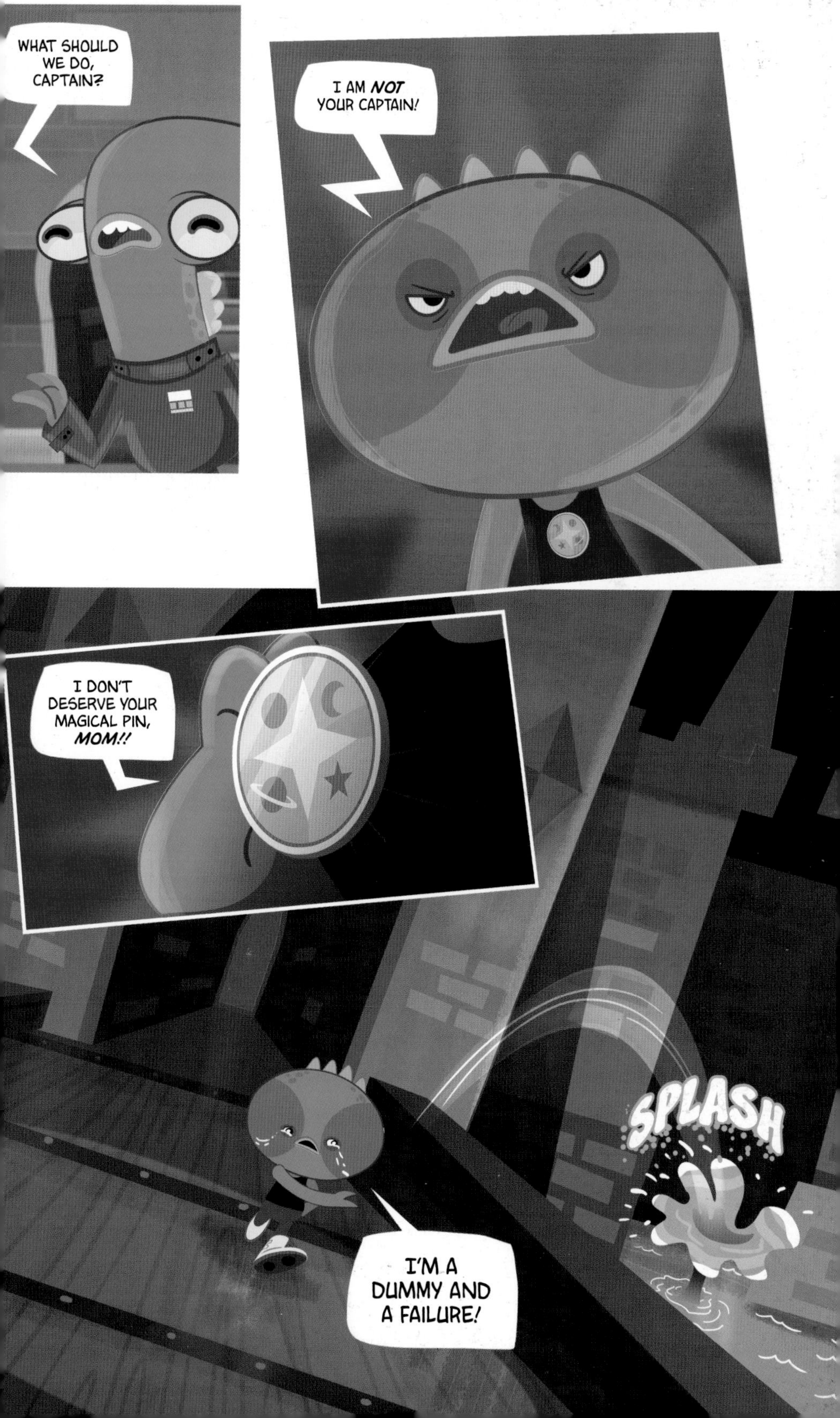
WHAT SHOULD WE DO, CAPTAIN?
I AM *NOT* YOUR CAPTAIN!
I DON'T DESERVE YOUR MAGICAL PIN, *MOM!!*
SPLASH
I'M A DUMMY AND A FAILURE!

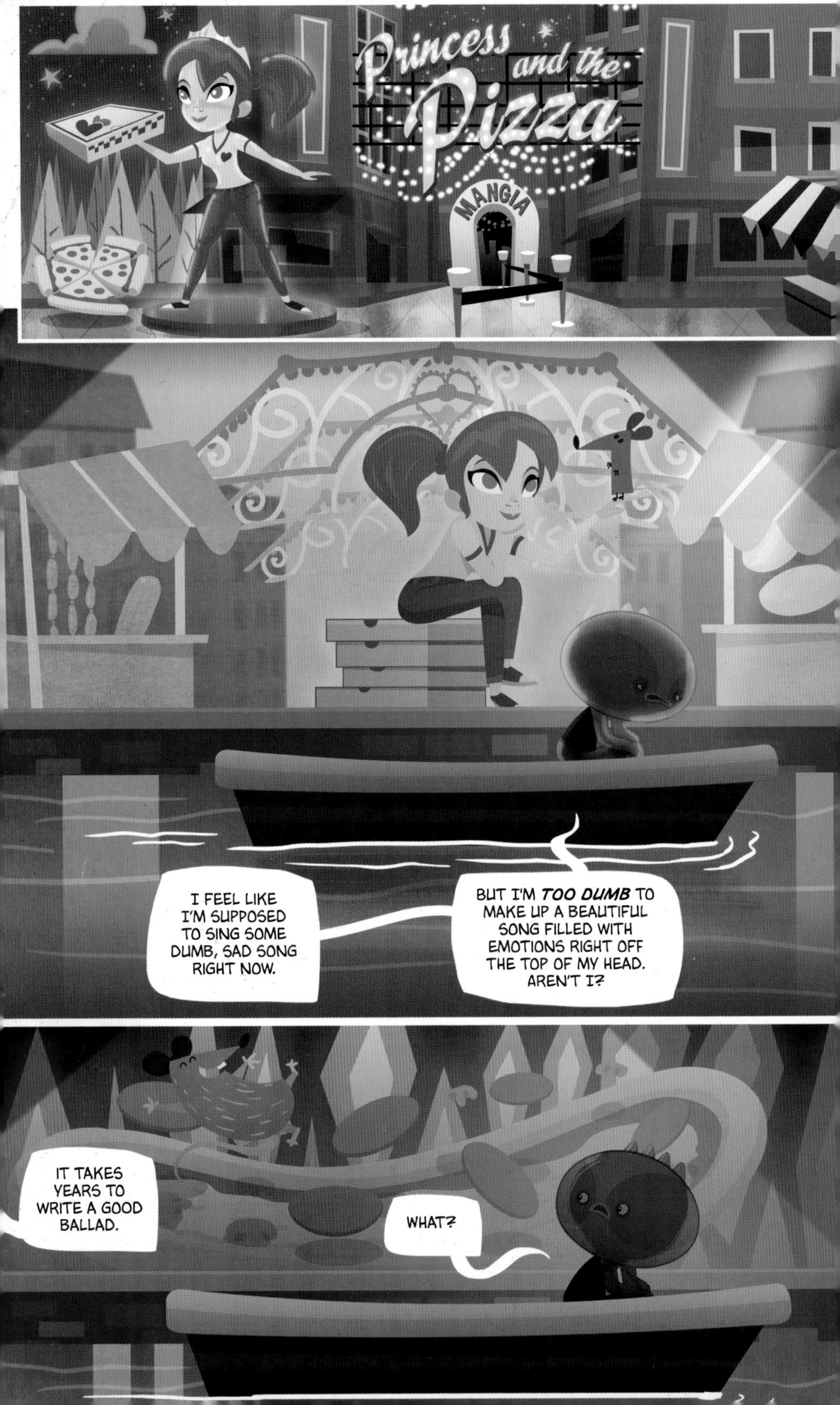
Princess and the Pizza
MANGIA
I FEEL LIKE I'M SUPPOSED TO SING SOME DUMB, SAD SONG RIGHT NOW.
BUT I'M *TOO DUMB* TO MAKE UP A BEAUTIFUL SONG FILLED WITH EMOTIONS RIGHT OFF THE TOP OF MY HEAD. AREN'T I?
IT TAKES YEARS TO WRITE A GOOD BALLAD.
WHAT?

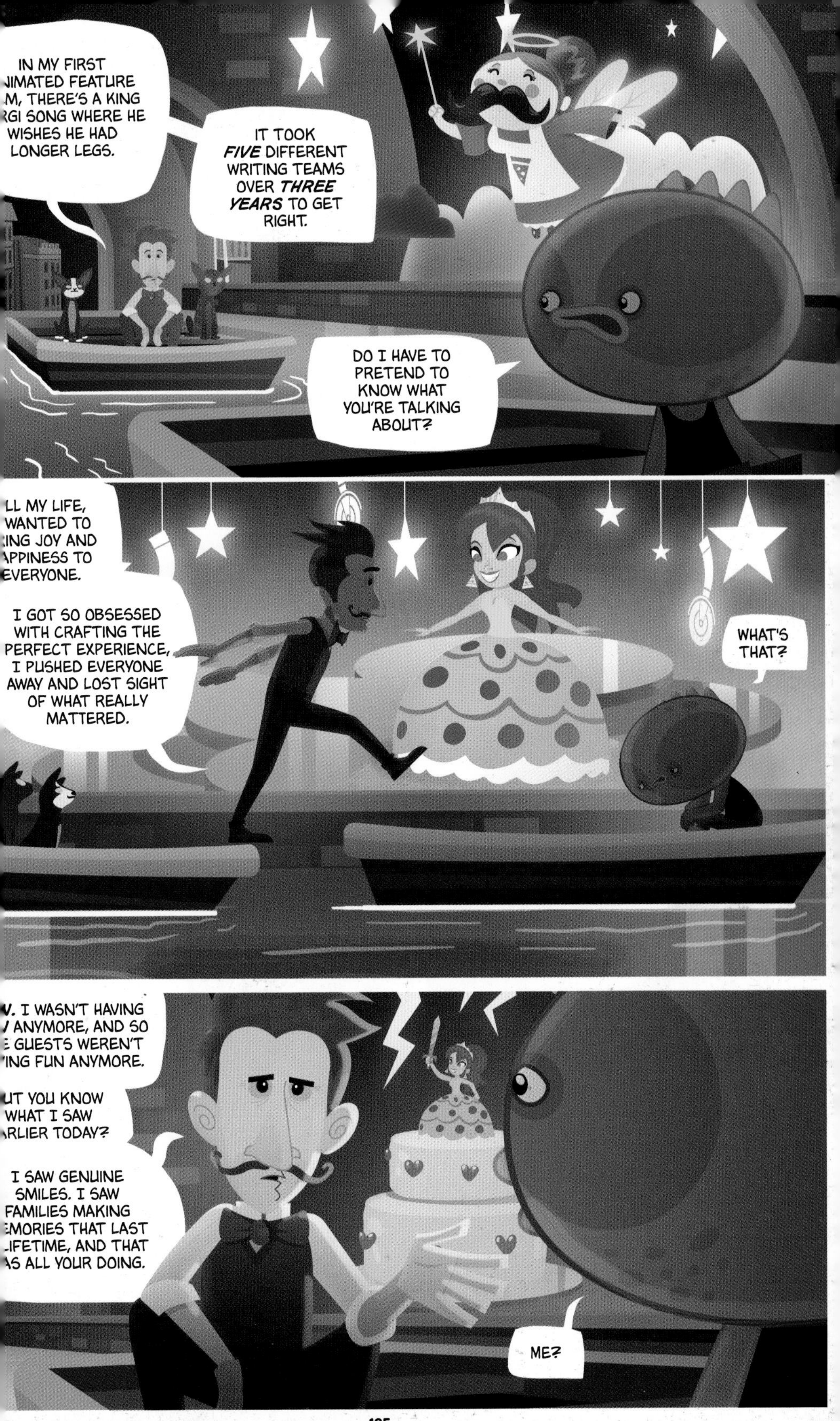

IN MY FIRST
NIMATED FEATURE
M, THERE'S A KING
RGI SONG WHERE HE
WISHES HE HAD
LONGER LEGS.
IT TOOK *FIVE* DIFFERENT WRITING TEAMS OVER *THREE YEARS* TO GET RIGHT.
DO I HAVE TO PRETEND TO KNOW WHAT YOU'RE TALKING ABOUT?
LL MY LIFE,
WANTED TO
ING JOY AND
APPINESS TO
EVERYONE.
I GOT SO OBSESSED WITH CRAFTING THE PERFECT EXPERIENCE, I PUSHED EVERYONE AWAY AND LOST SIGHT OF WHAT REALLY MATTERED.
WHAT'S THAT?
V. I WASN'T HAVING
/ ANYMORE, AND SO
E GUESTS WEREN'T
ING FUN ANYMORE.
UT YOU KNOW
WHAT I SAW
RLIER TODAY?
I SAW GENUINE
SMILES. I SAW
FAMILIES MAKING
EMORIES THAT LAST
LIFETIME, AND THAT
AS ALL YOUR DOING.
ME?

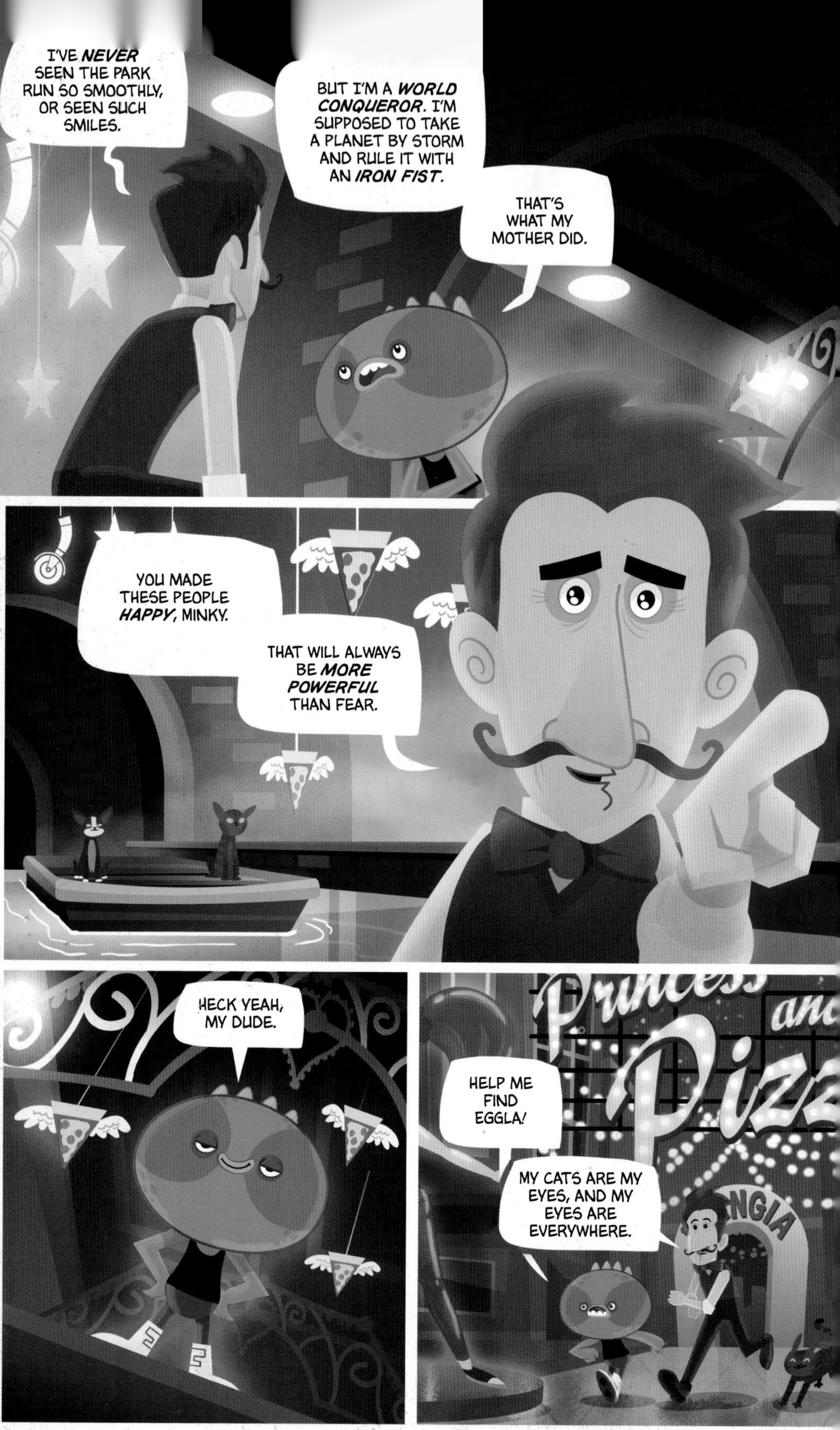

I'VE NEVER SEEN THE PARK RUN SO SMOOTHLY, OR SEEN SUCH SMILES.
BUT I'M A WORLD CONQUEROR. I'M SUPPOSED TO TAKE A PLANET BY STORM AND RULE IT WITH AN IRON FIST.
THAT'S WHAT MY MOTHER DID.
YOU MADE THESE PEOPLE HAPPY, MINKY.
THAT WILL ALWAYS BE MORE POWERFUL THAN FEAR.
HECK YEAH, MY DUDE.
HELP ME FIND EGGLA!
MY CATS ARE MY EYES, AND MY EYES ARE EVERYWHERE.

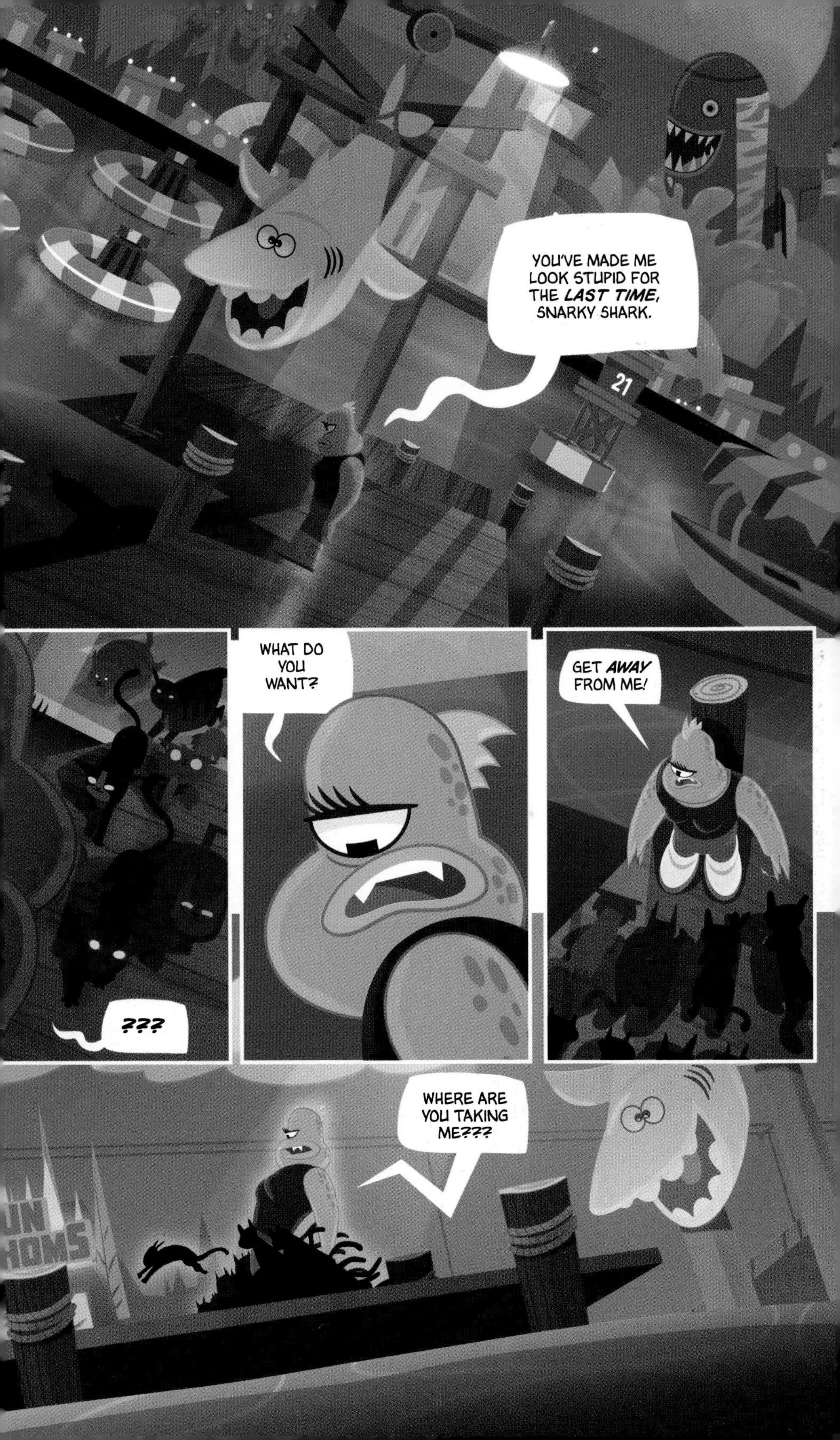
YOU'VE MADE ME LOOK STUPID FOR THE *LAST TIME*, SNARKY SHARK.
21
???
WHAT DO YOU WANT?
GET *AWAY* FROM ME!
WHERE ARE YOU TAKING ME???

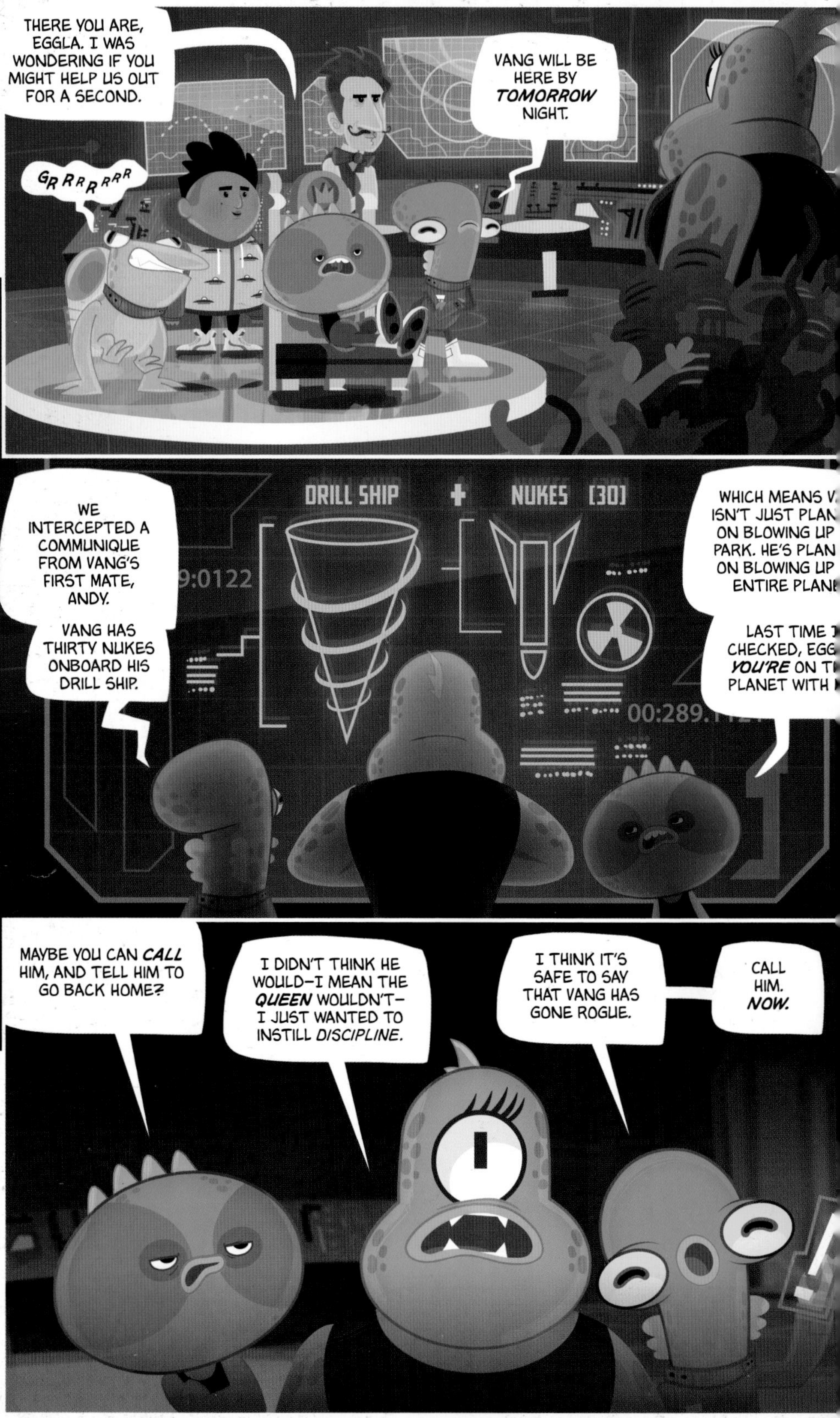
THERE YOU ARE, EGGLA. I WAS WONDERING IF YOU MIGHT HELP US OUT FOR A SECOND.
GRRRRRRR
VANG WILL BE HERE BY *TOMORROW* NIGHT.
DRILL SHIP + NUKES [30]
WE INTERCEPTED A COMMUNIQUE FROM VANG'S FIRST MATE, ANDY.
VANG HAS THIRTY NUKES ONBOARD HIS DRILL SHIP.
MAYBE YOU CAN *CALL* HIM, AND TELL HIM TO GO BACK HOME?
I DIDN'T THINK HE WOULD—I MEAN THE *QUEEN* WOULDN'T—I JUST WANTED TO INSTILL *DISCIPLINE.*
I THINK IT'S SAFE TO SAY THAT VANG HAS GONE ROGUE.
CALL HIM. *NOW.*

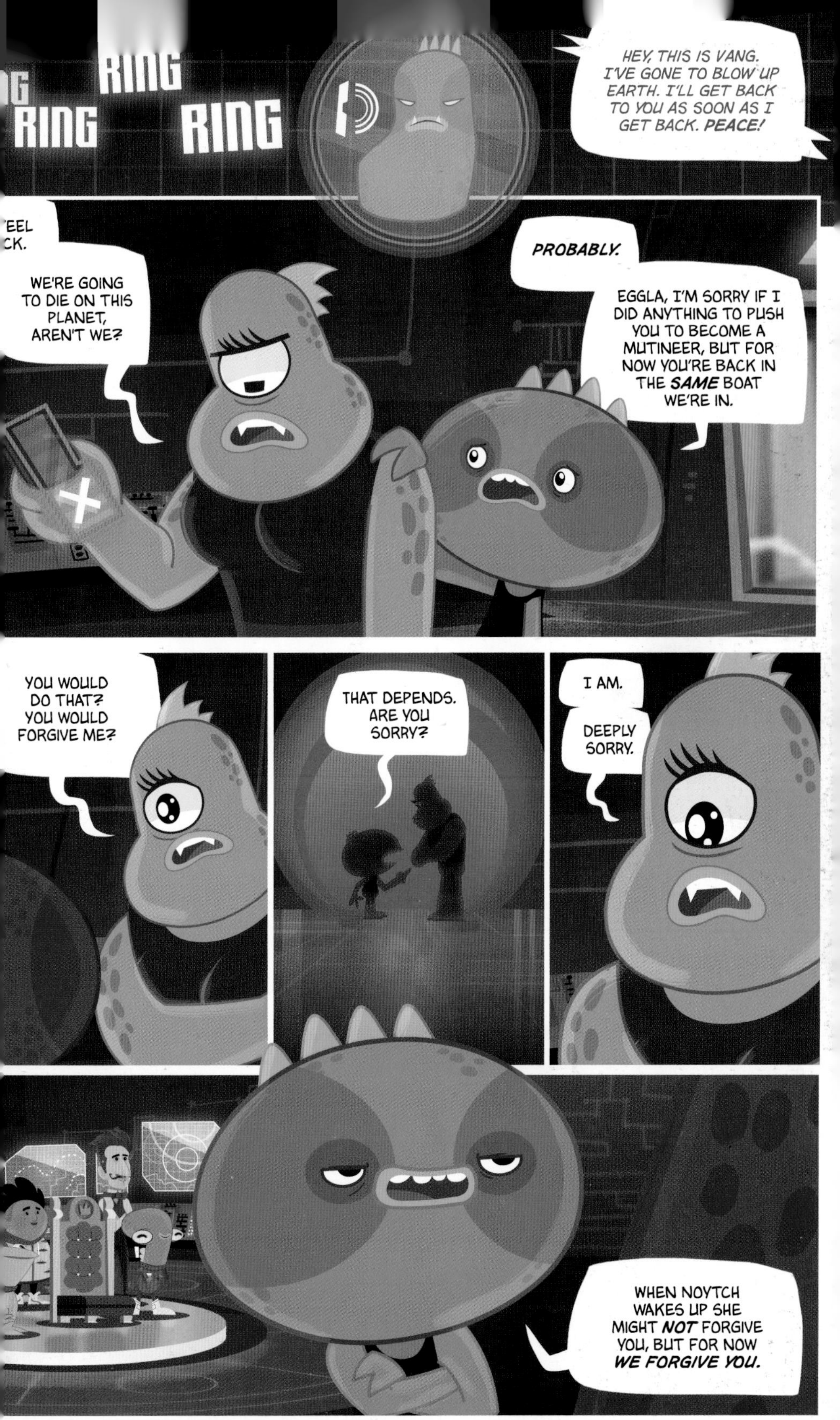
RING
RING
RING
RING
HEY, THIS IS VANG. I'VE GONE TO BLOW UP EARTH. I'LL GET BACK TO YOU AS SOON AS I GET BACK. PEACE!
WE'RE GOING TO DIE ON THIS PLANET, AREN'T WE?
PROBABLY.
EGGLA, I'M SORRY IF I DID ANYTHING TO PUSH YOU TO BECOME A MUTINEER, BUT FOR NOW YOU'RE BACK IN THE SAME BOAT WE'RE IN.
YOU WOULD DO THAT? YOU WOULD FORGIVE ME?
THAT DEPENDS. ARE YOU SORRY?
I AM.
DEEPLY SORRY.
WHEN NOYTCH WAKES UP SHE MIGHT NOT FORGIVE YOU, BUT FOR NOW WE FORGIVE YOU.

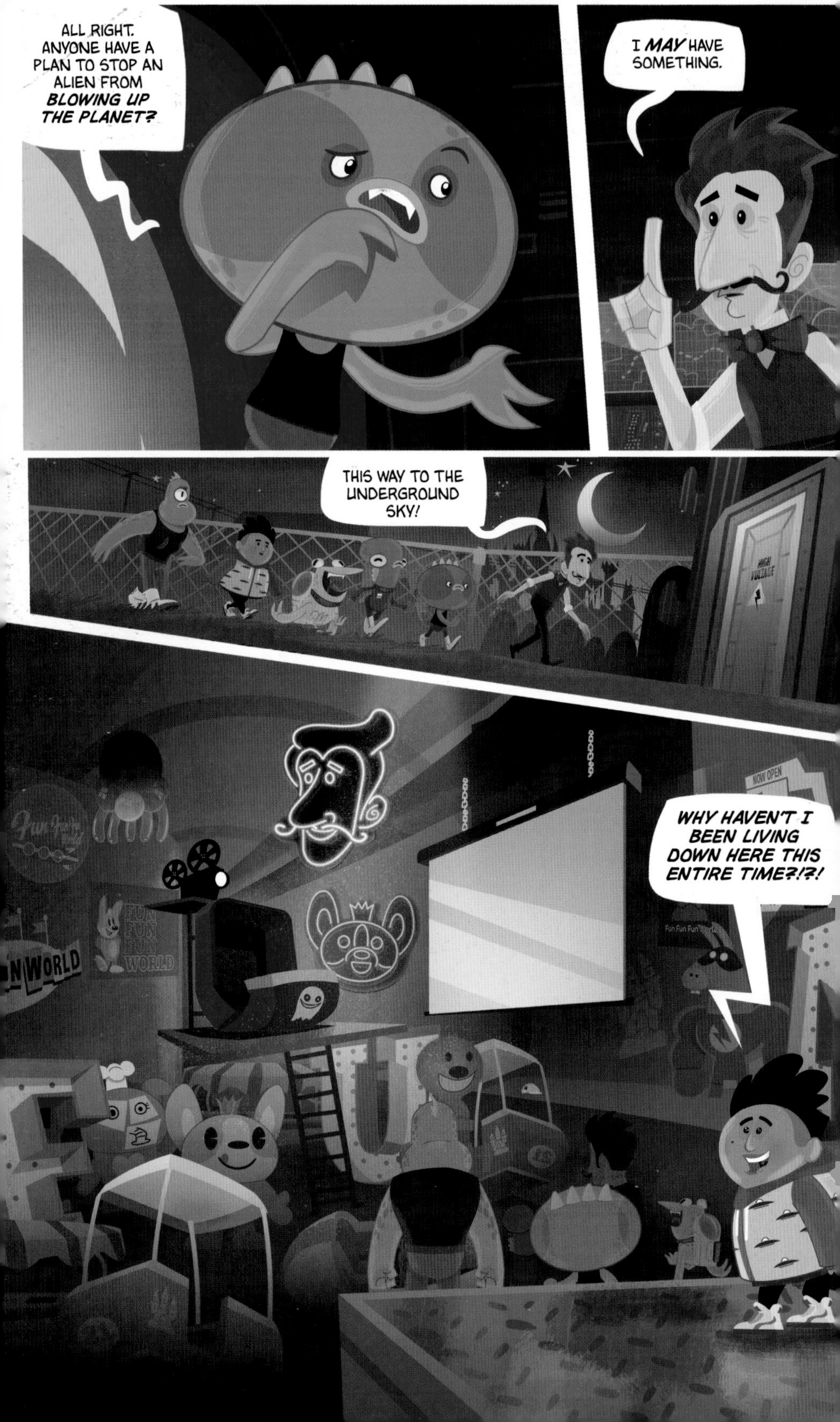
ALL RIGHT. ANYONE HAVE A PLAN TO STOP AN ALIEN FROM *BLOWING UP THE PLANET?*
I *MAY* HAVE SOMETHING.
THIS WAY TO THE UNDERGROUND SKY!
HIGH VOLTAGE
NOW OPEN
FUN FUN FUN WORLD
WHY HAVEN'T I BEEN LIVING DOWN HERE THIS ENTIRE TIME?!?!

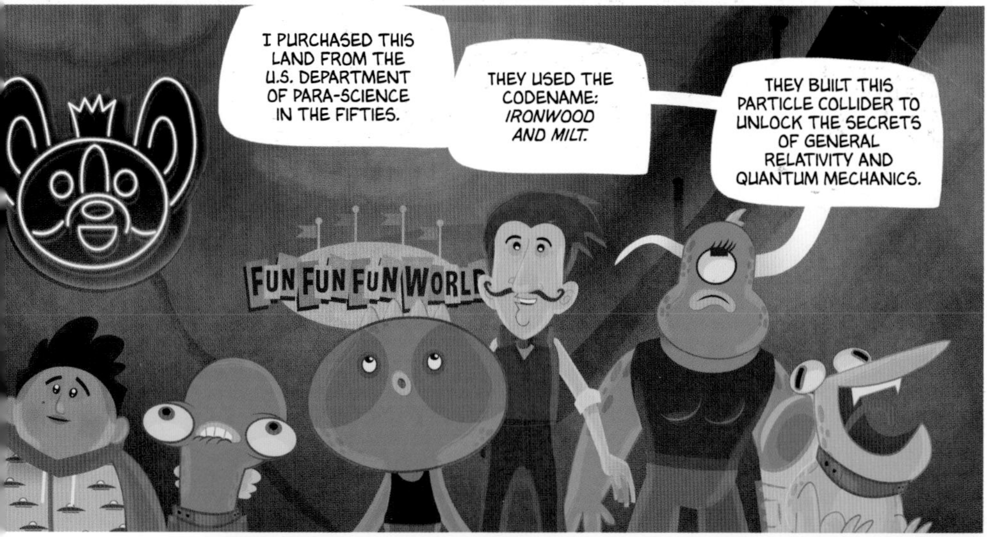
I PURCHASED THIS LAND FROM THE U.S. DEPARTMENT OF PARA-SCIENCE IN THE FIFTIES.
THEY USED THE CODENAME: *IRONWOOD AND MILT.*
THEY BUILT THIS PARTICLE COLLIDER TO UNLOCK THE SECRETS OF GENERAL RELATIVITY AND QUANTUM MECHANICS.
FUN FUN FUN WORLD

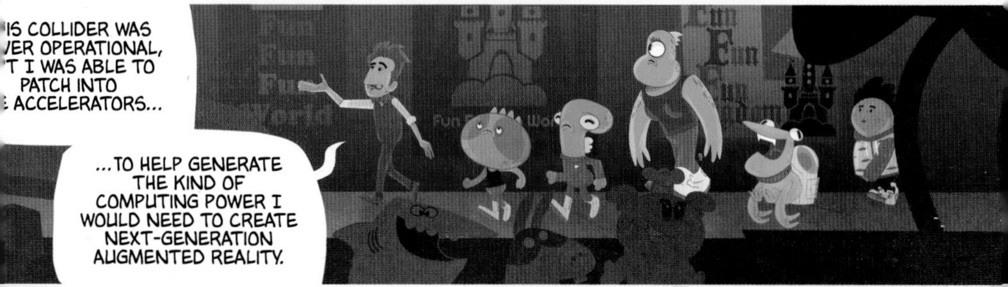
IS COLLIDER WAS VER OPERATIONAL, T I WAS ABLE TO PATCH INTO E ACCELERATORS...
...TO HELP GENERATE THE KIND OF COMPUTING POWER I WOULD NEED TO CREATE NEXT-GENERATION AUGMENTED REALITY.

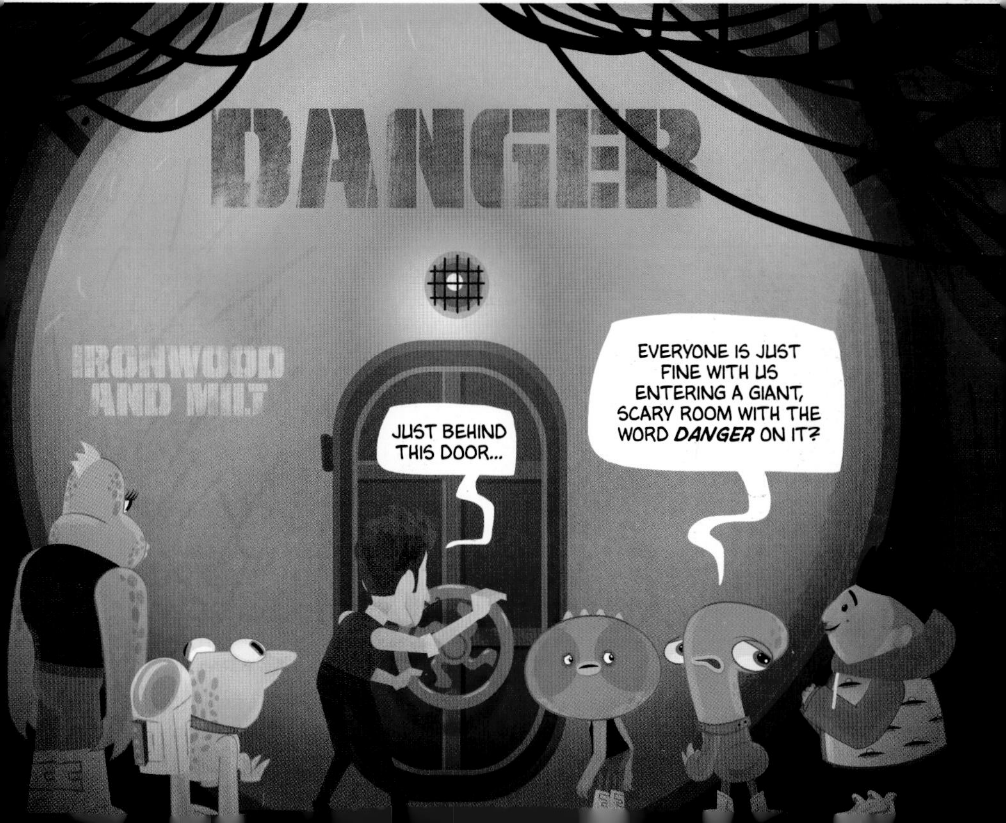
DANGER
IRONWOOD AND MILT
JUST BEHIND THIS DOOR...
EVERYONE IS JUST FINE WITH US ENTERING A GIANT, SCARY ROOM WITH THE WORD ***DANGER*** ON IT?

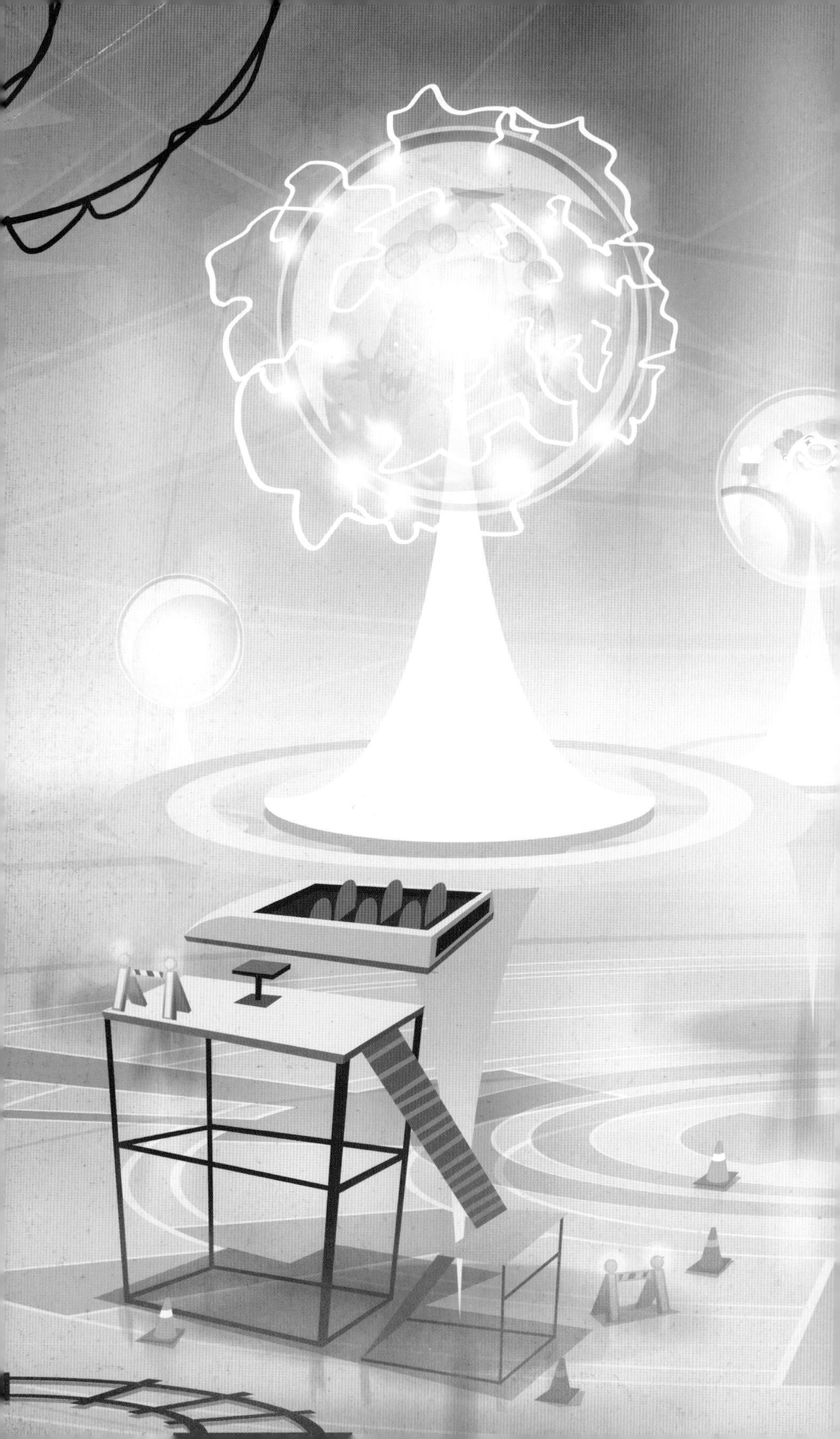

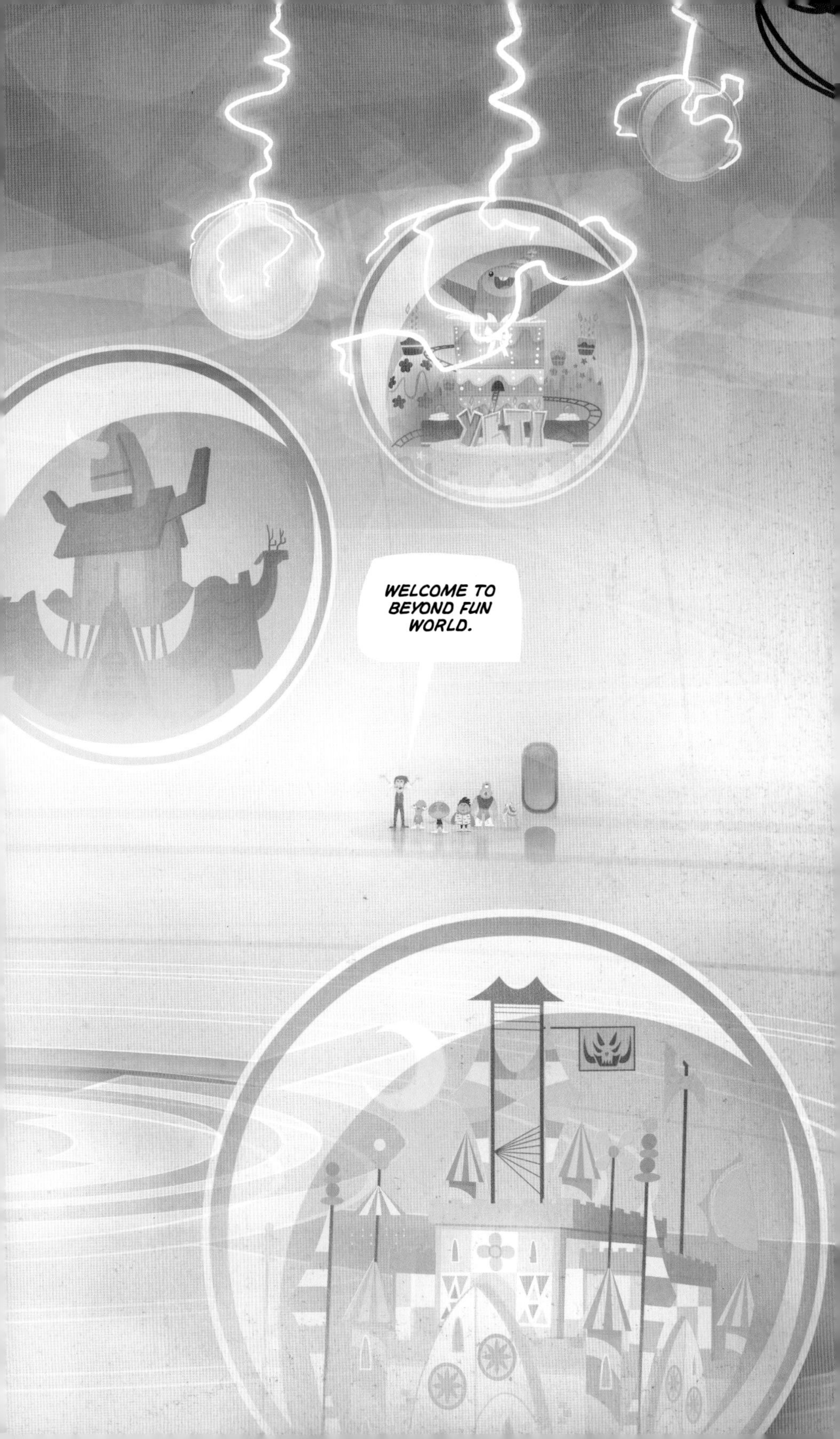
YETI
WELCOME TO BEYOND FUN WORLD.

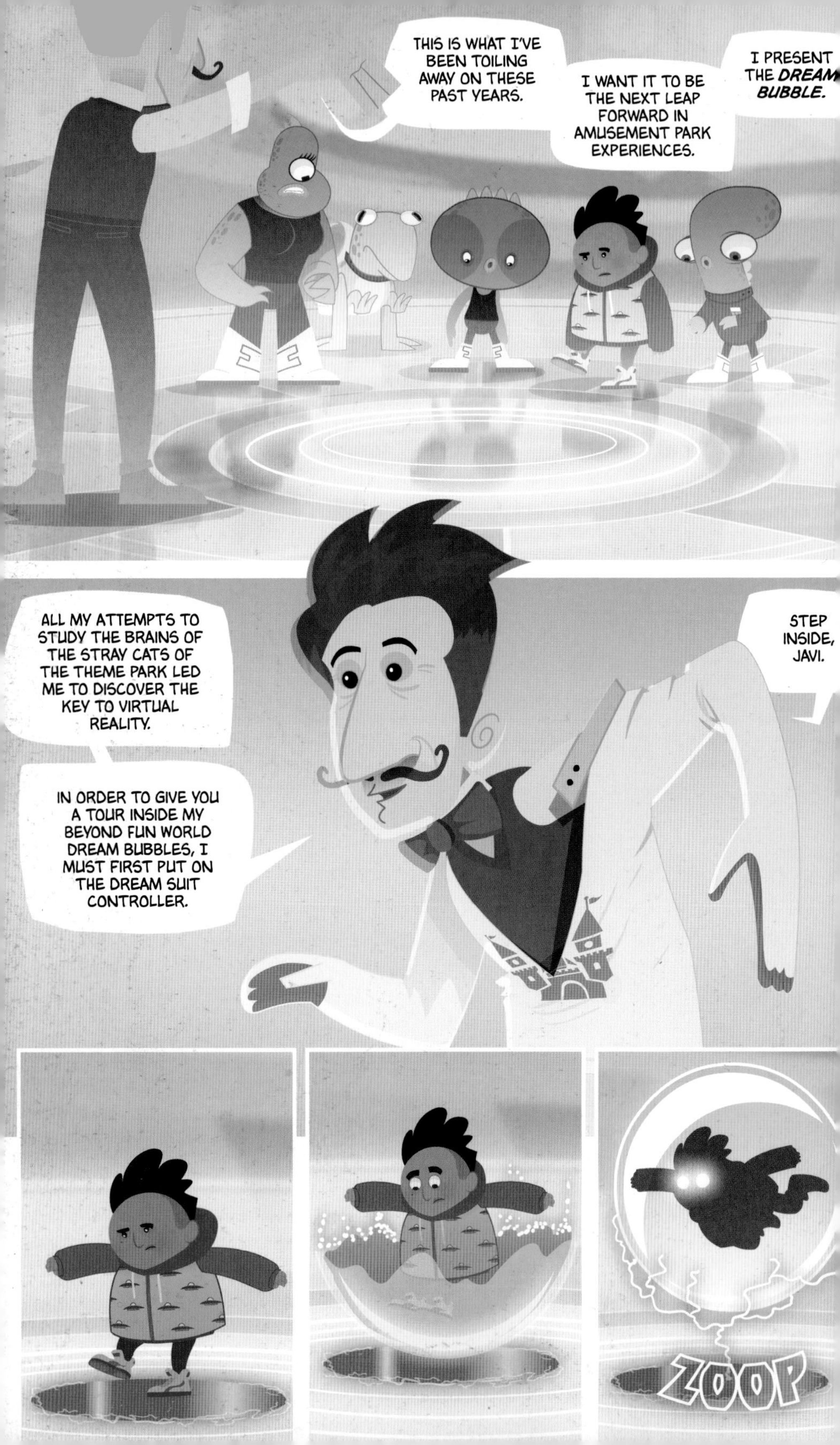
THIS IS WHAT I'VE BEEN TOILING AWAY ON THESE PAST YEARS.
I WANT IT TO BE THE NEXT LEAP FORWARD IN AMUSEMENT PARK EXPERIENCES.
I PRESENT THE *DREAM BUBBLE.*
ALL MY ATTEMPTS TO STUDY THE BRAINS OF THE STRAY CATS OF THE THEME PARK LED ME TO DISCOVER THE KEY TO VIRTUAL REALITY.
IN ORDER TO GIVE YOU A TOUR INSIDE MY BEYOND FUN WORLD DREAM BUBBLES, I MUST FIRST PUT ON THE DREAM SUIT CONTROLLER.
STEP INSIDE, JAVI.
ZOOP

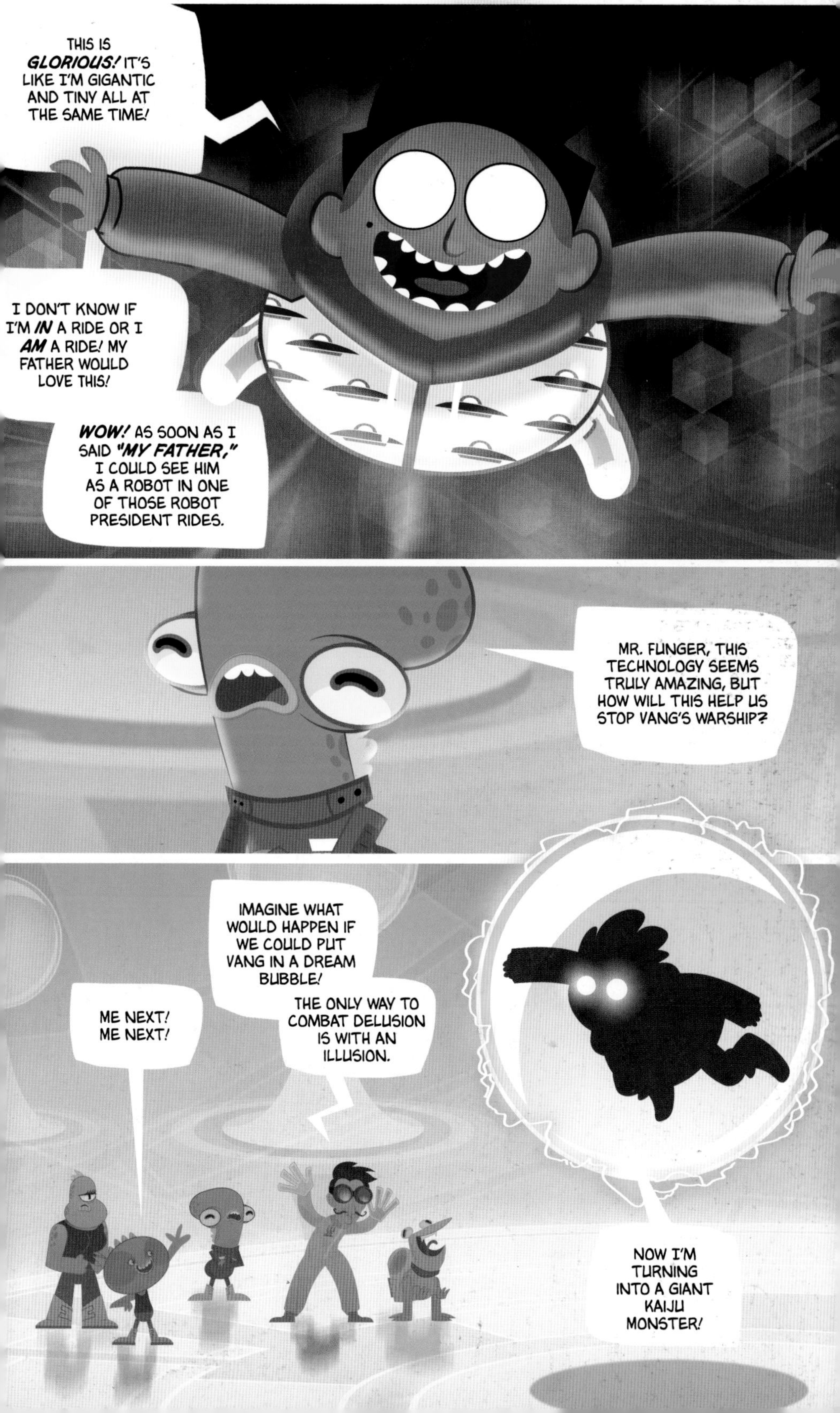
THIS IS GLORIOUS! IT'S LIKE I'M GIGANTIC AND TINY ALL AT THE SAME TIME!
I DON'T KNOW IF I'M IN A RIDE OR I AM A RIDE! MY FATHER WOULD LOVE THIS!
WOW! AS SOON AS I SAID "MY FATHER," I COULD SEE HIM AS A ROBOT IN ONE OF THOSE ROBOT PRESIDENT RIDES.
MR. FUNGER, THIS TECHNOLOGY SEEMS TRULY AMAZING, BUT HOW WILL THIS HELP US STOP VANG'S WARSHIP?
ME NEXT! ME NEXT!
IMAGINE WHAT WOULD HAPPEN IF WE COULD PUT VANG IN A DREAM BUBBLE!
THE ONLY WAY TO COMBAT DELUSION IS WITH AN ILLUSION.
NOW I'M TURNING INTO A GIANT KAIJU MONSTER!

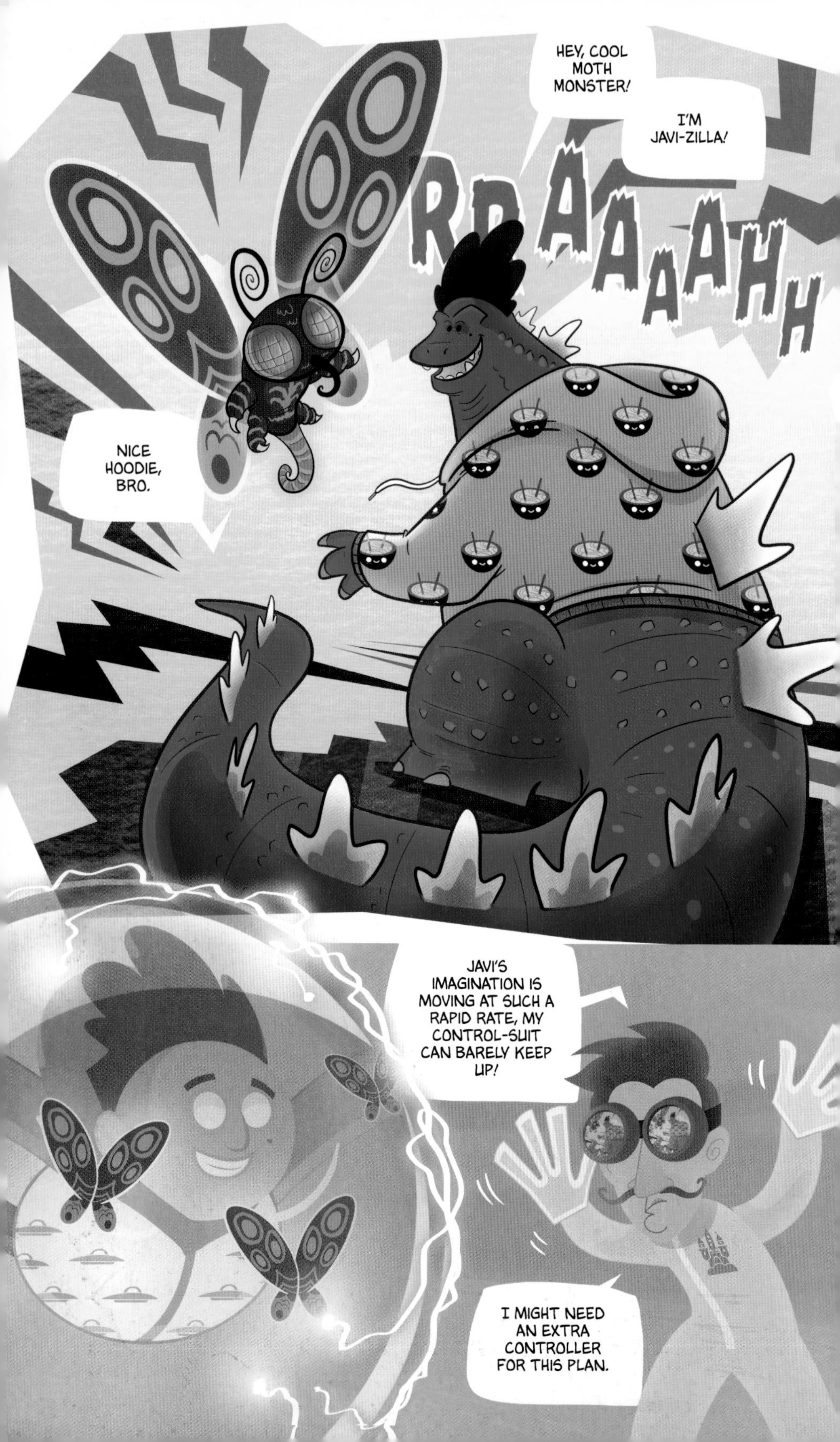
HEY, COOL MOTH MONSTER!
I'M JAVI-ZILLA!
RRAAAAAHH
NICE HOODIE, BRO.
JAVI'S IMAGINATION IS MOVING AT SUCH A RAPID RATE, MY CONTROL-SUIT CAN BARELY KEEP UP!
I MIGHT NEED AN EXTRA CONTROLLER FOR THIS PLAN.

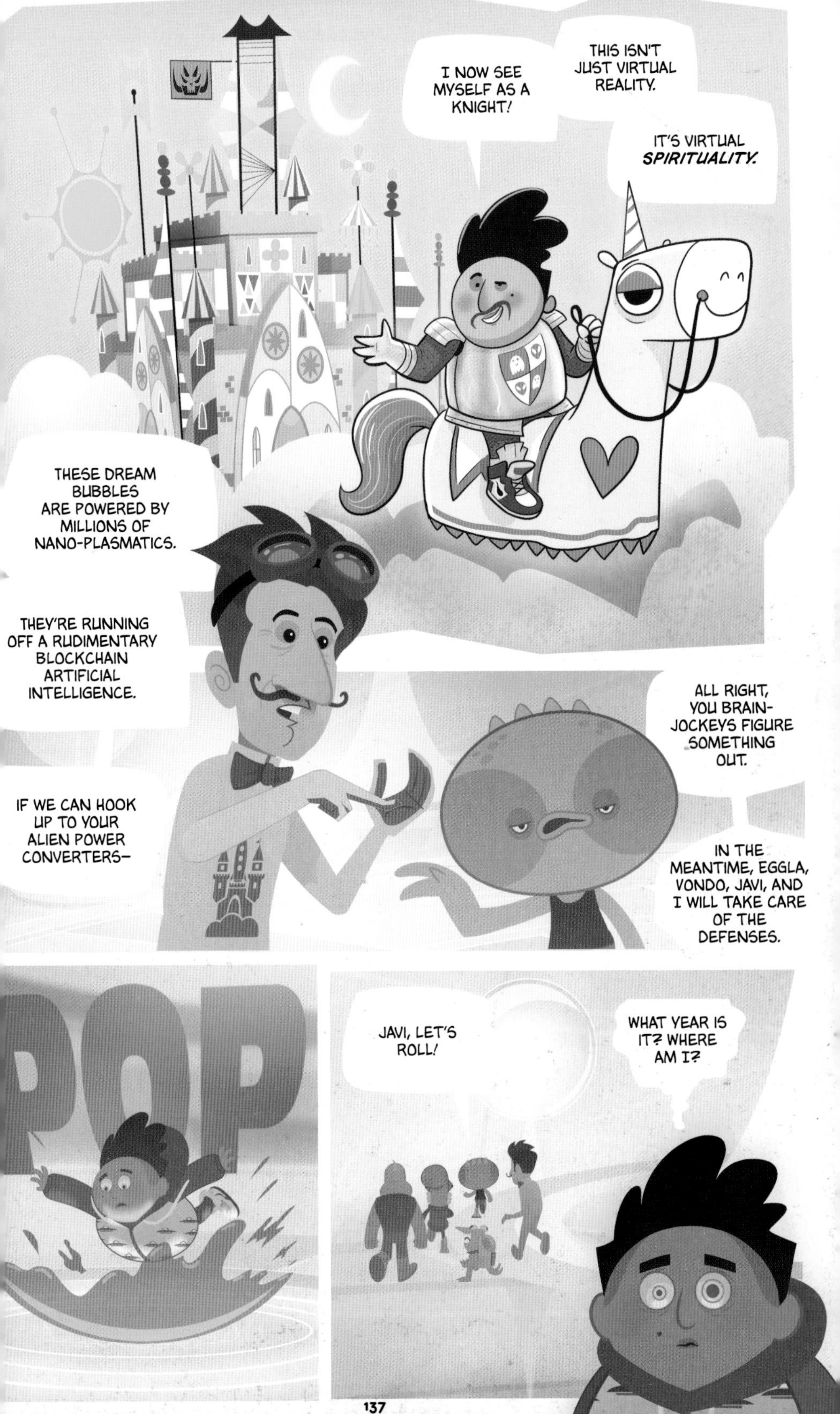
I NOW SEE MYSELF AS A KNIGHT!
THIS ISN'T JUST VIRTUAL REALITY.
IT'S VIRTUAL *SPIRITUALITY.*
THESE DREAM BUBBLES ARE POWERED BY MILLIONS OF NANO-PLASMATICS.
THEY'RE RUNNING OFF A RUDIMENTARY BLOCKCHAIN ARTIFICIAL INTELLIGENCE.
IF WE CAN HOOK UP TO YOUR ALIEN POWER CONVERTERS—
ALL RIGHT, YOU BRAIN-JOCKEYS FIGURE SOMETHING OUT.
IN THE MEANTIME, EGGLA, VONDO, JAVI, AND I WILL TAKE CARE OF THE DEFENSES.
POP
JAVI, LET'S ROLL!
WHAT YEAR IS IT? WHERE AM I?

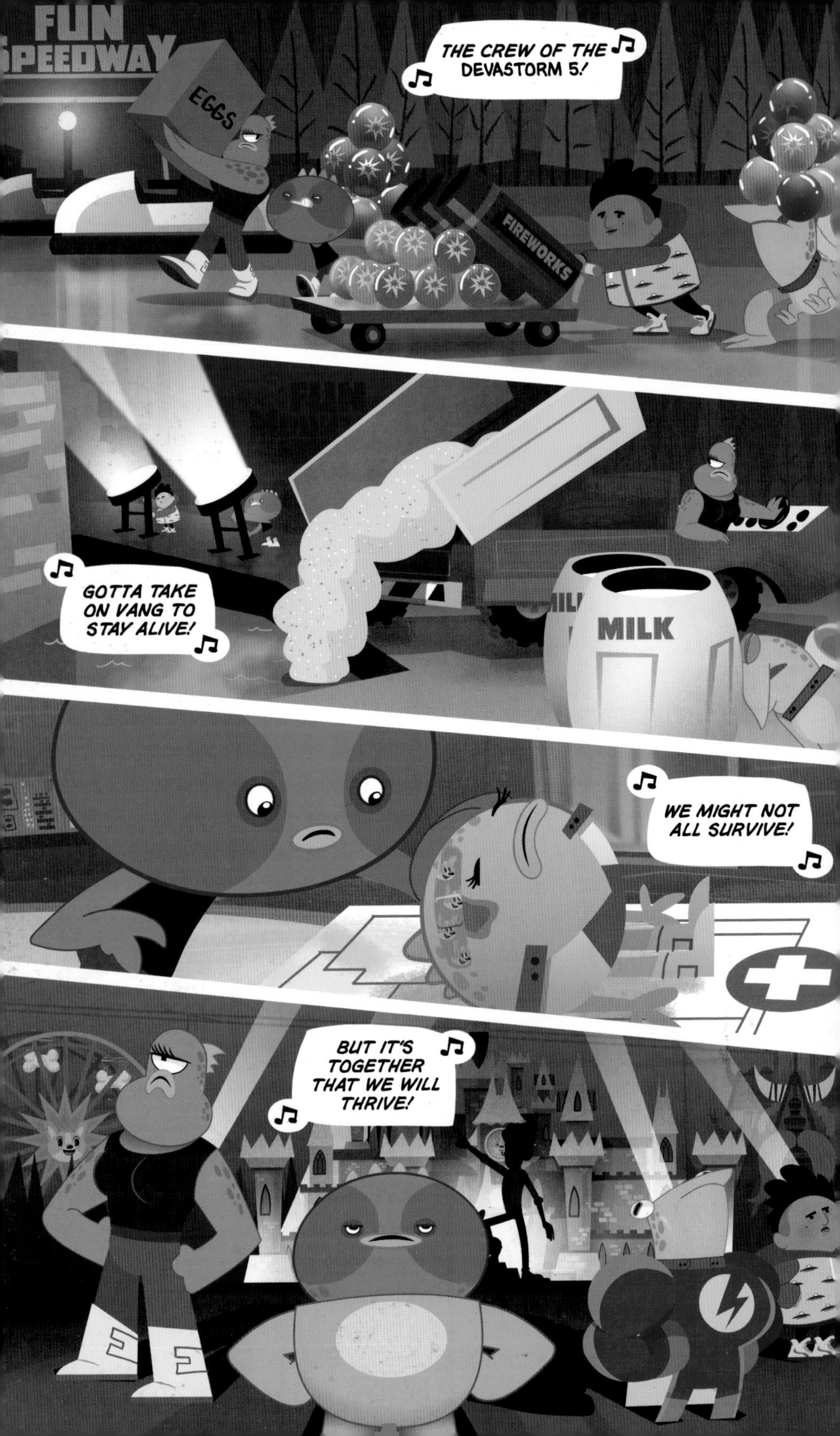
FUN SPEEDWAY
EGGS
THE CREW OF THE DEVASTORM 5!
FIREWORKS
GOTTA TAKE ON VANG TO STAY ALIVE!
MILK
WE MIGHT NOT ALL SURVIVE!
BUT IT'S TOGETHER THAT WE WILL THRIVE!

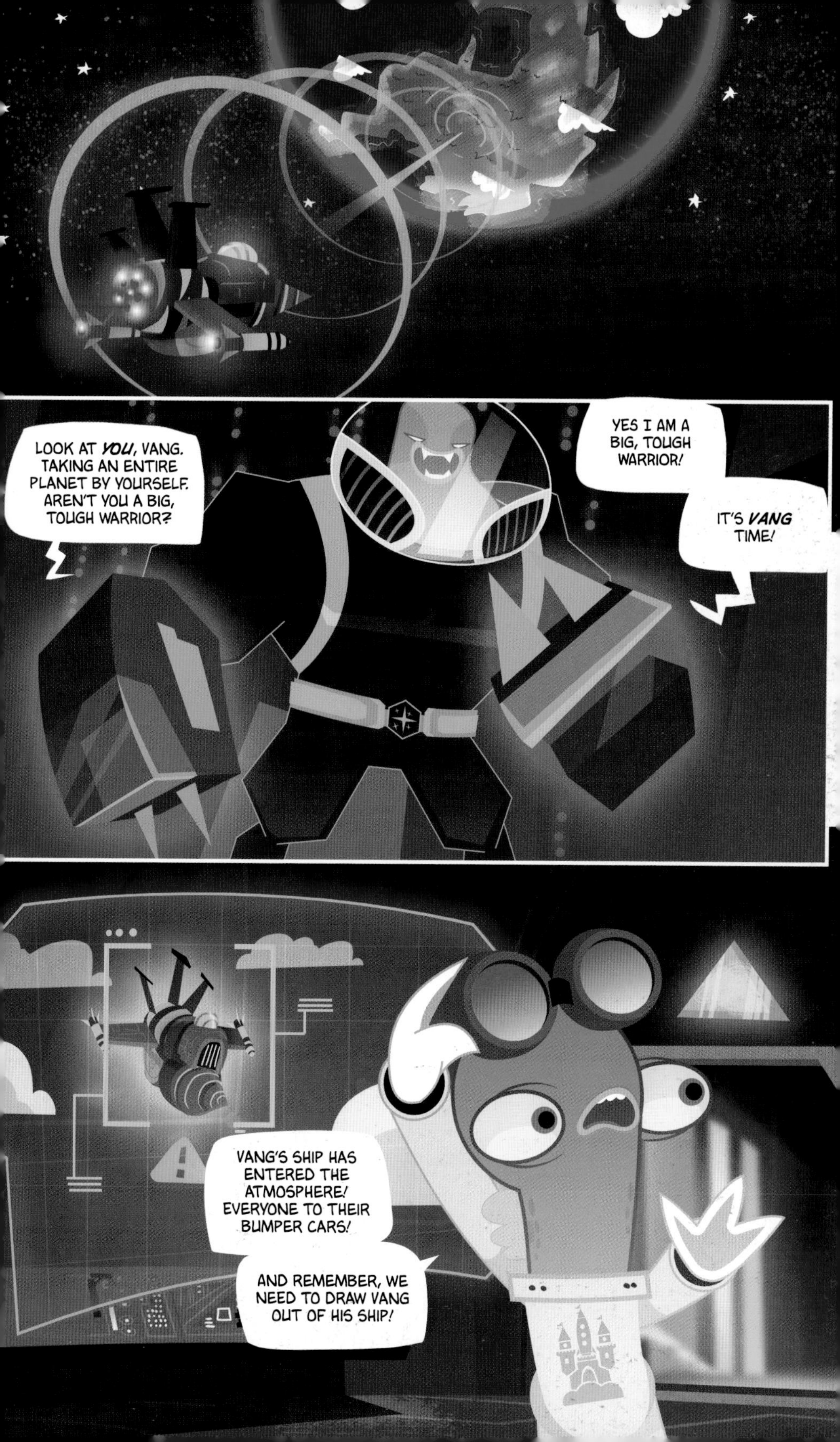
LOOK AT *YOU*, VANG. TAKING AN ENTIRE PLANET BY YOURSELF. AREN'T YOU A BIG, TOUGH WARRIOR?
YES I AM A BIG, TOUGH WARRIOR!
IT'S *VANG* TIME!
VANG'S SHIP HAS ENTERED THE ATMOSPHERE! EVERYONE TO THEIR BUMPER CARS!
AND REMEMBER, WE NEED TO DRAW VANG OUT OF HIS SHIP!

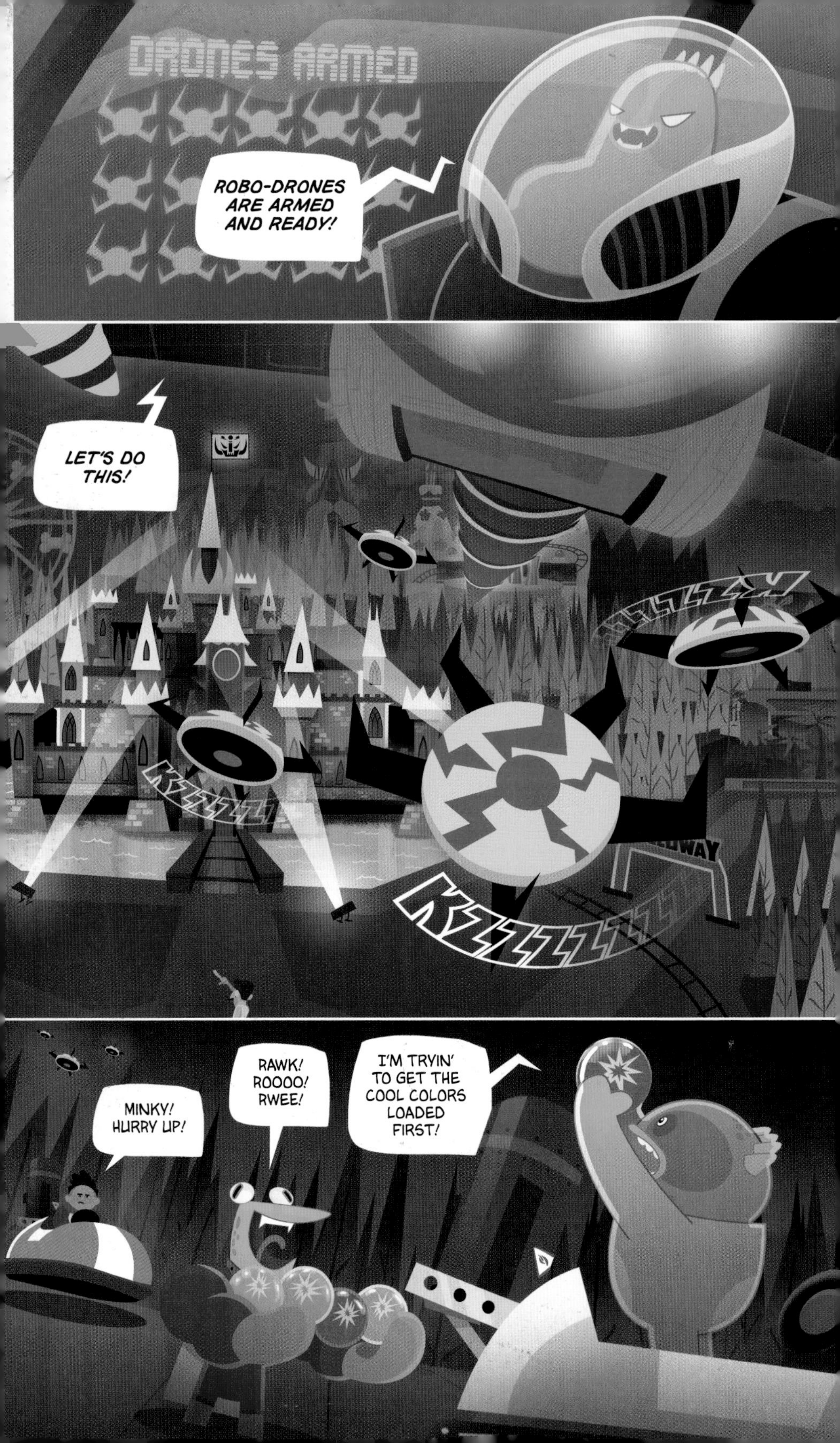
DRONES ARMED
ROBO-DRONES ARE ARMED AND READY!
LET'S DO THIS!
KZZZZ
KZZZZ
KZZZZZZZ
MINKY! HURRY UP!
RAWK! ROOOO! RWEE!
I'M TRYIN' TO GET THE COOL COLORS LOADED FIRST!

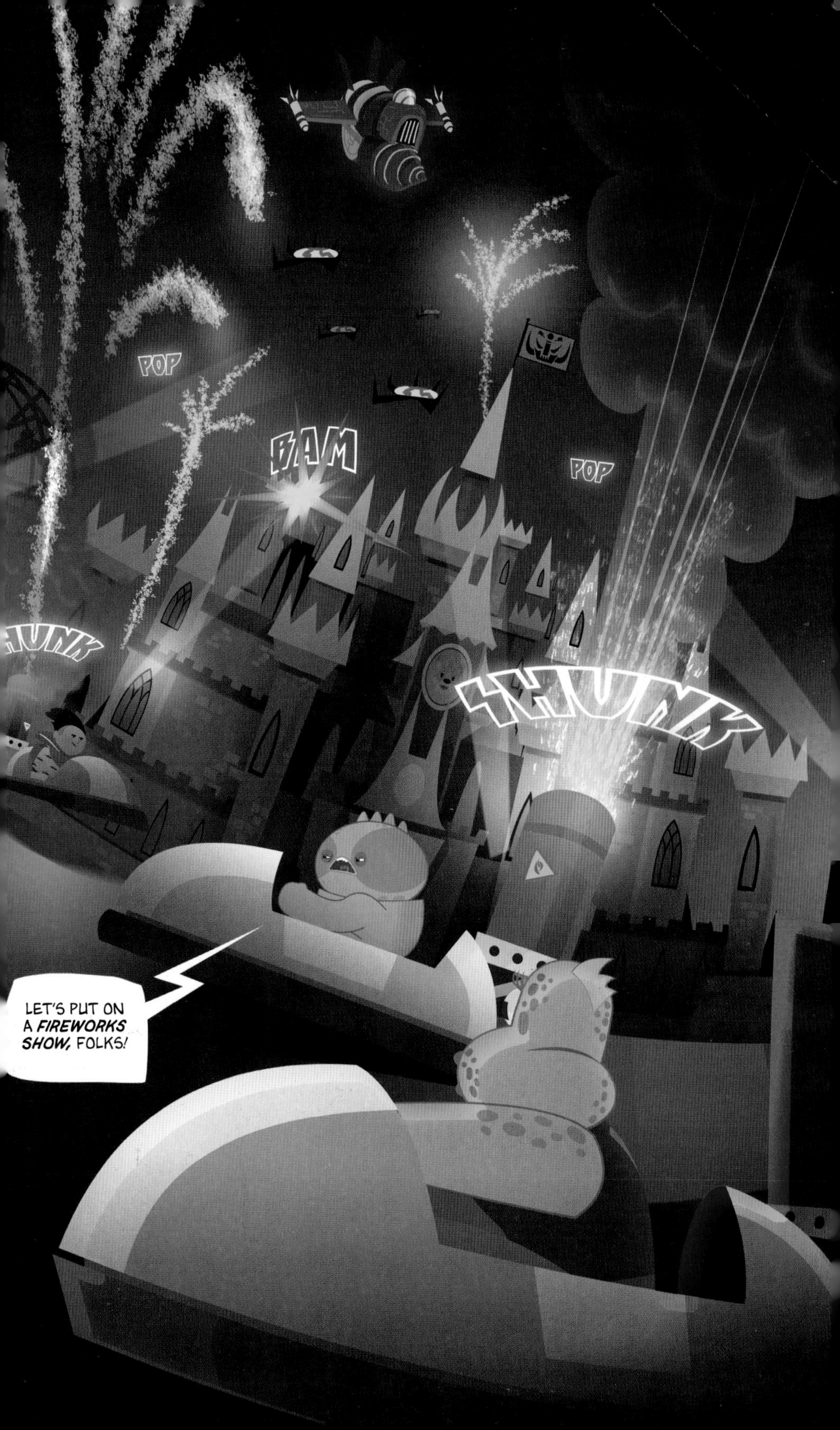

POP
BAM
POP
THUNK
THUNK
LET'S PUT ON A *FIREWORKS SHOW,* FOLKS!

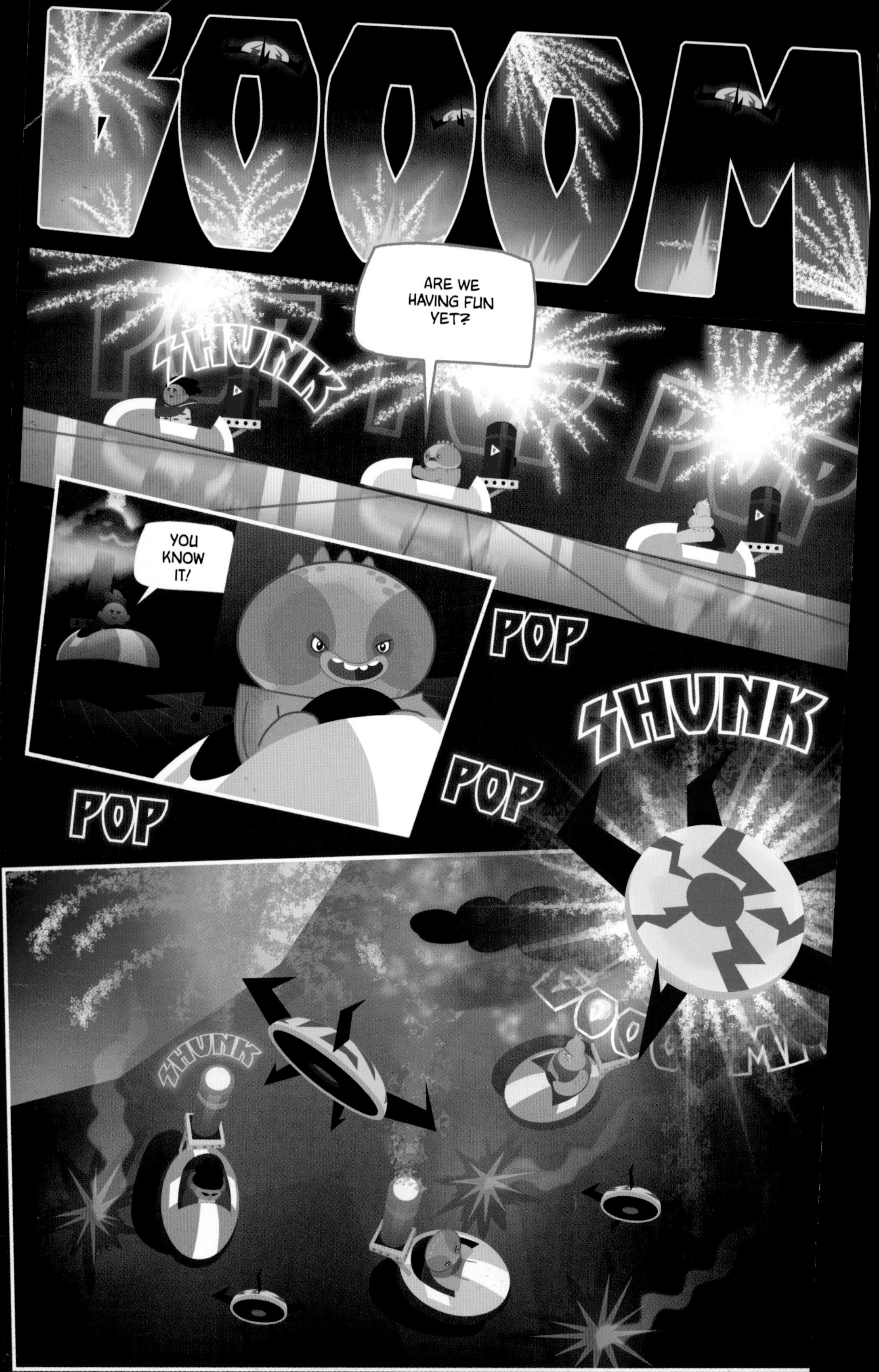
BOOOM
POP POP POP
SHUNK
ARE WE HAVING FUN YET?
YOU KNOW IT!
POP
SHUNK
POP
POP
SHUNK
BOOOM

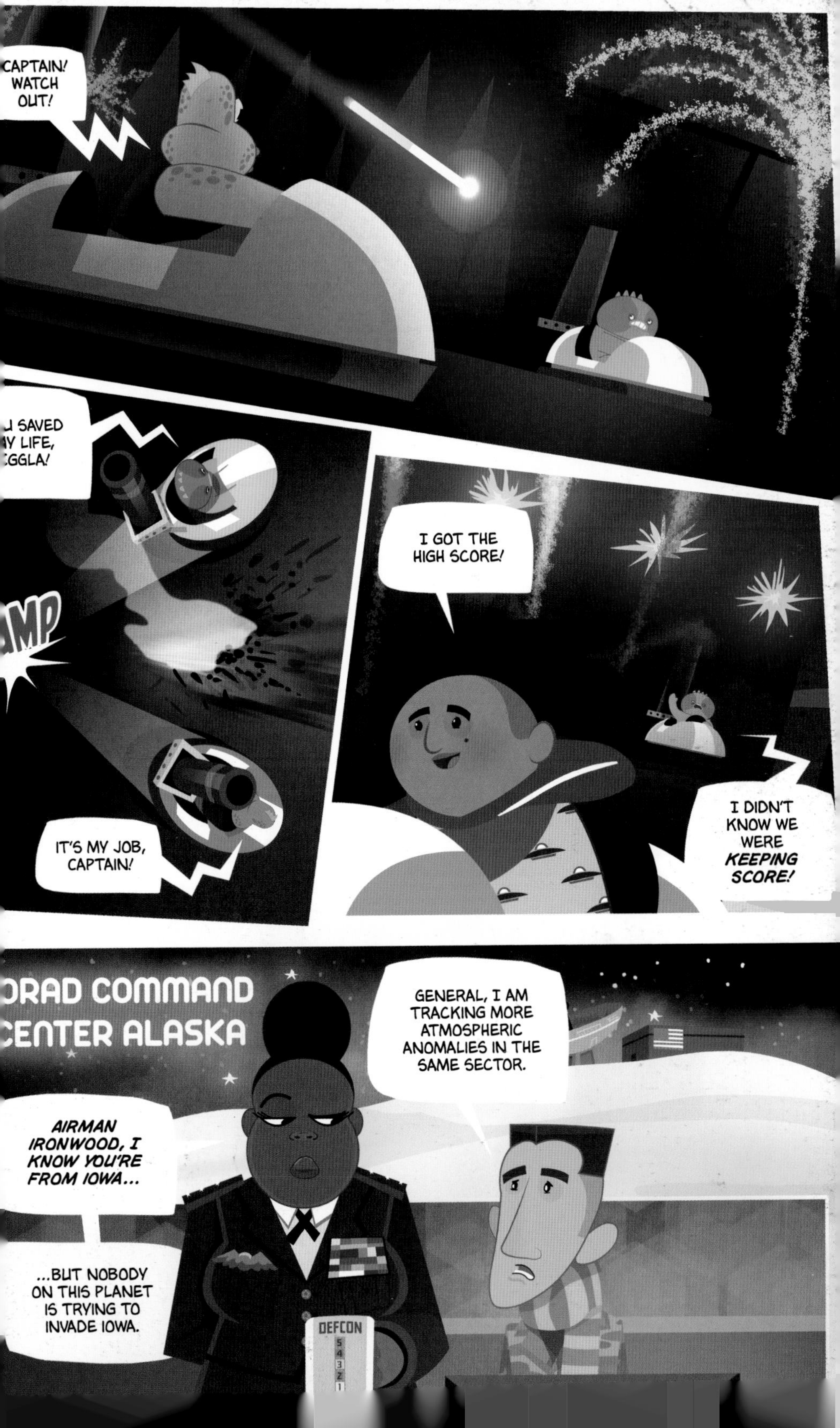
CAPTAIN! WATCH OUT!
U SAVED MY LIFE, CGGLA!
AMP
IT'S MY JOB, CAPTAIN!
I GOT THE HIGH SCORE!
I DIDN'T KNOW WE WERE *KEEPING SCORE!*
ORAD COMMAND CENTER ALASKA
GENERAL, I AM TRACKING MORE ATMOSPHERIC ANOMALIES IN THE SAME SECTOR.
AIRMAN IRONWOOD, I KNOW YOU'RE FROM IOWA...
...BUT NOBODY ON THIS PLANET IS TRYING TO INVADE IOWA.
DEFCON
5
4
3
2
1

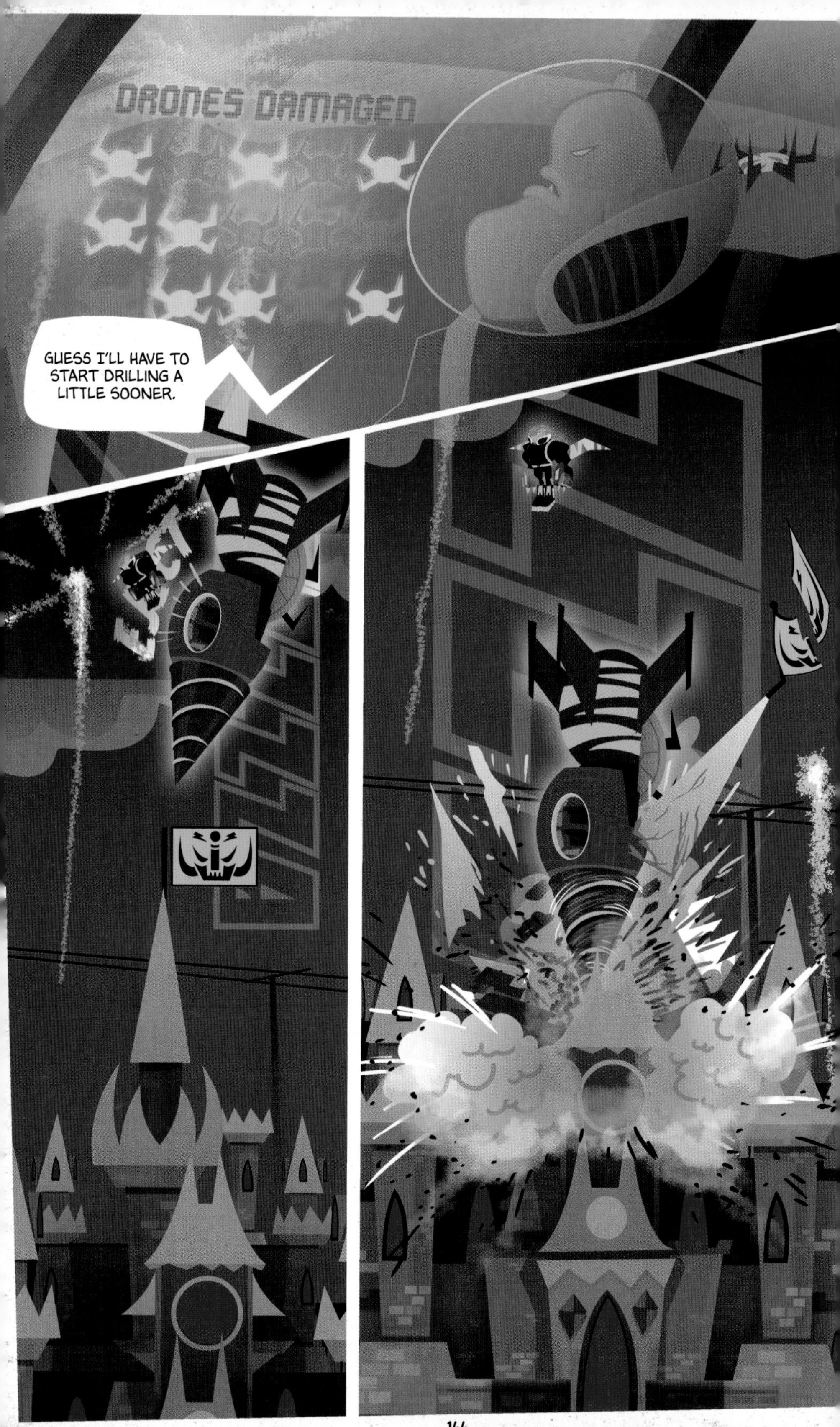
DRONES DAMAGED
GUESS I'LL HAVE TO START DRILLING A LITTLE SOONER.

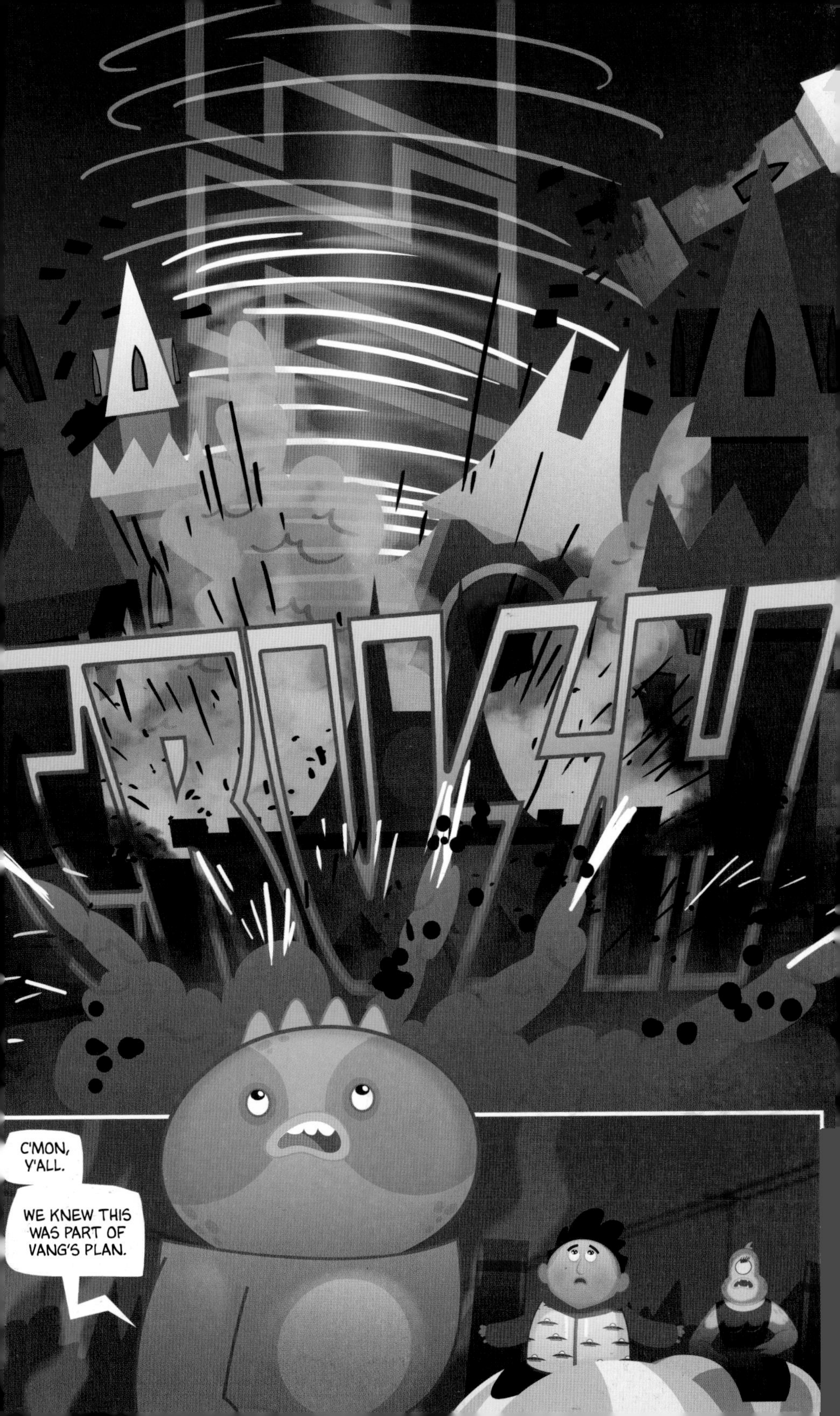
C'MON, Y'ALL.
WE KNEW THIS WAS PART OF VANG'S PLAN.

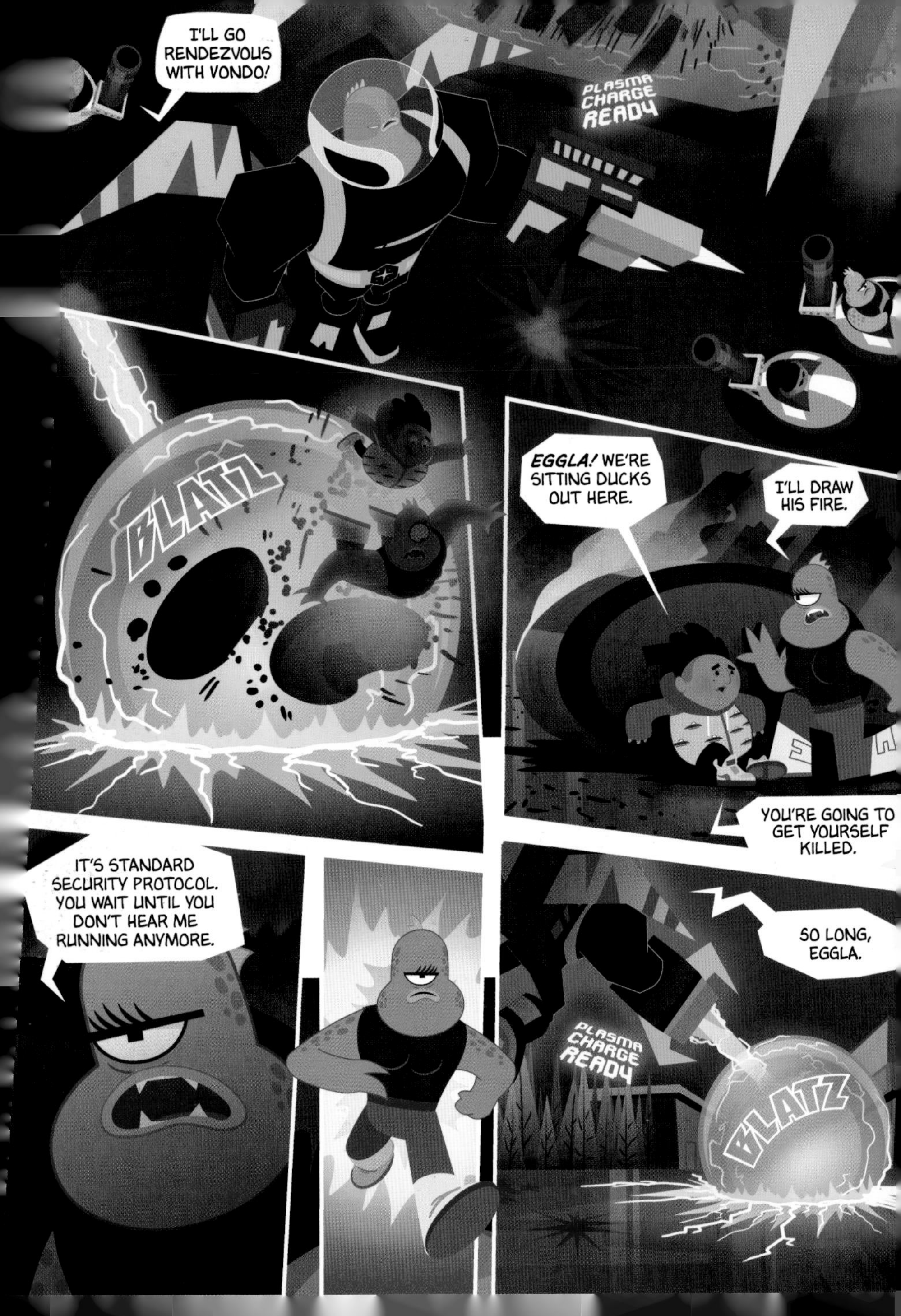
I'LL GO RENDEZVOUS WITH VONDO!
PLASMA CHARGE READY
BLATZ
EGGLA! WE'RE SITTING DUCKS OUT HERE.
I'LL DRAW HIS FIRE.
YOU'RE GOING TO GET YOURSELF KILLED.
IT'S STANDARD SECURITY PROTOCOL. YOU WAIT UNTIL YOU DON'T HEAR ME RUNNING ANYMORE.
SO LONG, EGGLA.
PLASMA CHARGE READY
BLATZ

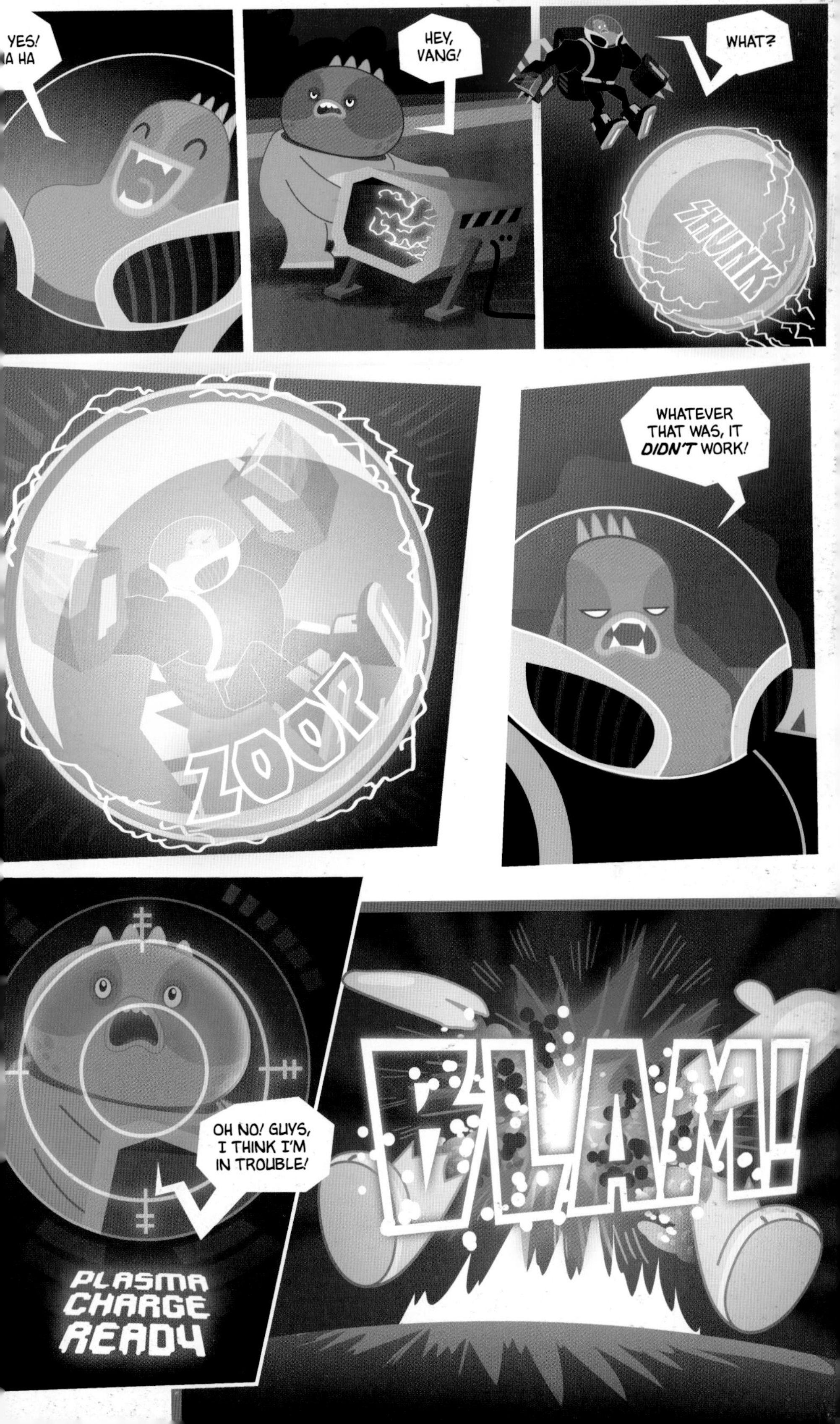

YES! A HA
HEY, VANG!
WHAT?
SHUNK
ZOOP
WHATEVER THAT WAS, IT *DIDN'T* WORK!
OH NO! GUYS, I THINK I'M IN TROUBLE!
PLASMA CHARGE READY
FLAM!

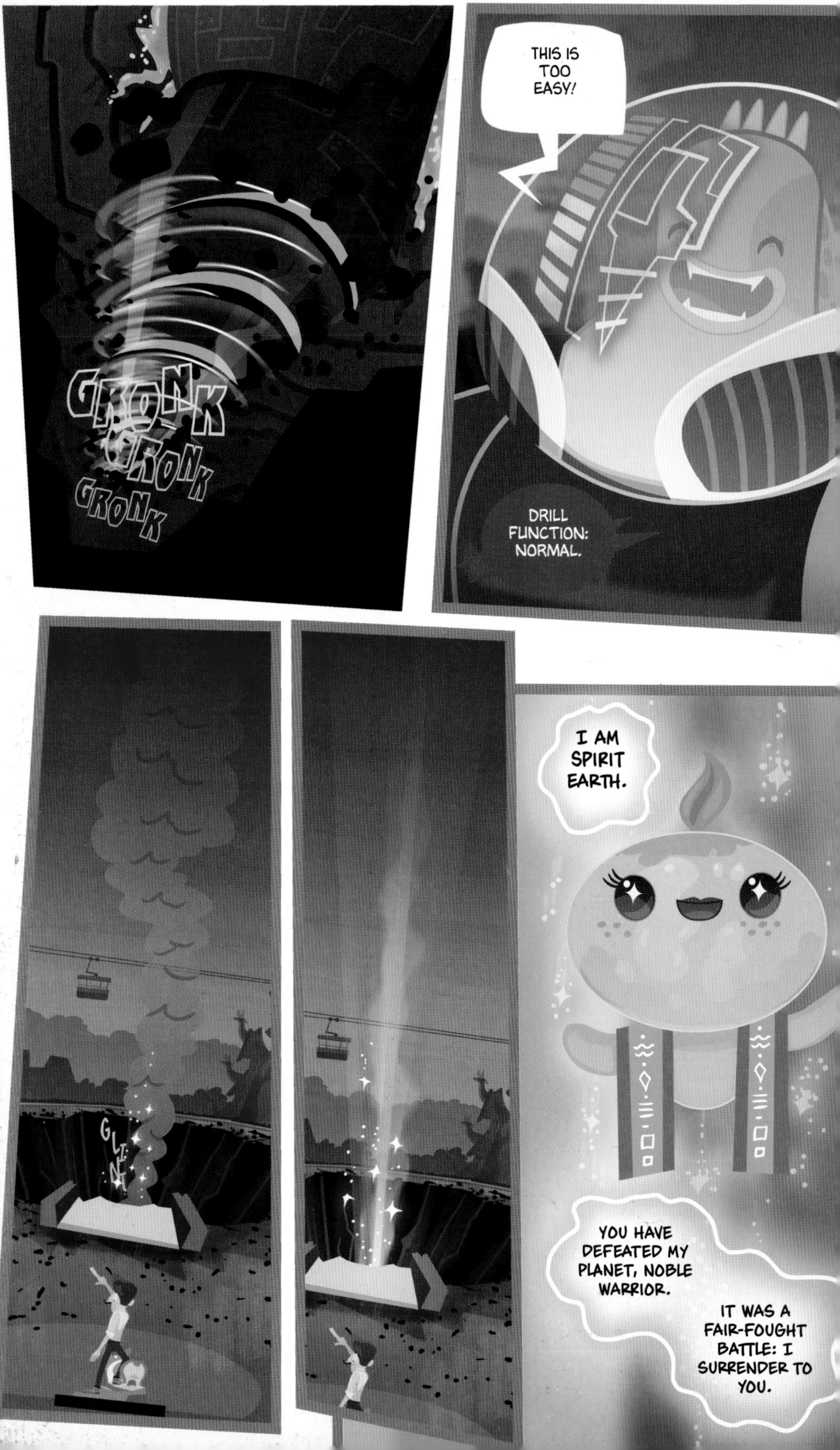
GRONK GRONK GRONK
THIS IS TOO EASY!
DRILL FUNCTION: NORMAL.
GLINT
I AM SPIRIT EARTH.
YOU HAVE DEFEATED MY PLANET, NOBLE WARRIOR.
IT WAS A FAIR-FOUGHT BATTLE: I SURRENDER TO YOU.

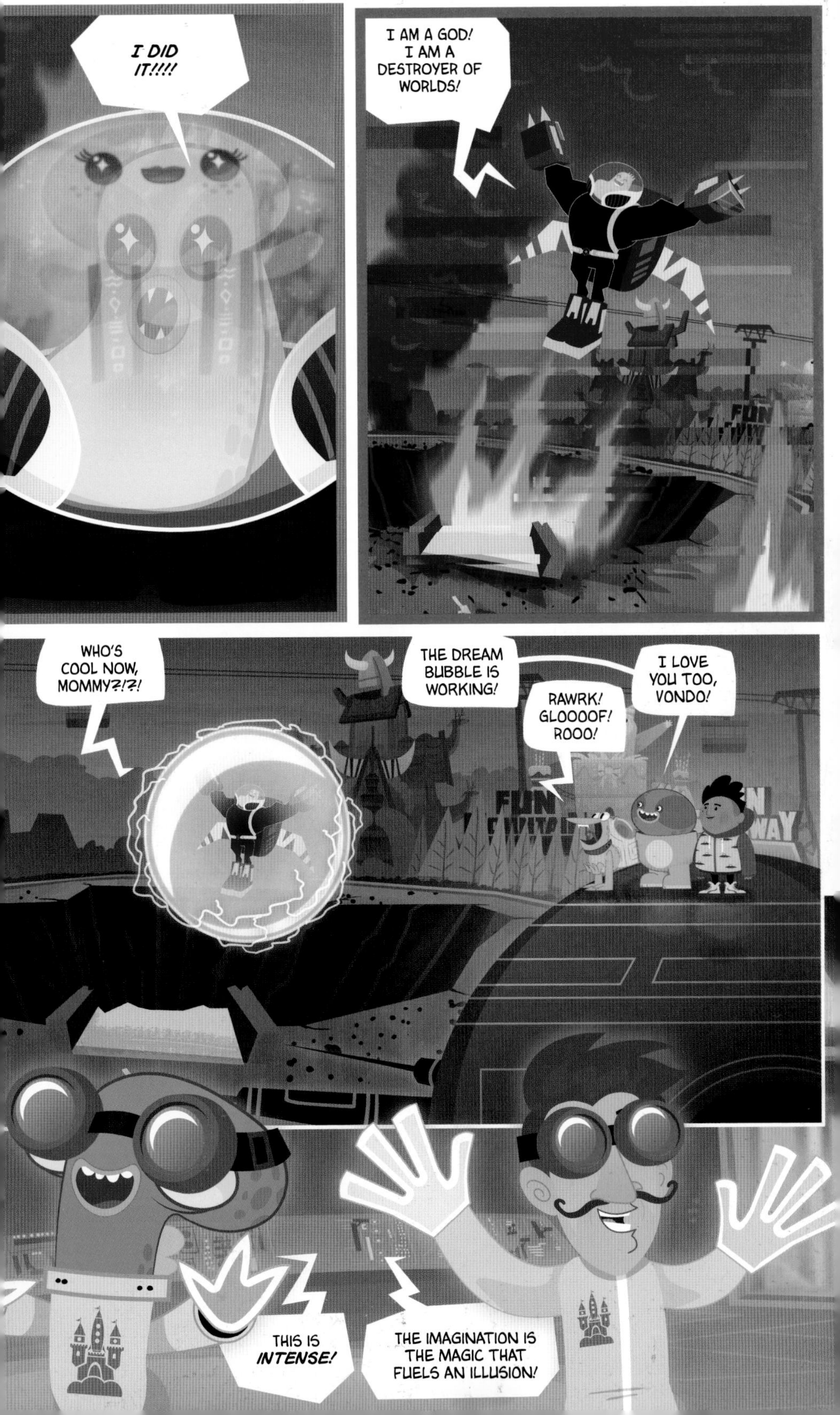
I DID IT!!!!
I AM A GOD! I AM A DESTROYER OF WORLDS!
WHO'S COOL NOW, MOMMY?!?!
THE DREAM BUBBLE IS WORKING!
RAWRK! GLOOOOF! ROOO!
I LOVE YOU TOO, VONDO!
FUN
THIS IS *INTENSE!*
THE IMAGINATION IS THE MAGIC THAT FUELS AN ILLUSION!

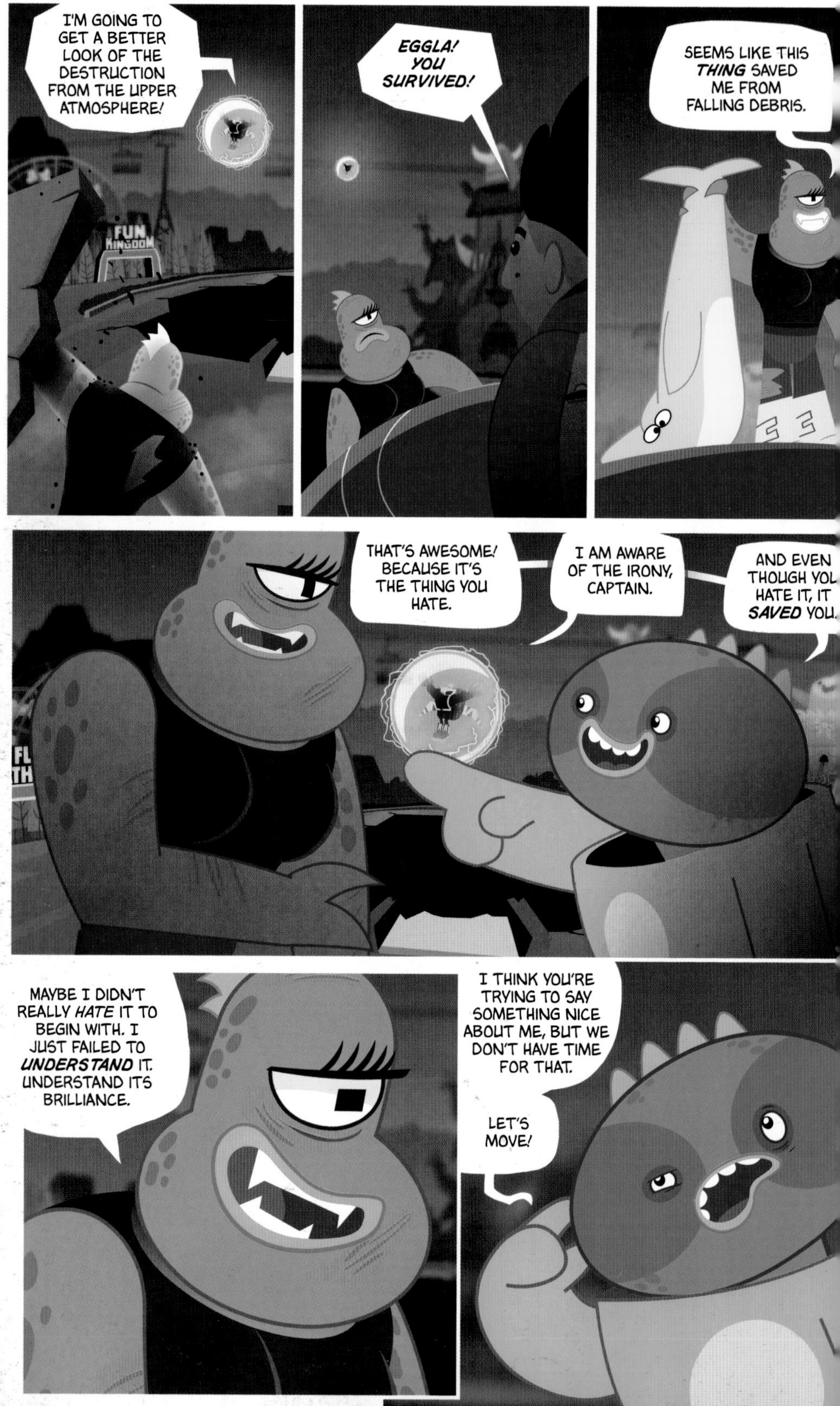

I'M GOING TO GET A BETTER LOOK OF THE DESTRUCTION FROM THE UPPER ATMOSPHERE!
FUN KINGDOM
EGGLA! YOU SURVIVED!
SEEMS LIKE THIS THING SAVED ME FROM FALLING DEBRIS.
THAT'S AWESOME! BECAUSE IT'S THE THING YOU HATE.
I AM AWARE OF THE IRONY, CAPTAIN.
AND EVEN THOUGH YOU HATE IT, IT SAVED YOU.
MAYBE I DIDN'T REALLY HATE IT TO BEGIN WITH. I JUST FAILED TO UNDERSTAND IT. UNDERSTAND ITS BRILLIANCE.
I THINK YOU'RE TRYING TO SAY SOMETHING NICE ABOUT ME, BUT WE DON'T HAVE TIME FOR THAT.
LET'S MOVE!

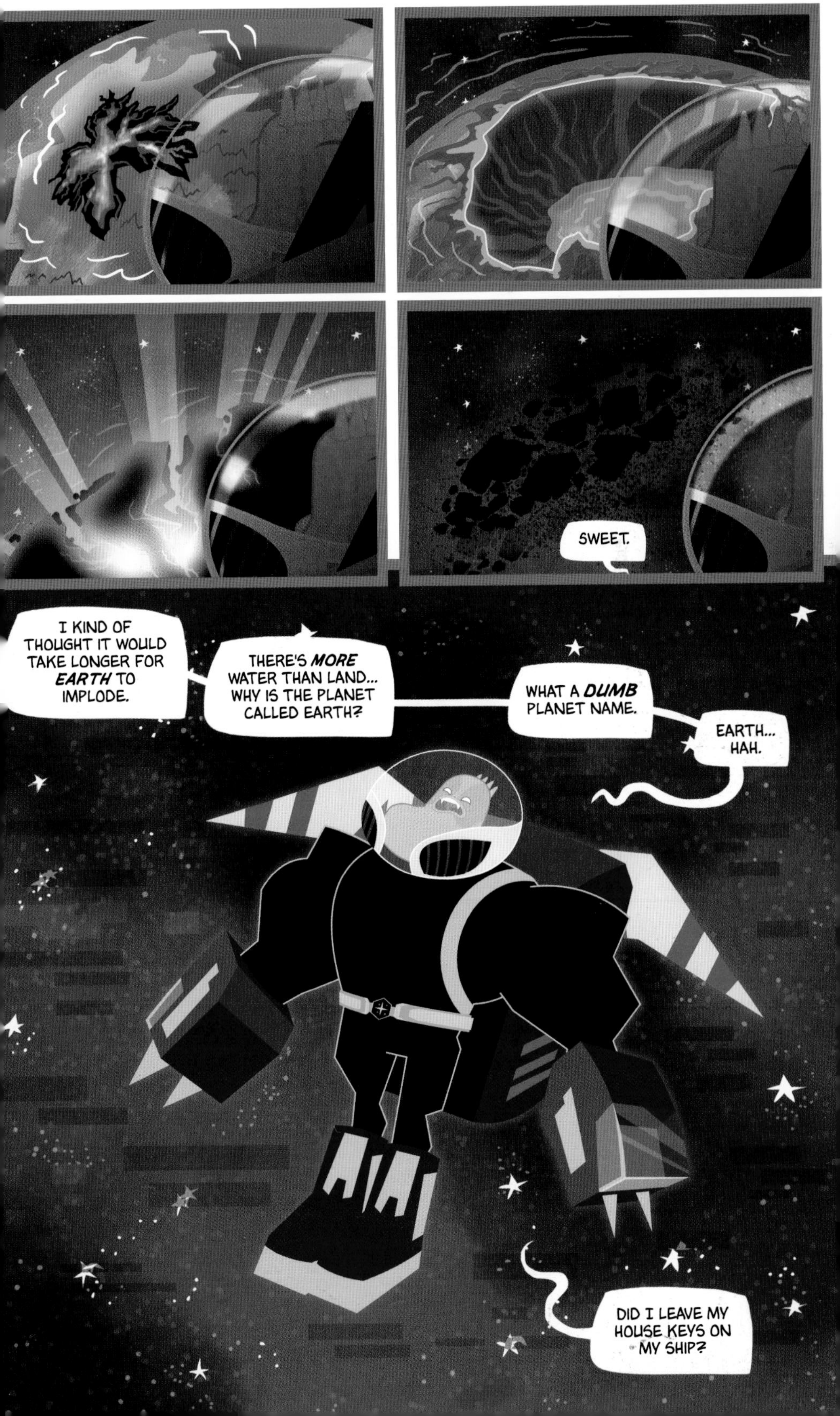
SWEET.
I KIND OF THOUGHT IT WOULD TAKE LONGER FOR EARTH TO IMPLODE.
THERE'S MORE WATER THAN LAND... WHY IS THE PLANET CALLED EARTH?
WHAT A DUMB PLANET NAME.
EARTH... HAH.
DID I LEAVE MY HOUSE KEYS ON MY SHIP?

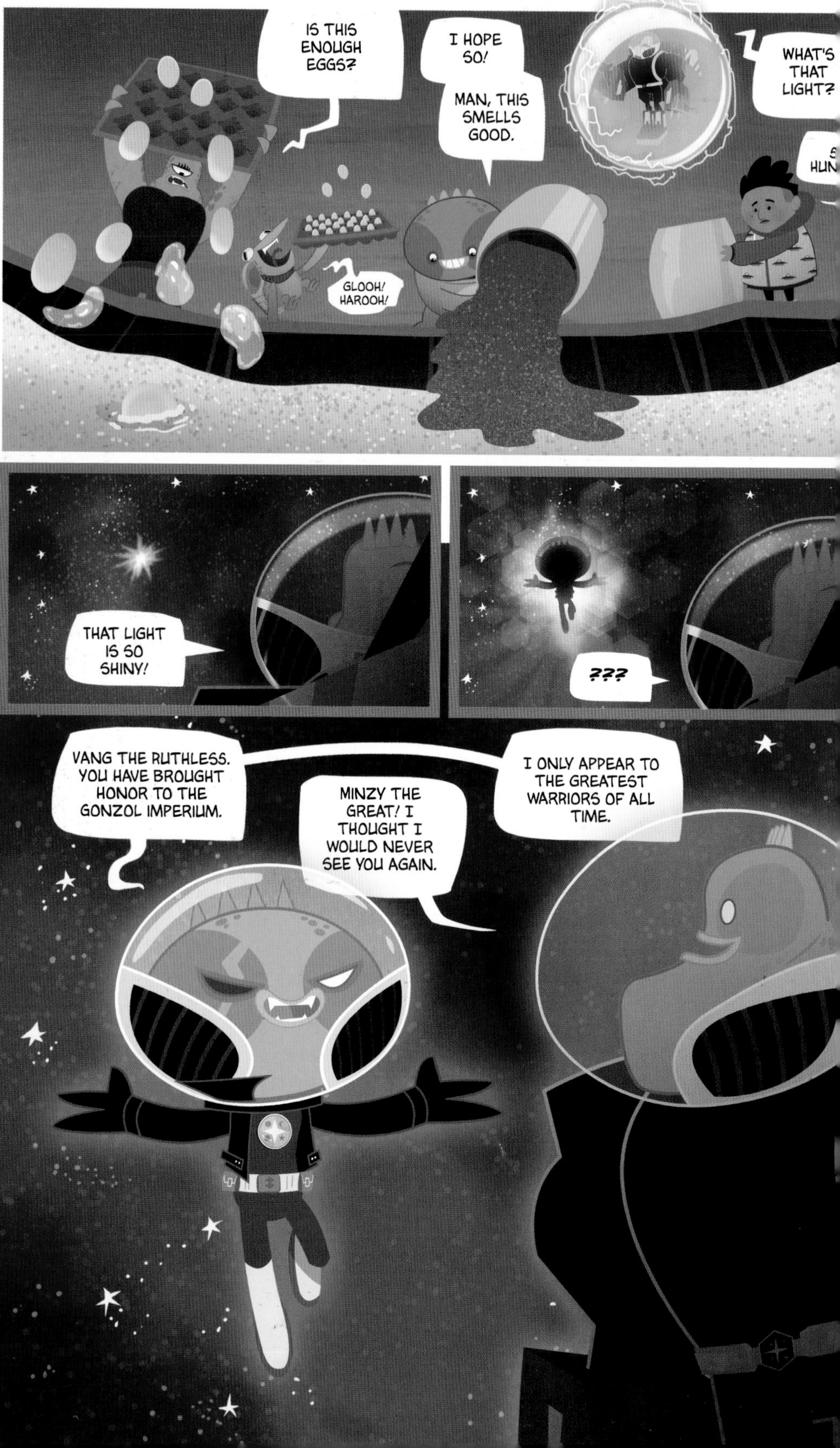
IS THIS ENOUGH EGGS?
I HOPE SO!
MAN, THIS SMELLS GOOD.
GLOOH! HAROOH!
WHAT'S THAT LIGHT?
THAT LIGHT IS SO SHINY!
???
VANG THE RUTHLESS. YOU HAVE BROUGHT HONOR TO THE GONZOL IMPERIUM.
I ONLY APPEAR TO THE GREATEST WARRIORS OF ALL TIME.
MINZY THE GREAT! I THOUGHT I WOULD NEVER SEE YOU AGAIN.

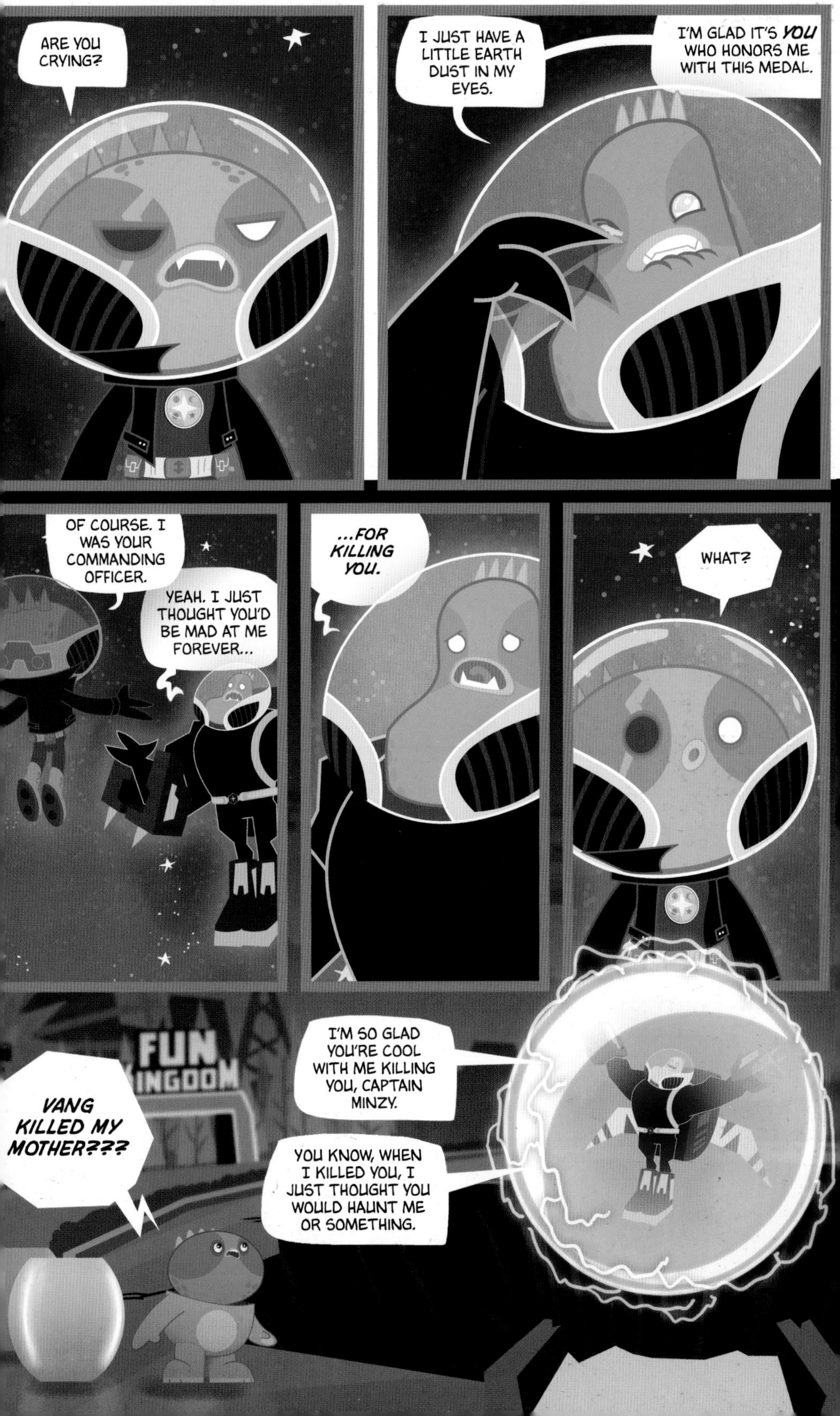

ARE YOU CRYING?
I JUST HAVE A LITTLE EARTH DUST IN MY EYES.
I'M GLAD IT'S *YOU* WHO HONORS ME WITH THIS MEDAL.
OF COURSE. I WAS YOUR COMMANDING OFFICER.
YEAH. I JUST THOUGHT YOU'D BE MAD AT ME FOREVER...
...FOR KILLING YOU.
WHAT?
FUN KINGDOM
VANG KILLED MY MOTHER???
I'M SO GLAD YOU'RE COOL WITH ME KILLING YOU, CAPTAIN MINZY.
YOU KNOW, WHEN I KILLED YOU, I JUST THOUGHT YOU WOULD HAUNT ME OR SOMETHING.

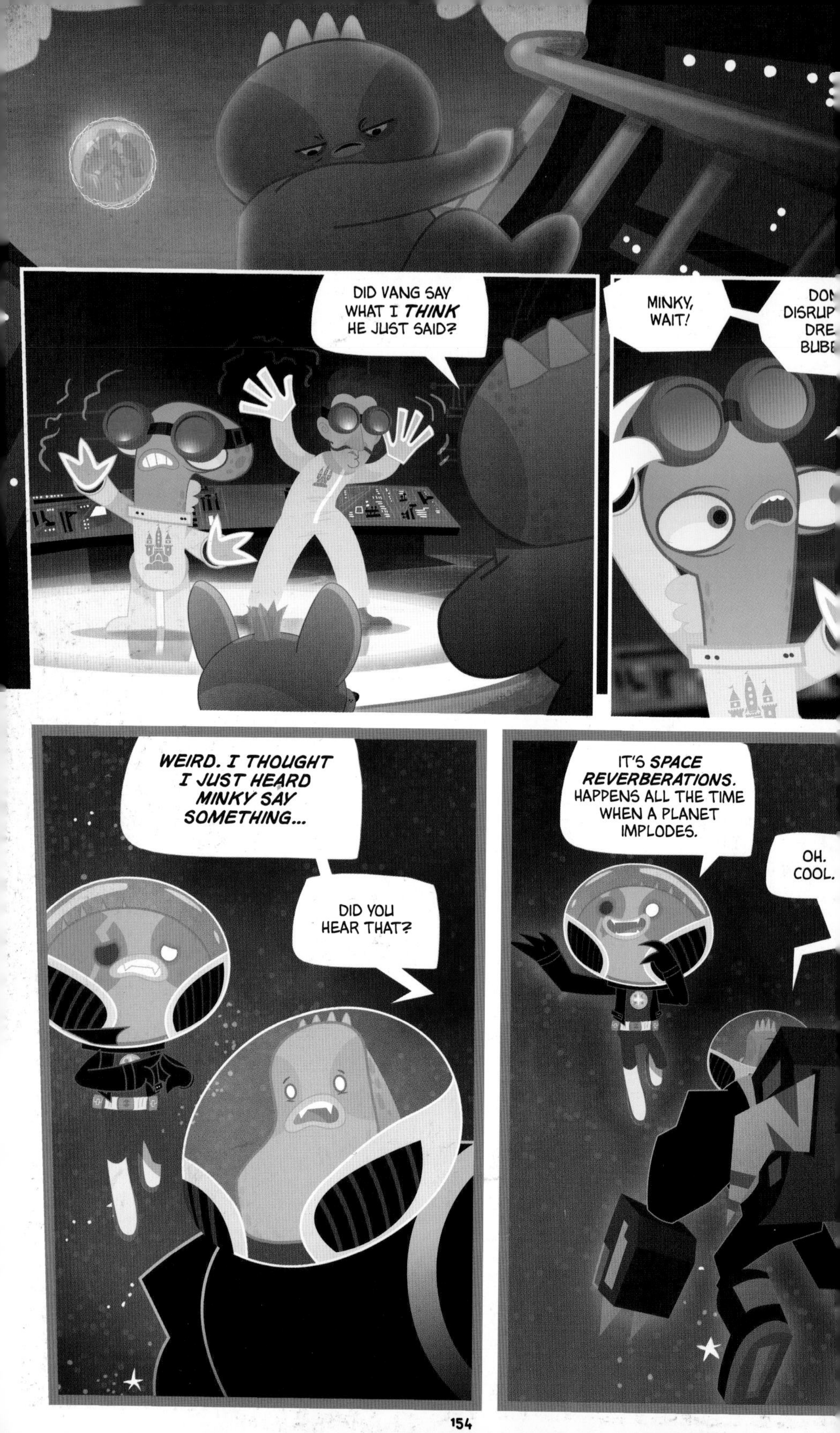
DID VANG SAY WHAT I *THINK* HE JUST SAID?
MINKY, WAIT!
WEIRD. I THOUGHT I JUST HEARD MINKY SAY SOMETHING...
DID YOU HEAR THAT?
IT'S *SPACE REVERBERATIONS.* HAPPENS ALL THE TIME WHEN A PLANET IMPLODES.
OH. COOL.

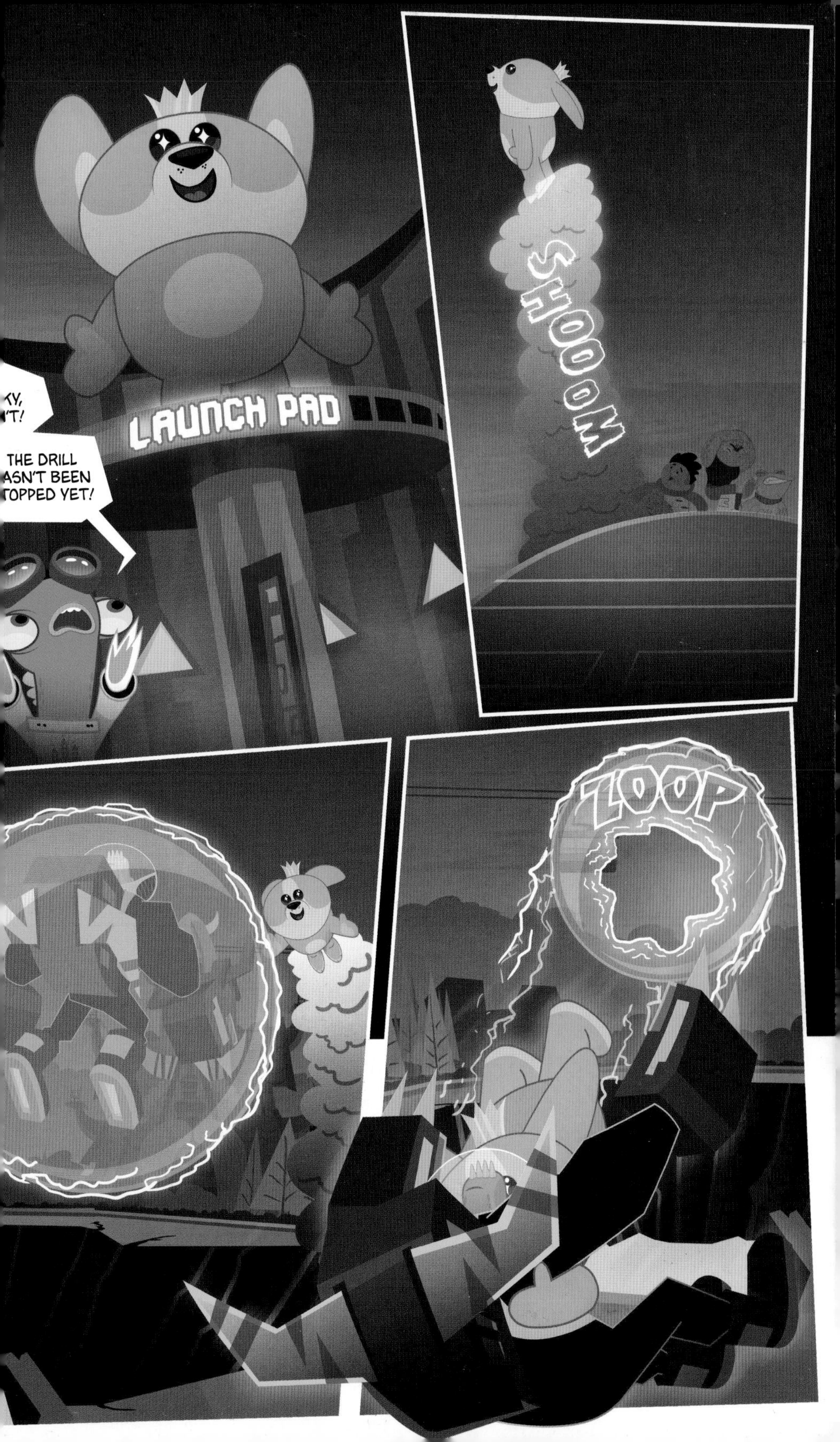
THE DRILL ASN'T BEEN TOPPED YET!
LAUNCH PAD
SHOOOM
ZOOP

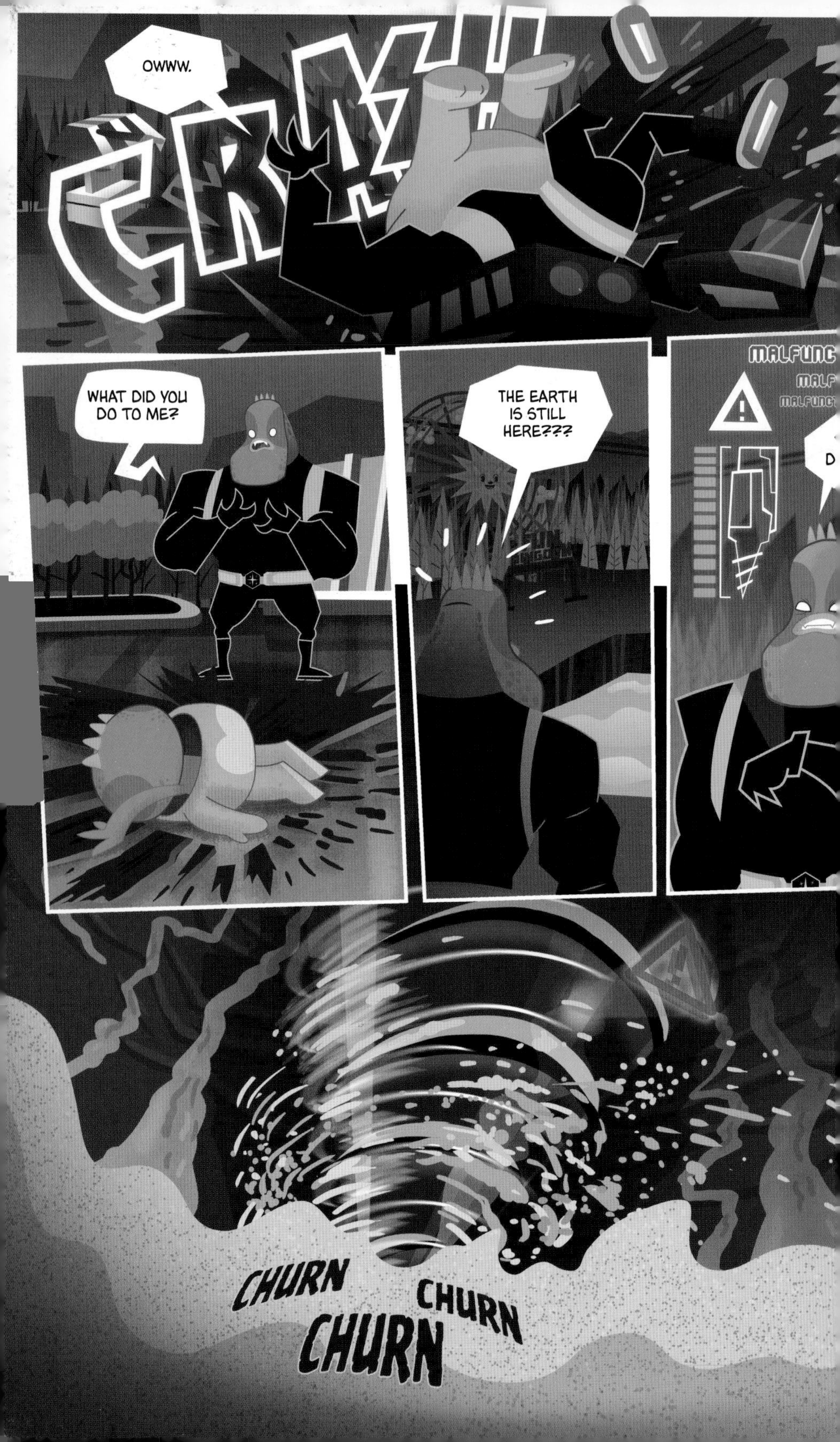
OWWW.
WHAT DID YOU DO TO ME?
THE EARTH IS STILL HERE???
MALFUNC
CHURN
CHURN
CHURN

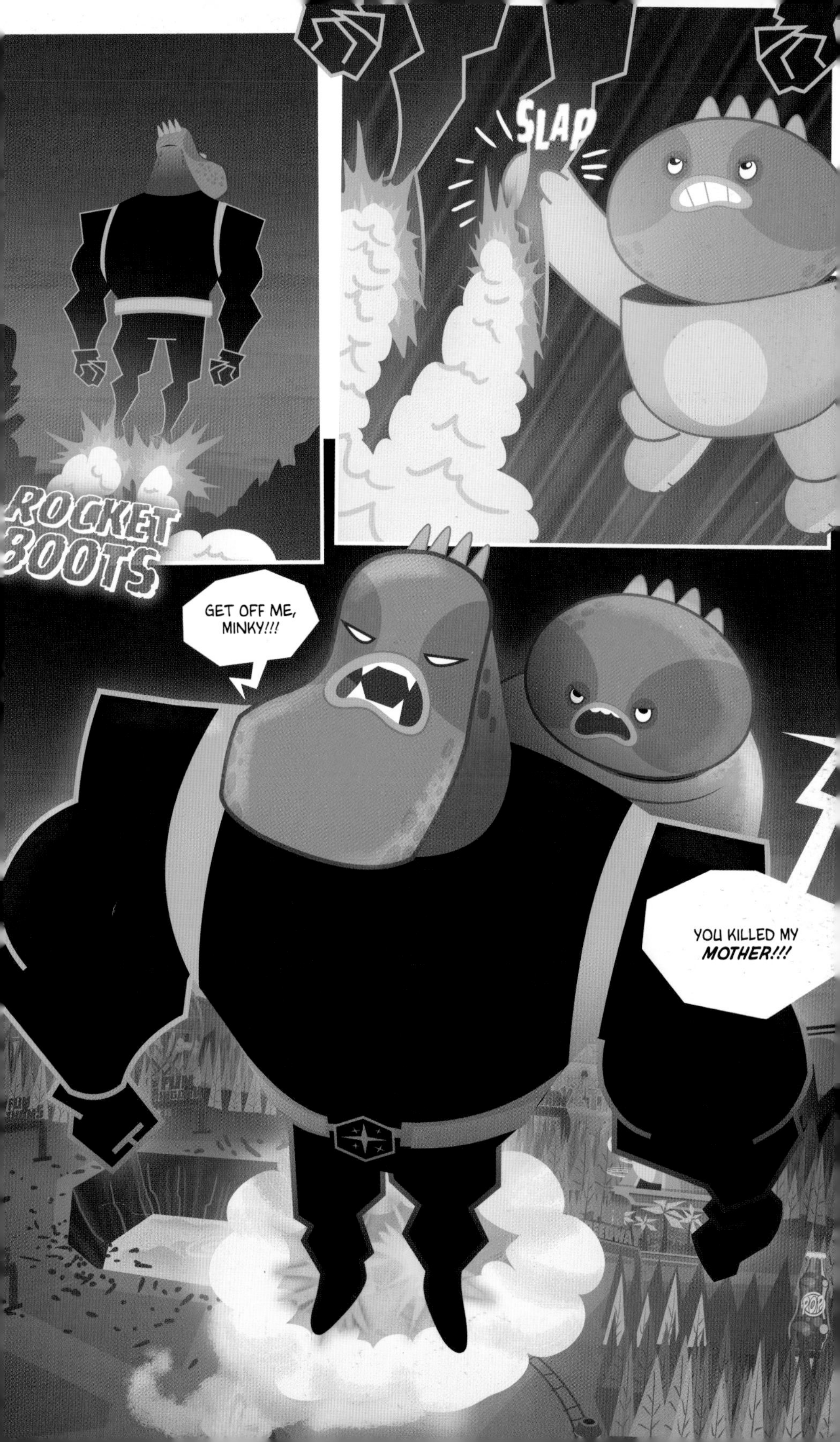
ROCKET BOOTS
SLAP
GET OFF ME, MINKY!!!
YOU KILLED MY *MOTHER!!!*

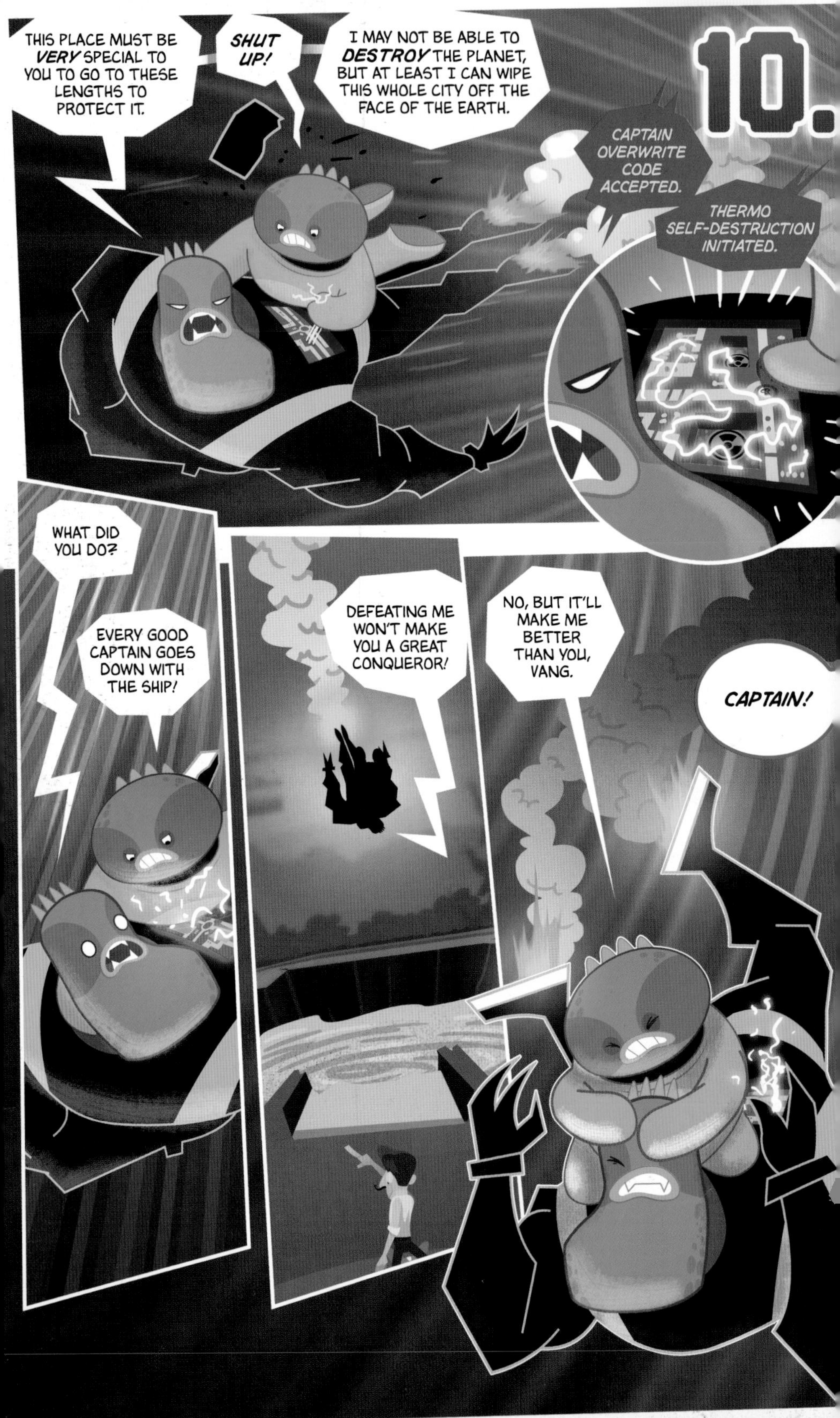
THIS PLACE MUST BE VERY SPECIAL TO YOU TO GO TO THESE LENGTHS TO PROTECT IT.
SHUT UP!
I MAY NOT BE ABLE TO DESTROY THE PLANET, BUT AT LEAST I CAN WIPE THIS WHOLE CITY OFF THE FACE OF THE EARTH.
10.
CAPTAIN OVERWRITE CODE ACCEPTED.
THERMO SELF-DESTRUCTION INITIATED.
WHAT DID YOU DO?
EVERY GOOD CAPTAIN GOES DOWN WITH THE SHIP!
DEFEATING ME WON'T MAKE YOU A GREAT CONQUEROR!
NO, BUT IT'LL MAKE ME BETTER THAN YOU, VANG.
CAPTAIN!

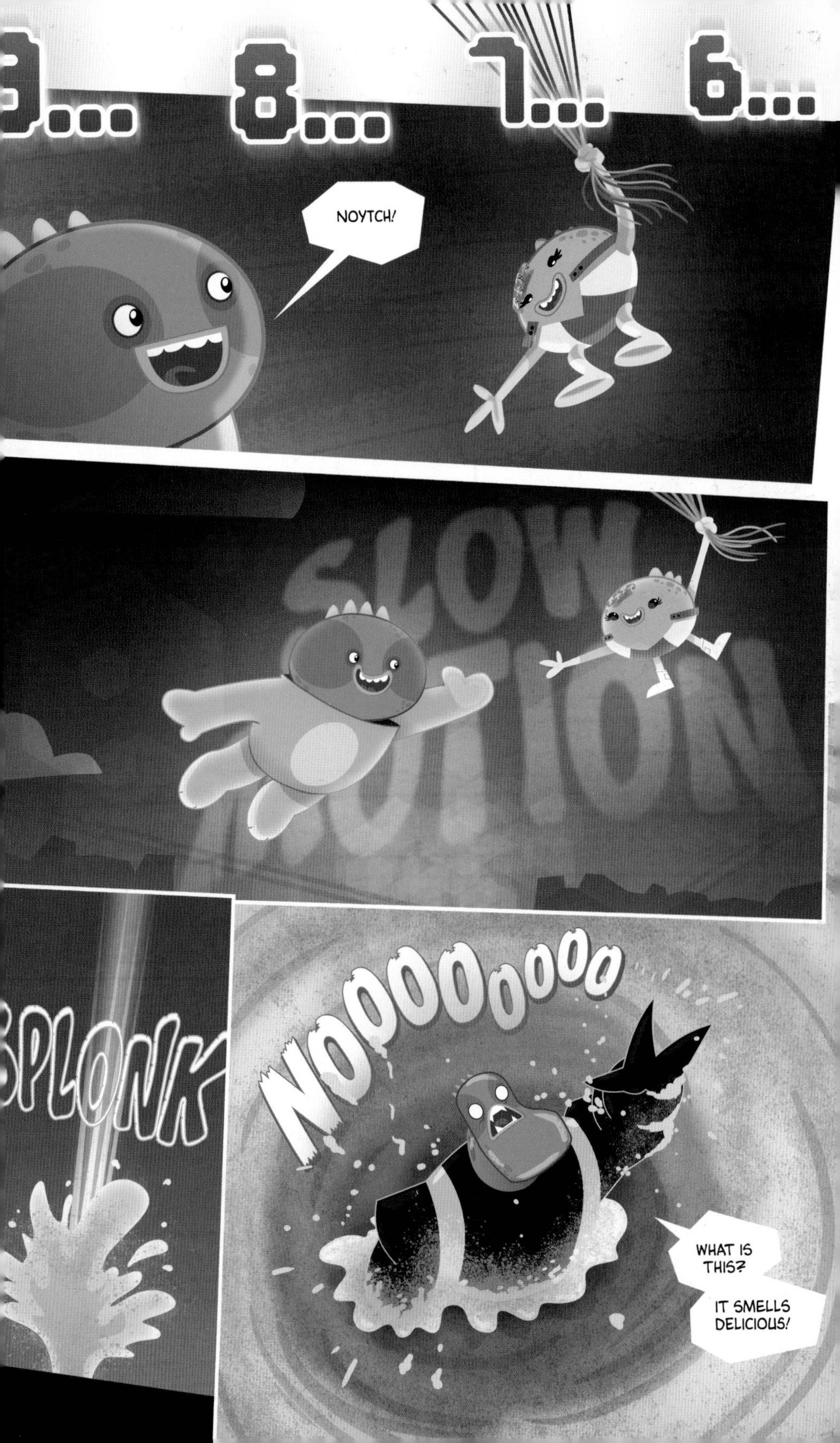
9... 8... 7... 6...
NOYTCH!
SLOW MOTION
SPLONK
NOOOOOOOO
WHAT IS THIS?
IT SMELLS DELICIOUS!

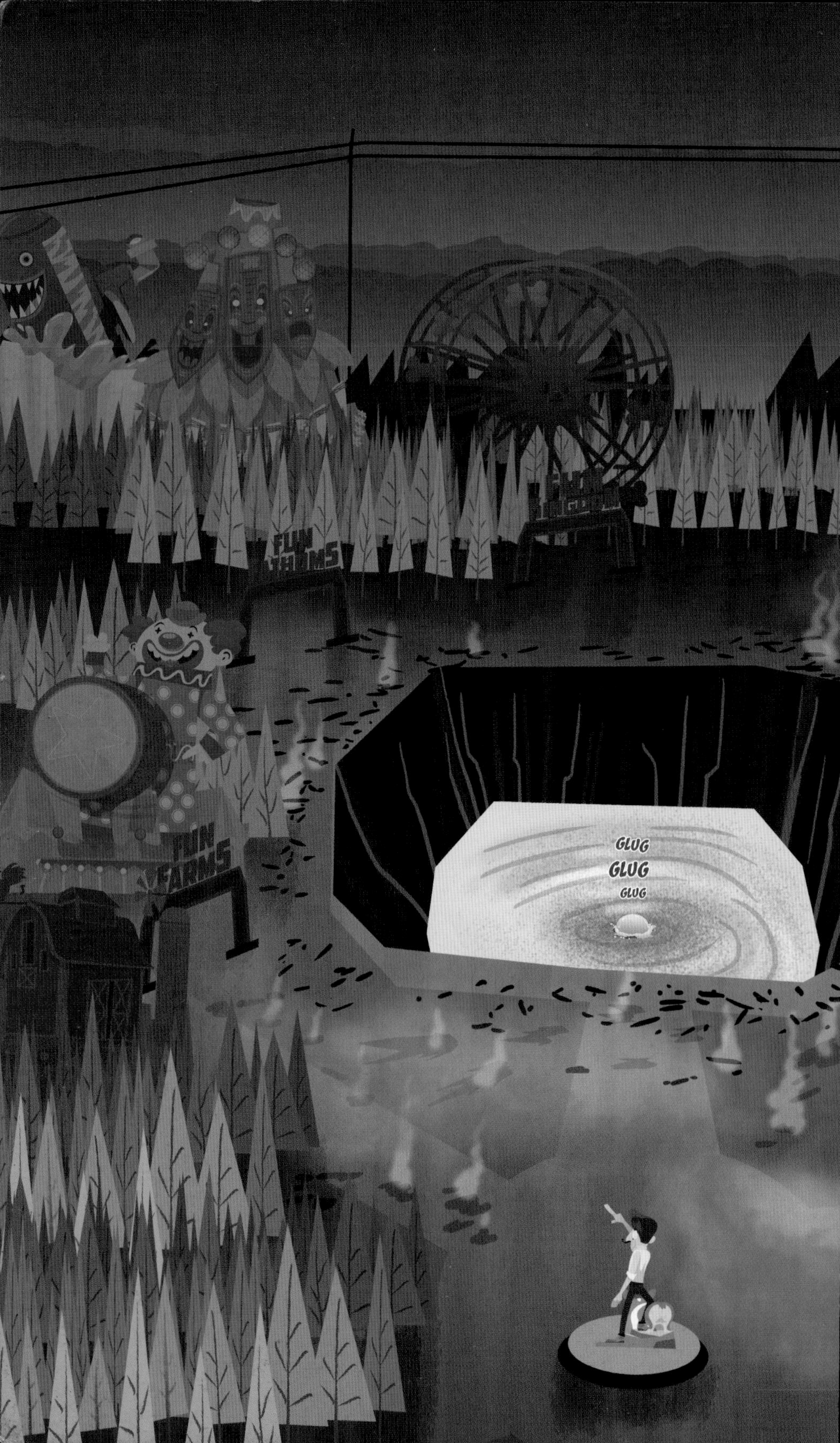
FUN FARMS
GLUG
GLUG
GLUG

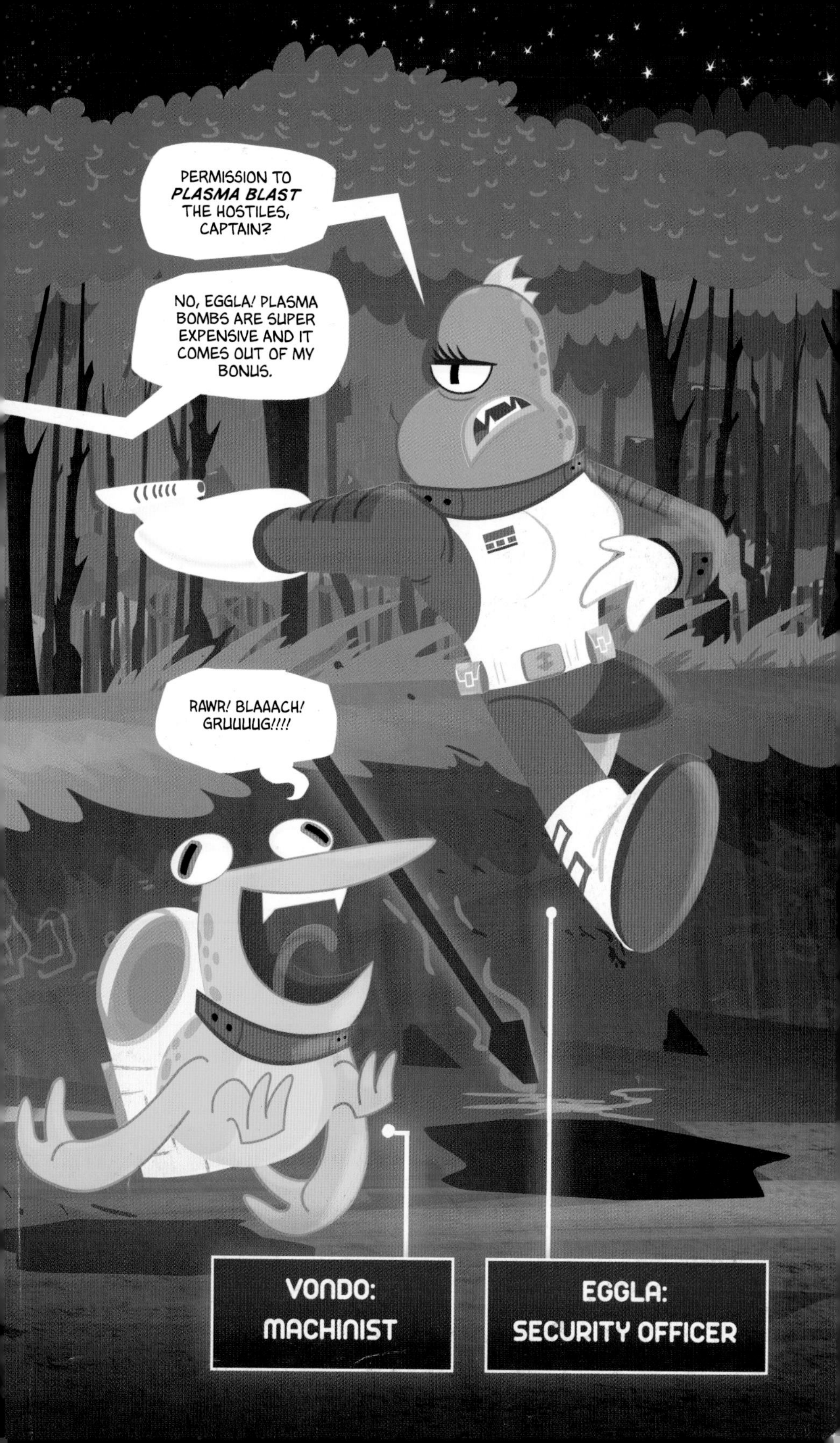
PERMISSION TO *PLASMA BLAST* THE HOSTILES, CAPTAIN?
NO, EGGLA! PLASMA BOMBS ARE SUPER EXPENSIVE AND IT COMES OUT OF MY BONUS.
RAWR! BLAAACH! GRUUUUG!!!!
VONDO: MACHINIST
EGGLA: SECURITY OFFICER

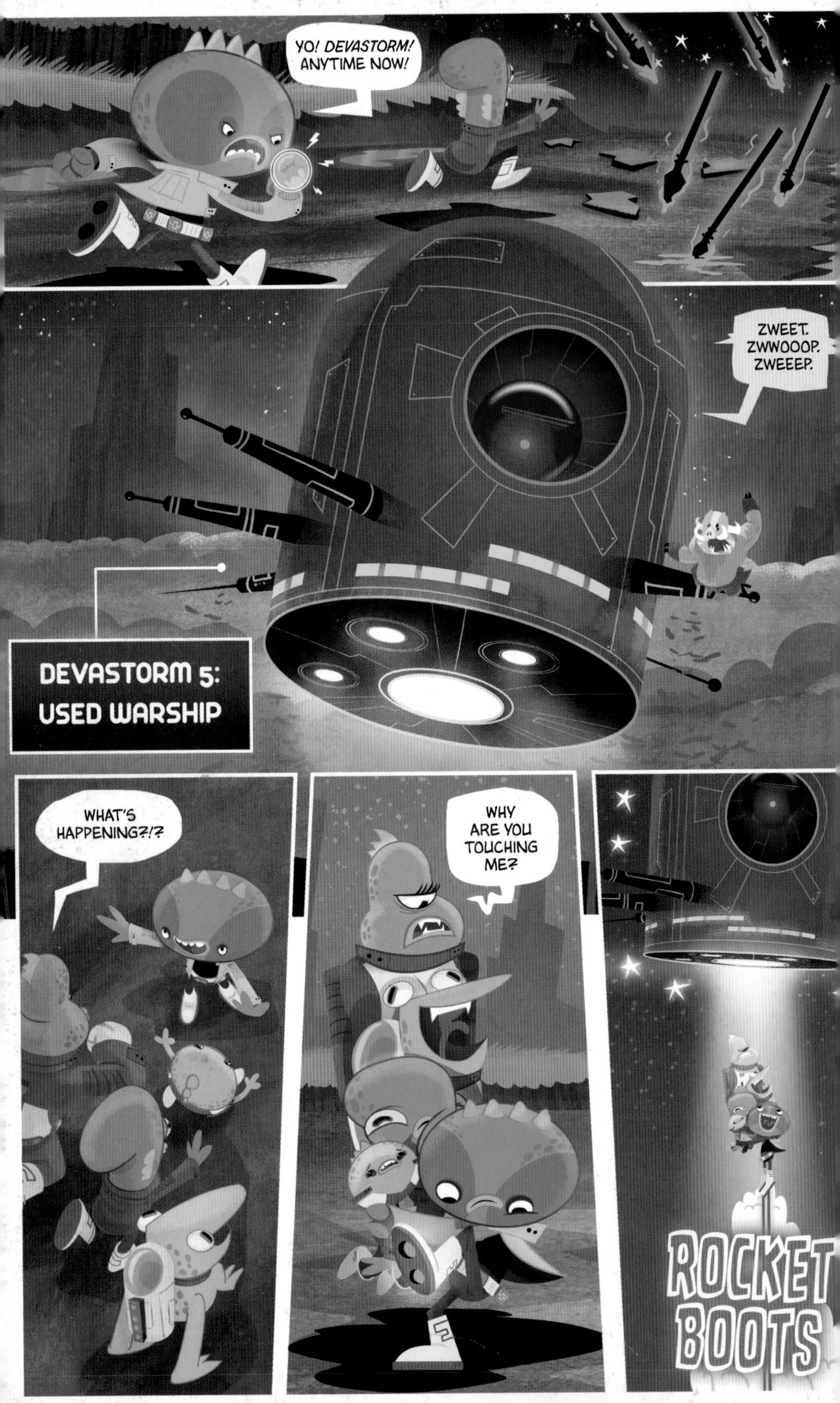
YO! DEVASTORM! ANYTIME NOW!
ZWEET. ZWWOOOP. ZWEEEP.
DEVASTORM 5: USED WARSHIP
WHAT'S HAPPENING?!?
WHY ARE YOU TOUCHING ME?
ROCKET BOOTS

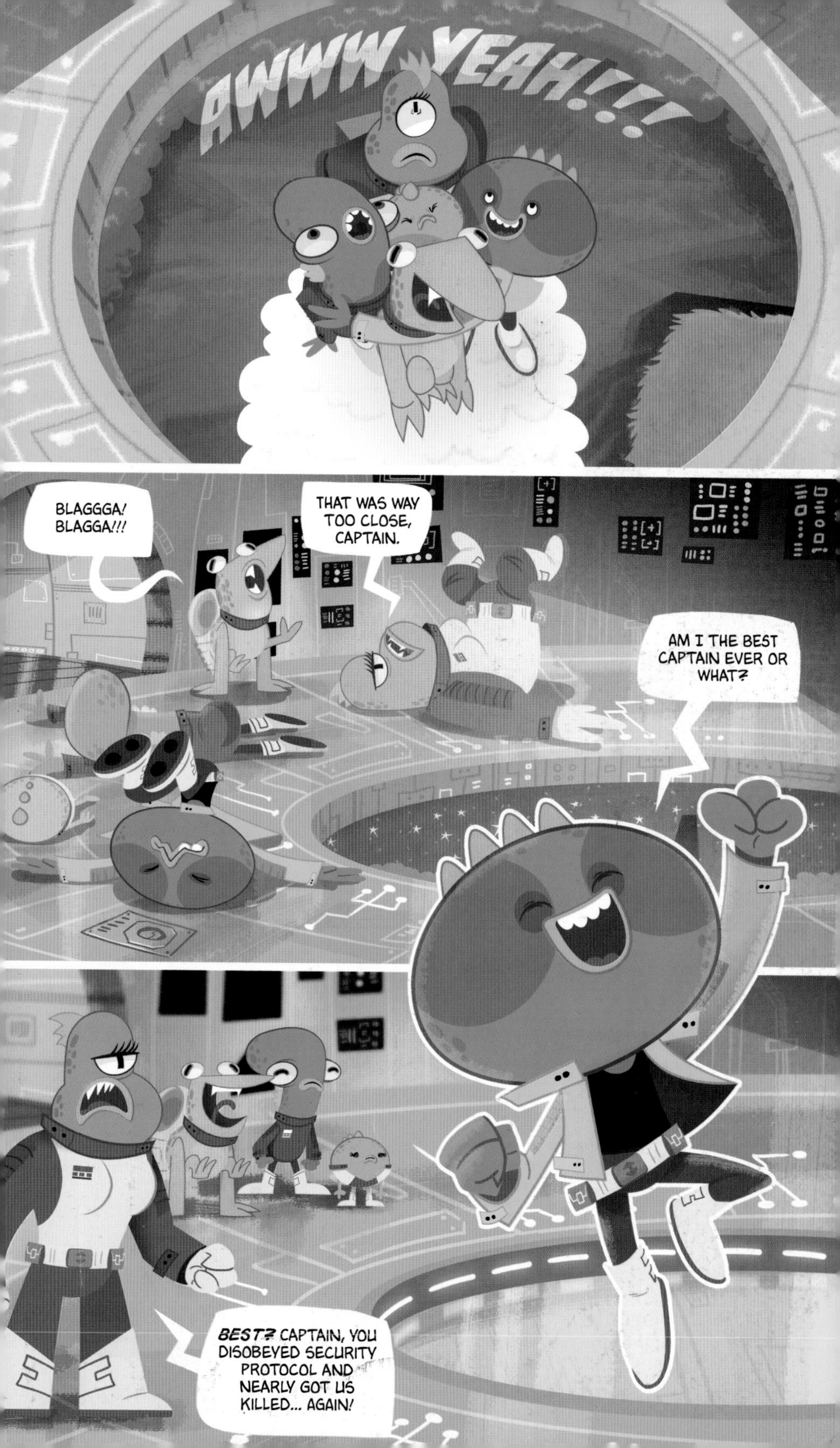
AWWW YEAH!!!
BLAGGGA! BLAGGA!!!
THAT WAS WAY TOO CLOSE, CAPTAIN.
AM I THE BEST CAPTAIN EVER OR WHAT?
BEST? CAPTAIN, YOU DISOBEYED SECURITY PROTOCOL AND NEARLY GOT US KILLED... AGAIN!

THE MISSION WAS TO *INVADE* CONQUER, AND ANNEX THE PLANET FOR OUR QUEEN.

ANY MISSION ACCOMPLISHED IS A *WIN* IN MY BOOK.

THAT MISSION WAS NOT ACHIEVED.

AS YOUR CAPTAIN, ILLY, MY MISSION IS TO BRING MY CREW BACK ALIVE... SO I'D RATHER Y'ALL THANK ME. MAYBE EVEN GET ME A TOOKER BAR.

RUCK, RAWK, ROOOK!!!

YOU'RE WELCO VONDO. I KN I'M THE BES

MISSION FAILED.

ONE DAY YOU DUMMIES ARE GONNA APPRECIATE ME.

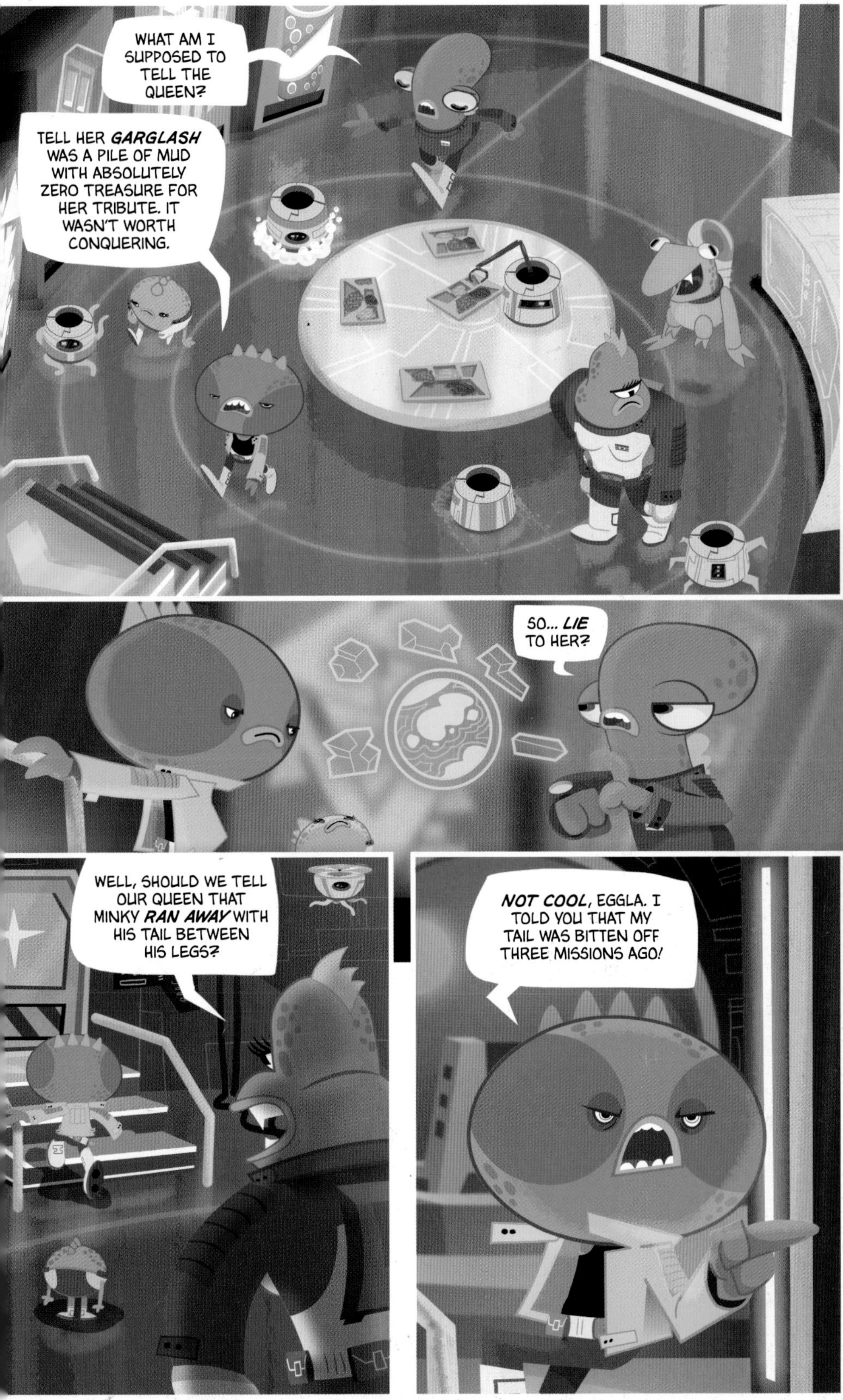
WHAT AM I SUPPOSED TO TELL THE QUEEN?
TELL HER ***GARGLASH*** WAS A PILE OF MUD WITH ABSOLUTELY ZERO TREASURE FOR HER TRIBUTE. IT WASN'T WORTH CONQUERING.
SO... ***LIE*** TO HER?
WELL, SHOULD WE TELL OUR QUEEN THAT MINKY ***RAN AWAY*** WITH HIS TAIL BETWEEN HIS LEGS?
NOT COOL, EGGLA. I TOLD YOU THAT MY TAIL WAS BITTEN OFF THREE MISSIONS AGO!

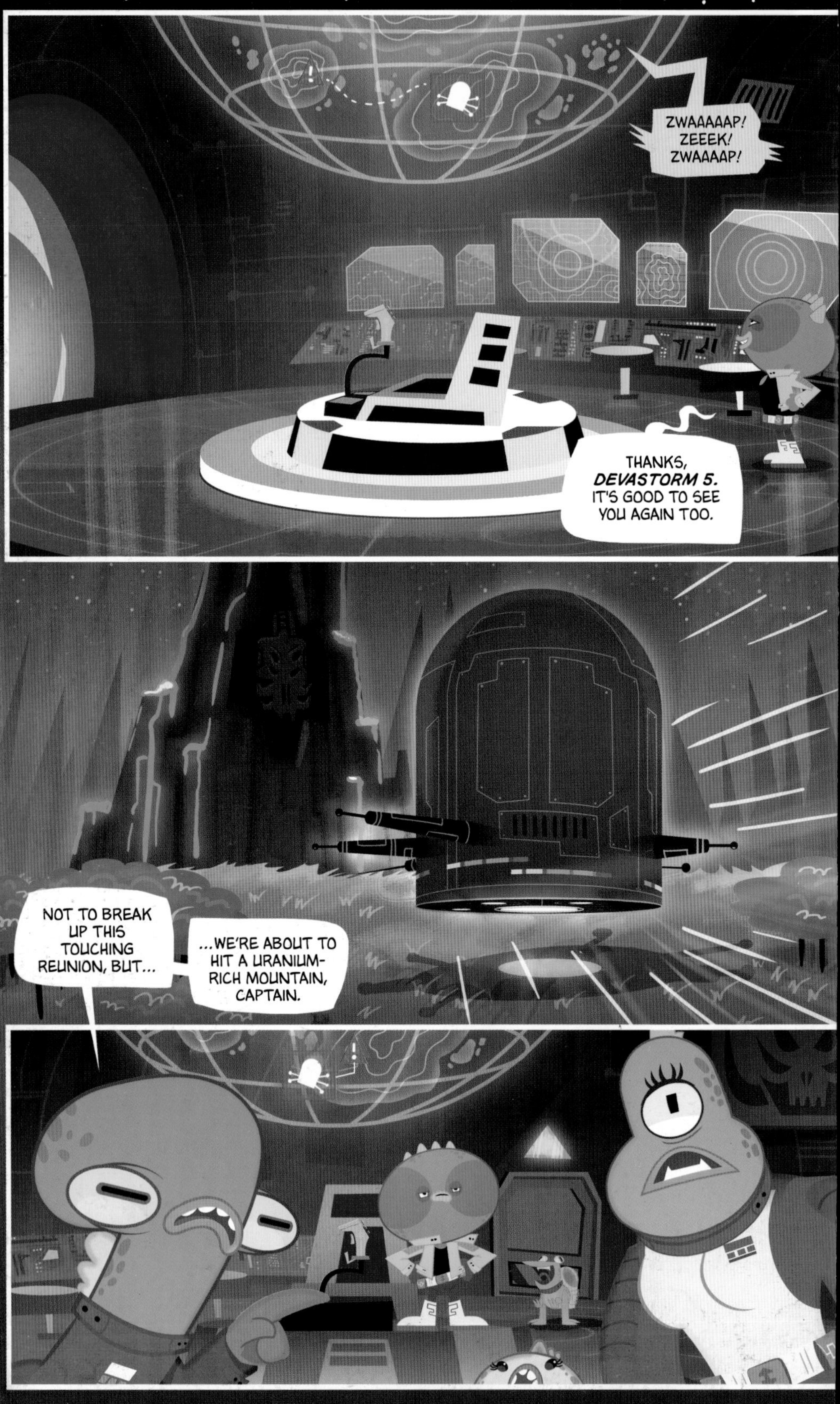
ZWAAAAAP! ZEEEK! ZWAAAAP!
THANKS, DEVASTORM 5. IT'S GOOD TO SEE YOU AGAIN TOO.
NOT TO BREAK UP THIS TOUCHING REUNION, BUT...
...WE'RE ABOUT TO HIT A URANIUM-RICH MOUNTAIN, CAPTAIN.

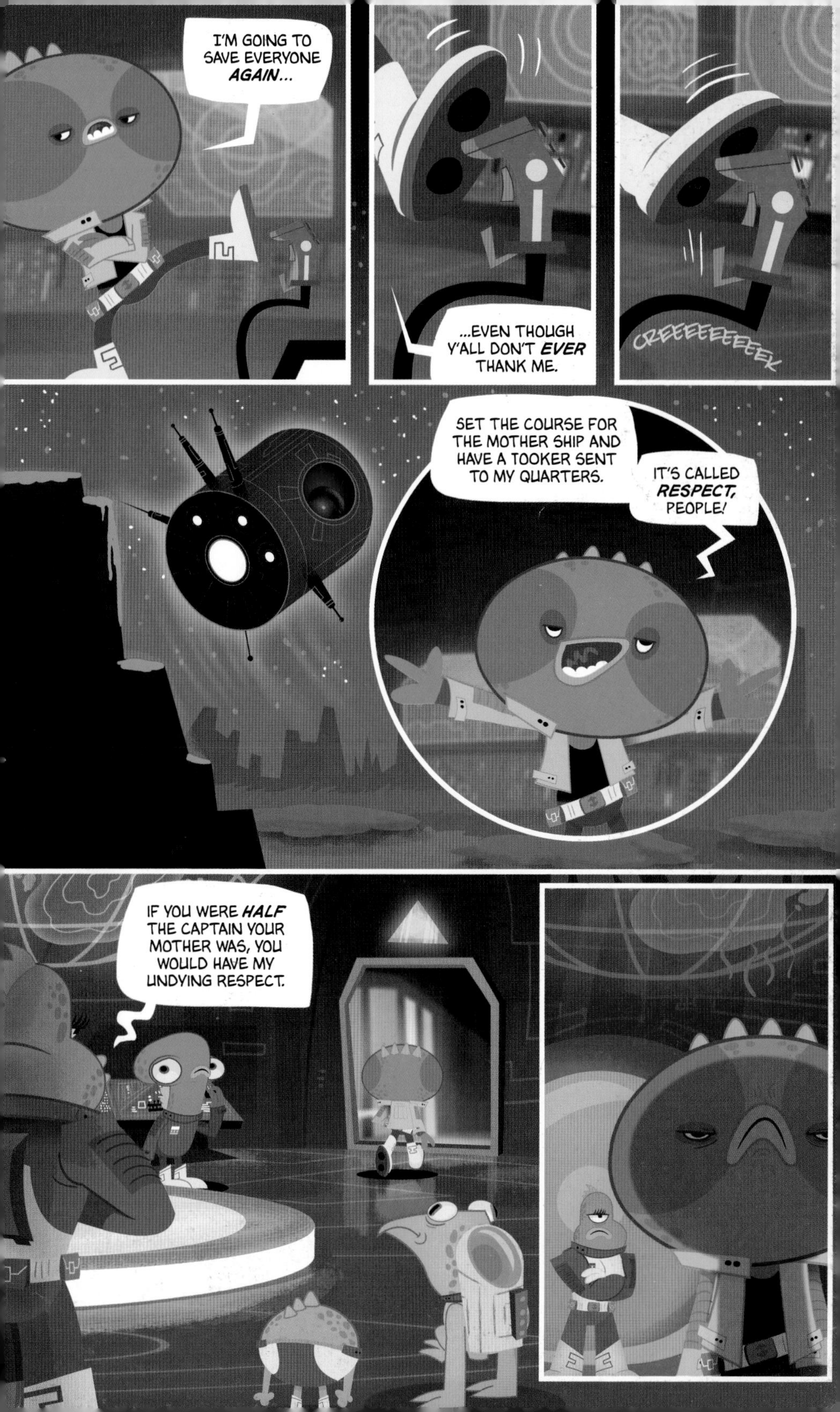
I'M GOING TO SAVE EVERYONE ***AGAIN...***
...EVEN THOUGH Y'ALL DON'T ***EVER*** THANK ME.
CREEEEEEEEEEK
SET THE COURSE FOR THE MOTHER SHIP AND HAVE A TOOKER SENT TO MY QUARTERS.
IT'S CALLED ***RESPECT,*** PEOPLE!
IF YOU WERE ***HALF*** THE CAPTAIN YOUR MOTHER WAS, YOU WOULD HAVE MY UNDYING RESPECT.

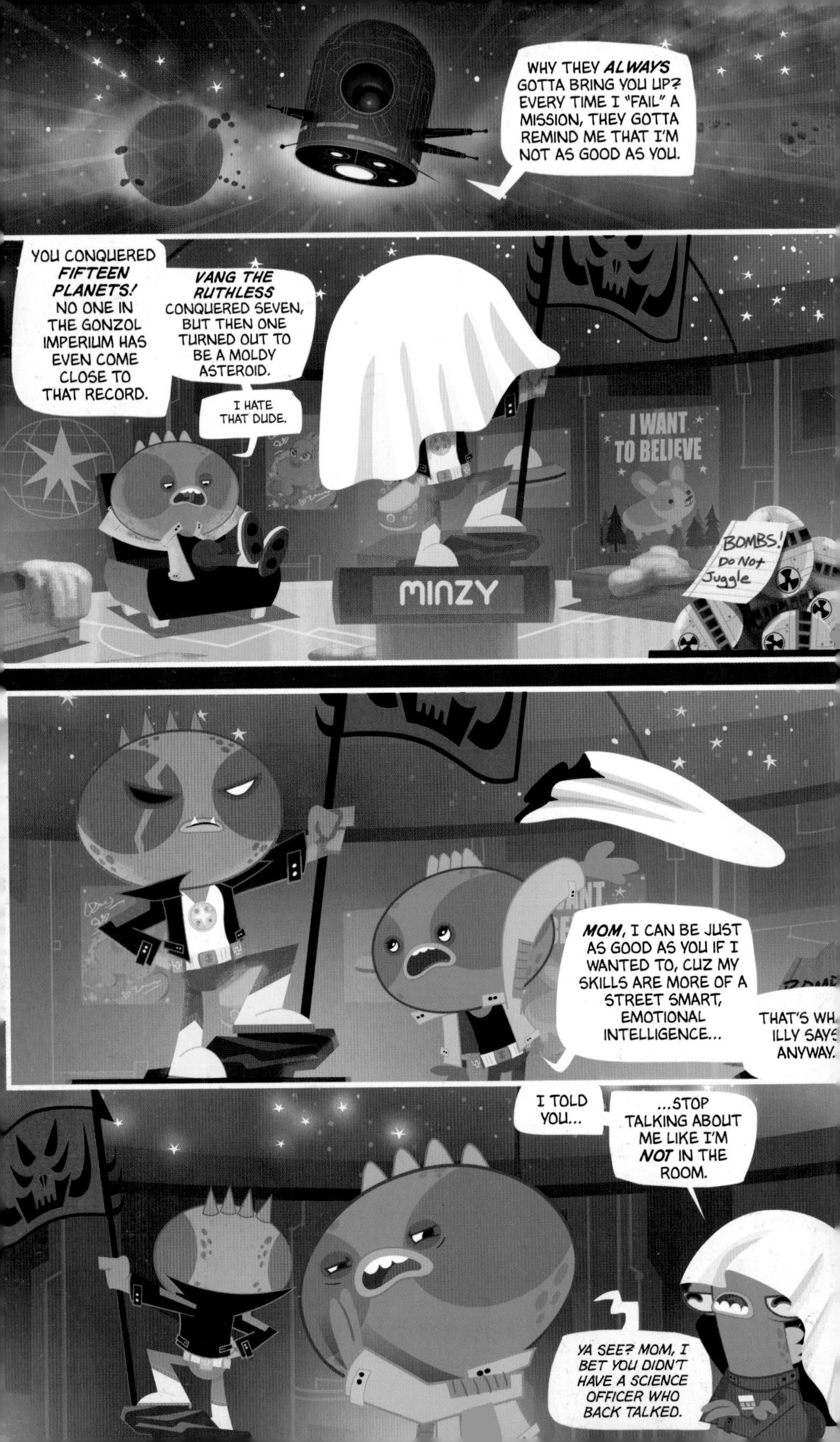
WHY THEY *ALWAYS* GOTTA BRING YOU UP? EVERY TIME I "FAIL" A MISSION, THEY GOTTA REMIND ME THAT I'M NOT AS GOOD AS YOU.
YOU CONQUERED *FIFTEEN PLANETS!* NO ONE IN THE GONZOL IMPERIUM HAS EVEN COME CLOSE TO THAT RECORD.
VANG THE RUTHLESS CONQUERED SEVEN, BUT THEN ONE TURNED OUT TO BE A MOLDY ASTEROID.
I HATE THAT DUDE.
I WANT TO BELIEVE
MINZY
BOMBS! Do Not Juggle
MOM, I CAN BE JUST AS GOOD AS YOU IF I WANTED TO, CUZ MY SKILLS ARE MORE OF A STREET SMART, EMOTIONAL INTELLIGENCE...
THAT'S WH ILLY SAYS ANYWAY.
I TOLD YOU...
...STOP TALKING ABOUT ME LIKE I'M *NOT* IN THE ROOM.
YA SEE? MOM, I BET YOU DIDN'T HAVE A SCIENCE OFFICER WHO BACK TALKED.

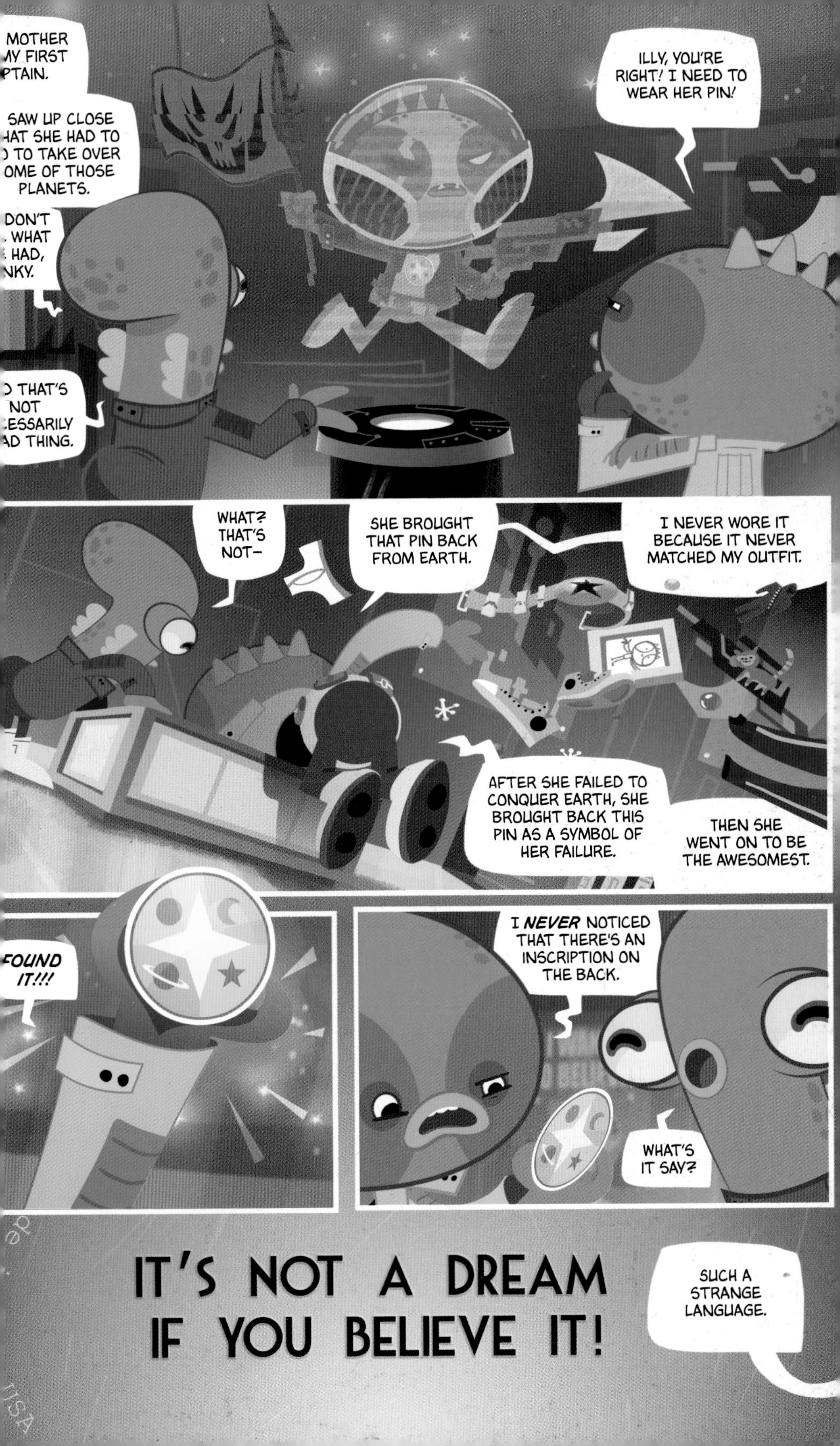

MOTHER
MY FIRST
PTAIN.
SAW UP CLOSE
HAT SHE HAD TO
TO TAKE OVER
OME OF THOSE
PLANETS.
ILLY, YOU'RE RIGHT! I NEED TO WEAR HER PIN!
DON'T
WHAT
HAD,
NKY.
THAT'S
NOT
CESSARILY
AD THING.
WHAT? THAT'S NOT—
SHE BROUGHT THAT PIN BACK FROM EARTH.
I NEVER WORE IT BECAUSE IT NEVER MATCHED MY OUTFIT.
AFTER SHE FAILED TO CONQUER EARTH, SHE BROUGHT BACK THIS PIN AS A SYMBOL OF HER FAILURE.
THEN SHE WENT ON TO BE THE AWESOMEST.
FOUND IT!!!
I *NEVER* NOTICED THAT THERE'S AN INSCRIPTION ON THE BACK.
WHAT'S IT SAY?
IT'S NOT A DREAM IF YOU BELIEVE IT!
SUCH A STRANGE LANGUAGE.

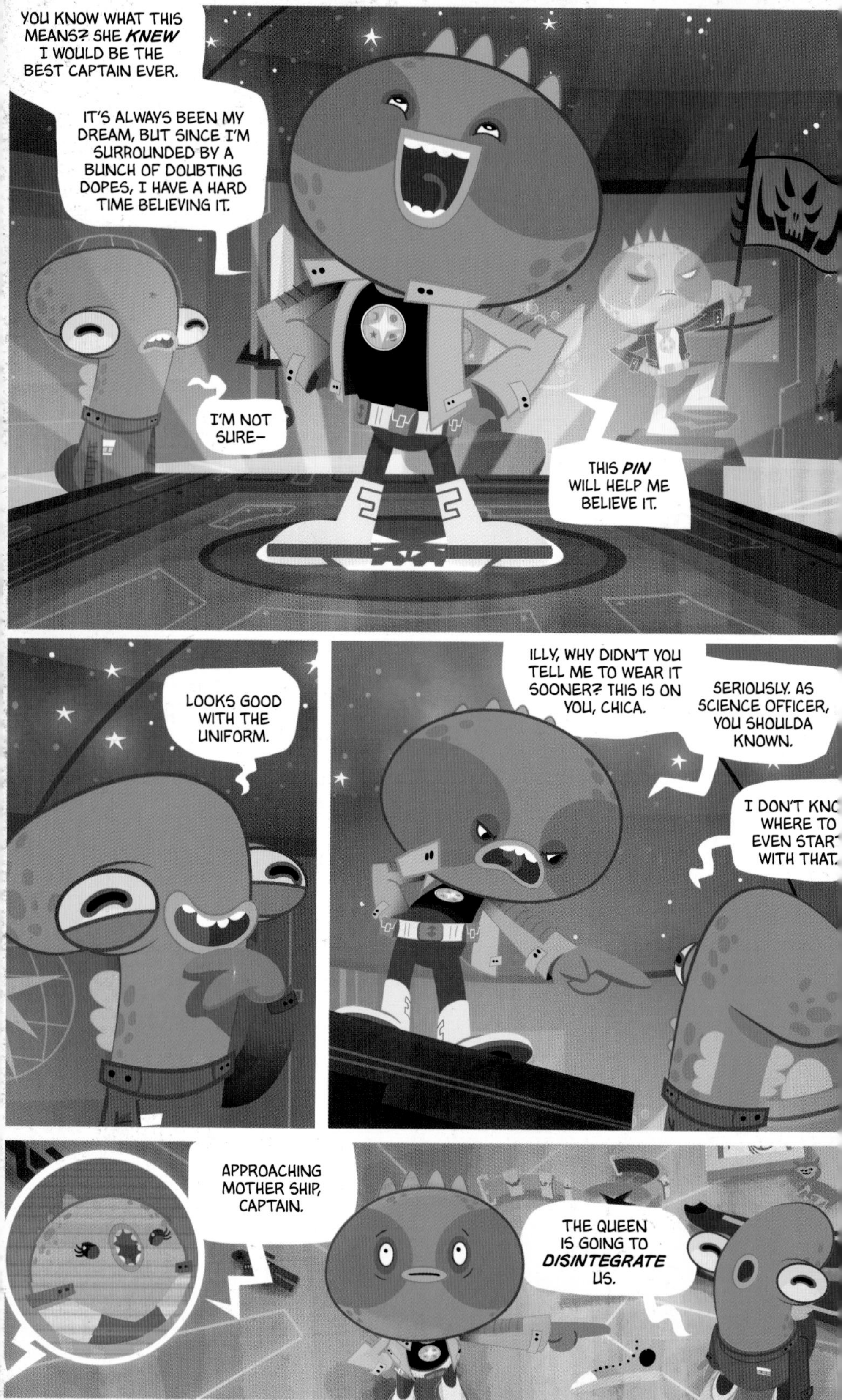
YOU KNOW WHAT THIS MEANS? SHE *KNEW* I WOULD BE THE BEST CAPTAIN EVER.
IT'S ALWAYS BEEN MY DREAM, BUT SINCE I'M SURROUNDED BY A BUNCH OF DOUBTING DOPES, I HAVE A HARD TIME BELIEVING IT.
I'M NOT SURE–
THIS *PIN* WILL HELP ME BELIEVE IT.
LOOKS GOOD WITH THE UNIFORM.
ILLY, WHY DIDN'T YOU TELL ME TO WEAR IT SOONER? THIS IS ON YOU, CHICA.
SERIOUSLY. AS SCIENCE OFFICER, YOU SHOULDA KNOWN.
I DON'T KNO WHERE TO EVEN STAR WITH THAT.
APPROACHING MOTHER SHIP, CAPTAIN.
THE QUEEN IS GOING TO ***DISINTEGRATE*** US.

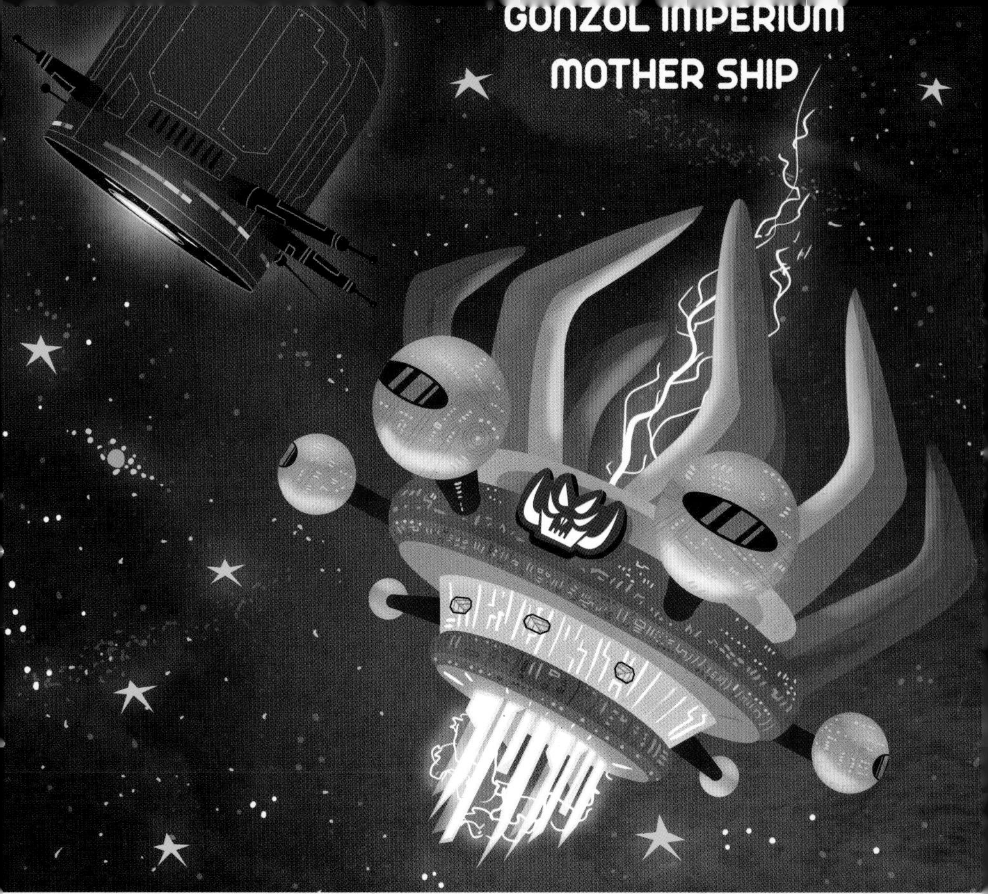
GONZOL IMPERIUM
MOTHER SHIP

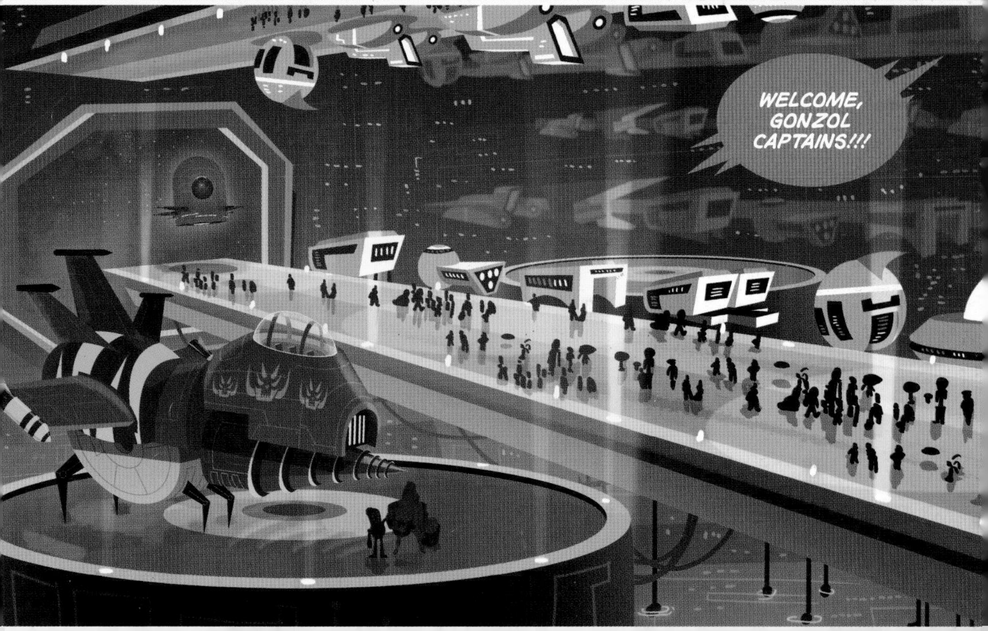
WELCOME, GONZOL CAPTAINS!!!

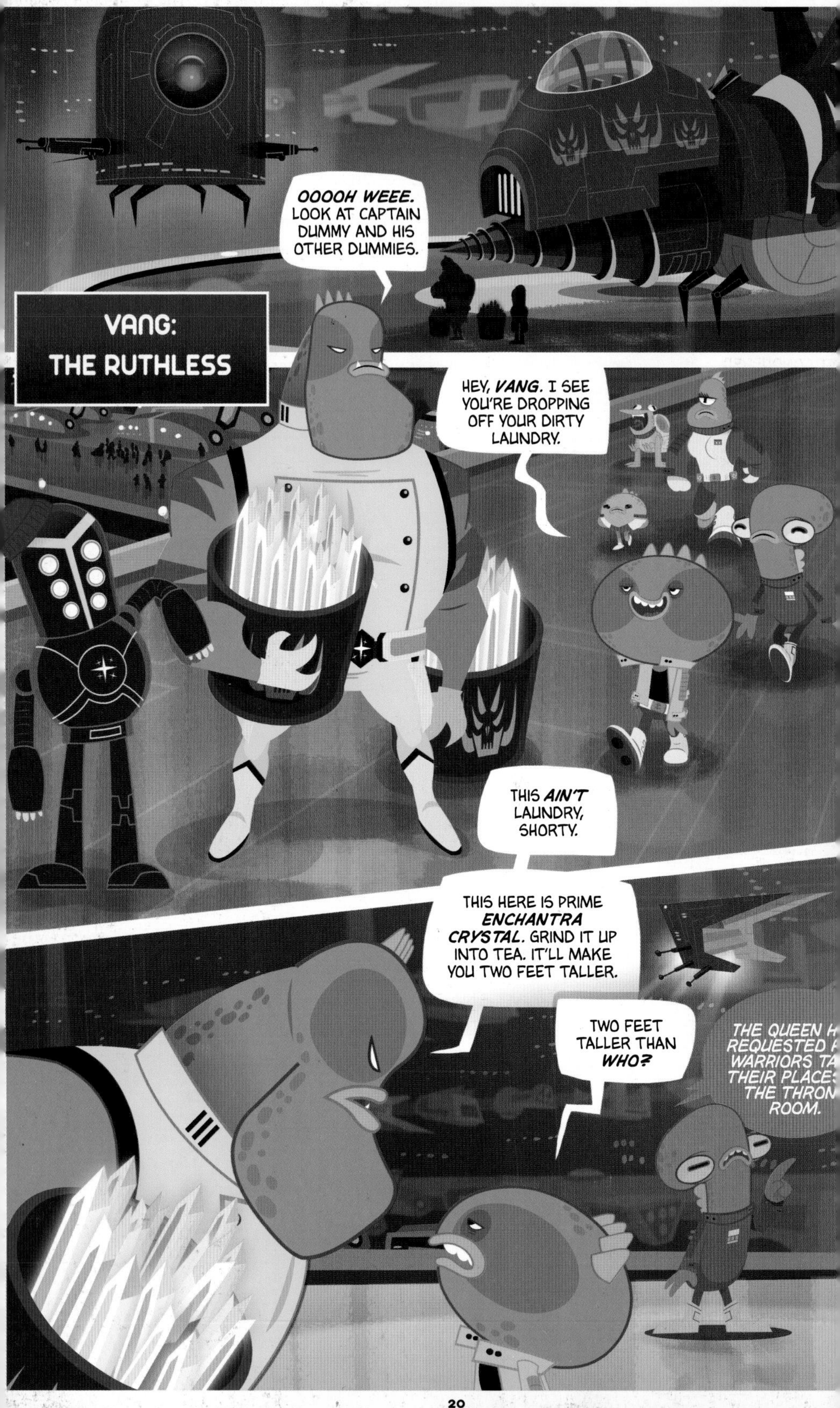

OOOOH WEEE. LOOK AT CAPTAIN DUMMY AND HIS OTHER DUMMIES.
VANG: THE RUTHLESS
HEY, VANG. I SEE YOU'RE DROPPING OFF YOUR DIRTY LAUNDRY.
THIS AIN'T LAUNDRY, SHORTY.
THIS HERE IS PRIME ENCHANTRA CRYSTAL. GRIND IT UP INTO TEA. IT'LL MAKE YOU TWO FEET TALLER.
TWO FEET TALLER THAN WHO?

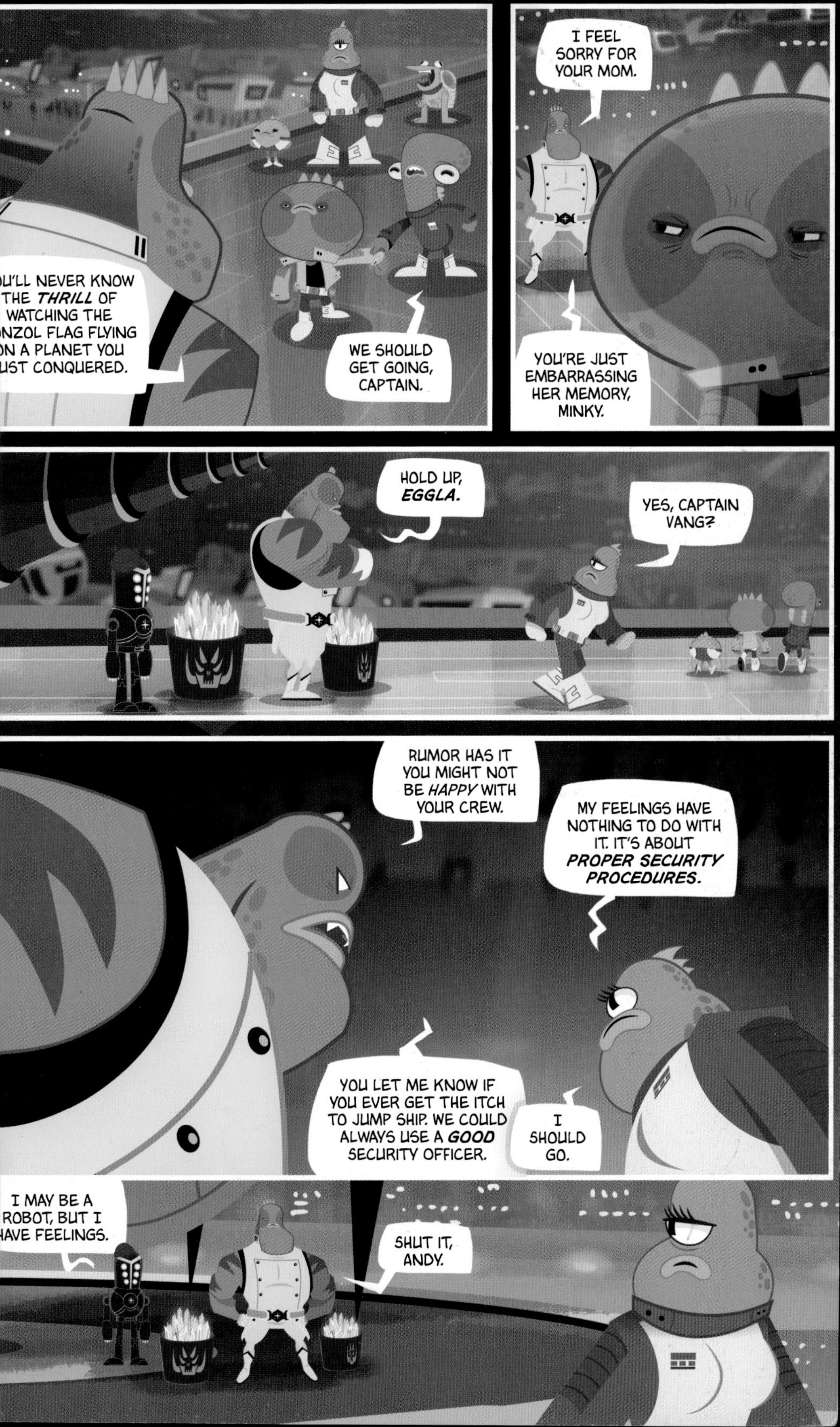

OU'LL NEVER KNOW THE *THRILL* OF WATCHING THE NZOL FLAG FLYING ON A PLANET YOU UST CONQUERED.
WE SHOULD GET GOING, CAPTAIN.
I FEEL SORRY FOR YOUR MOM.
YOU'RE JUST EMBARRASSING HER MEMORY, MINKY.
HOLD UP, ***EGGLA.***
YES, CAPTAIN VANG?
RUMOR HAS IT YOU MIGHT NOT BE *HAPPY* WITH YOUR CREW.
MY FEELINGS HAVE NOTHING TO DO WITH IT. IT'S ABOUT ***PROPER SECURITY PROCEDURES.***
YOU LET ME KNOW IF YOU EVER GET THE ITCH TO JUMP SHIP. WE COULD ALWAYS USE A ***GOOD*** SECURITY OFFICER.
I SHOULD GO.
I MAY BE A ROBOT, BUT I HAVE FEELINGS.
SHUT IT, ANDY.

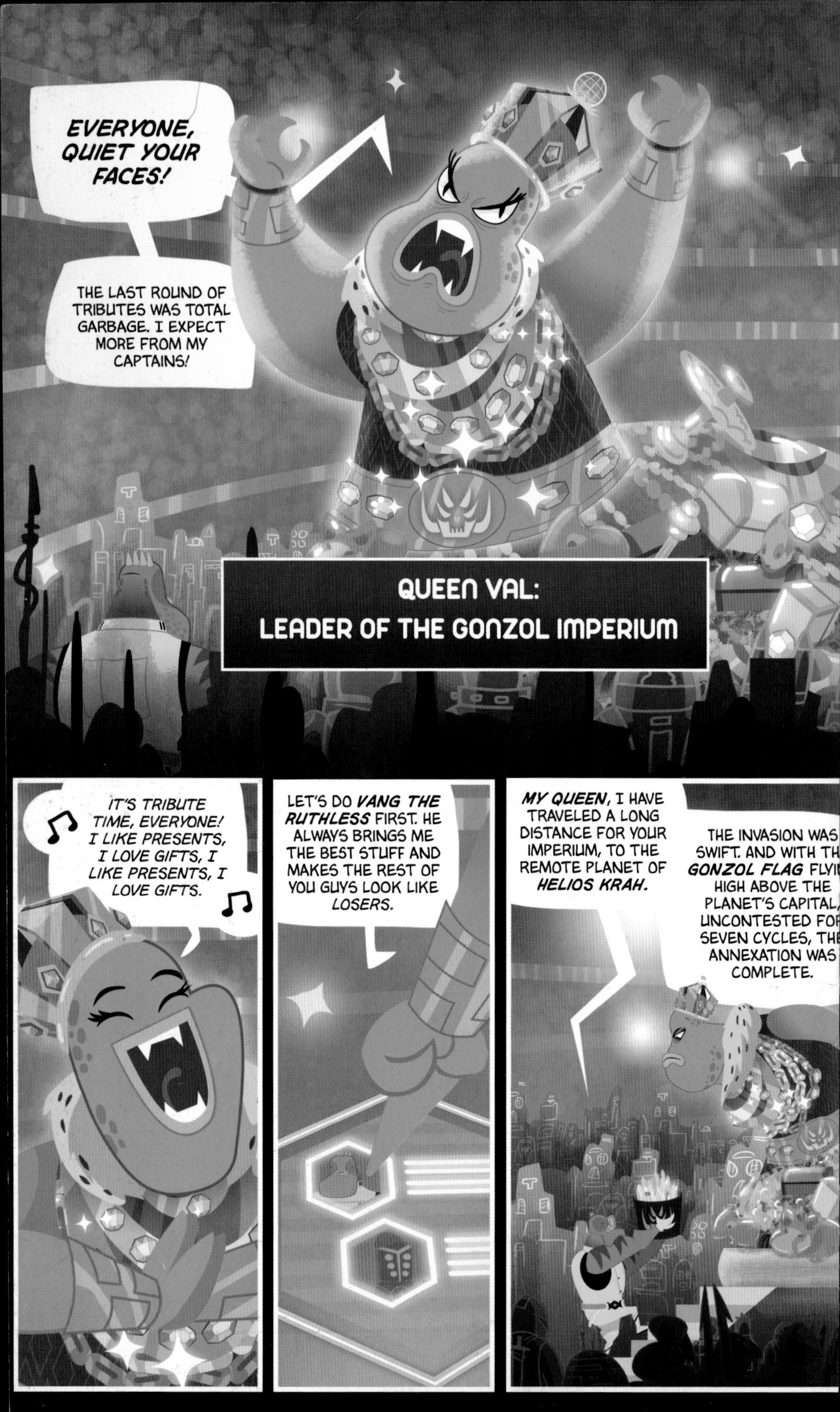
EVERYONE, QUIET YOUR FACES!
THE LAST ROUND OF TRIBUTES WAS TOTAL GARBAGE. I EXPECT MORE FROM MY CAPTAINS!
QUEEN VAL: LEADER OF THE GONZOL IMPERIUM
IT'S TRIBUTE TIME, EVERYONE! I LIKE PRESENTS, I LOVE GIFTS, I LIKE PRESENTS, I LOVE GIFTS.
LET'S DO VANG THE RUTHLESS FIRST. HE ALWAYS BRINGS ME THE BEST STUFF AND MAKES THE REST OF YOU GUYS LOOK LIKE LOSERS.
MY QUEEN, I HAVE TRAVELED A LONG DISTANCE FOR YOUR IMPERIUM, TO THE REMOTE PLANET OF HELIOS KRAH.
THE INVASION WAS SWIFT. AND WITH TH GONZOL FLAG FLYI HIGH ABOVE THE PLANET'S CAPITAL, UNCONTESTED FOR SEVEN CYCLES, THE ANNEXATION WAS COMPLETE.

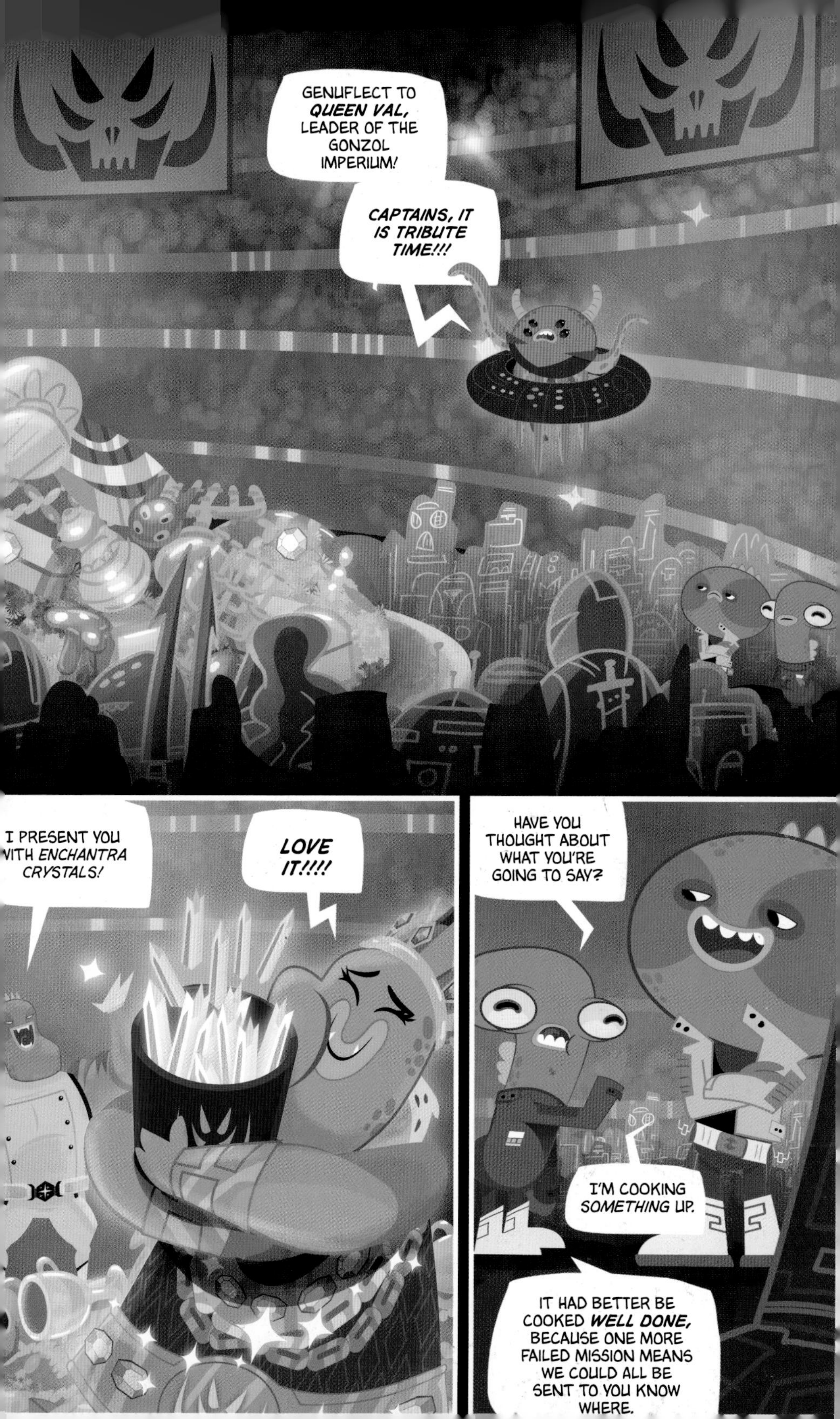
GENUFLECT TO **QUEEN VAL,** LEADER OF THE GONZOL IMPERIUM!
CAPTAINS, IT IS TRIBUTE TIME!!!
I PRESENT YOU WITH *ENCHANTRA CRYSTALS!*
LOVE IT!!!!
HAVE YOU THOUGHT ABOUT WHAT YOU'RE GOING TO SAY?
I'M COOKING *SOMETHING* UP.
IT HAD BETTER BE COOKED ***WELL DONE,*** BECAUSE ONE MORE FAILED MISSION MEANS WE COULD ALL BE SENT TO YOU KNOW WHERE.

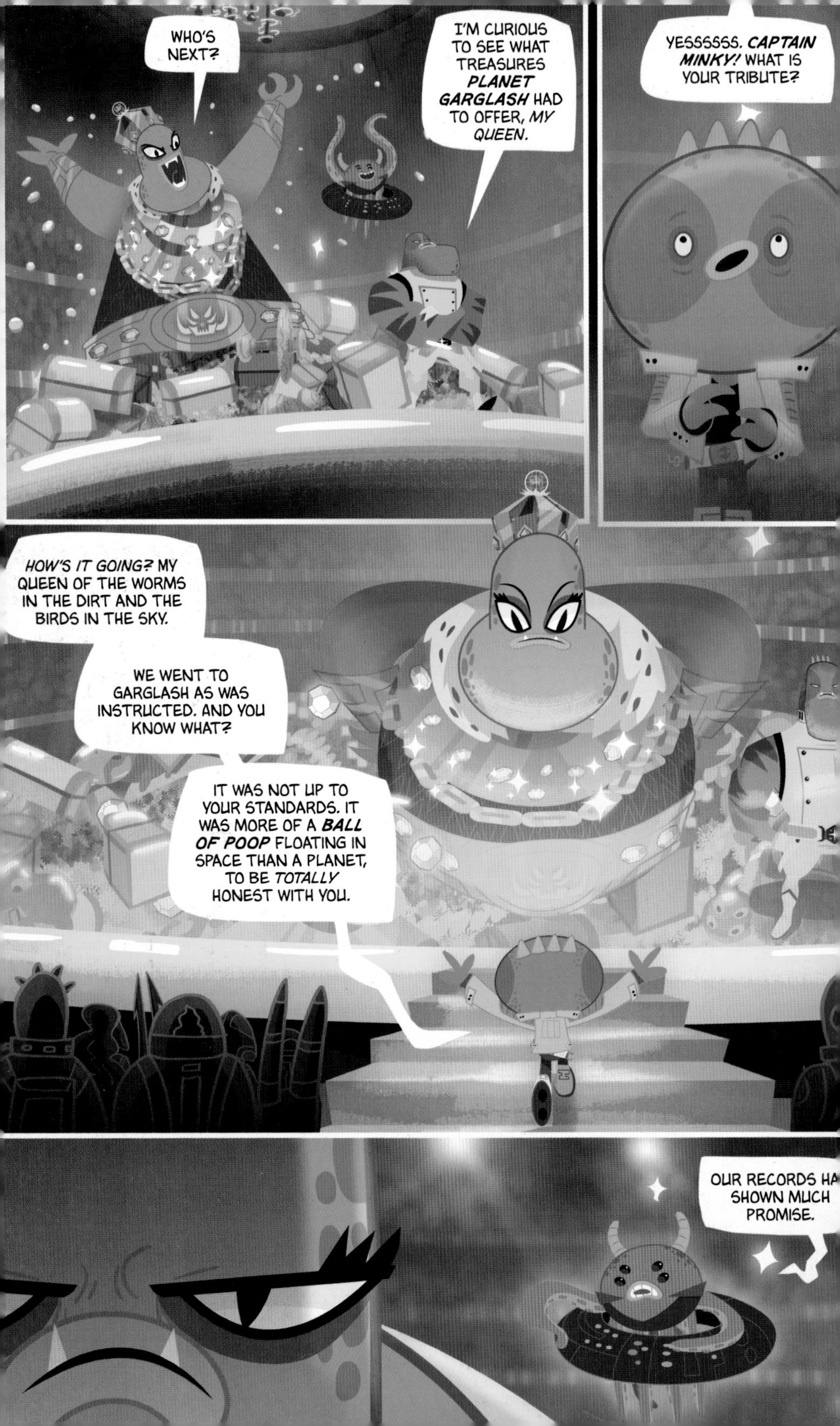
WHO'S NEXT?
I'M CURIOUS TO SEE WHAT TREASURES *PLANET GARGLASH* HAD TO OFFER, *MY QUEEN.*
YESSSSSS. *CAPTAIN MINKY!* WHAT IS YOUR TRIBUTE?
HOW'S IT GOING? MY QUEEN OF THE WORMS IN THE DIRT AND THE BIRDS IN THE SKY.
WE WENT TO GARGLASH AS WAS INSTRUCTED. AND YOU KNOW WHAT?
IT WAS NOT UP TO YOUR STANDARDS. IT WAS MORE OF A *BALL OF POOP* FLOATING IN SPACE THAN A PLANET, TO BE *TOTALLY* HONEST WITH YOU.
SHOWN MUCH PROMISE.

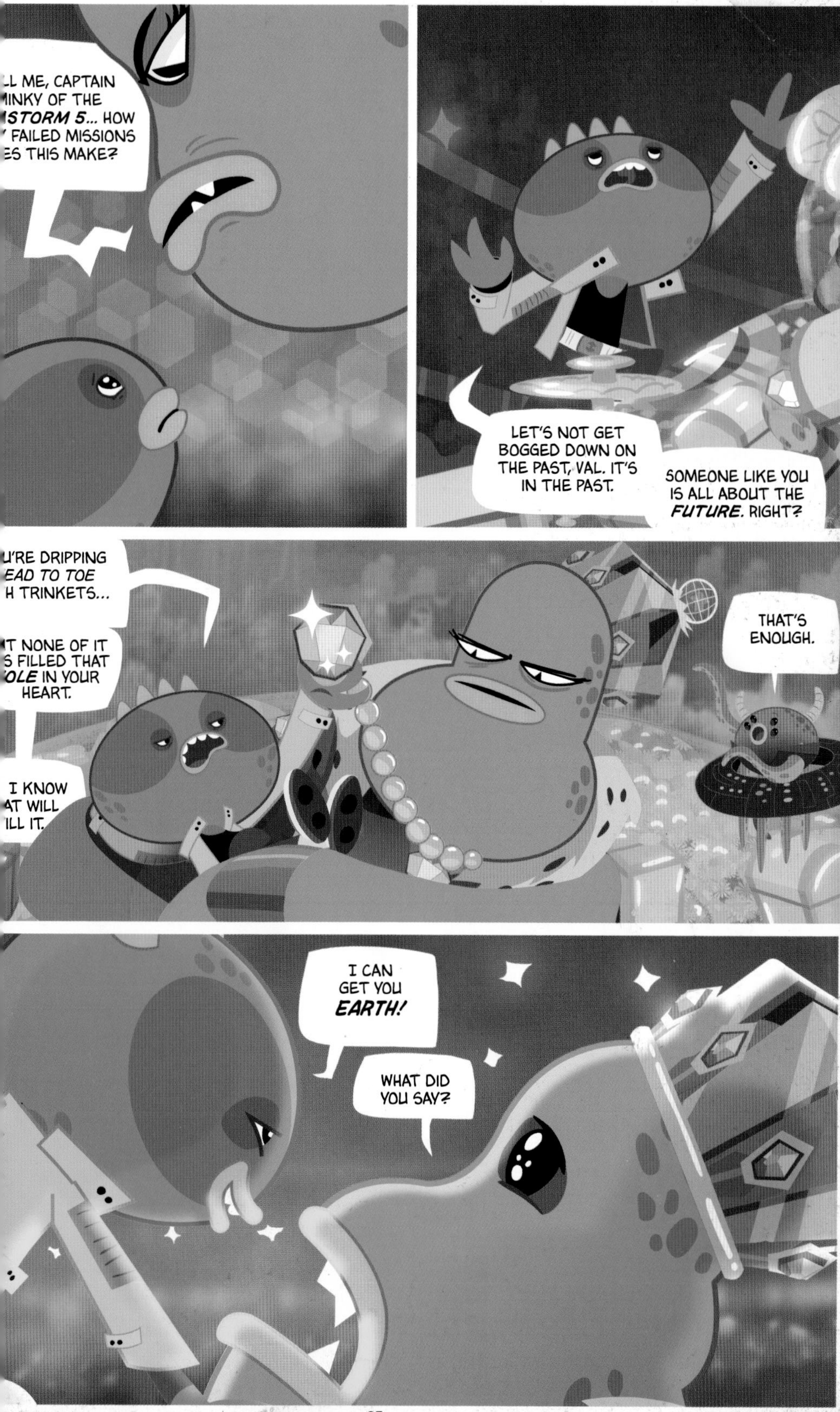

LL ME, CAPTAIN
MINKY OF THE
STORM 5... HOW
FAILED MISSIONS
ES THIS MAKE?
LET'S NOT GET BOGGED DOWN ON THE PAST, VAL. IT'S IN THE PAST.
SOMEONE LIKE YOU IS ALL ABOUT THE FUTURE, RIGHT?
U'RE DRIPPING
EAD TO TOE
H TRINKETS...
T NONE OF IT
S FILLED THAT
OLE IN YOUR
HEART.
I KNOW
AT WILL
LL IT.
THAT'S ENOUGH.
I CAN GET YOU EARTH!
WHAT DID YOU SAY?

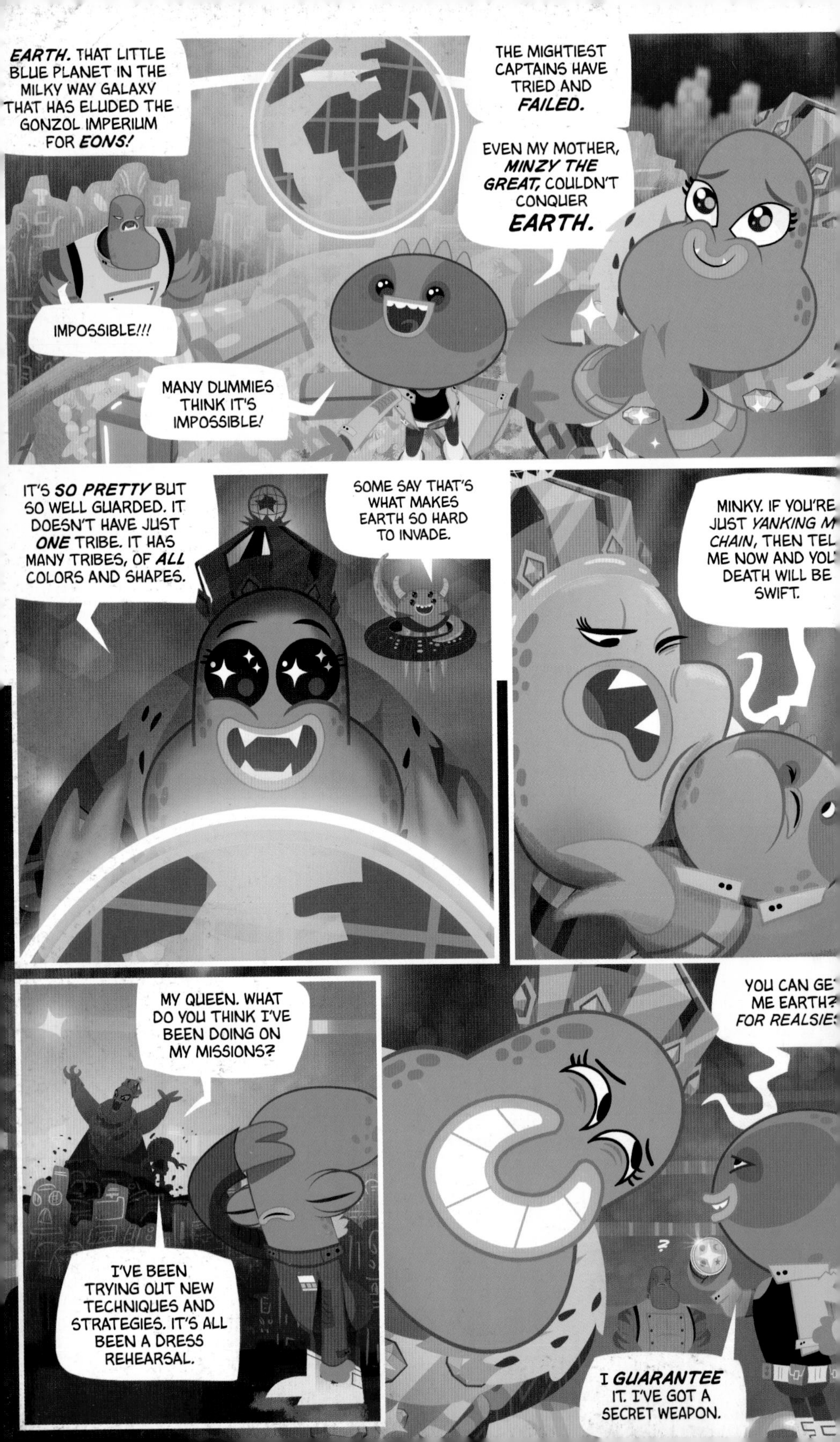
EARTH. THAT LITTLE BLUE PLANET IN THE MILKY WAY GALAXY THAT HAS ELUDED THE GONZOL IMPERIUM FOR EONS!
IMPOSSIBLE!!!
MANY DUMMIES THINK IT'S IMPOSSIBLE!
THE MIGHTIEST CAPTAINS HAVE TRIED AND FAILED.
EVEN MY MOTHER, MINZY THE GREAT, COULDN'T CONQUER EARTH.
IT'S SO PRETTY BUT SO WELL GUARDED. IT DOESN'T HAVE JUST ONE TRIBE. IT HAS MANY TRIBES, OF ALL COLORS AND SHAPES.
SOME SAY THAT'S WHAT MAKES EARTH SO HARD TO INVADE.
MINKY. IF YOU'RE JUST YANKING M CHAIN, THEN TEL ME NOW AND YO DEATH WILL BE SWIFT.
MY QUEEN. WHAT DO YOU THINK I'VE BEEN DOING ON MY MISSIONS?
I'VE BEEN TRYING OUT NEW TECHNIQUES AND STRATEGIES. IT'S ALL BEEN A DRESS REHEARSAL.
YOU CAN GE ME EARTH? FOR REALSIE
I GUARANTEE IT. I'VE GOT A SECRET WEAPON.

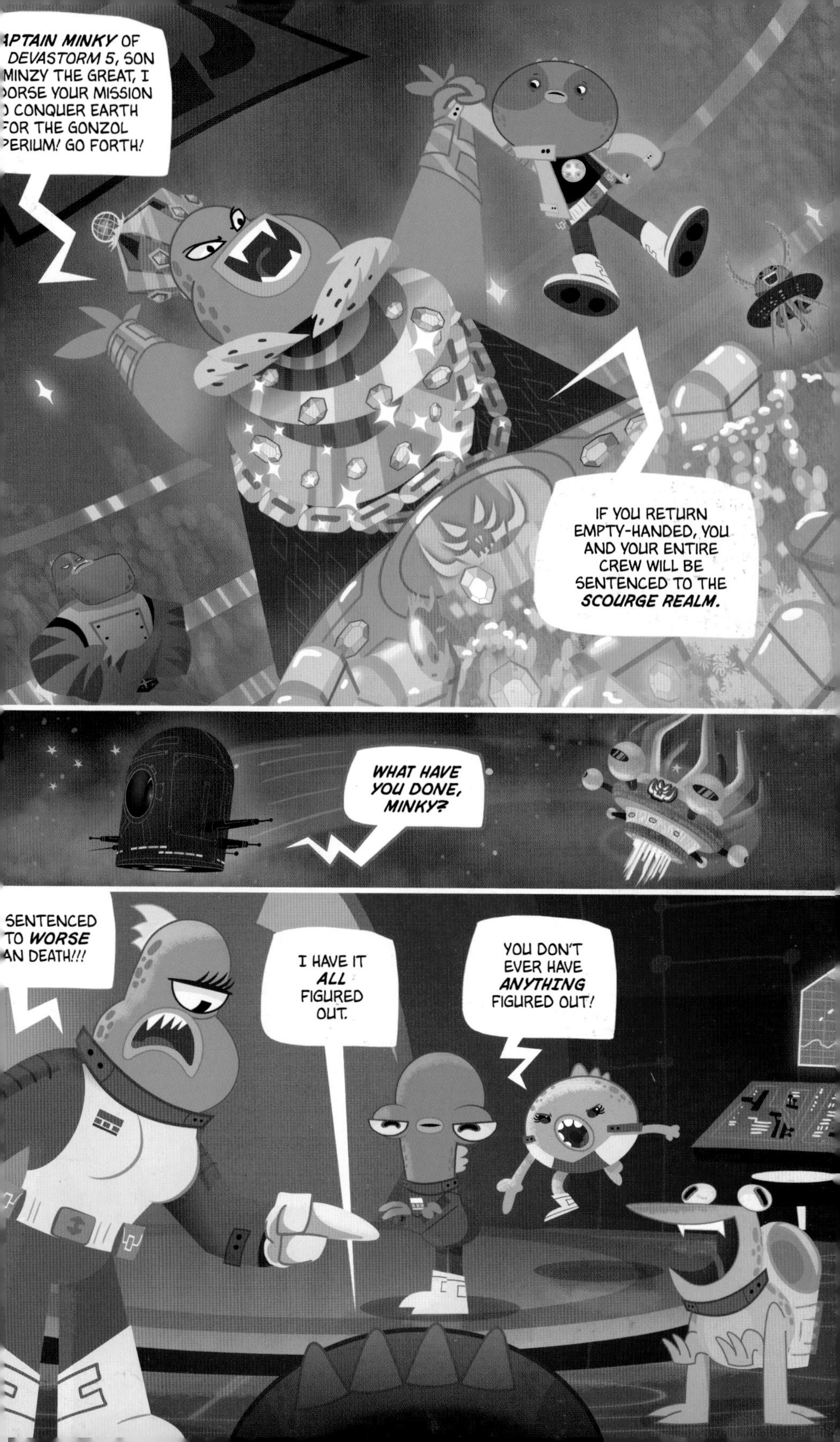

APTAIN MINKY OF DEVASTORM 5, SON MINZY THE GREAT, I DORSE YOUR MISSION O CONQUER EARTH FOR THE GONZOL PERIUM! GO FORTH!
IF YOU RETURN EMPTY-HANDED, YOU AND YOUR ENTIRE CREW WILL BE SENTENCED TO THE SCOURGE REALM.
WHAT HAVE YOU DONE, MINKY?
SENTENCED TO WORSE AN DEATH!!!
I HAVE IT ALL FIGURED OUT.
YOU DON'T EVER HAVE ANYTHING FIGURED OUT!

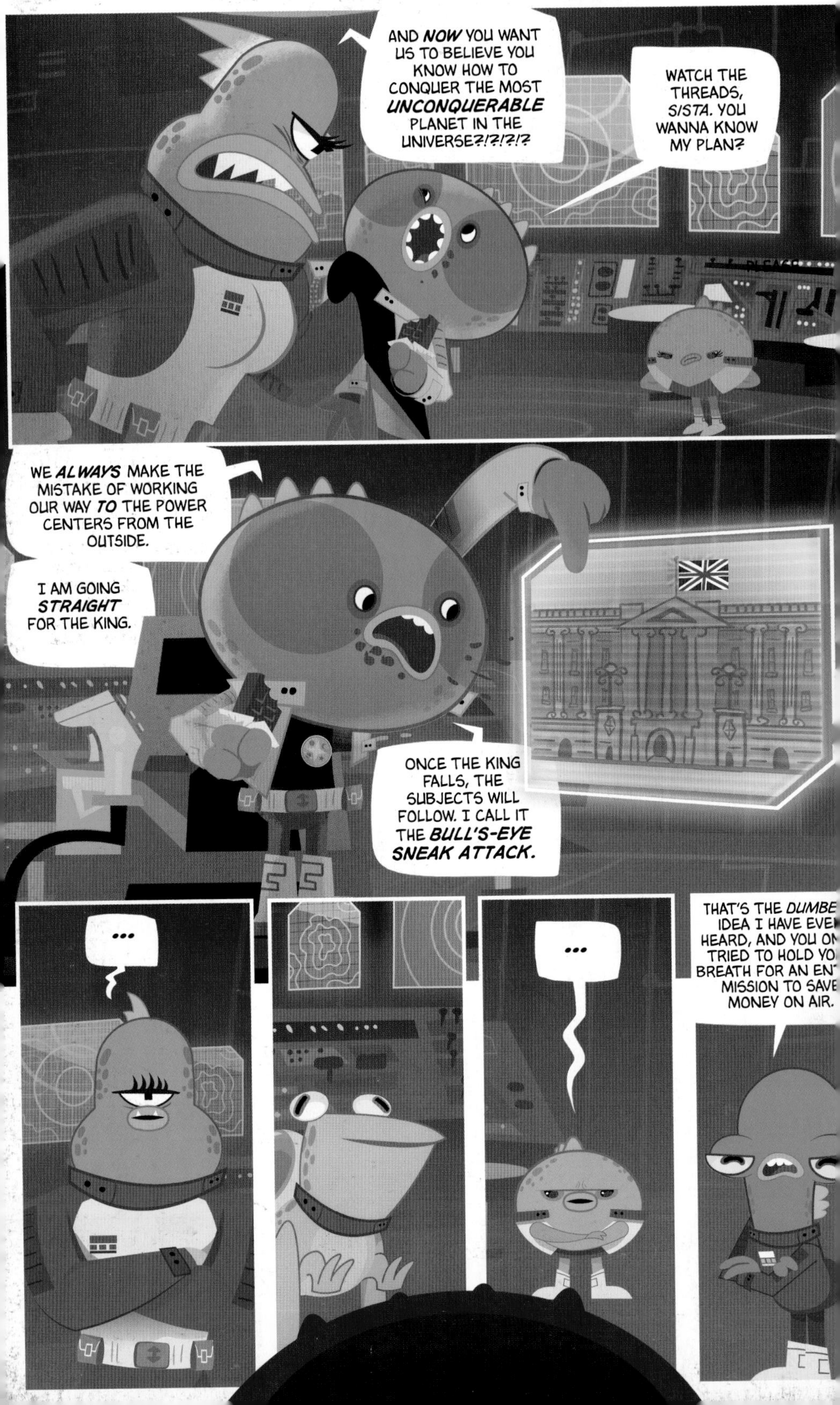
AND NOW YOU WANT US TO BELIEVE YOU KNOW HOW TO CONQUER THE MOST UNCONQUERABLE PLANET IN THE UNIVERSE?!?!?!?
WATCH THE THREADS, SISTA. YOU WANNA KNOW MY PLAN?
WE ALWAYS MAKE THE MISTAKE OF WORKING OUR WAY TO THE POWER CENTERS FROM THE OUTSIDE.
I AM GOING STRAIGHT FOR THE KING.
ONCE THE KING FALLS, THE SUBJECTS WILL FOLLOW. I CALL IT THE BULL'S-EYE SNEAK ATTACK.
...
...
THAT'S THE DUMBE IDEA I HAVE EVE HEARD, AND YOU ON TRIED TO HOLD YO BREATH FOR AN EN MISSION TO SAVE MONEY ON AIR.

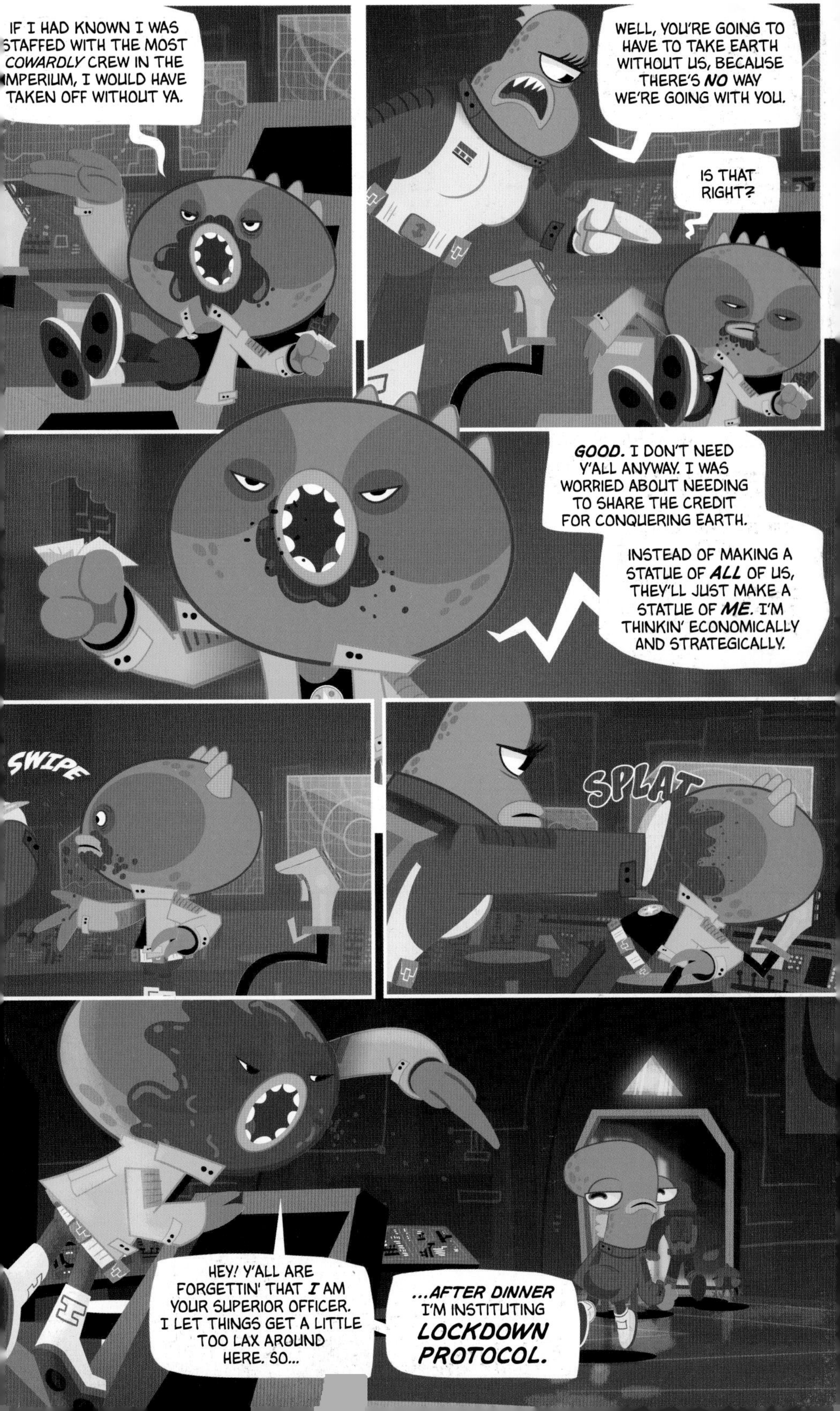
IF I HAD KNOWN I WAS STAFFED WITH THE MOST *COWARDLY* CREW IN THE IMPERIUM, I WOULD HAVE TAKEN OFF WITHOUT YA.
WELL, YOU'RE GOING TO HAVE TO TAKE EARTH WITHOUT US, BECAUSE THERE'S **NO** WAY WE'RE GOING WITH YOU.
IS THAT RIGHT?
GOOD. I DON'T NEED Y'ALL ANYWAY. I WAS WORRIED ABOUT NEEDING TO SHARE THE CREDIT FOR CONQUERING EARTH.
INSTEAD OF MAKING A STATUE OF **ALL** OF US, THEY'LL JUST MAKE A STATUE OF **ME**. I'M THINKIN' ECONOMICALLY AND STRATEGICALLY.
SWIPE
SPLAT
HEY! Y'ALL ARE FORGETTIN' THAT *I* AM YOUR SUPERIOR OFFICER. I LET THINGS GET A LITTLE TOO LAX AROUND HERE. SO...
...*AFTER DINNER* I'M INSTITUTING ***LOCKDOWN PROTOCOL.***

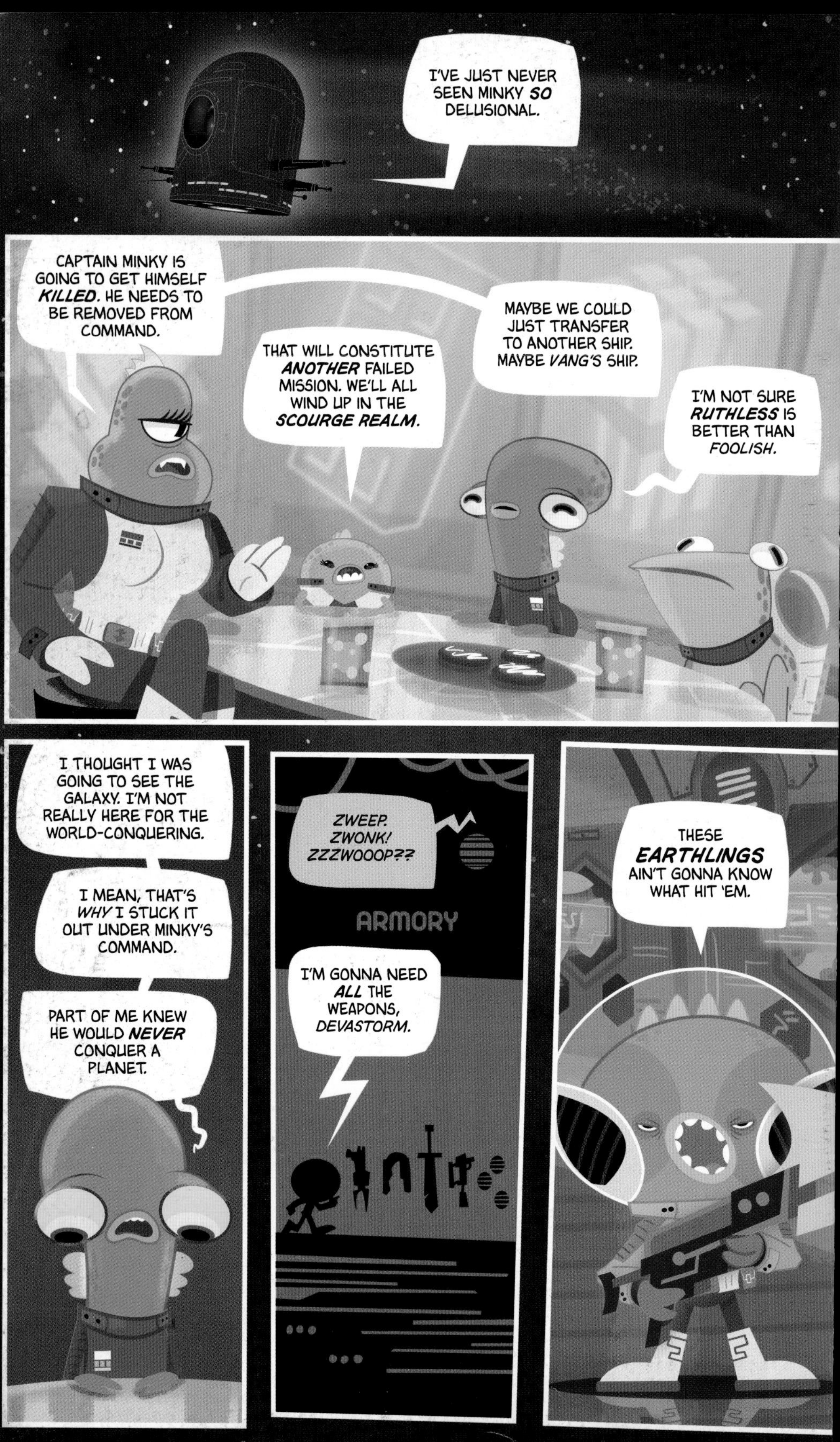
I'VE JUST NEVER SEEN MINKY *SO* DELUSIONAL.
CAPTAIN MINKY IS GOING TO GET HIMSELF *KILLED*. HE NEEDS TO BE REMOVED FROM COMMAND.
THAT WILL CONSTITUTE *ANOTHER* FAILED MISSION. WE'LL ALL WIND UP IN THE *SCOURGE REALM*.
MAYBE WE COULD JUST TRANSFER TO ANOTHER SHIP. MAYBE *VANG'S* SHIP.
I'M NOT SURE *RUTHLESS* IS BETTER THAN *FOOLISH*.
I THOUGHT I WAS GOING TO SEE THE GALAXY. I'M NOT REALLY HERE FOR THE WORLD-CONQUERING.
I MEAN, THAT'S *WHY* I STUCK IT OUT UNDER MINKY'S COMMAND.
PART OF ME KNEW HE WOULD *NEVER* CONQUER A PLANET.
ZWEEP. ZWONK! ZZZWOOOP??
ARMORY
I'M GONNA NEED *ALL* THE WEAPONS, *DEVASTORM*.
THESE *EARTHLINGS* AIN'T GONNA KNOW WHAT HIT 'EM.

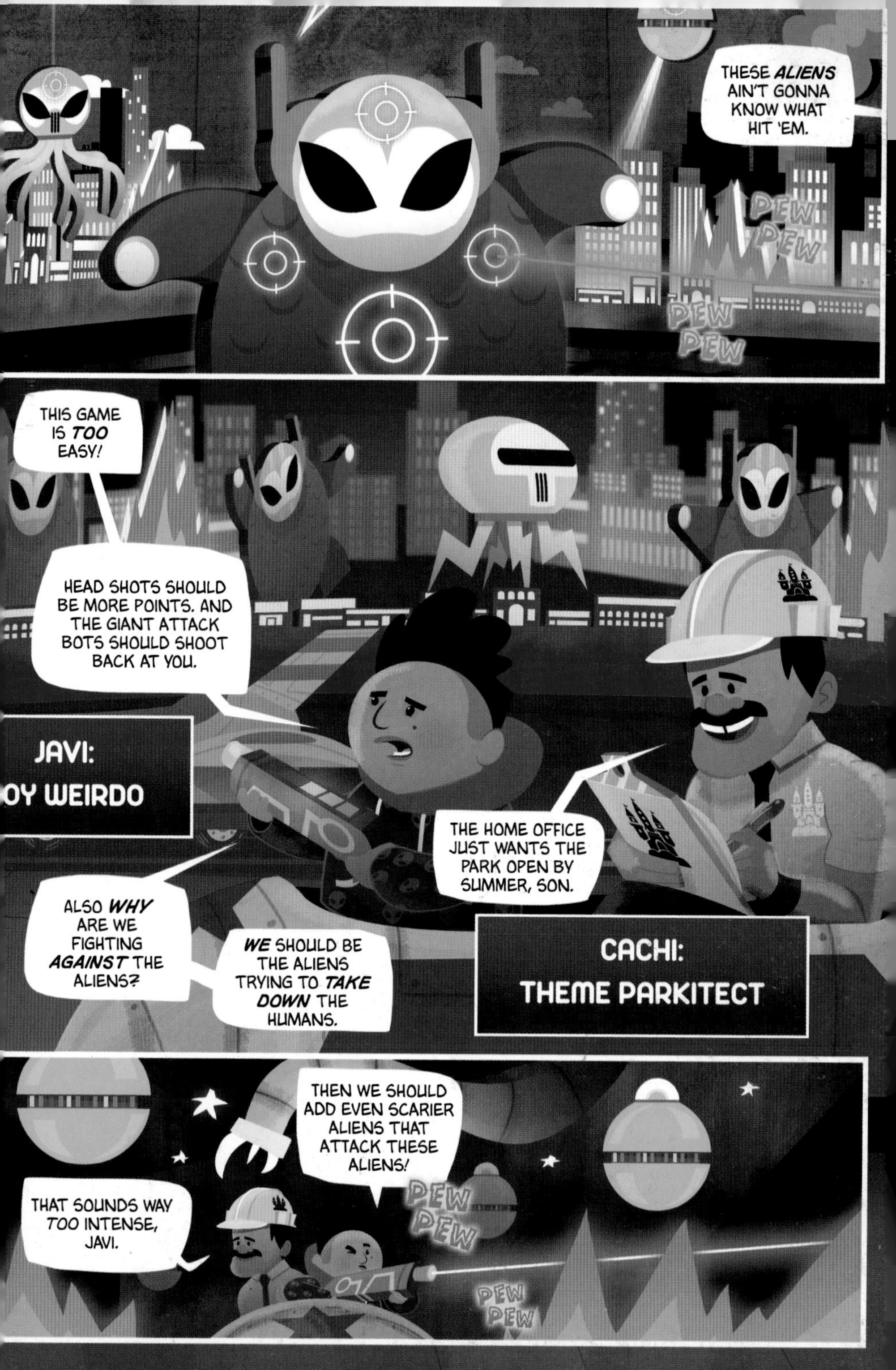
THESE ALIENS AIN'T GONNA KNOW WHAT HIT 'EM.
PEW PEW
PEW PEW
THIS GAME IS TOO EASY!
HEAD SHOTS SHOULD BE MORE POINTS. AND THE GIANT ATTACK BOTS SHOULD SHOOT BACK AT YOU.
JAVI:
OY WEIRDO
THE HOME OFFICE JUST WANTS THE PARK OPEN BY SUMMER, SON.
ALSO WHY ARE WE FIGHTING AGAINST THE ALIENS?
WE SHOULD BE THE ALIENS TRYING TO TAKE DOWN THE HUMANS.
CACHI:
THEME PARKITECT
THEN WE SHOULD ADD EVEN SCARIER ALIENS THAT ATTACK THESE ALIENS!
THAT SOUNDS WAY TOO INTENSE, JAVI.
PEW PEW
PEW PEW

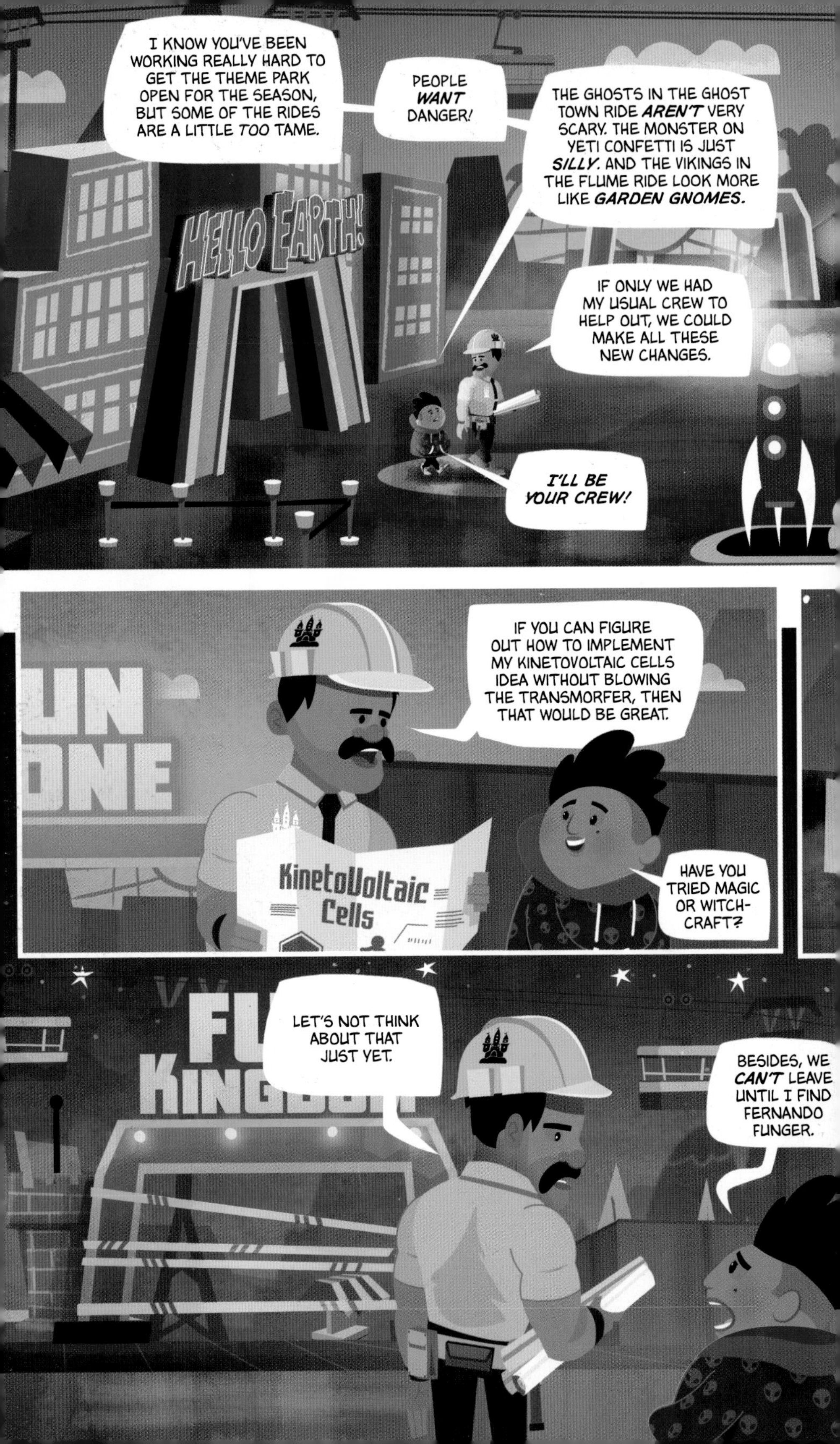
HELLO EARTH!
I KNOW YOU'VE BEEN WORKING REALLY HARD TO GET THE THEME PARK OPEN FOR THE SEASON, BUT SOME OF THE RIDES ARE A LITTLE *TOO* TAME.
PEOPLE ***WANT*** DANGER!
THE GHOSTS IN THE GHOST TOWN RIDE ***AREN'T*** VERY SCARY. THE MONSTER ON YETI CONFETTI IS JUST ***SILLY***. AND THE VIKINGS IN THE FLUME RIDE LOOK MORE LIKE ***GARDEN GNOMES.***
IF ONLY WE HAD MY USUAL CREW TO HELP OUT, WE COULD MAKE ALL THESE NEW CHANGES.
I'LL BE YOUR CREW!
IF YOU CAN FIGURE OUT HOW TO IMPLEMENT MY KINETOVOLTAIC CELLS IDEA WITHOUT BLOWING THE TRANSMORFER, THEN THAT WOULD BE GREAT.
KinetoVoltaic Cells
HAVE YOU TRIED MAGIC OR WITCH-CRAFT?
LET'S NOT THINK ABOUT THAT JUST YET.
BESIDES, WE ***CAN'T*** LEAVE UNTIL I FIND FERNANDO FUNGER.

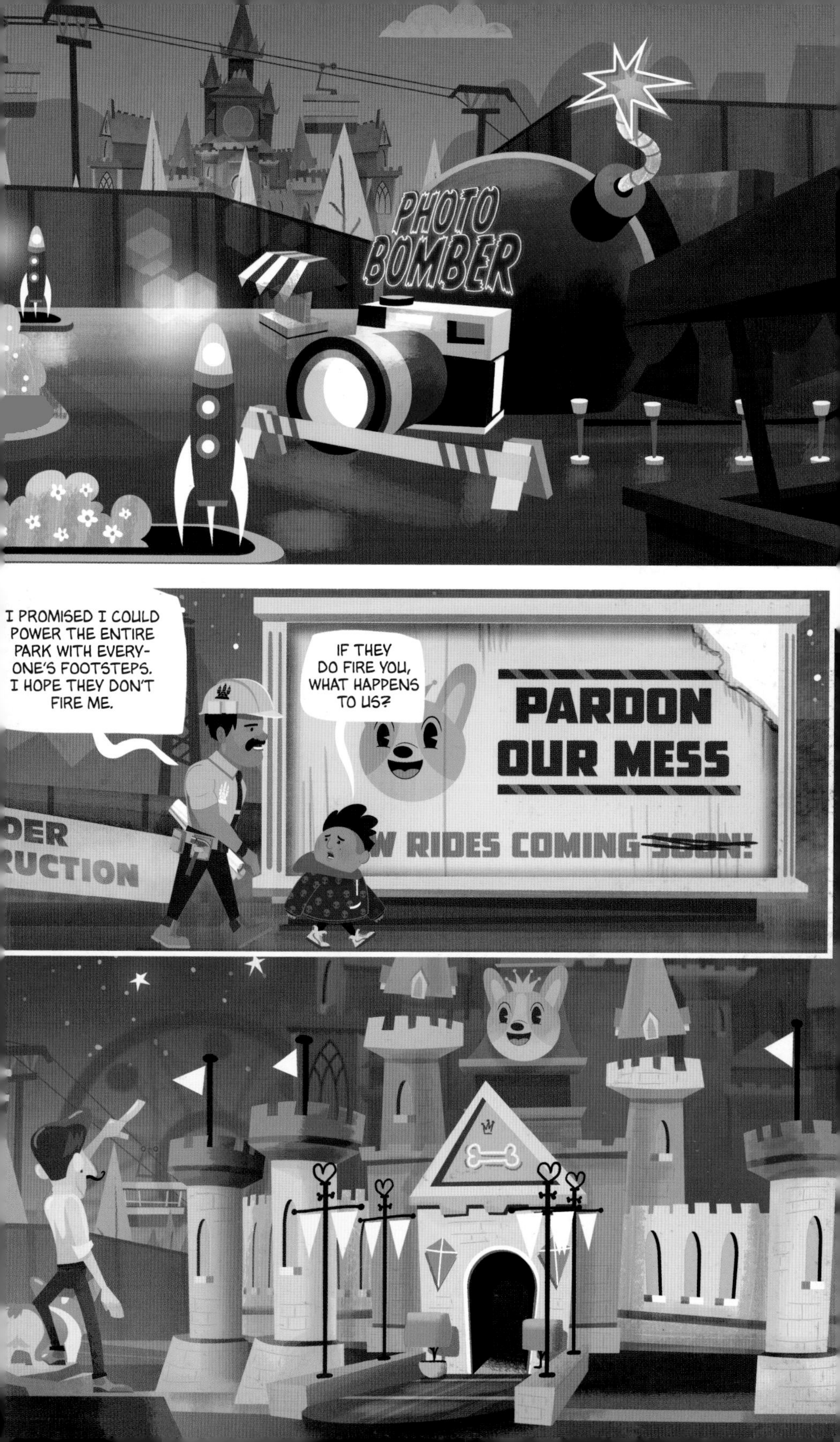
PHOTO BOMBER
I PROMISED I COULD POWER THE ENTIRE PARK WITH EVERY-ONE'S FOOTSTEPS. I HOPE THEY DON'T FIRE ME.
IF THEY DO FIRE YOU, WHAT HAPPENS TO US?
PARDON OUR MESS
W RIDES COMING SOON!

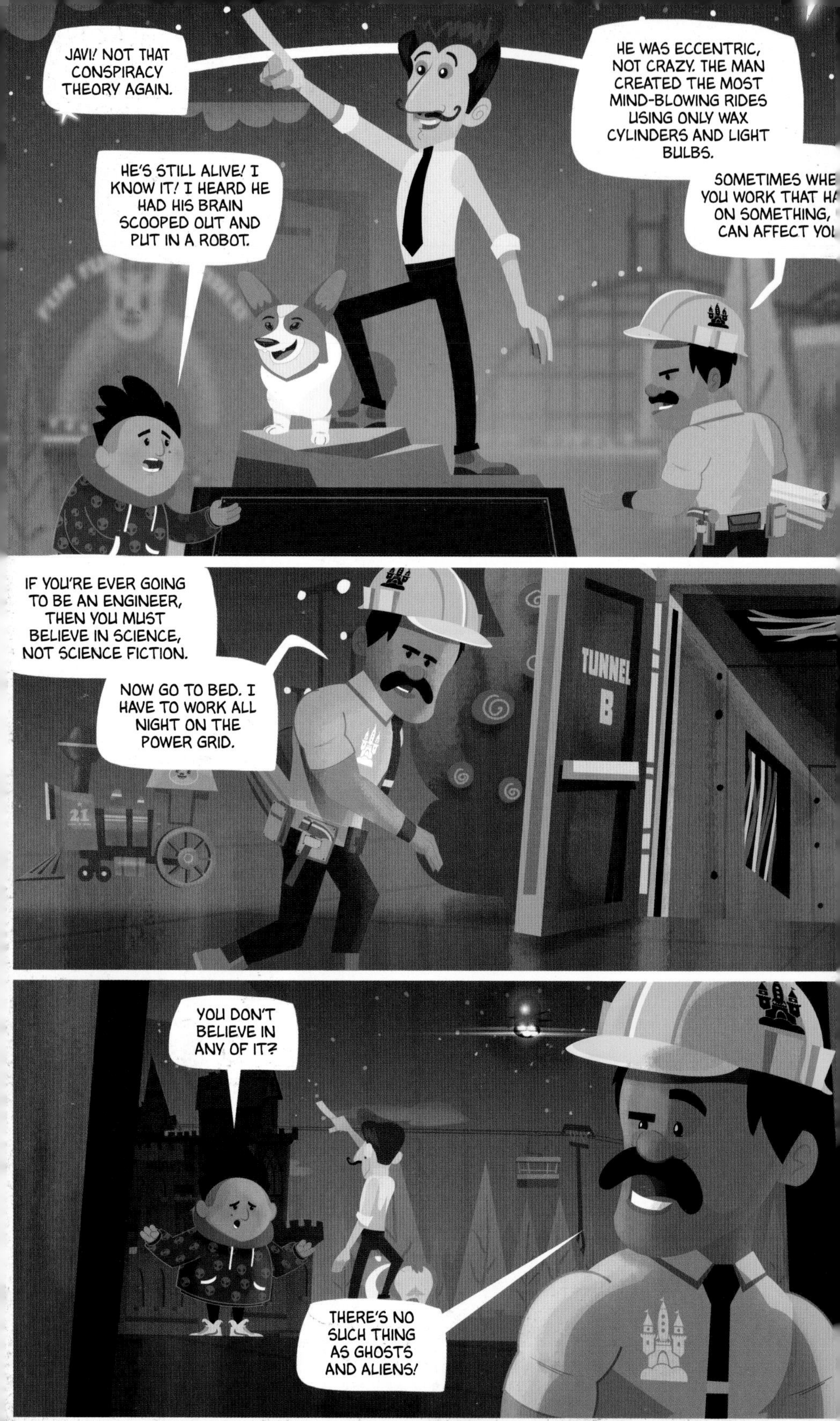
JAVI! NOT THAT CONSPIRACY THEORY AGAIN.
HE'S STILL ALIVE! I KNOW IT! I HEARD HE HAD HIS BRAIN SCOOPED OUT AND PUT IN A ROBOT.
HE WAS ECCENTRIC, NOT CRAZY. THE MAN CREATED THE MOST MIND-BLOWING RIDES USING ONLY WAX CYLINDERS AND LIGHT BULBS.
SOMETIMES WHE YOU WORK THAT H ON SOMETHING, CAN AFFECT YO
IF YOU'RE EVER GOING TO BE AN ENGINEER, THEN YOU MUST BELIEVE IN SCIENCE, NOT SCIENCE FICTION.
NOW GO TO BED. I HAVE TO WORK ALL NIGHT ON THE POWER GRID.
TUNNEL B
21
YOU DON'T BELIEVE IN ANY OF IT?
THERE'S NO SUCH THING AS GHOSTS AND ALIENS!

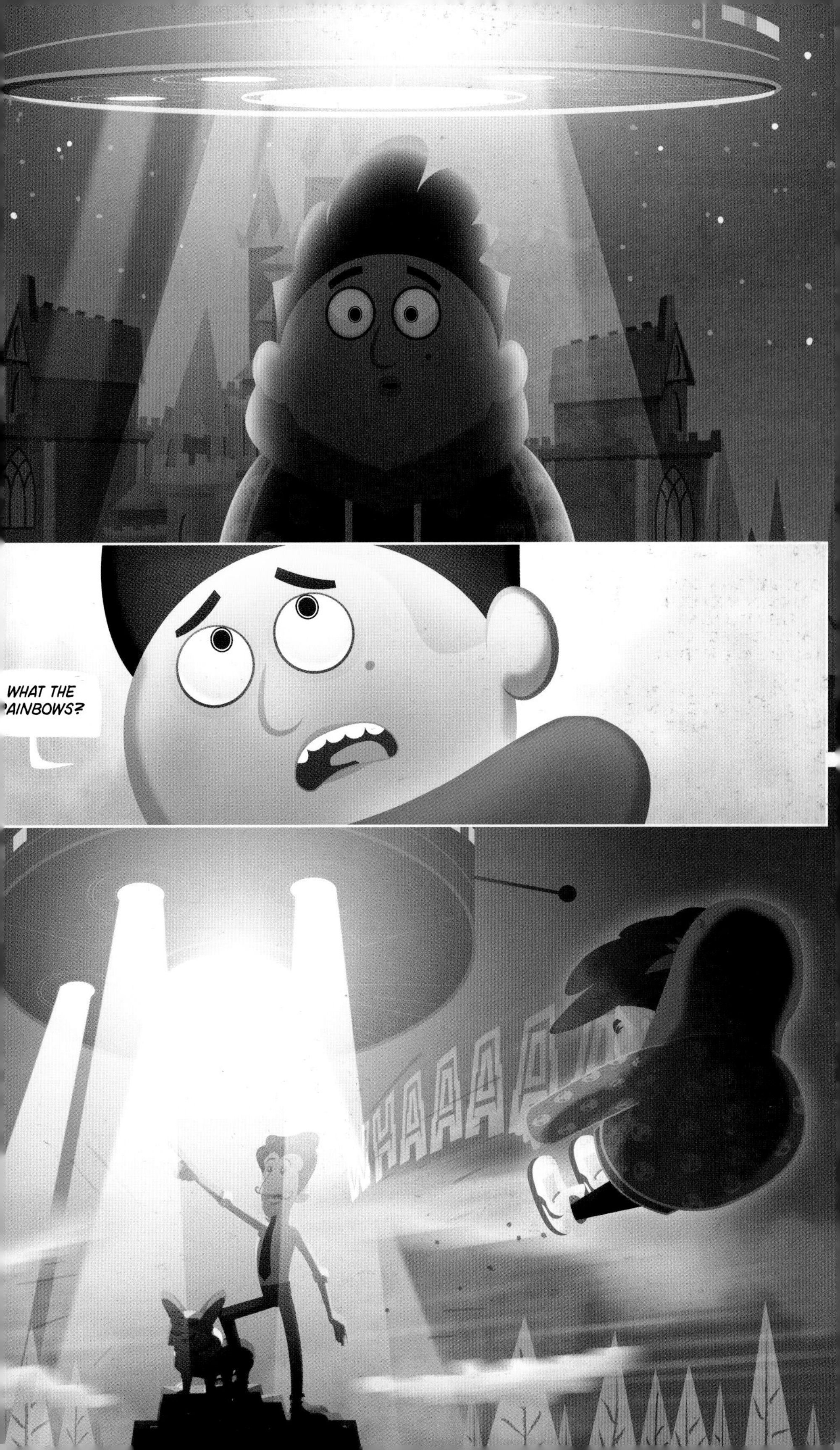
WHAT THE
AINBOWS?
WHAAAA

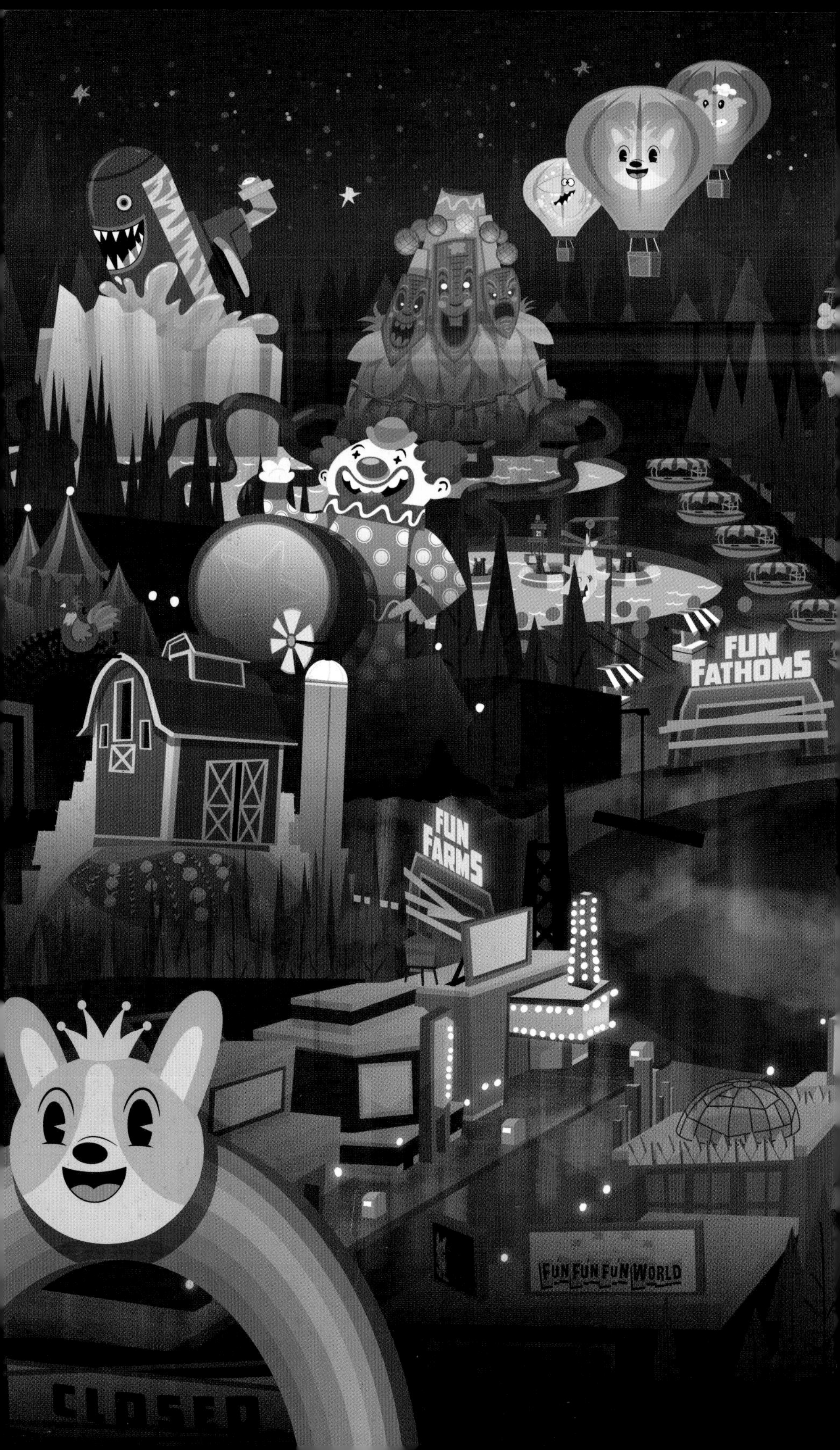
FUN FATHOMS
FUN FARMS
FUN FUN FUN WORLD
CLOSED

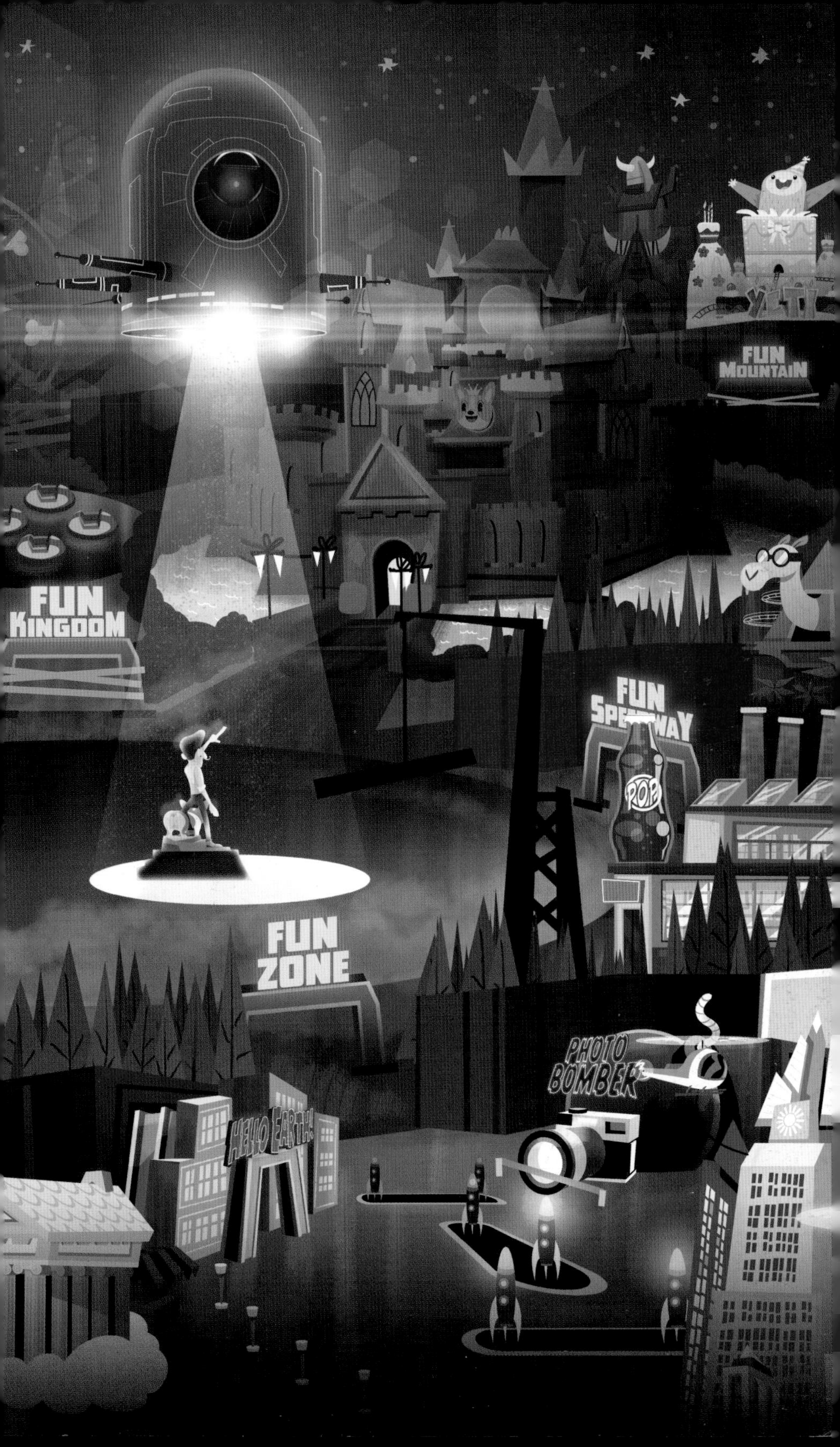
FUN MOUNTAIN
FUN KINGDOM
FUN
POP
FUN ZONE
HELLO EARTH!
PHOTO BOMBER

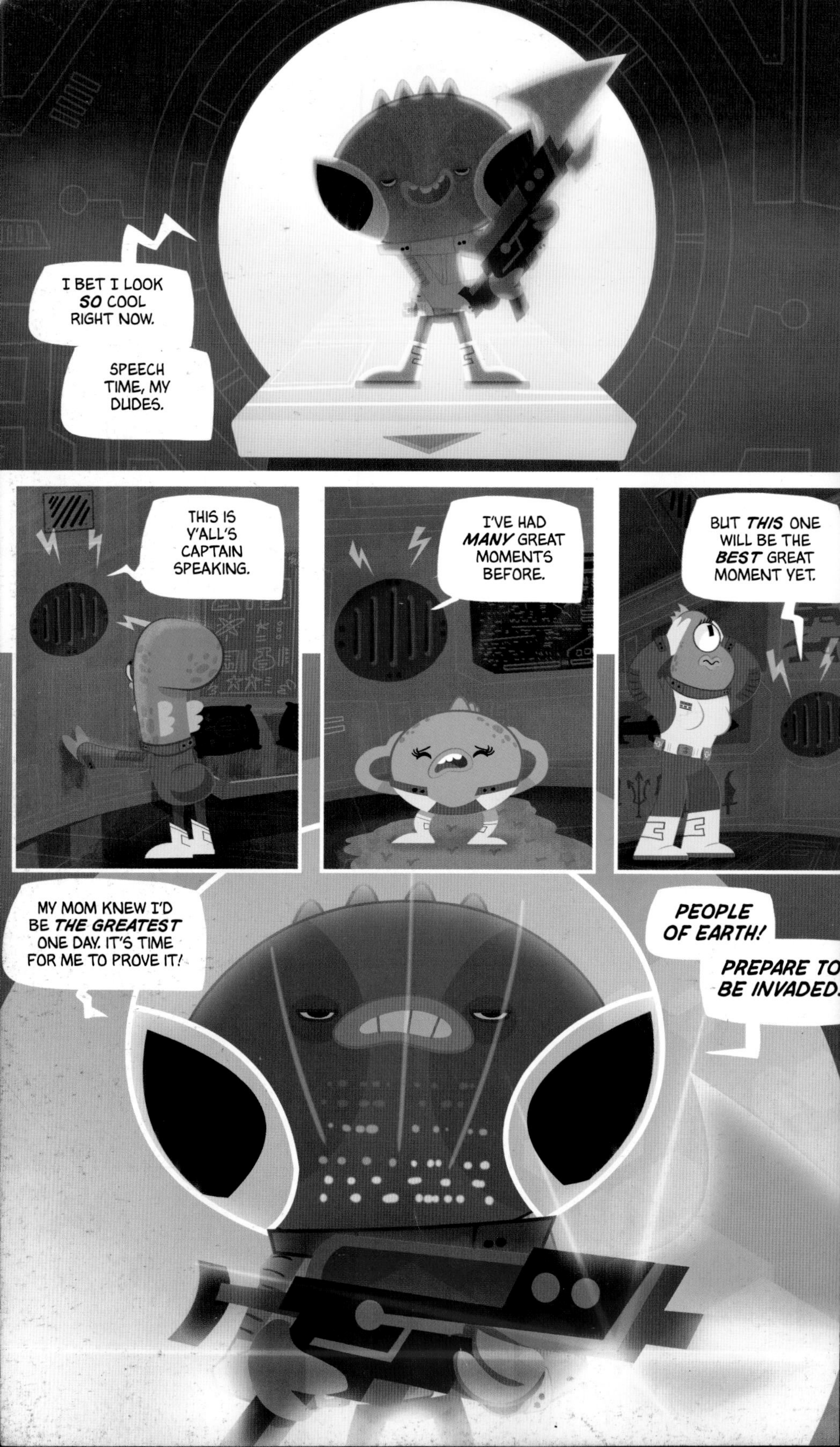

I BET I LOOK *SO* COOL RIGHT NOW.
SPEECH TIME, MY DUDES.
THIS IS Y'ALL'S CAPTAIN SPEAKING.
I'VE HAD *MANY* GREAT MOMENTS BEFORE.
BUT *THIS* ONE WILL BE THE *BEST* GREAT MOMENT YET.
MY MOM KNEW I'D BE *THE GREATEST* ONE DAY. IT'S TIME FOR ME TO PROVE IT!
PEOPLE OF EARTH!
PREPARE TO BE INVADED.

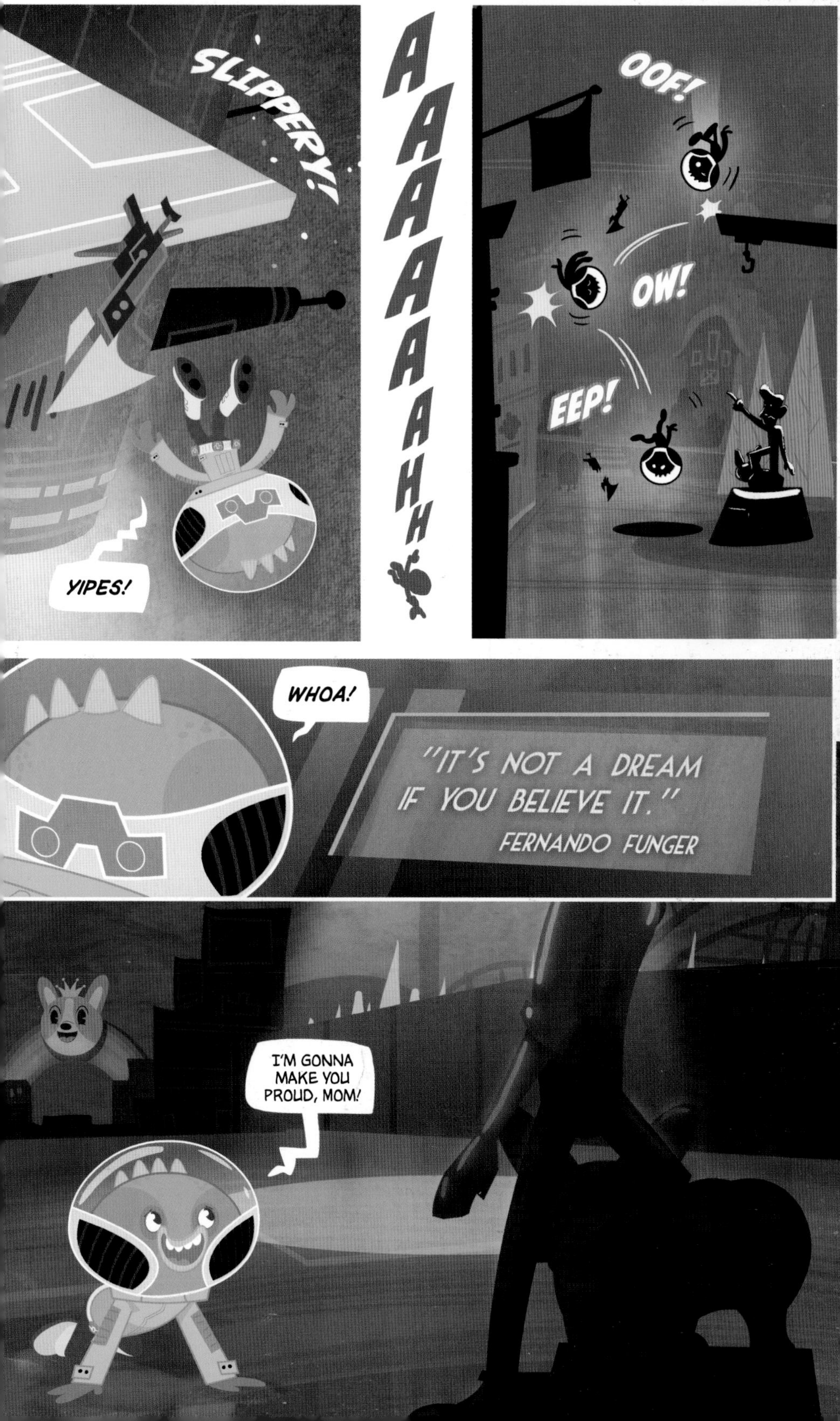
SLIPPERY!
YIPES!
AAAAAAAAAHH
OOF!
OW!
EEP!
WHOA!
"IT'S NOT A DREAM IF YOU BELIEVE IT."
FERNANDO FUNGER
I'M GONNA MAKE YOU PROUD, MOM!

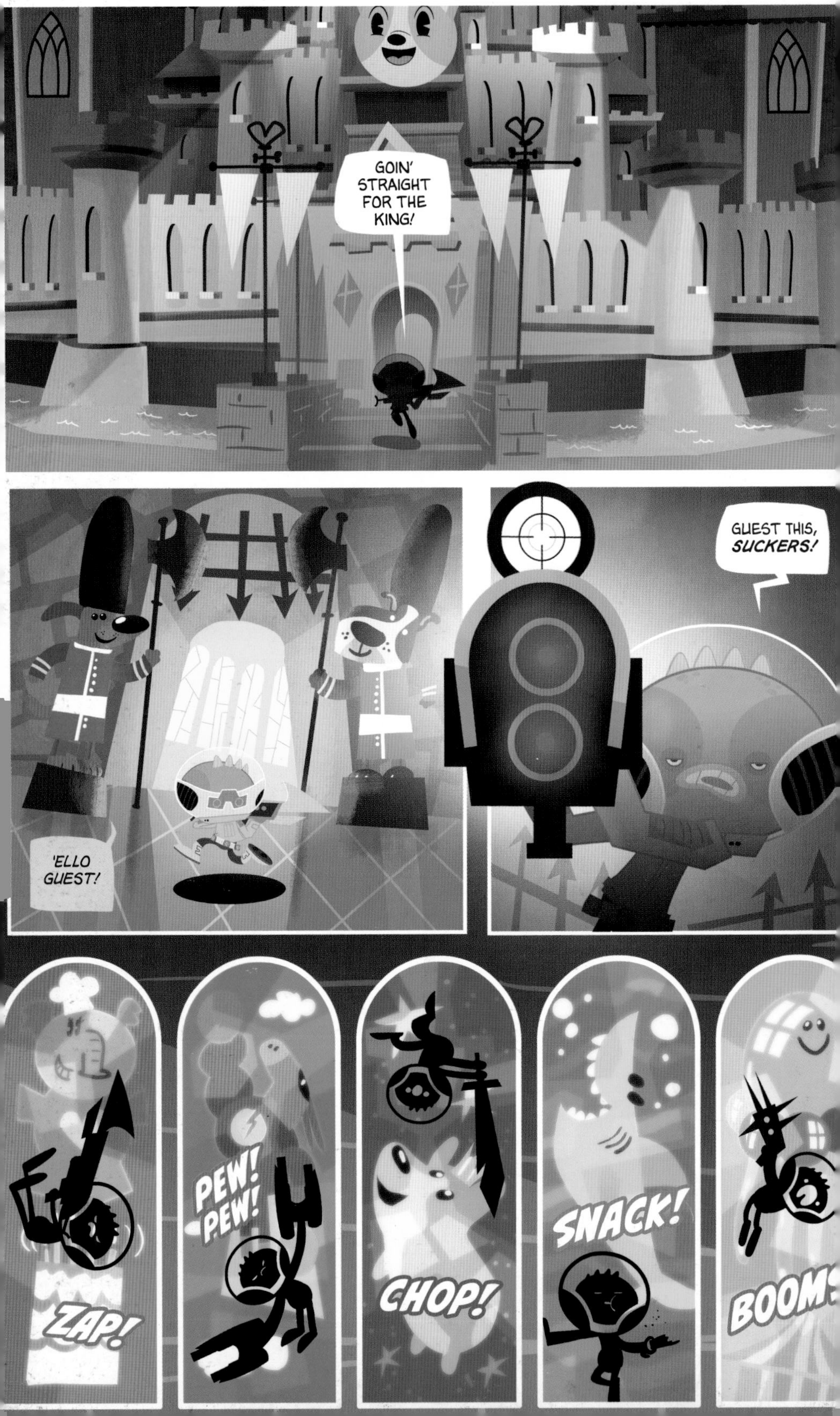
GOIN' STRAIGHT FOR THE KING!
'ELLO GUEST!
GUEST THIS, SUCKERS!
ZAP!
PEW! PEW!
CHOP!
SNACK!
BOOM!

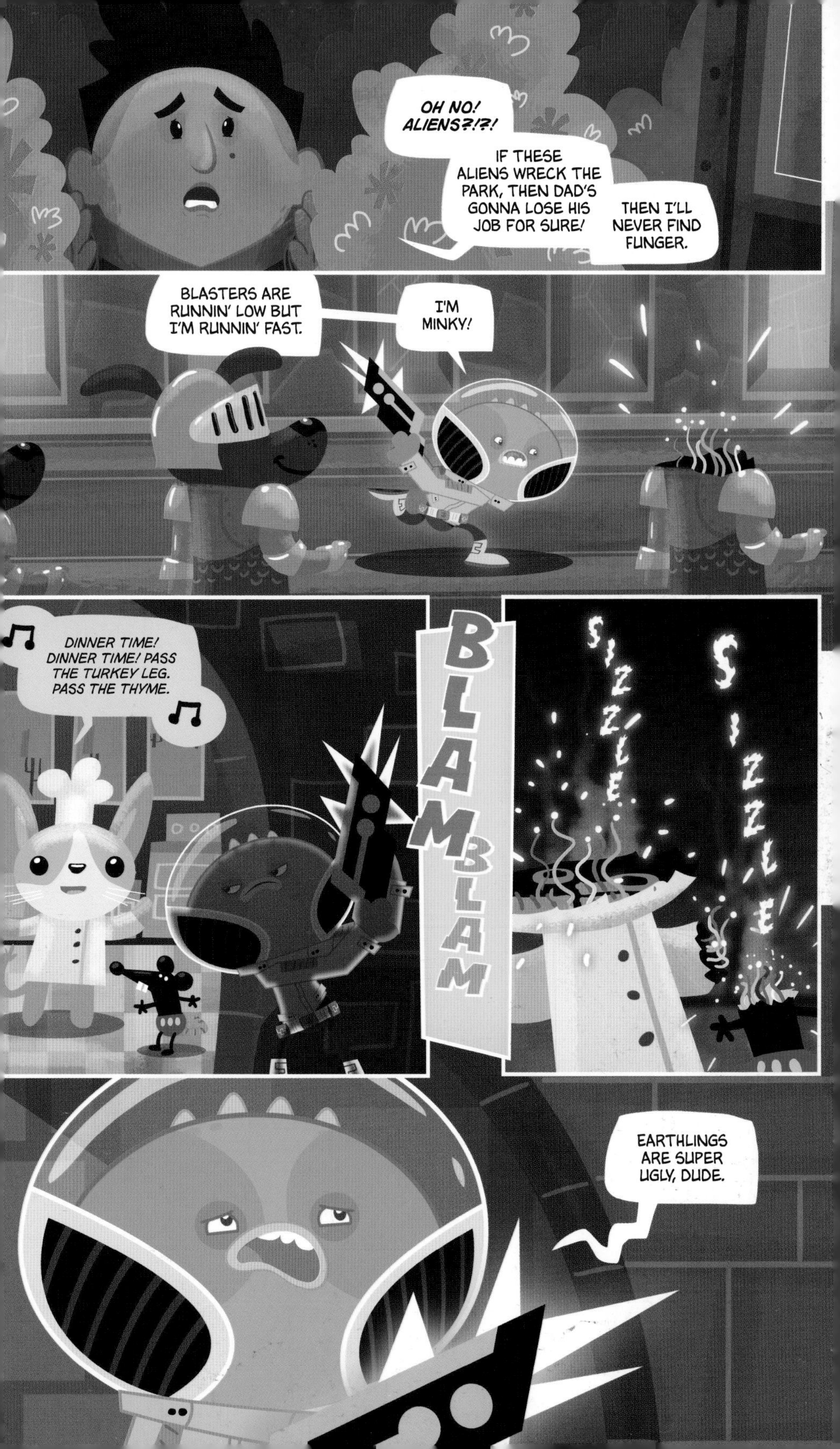

OH NO! ALIENS?!?!
IF THESE ALIENS WRECK THE PARK, THEN DAD'S GONNA LOSE HIS JOB FOR SURE!
THEN I'LL NEVER FIND FUNGER.
BLASTERS ARE RUNNIN' LOW BUT I'M RUNNIN' FAST.
I'M MINKY!
DINNER TIME! DINNER TIME! PASS THE TURKEY LEG. PASS THE THYME.
BLAM BLAM
SIZZLE
SIZZLE
EARTHLINGS ARE SUPER UGLY, DUDE.

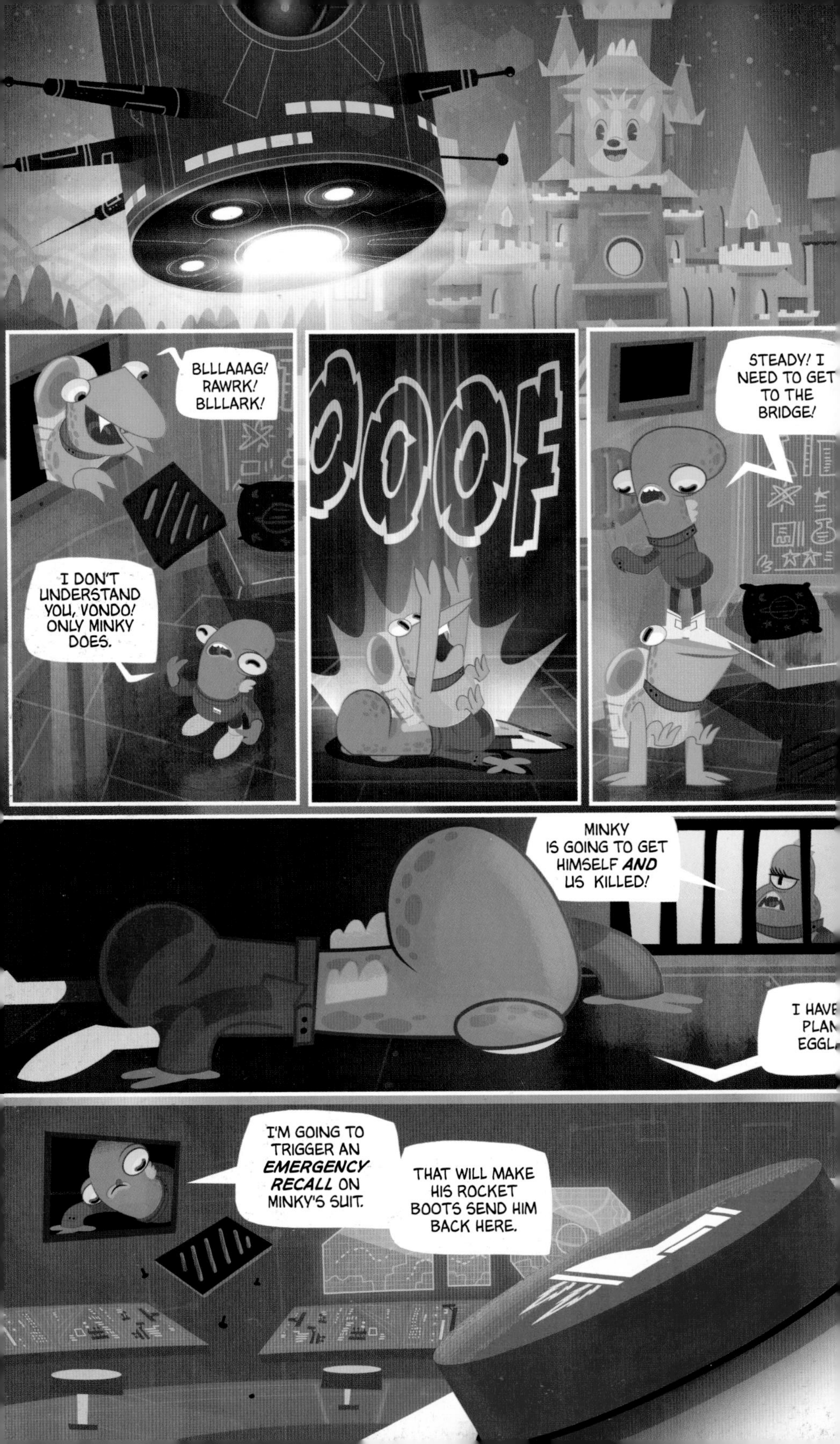

BLLLAAAG! RAWRK! BLLLARK!
I DON'T UNDERSTAND YOU, VONDO! ONLY MINKY DOES.
OOOF
STEADY! I NEED TO GET TO THE BRIDGE!
MINKY IS GOING TO GET HIMSELF *AND* US KILLED!
I'M GOING TO TRIGGER AN ***EMERGENCY RECALL*** ON MINKY'S SUIT.
THAT WILL MAKE HIS ROCKET BOOTS SEND HIM BACK HERE.

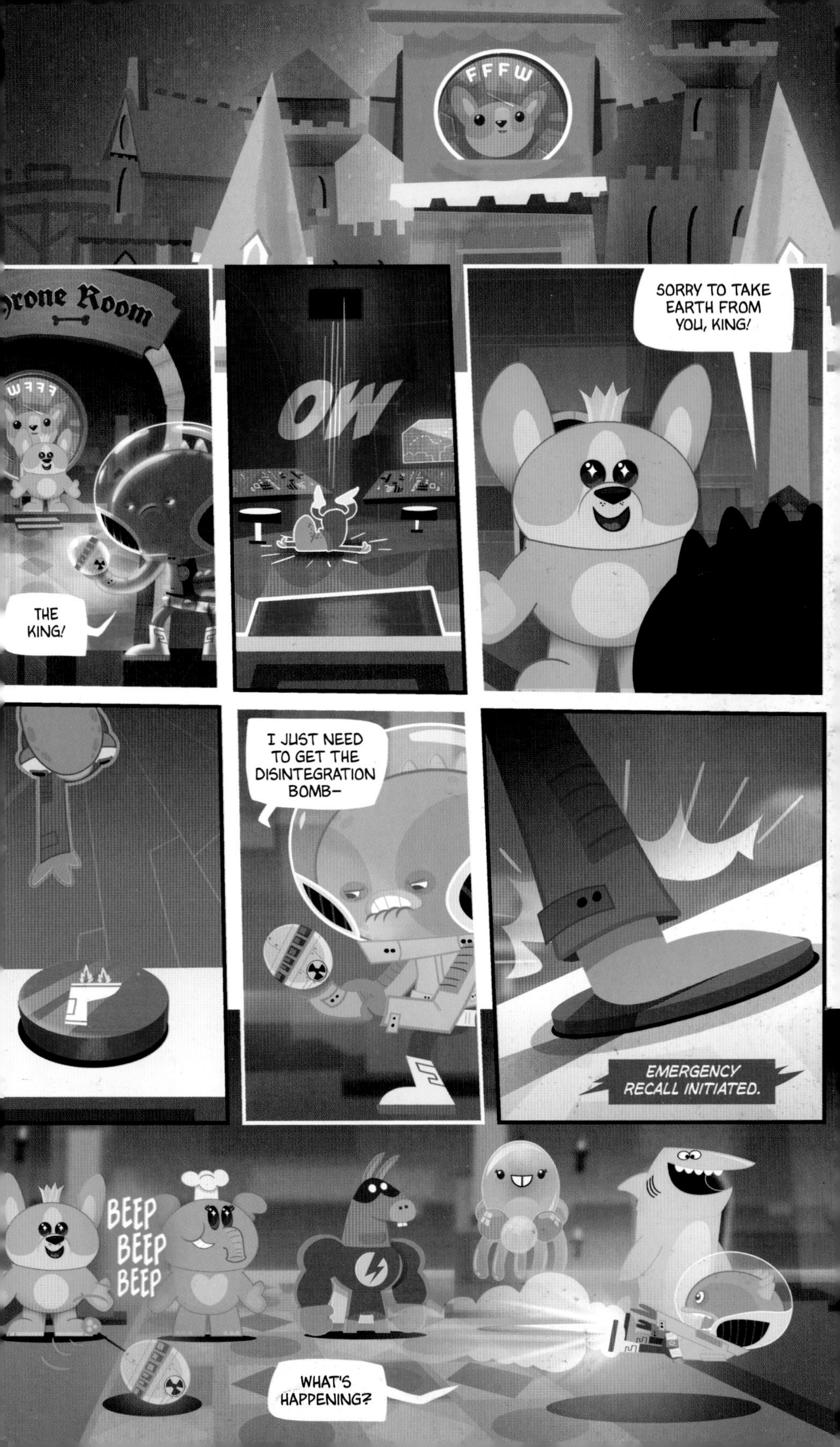
FFFW
Throne Room
THE KING!
OW
SORRY TO TAKE EARTH FROM YOU, KING!
I JUST NEED TO GET THE DISINTEGRATION BOMB–
EMERGENCY RECALL INITIATED.
BEEP BEEP BEEP
WHAT'S HAPPENING?

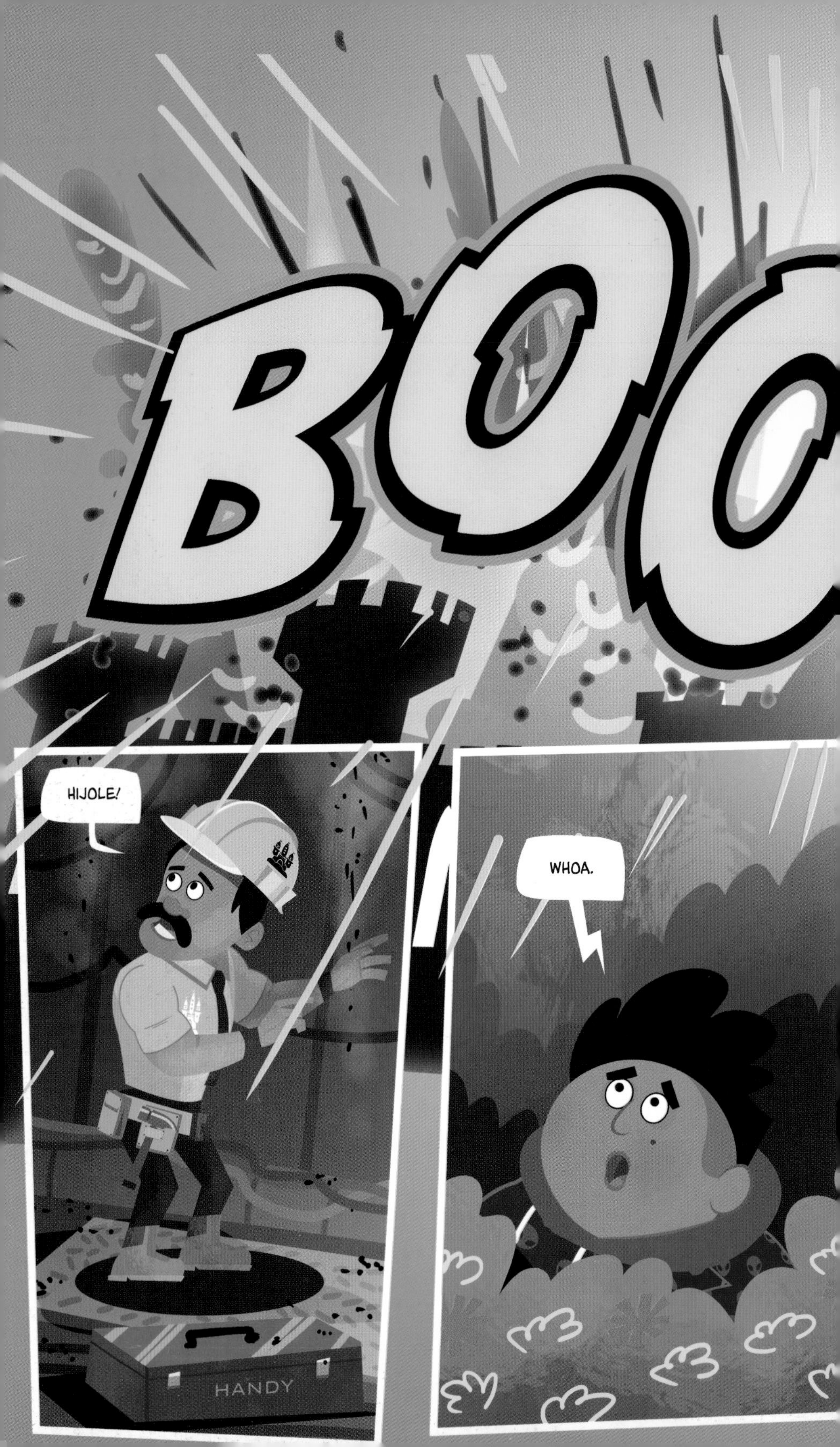
BOO
HIJOLE!
HANDY
WHOA.

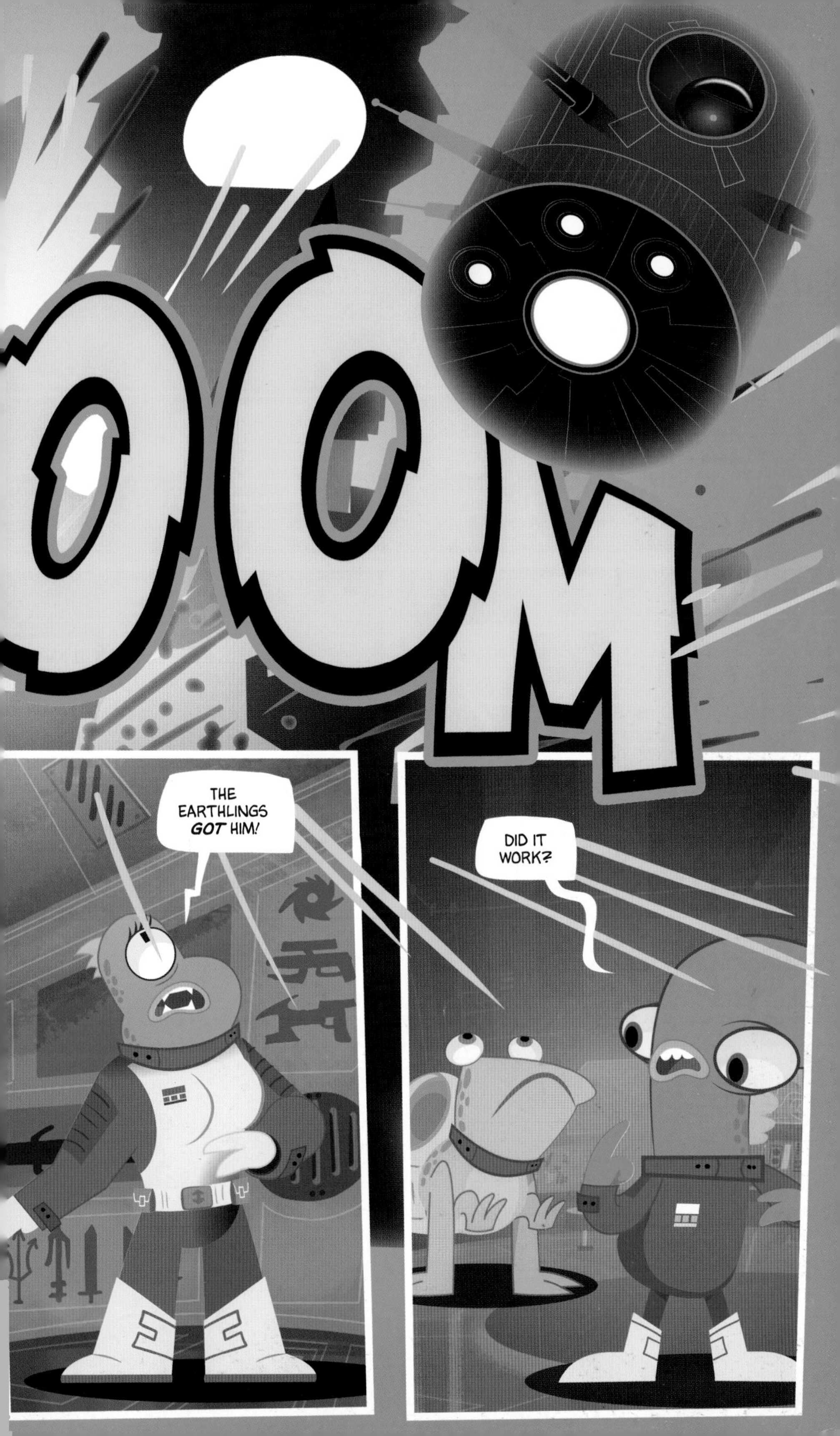
OOM
THE EARTHLINGS GOT HIM!
DID IT WORK?

NORAD COMMAND CENTER
ALASKA

GENERAL WEST, THE RADAR PICKED UP ANOTHER ATMOSPHERIC ANOMALY.

IT'S IOWA.

BUT—

YOU THINK SOMEONE IS TRYING TO INVADE IOWA?

I KNOW, BUT—

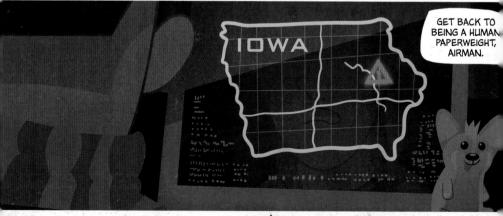

GET BACK TO BEING A HUMAN PAPERWEIGHT, AIRMAN.

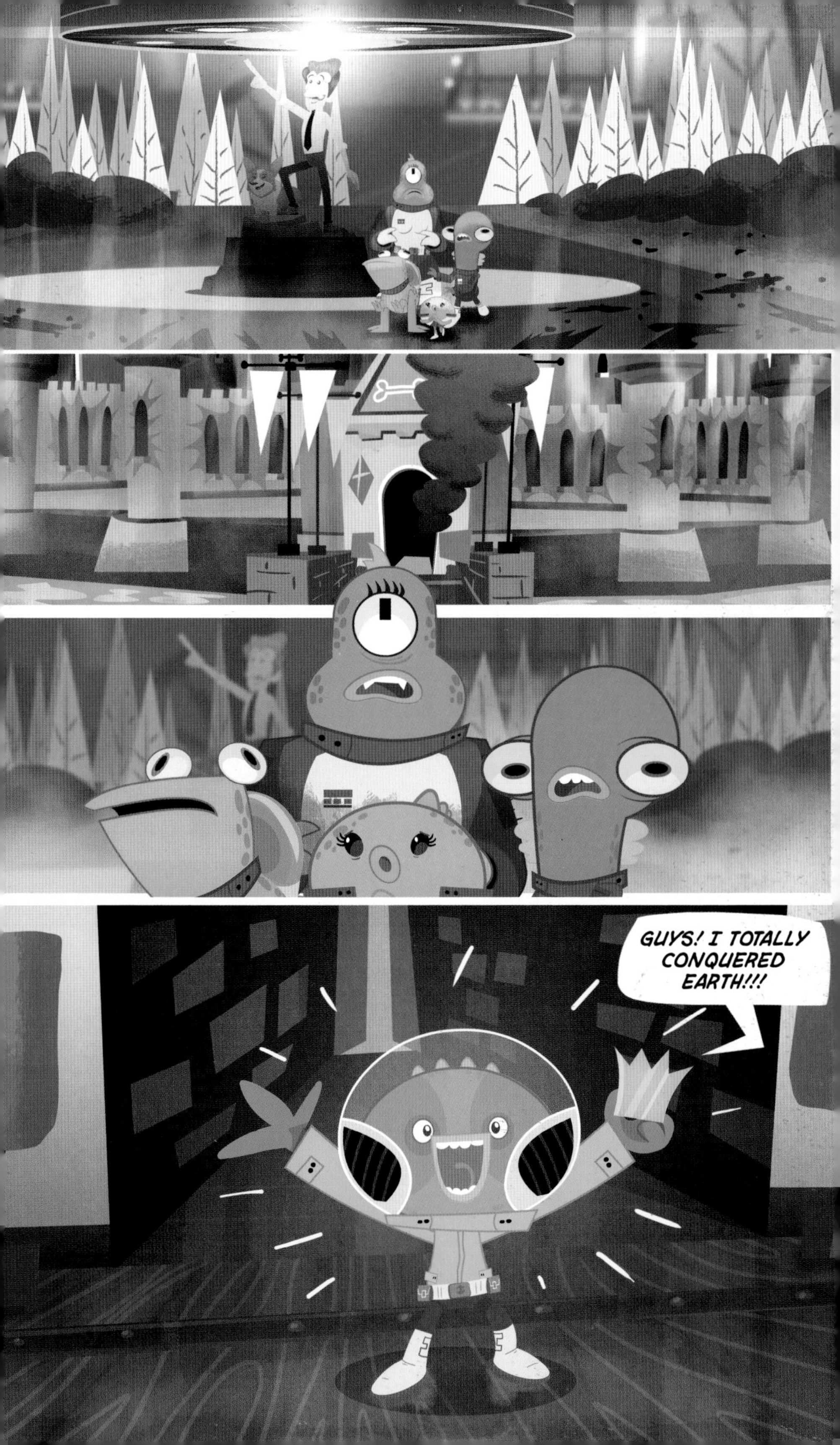
GUYS! I TOTALLY CONQUERED EARTH!!!

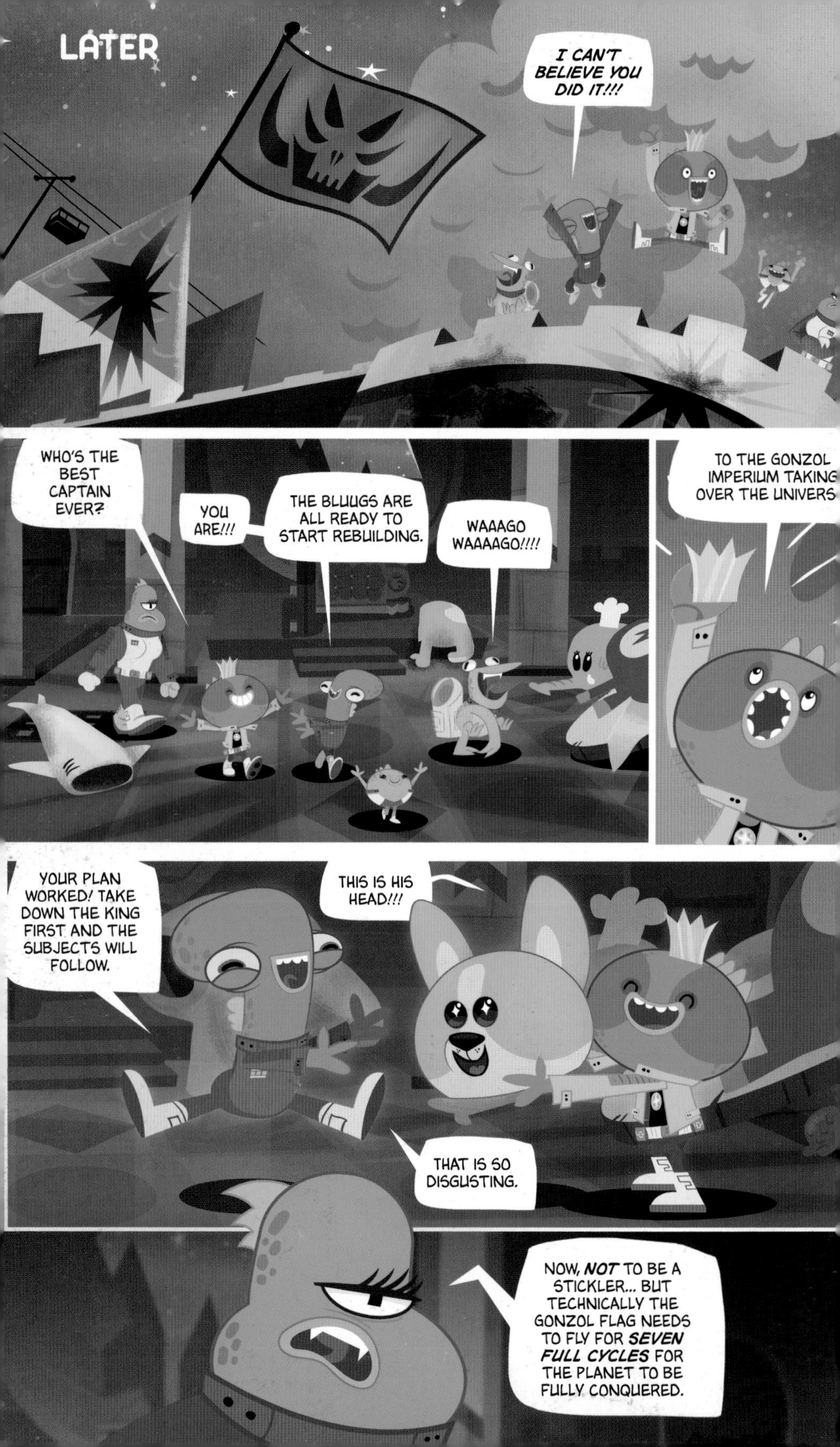

LATER
I CAN'T BELIEVE YOU DID IT!!!
WHO'S THE BEST CAPTAIN EVER?
YOU ARE!!!
THE BLUUGS ARE ALL READY TO START REBUILDING.
WAAAGO WAAAAGO!!!!
TO THE GONZOL IMPERIUM TAKING OVER THE UNIVERS
YOUR PLAN WORKED! TAKE DOWN THE KING FIRST AND THE SUBJECTS WILL FOLLOW.
THIS IS HIS HEAD!!!
THAT IS SO DISGUSTING.
NOW, *NOT* TO BE A STICKLER... BUT TECHNICALLY THE GONZOL FLAG NEEDS TO FLY FOR ***SEVEN FULL CYCLES*** FOR THE PLANET TO BE FULLY CONQUERED.

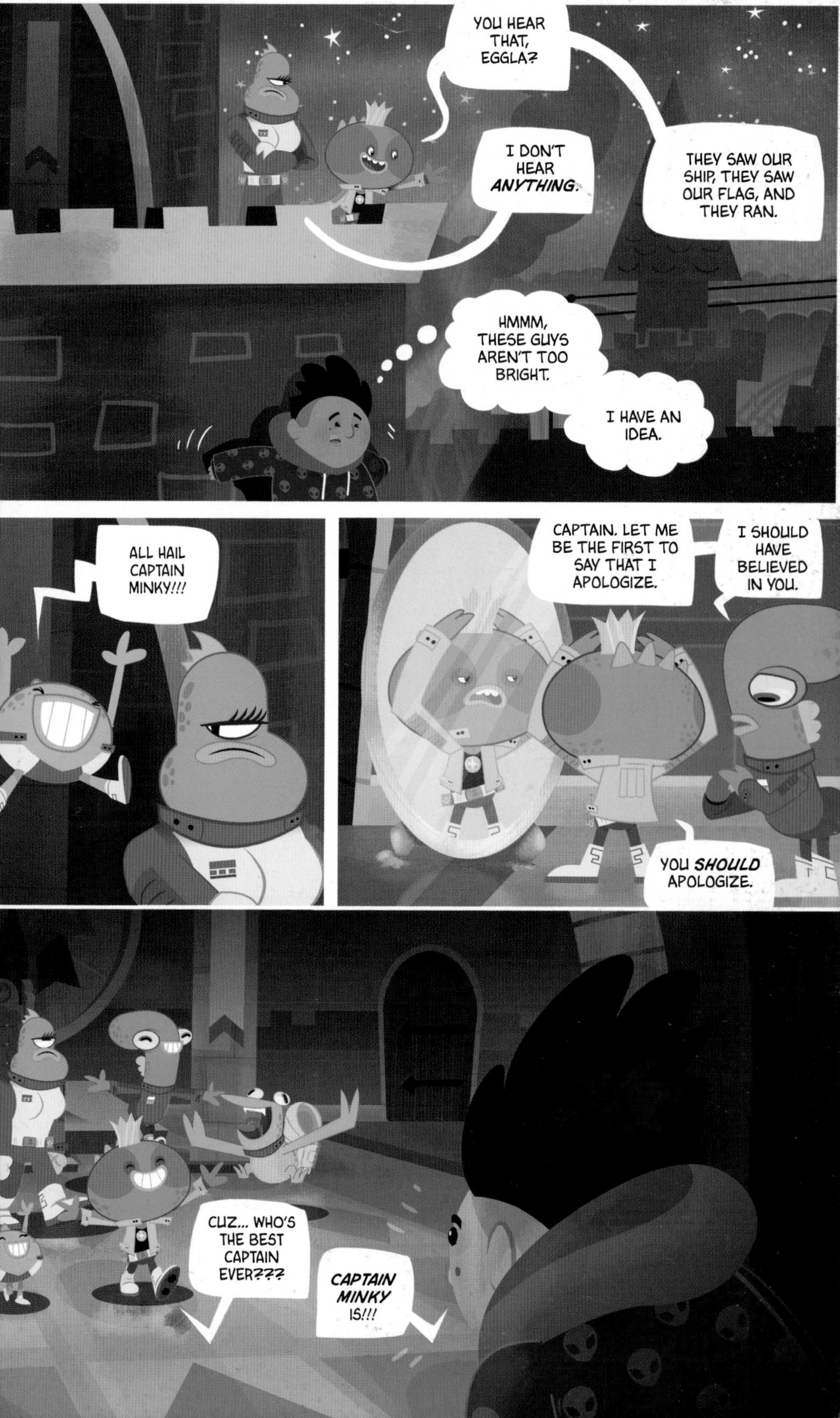
YOU HEAR THAT, EGGLA?
I DON'T HEAR *ANYTHING*.
THEY SAW OUR SHIP, THEY SAW OUR FLAG, AND THEY RAN.
HMMM, THESE GUYS AREN'T TOO BRIGHT.
I HAVE AN IDEA.
ALL HAIL CAPTAIN MINKY!!!
CAPTAIN. LET ME BE THE FIRST TO SAY THAT I APOLOGIZE.
I SHOULD HAVE BELIEVED IN YOU.
YOU *SHOULD* APOLOGIZE.
CUZ... WHO'S THE BEST CAPTAIN EVER???
CAPTAIN MINKY IS!!!

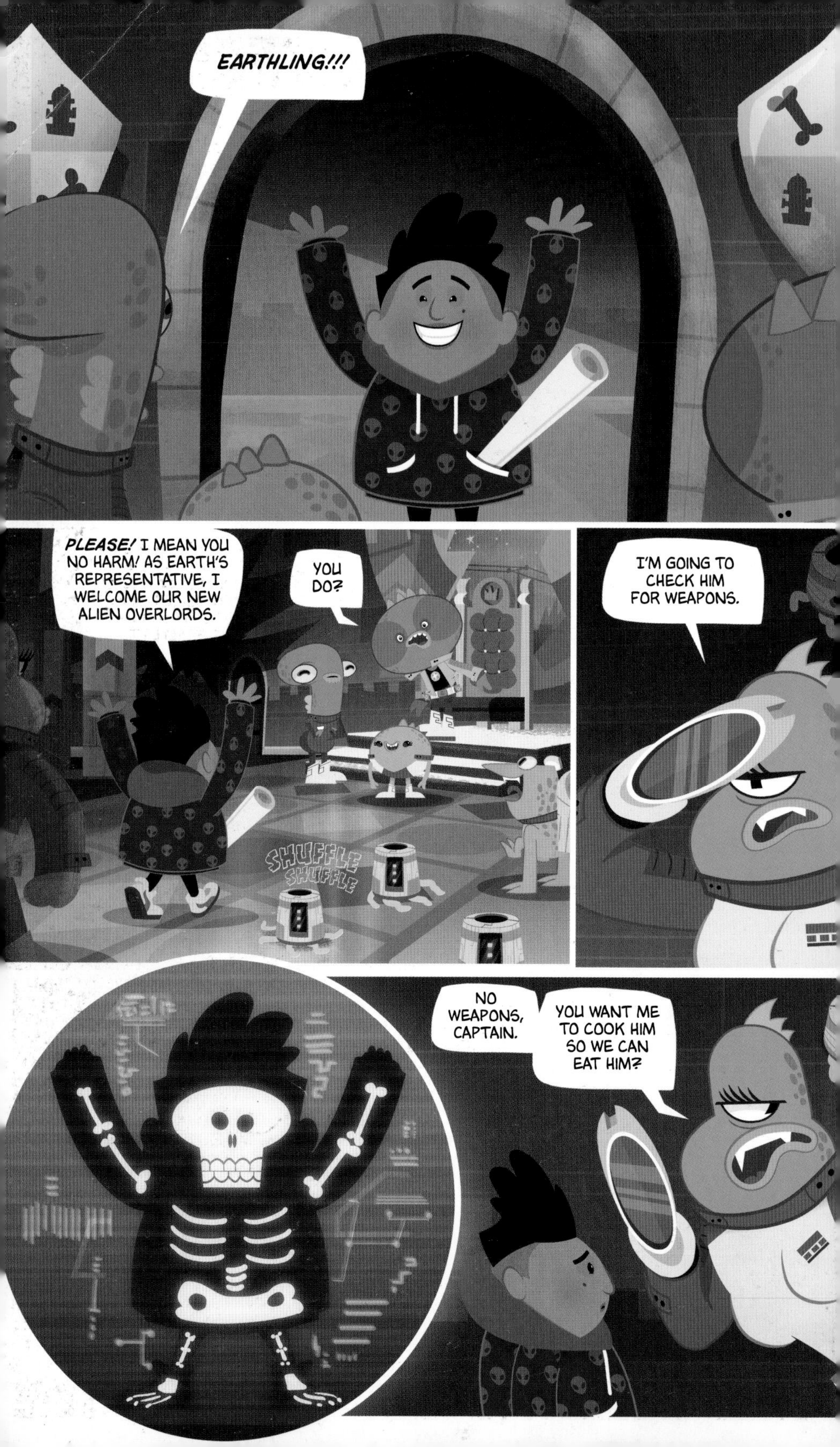
EARTHLING!!!
PLEASE! I MEAN YOU NO HARM! AS EARTH'S REPRESENTATIVE, I WELCOME OUR NEW ALIEN OVERLORDS.
YOU DO?
SHUFFLE SHUFFLE
I'M GOING TO CHECK HIM FOR WEAPONS.
NO WEAPONS, CAPTAIN.
YOU WANT ME TO COOK HIM SO WE CAN EAT HIM?

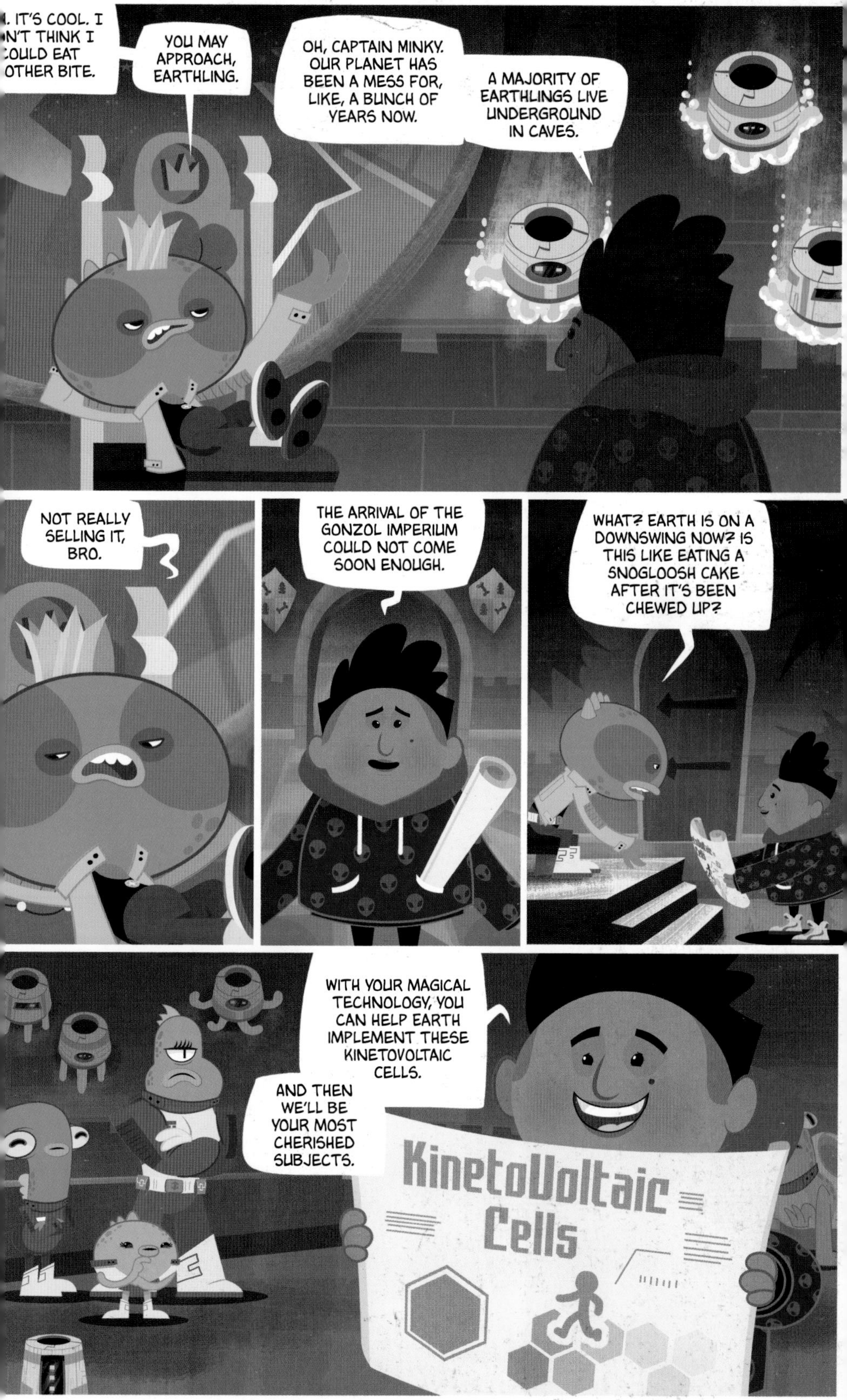

. IT'S COOL. I
N'T THINK I
COULD EAT
OTHER BITE.
YOU MAY APPROACH, EARTHLING.
OH, CAPTAIN MINKY. OUR PLANET HAS BEEN A MESS FOR, LIKE, A BUNCH OF YEARS NOW.
A MAJORITY OF EARTHLINGS LIVE UNDERGROUND IN CAVES.
NOT REALLY SELLING IT, BRO.
THE ARRIVAL OF THE GONZOL IMPERIUM COULD NOT COME SOON ENOUGH.
WHAT? EARTH IS ON A DOWNSWING NOW? IS THIS LIKE EATING A SNOGLOOSH CAKE AFTER IT'S BEEN CHEWED UP?
WITH YOUR MAGICAL TECHNOLOGY, YOU CAN HELP EARTH IMPLEMENT THESE KINETOVOLTAIC CELLS.
AND THEN WE'LL BE YOUR MOST CHERISHED SUBJECTS.
KinetoVoltaic Cells

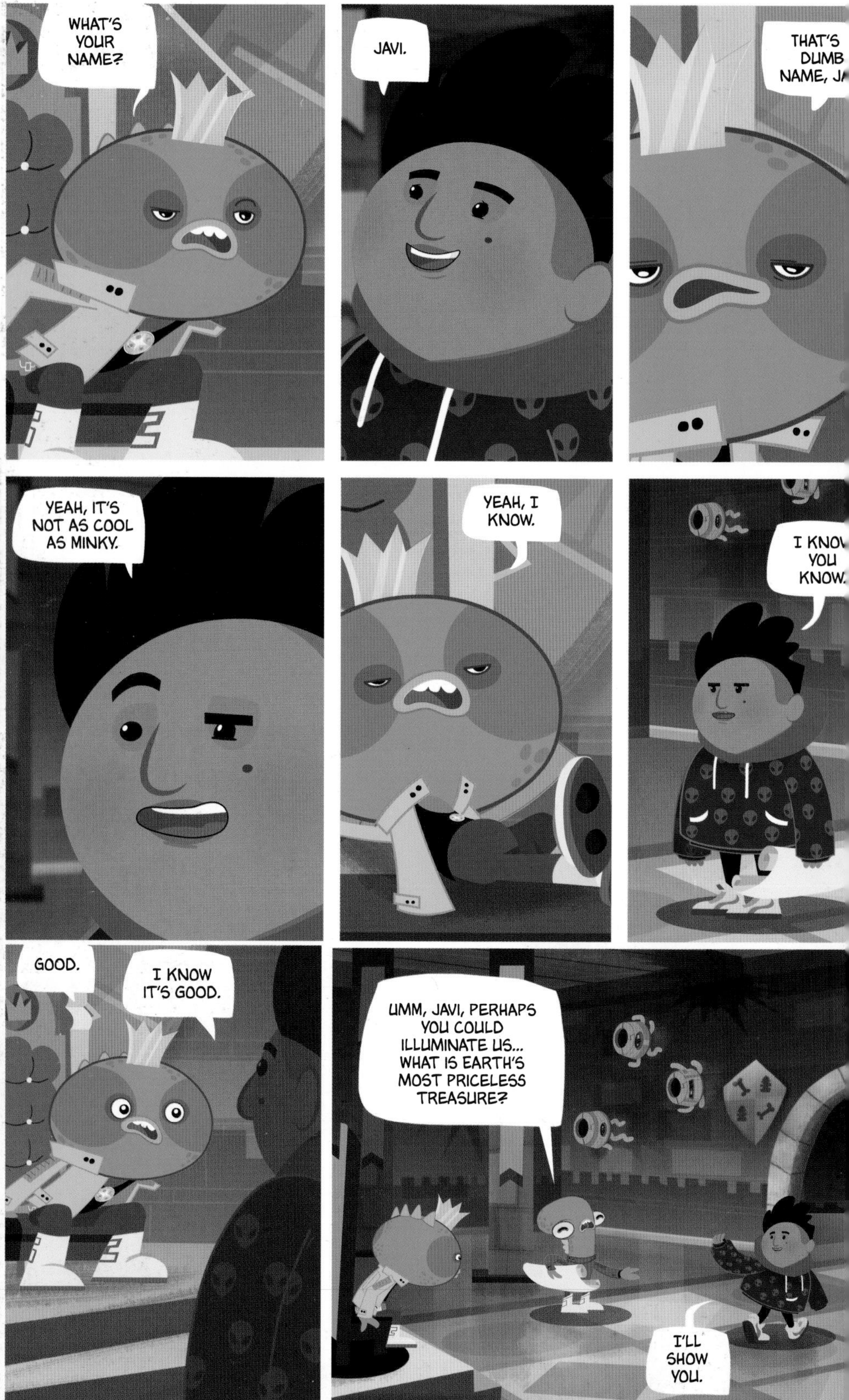
WHAT'S YOUR NAME?
JAVI.
THAT'S DUMB NAME, JA
YEAH, IT'S NOT AS COOL AS MINKY.
YEAH, I KNOW.
I KNOW YOU KNOW.
GOOD.
I KNOW IT'S GOOD.
UMM, JAVI, PERHAPS YOU COULD ILLUMINATE US... WHAT IS EARTH'S MOST PRICELESS TREASURE?
I'LL SHOW YOU.

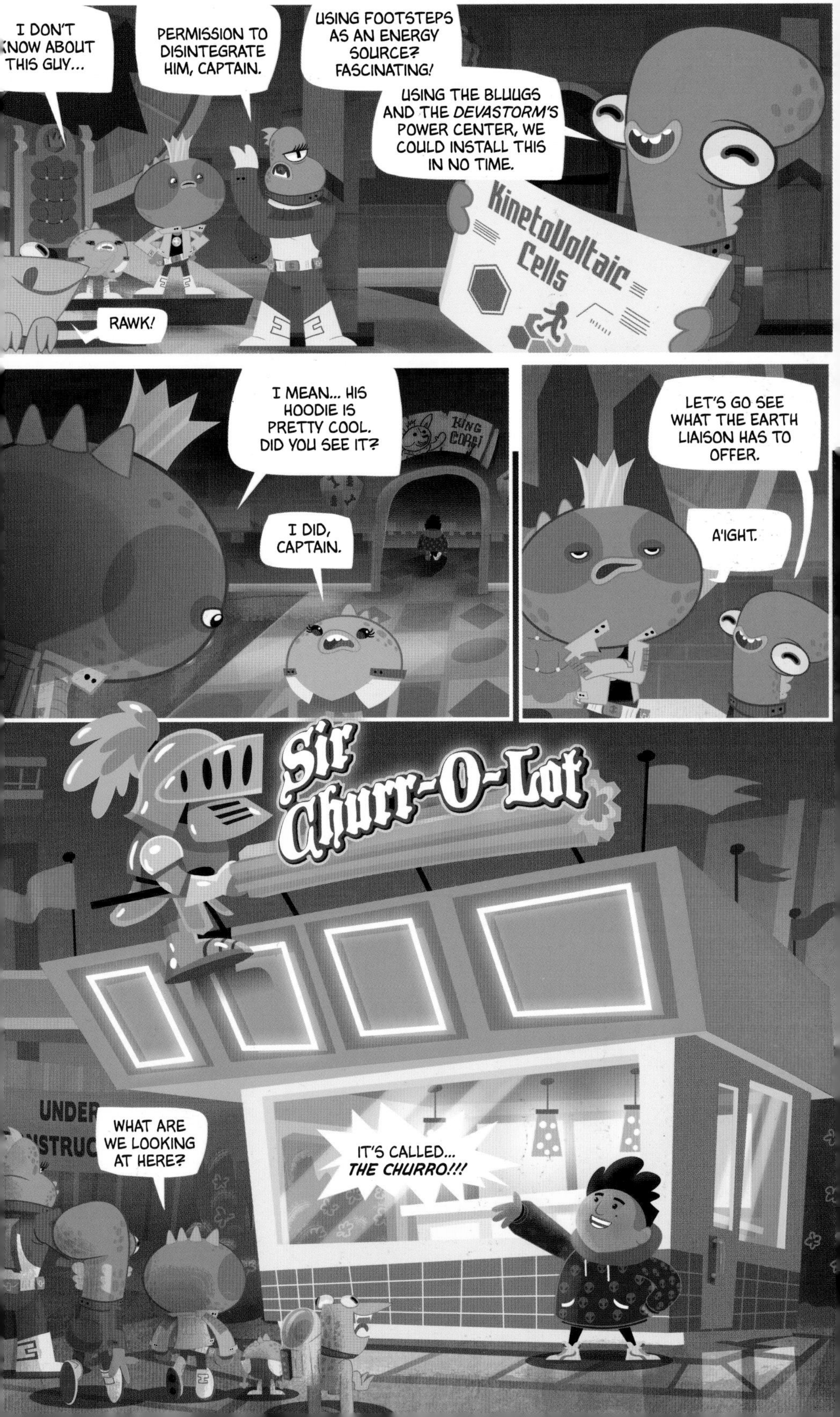
I DON'T KNOW ABOUT THIS GUY...
PERMISSION TO DISINTEGRATE HIM, CAPTAIN.
USING FOOTSTEPS AS AN ENERGY SOURCE? FASCINATING!
USING THE BLUUGS AND THE *DEVASTORM'S* POWER CENTER, WE COULD INSTALL THIS IN NO TIME.
KinetoVoltaic Cells
RAWK!
I MEAN... HIS HOODIE IS PRETTY COOL. DID YOU SEE IT?
I DID, CAPTAIN.
LET'S GO SEE WHAT THE EARTH LIAISON HAS TO OFFER.
A'IGHT.
Sir Churr-O-Lot
WHAT ARE WE LOOKING AT HERE?
IT'S CALLED... *THE CHURRO!!!*

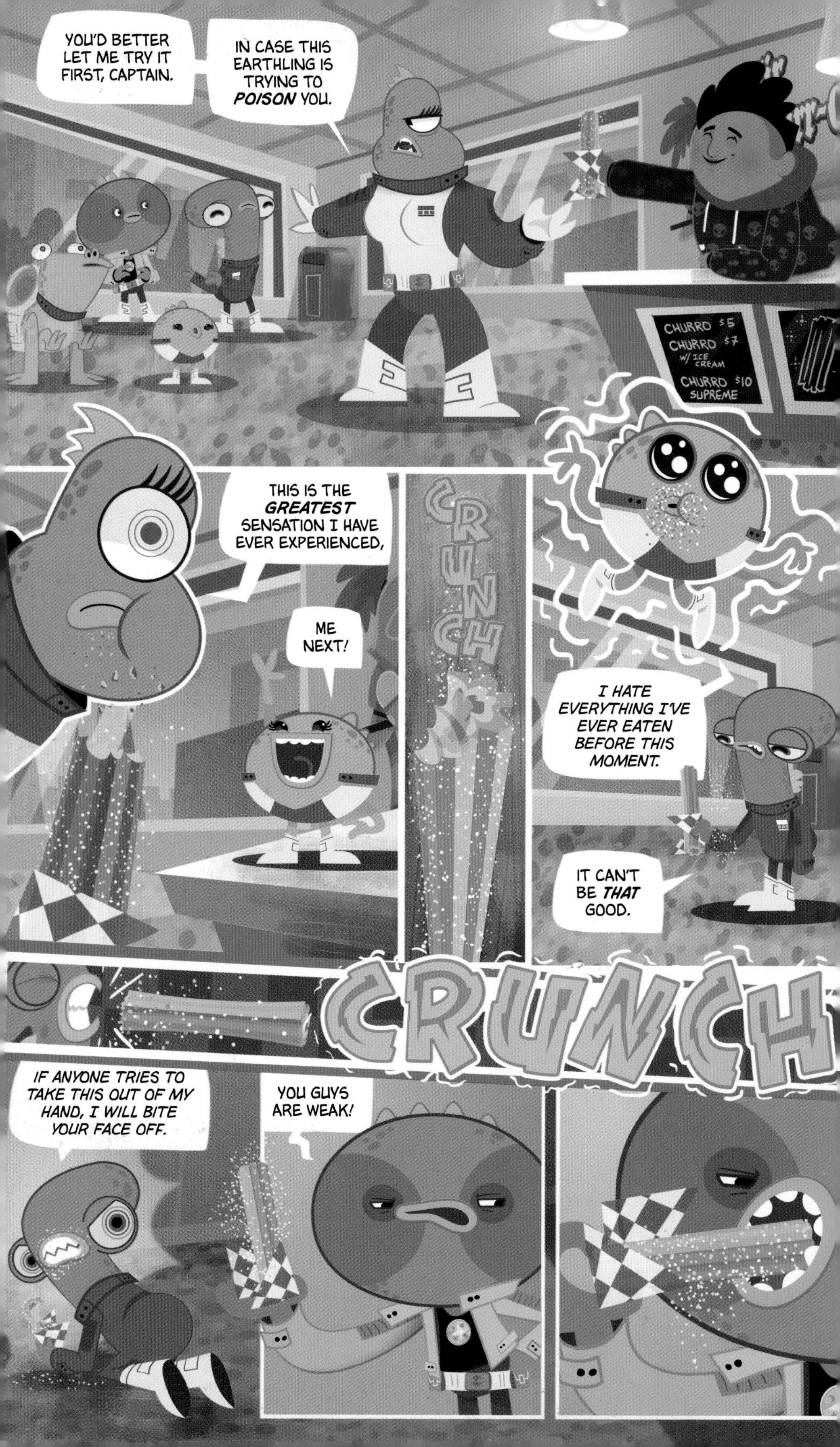
YOU'D BETTER LET ME TRY IT FIRST, CAPTAIN.
IN CASE THIS EARTHLING IS TRYING TO *POISON* YOU.
CHURRO $5
CHURRO $7 W/ ICE CREAM
CHURRO $10 SUPREME
THIS IS THE *GREATEST* SENSATION I HAVE EVER EXPERIENCED,
ME NEXT!
CRUNCH
I HATE EVERYTHING I'VE EVER EATEN BEFORE THIS MOMENT.
IT CAN'T BE *THAT* GOOD.
CRUNCH
IF ANYONE TRIES TO TAKE THIS OUT OF MY HAND, I WILL BITE YOUR FACE OFF.
YOU GUYS ARE WEAK!

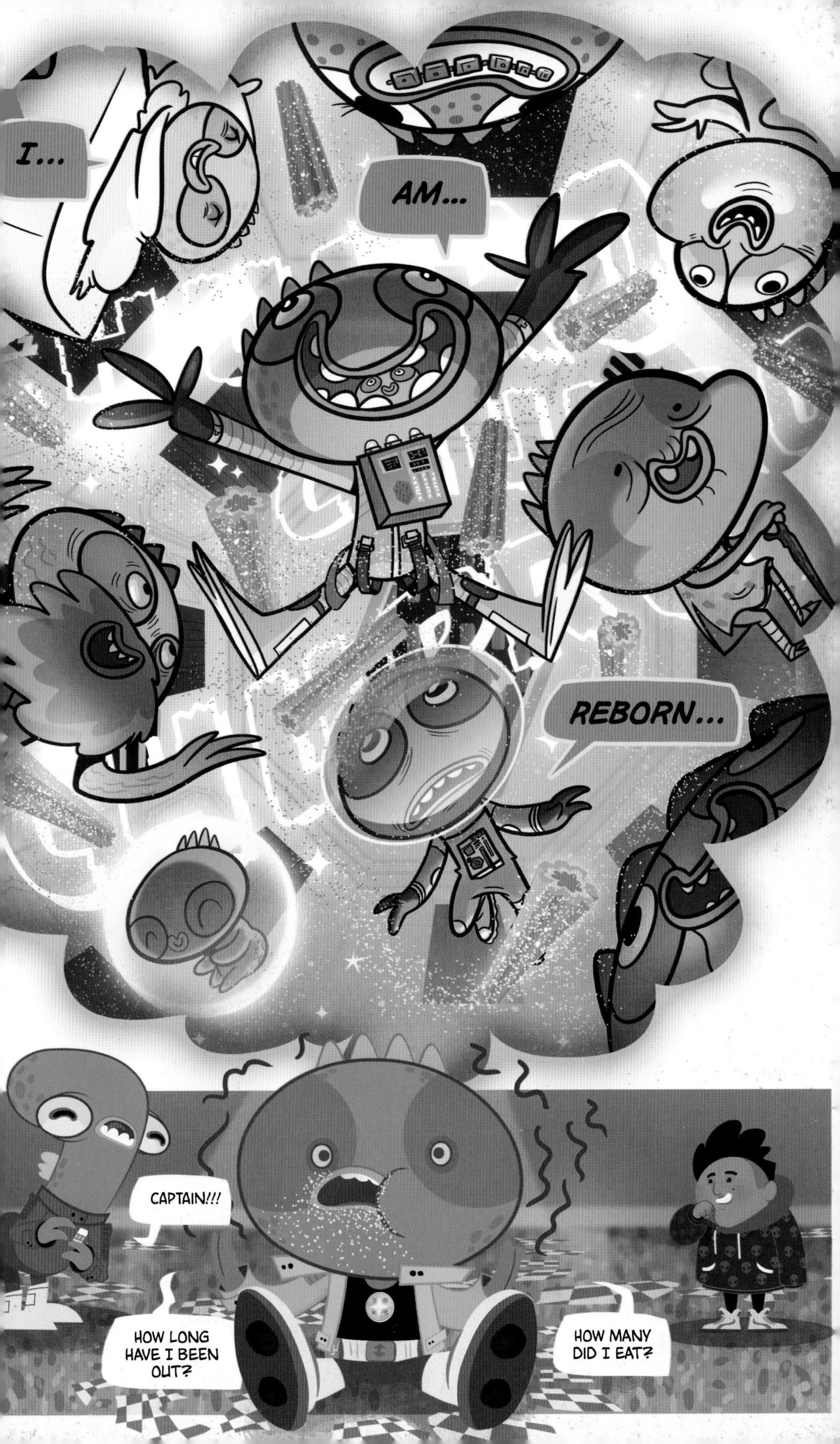
I...
AM...
REBORN...
CAPTAIN!!!
HOW LONG HAVE I BEEN OUT?
HOW MANY DID I EAT?

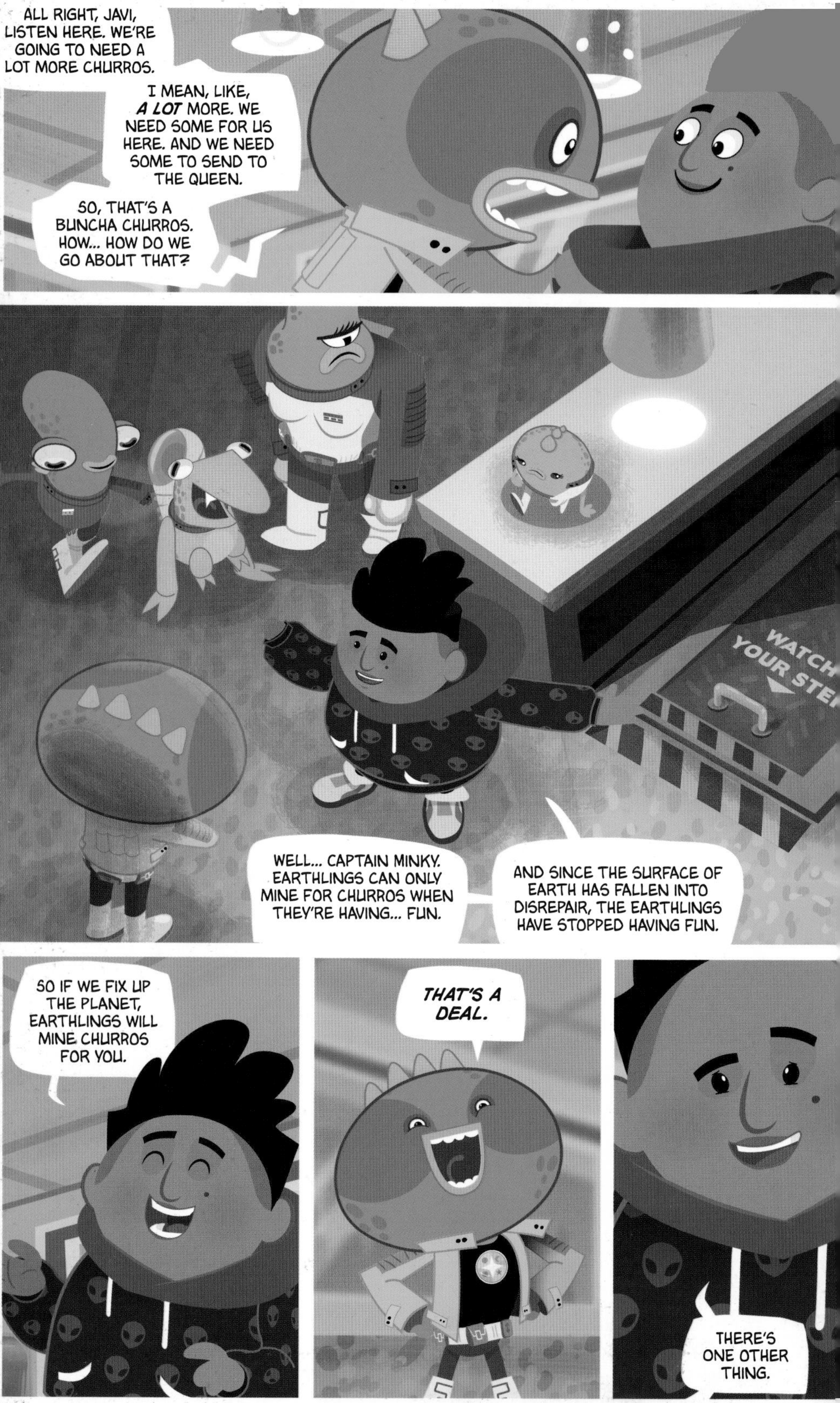
ALL RIGHT, JAVI, LISTEN HERE. WE'RE GOING TO NEED A LOT MORE CHURROS.
I MEAN, LIKE, *A LOT* MORE. WE NEED SOME FOR US HERE. AND WE NEED SOME TO SEND TO THE QUEEN.
SO, THAT'S A BUNCHA CHURROS. HOW... HOW DO WE GO ABOUT THAT?
WATCH YOUR STEP
WELL... CAPTAIN MINKY. EARTHLINGS CAN ONLY MINE FOR CHURROS WHEN THEY'RE HAVING... FUN.
AND SINCE THE SURFACE OF EARTH HAS FALLEN INTO DISREPAIR, THE EARTHLINGS HAVE STOPPED HAVING FUN.
SO IF WE FIX UP THE PLANET, EARTHLINGS WILL MINE CHURROS FOR YOU.
THAT'S A DEAL.
THERE'S ONE OTHER THING.

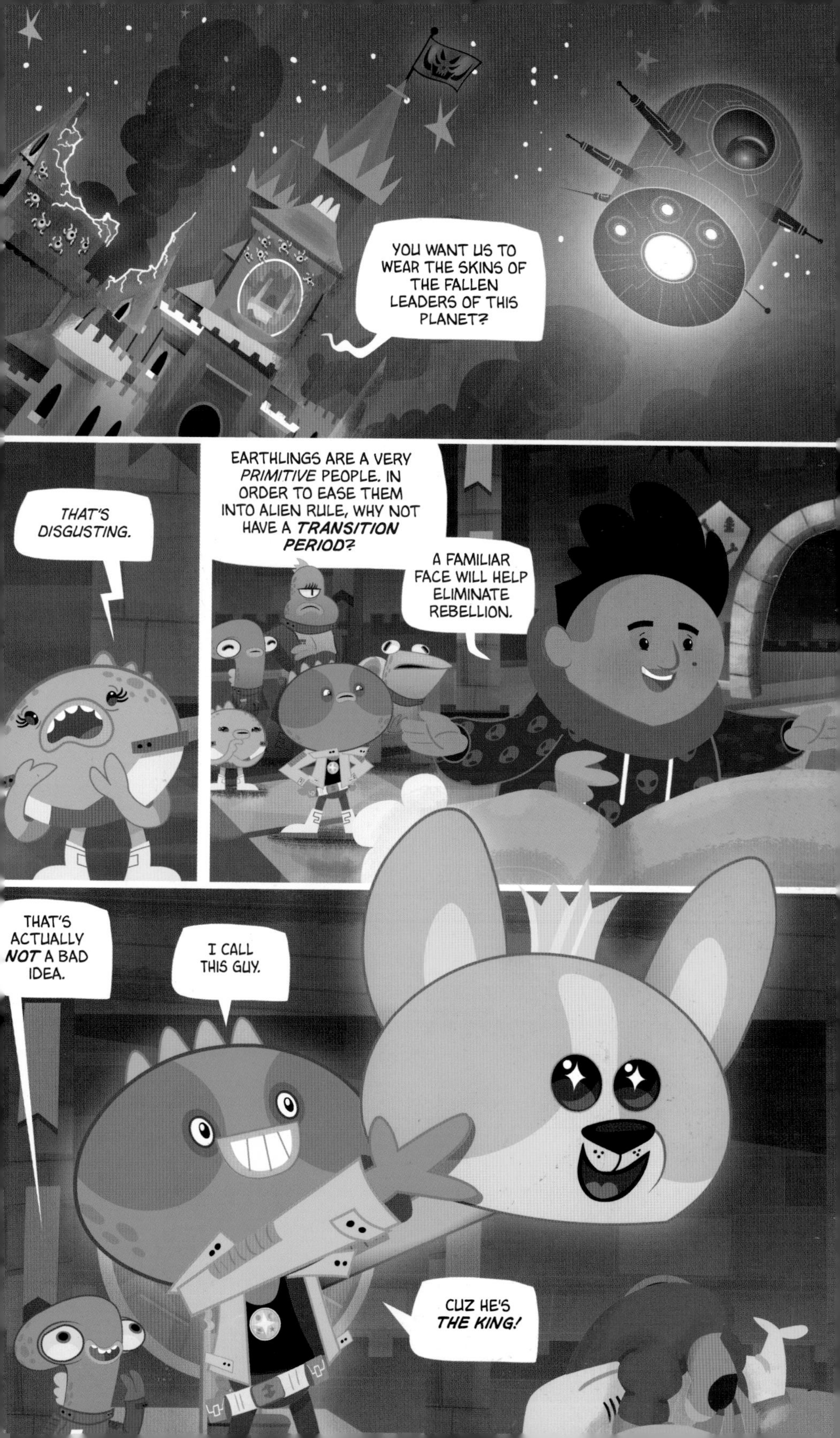
YOU WANT US TO WEAR THE SKINS OF THE FALLEN LEADERS OF THIS PLANET?
THAT'S DISGUSTING.
EARTHLINGS ARE A VERY *PRIMITIVE* PEOPLE. IN ORDER TO EASE THEM INTO ALIEN RULE, WHY NOT HAVE A ***TRANSITION PERIOD***?
A FAMILIAR FACE WILL HELP ELIMINATE REBELLION.
THAT'S ACTUALLY ***NOT*** A BAD IDEA.
I CALL THIS GUY.
CUZ HE'S ***THE KING!***

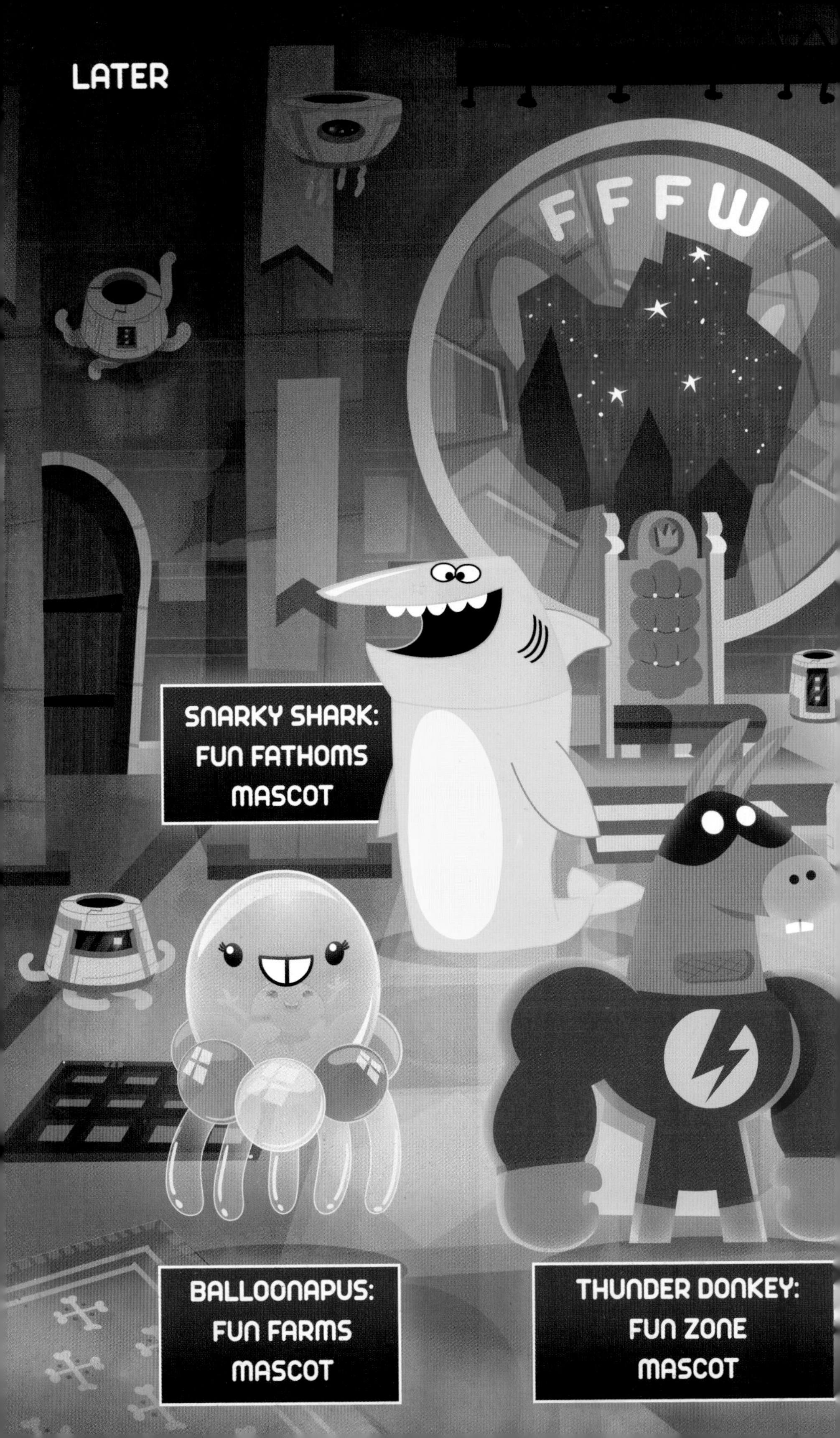
LATER
FFFW
SNARKY SHARK:
FUN FATHOMS
MASCOT
BALLOONAPUS:
FUN FARMS
MASCOT
THUNDER DONKEY:
FUN ZONE
MASCOT

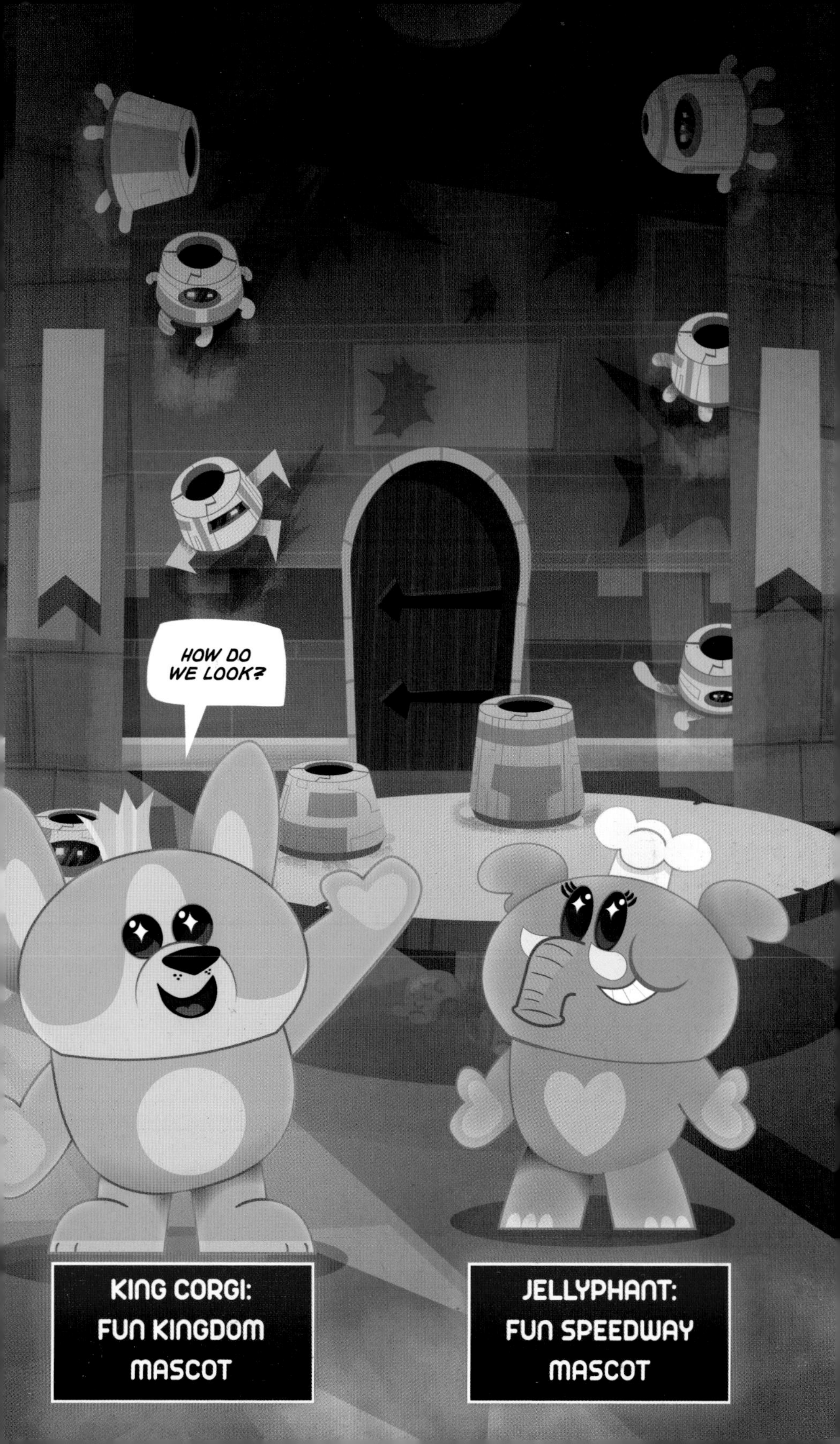
HOW DO WE LOOK?
KING CORGI: FUN KINGDOM MASCOT
JELLYPHANT: FUN SPEEDWAY MASCOT

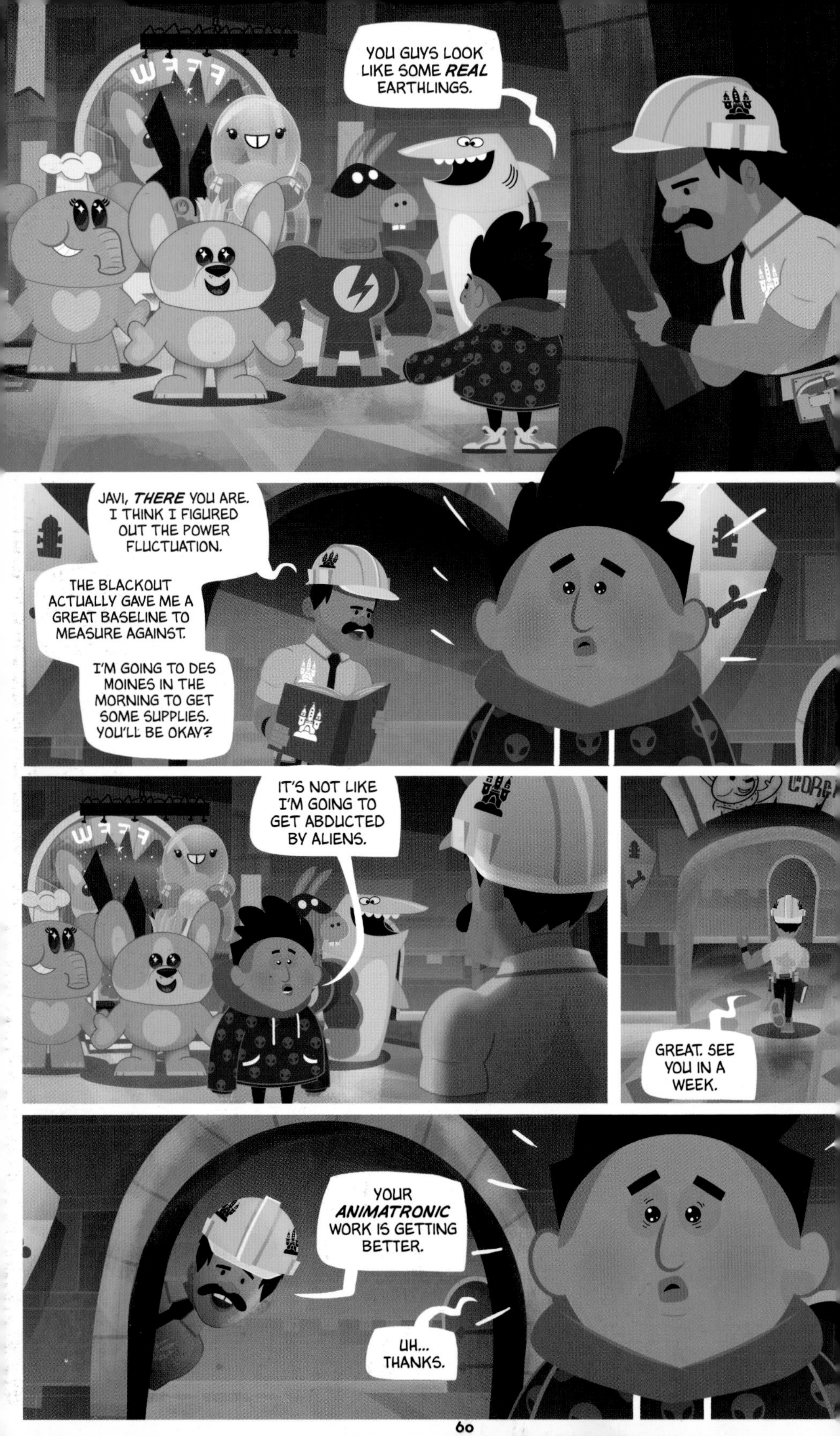
YOU GUYS LOOK LIKE SOME *REAL* EARTHLINGS.
JAVI, *THERE* YOU ARE. I THINK I FIGURED OUT THE POWER FLUCTUATION.
THE BLACKOUT ACTUALLY GAVE ME A GREAT BASELINE TO MEASURE AGAINST.
I'M GOING TO DES MOINES IN THE MORNING TO GET SOME SUPPLIES. YOU'LL BE OKAY?
IT'S NOT LIKE I'M GOING TO GET ABDUCTED BY ALIENS.
GREAT. SEE YOU IN A WEEK.
YOUR *ANIMATRONIC* WORK IS GETTING BETTER.
UH... THANKS.

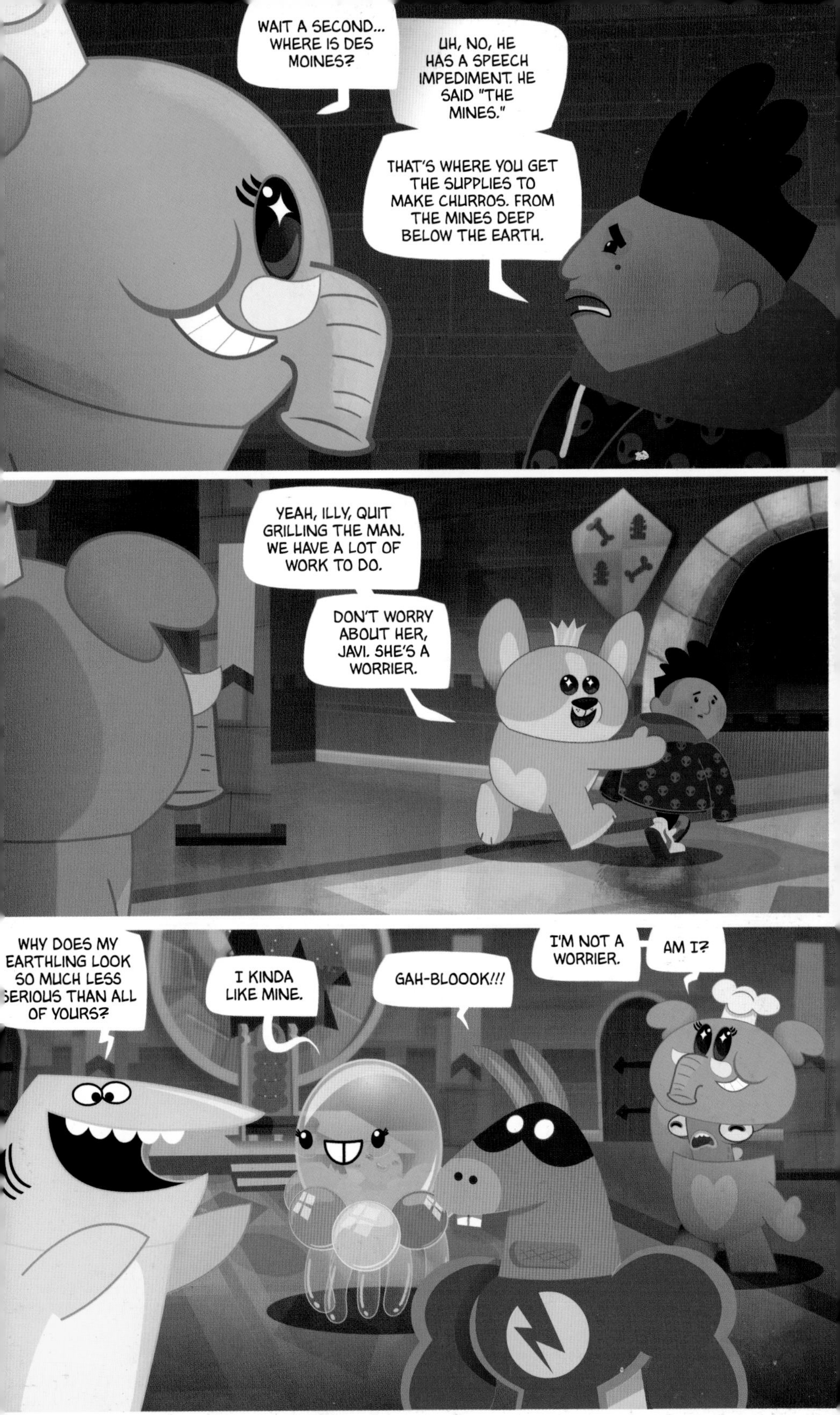
WAIT A SECOND... WHERE IS DES MOINES?
UH, NO, HE HAS A SPEECH IMPEDIMENT. HE SAID "THE MINES."
THAT'S WHERE YOU GET THE SUPPLIES TO MAKE CHURROS. FROM THE MINES DEEP BELOW THE EARTH.
YEAH, ILLY, QUIT GRILLING THE MAN. WE HAVE A LOT OF WORK TO DO.
DON'T WORRY ABOUT HER, JAVI. SHE'S A WORRIER.
WHY DOES MY EARTHLING LOOK SO MUCH LESS SERIOUS THAN ALL OF YOURS?
I KINDA LIKE MINE.
GAH-BLOOOK!!!
I'M NOT A WORRIER.
AM I?

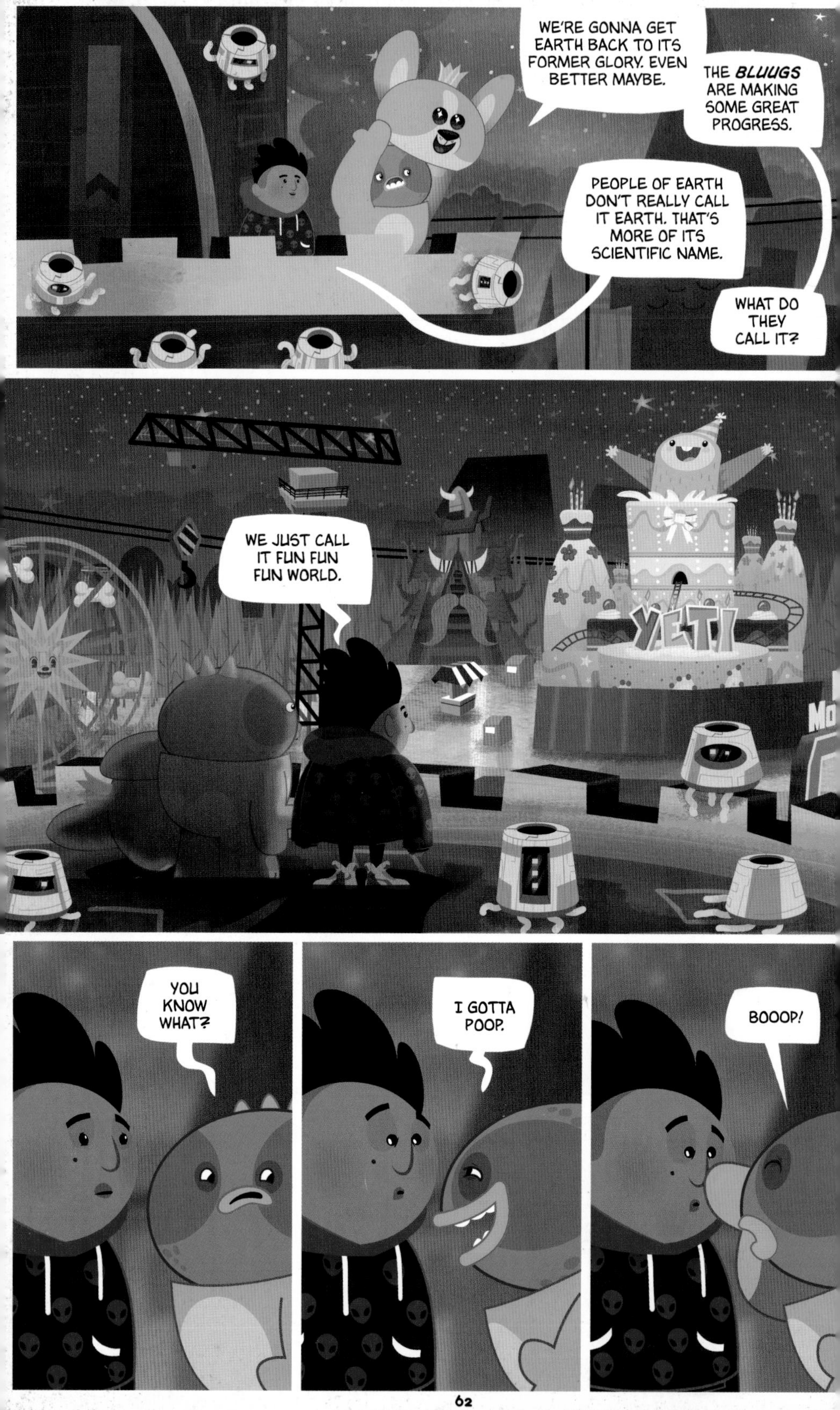
WE'RE GONNA GET EARTH BACK TO ITS FORMER GLORY. EVEN BETTER MAYBE.
THE ***BLUUGS*** ARE MAKING SOME GREAT PROGRESS.
PEOPLE OF EARTH DON'T REALLY CALL IT EARTH. THAT'S MORE OF ITS SCIENTIFIC NAME.
WHAT DO THEY CALL IT?
WE JUST CALL IT FUN FUN FUN WORLD.
YETI
YOU KNOW WHAT?
I GOTTA POOP.
BOOOP!

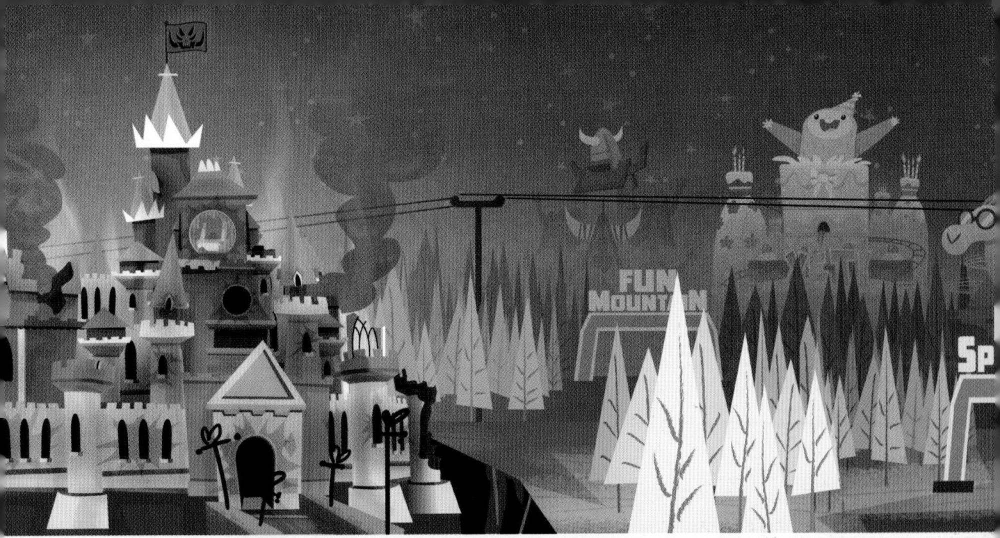
FUN

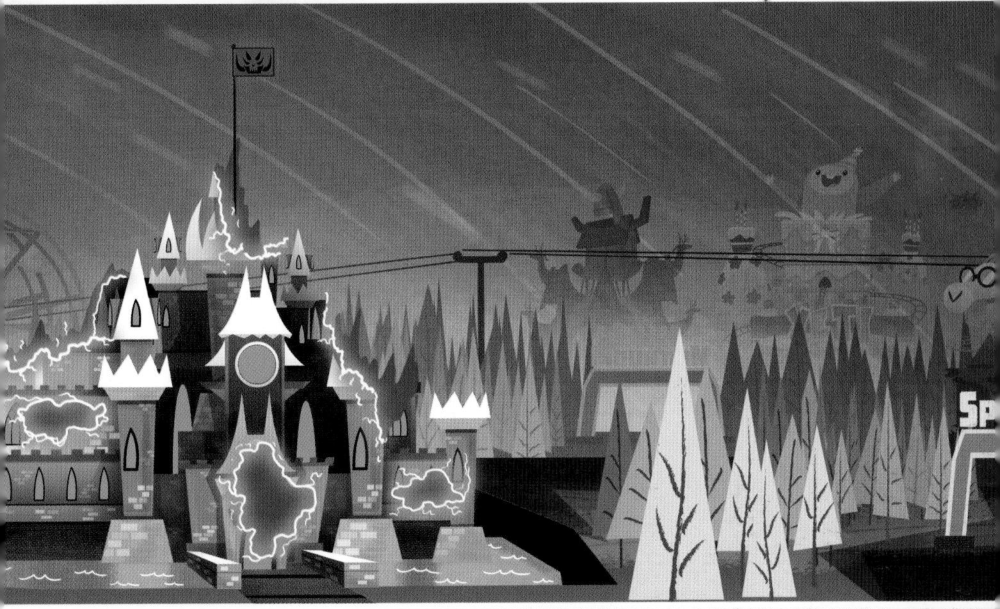

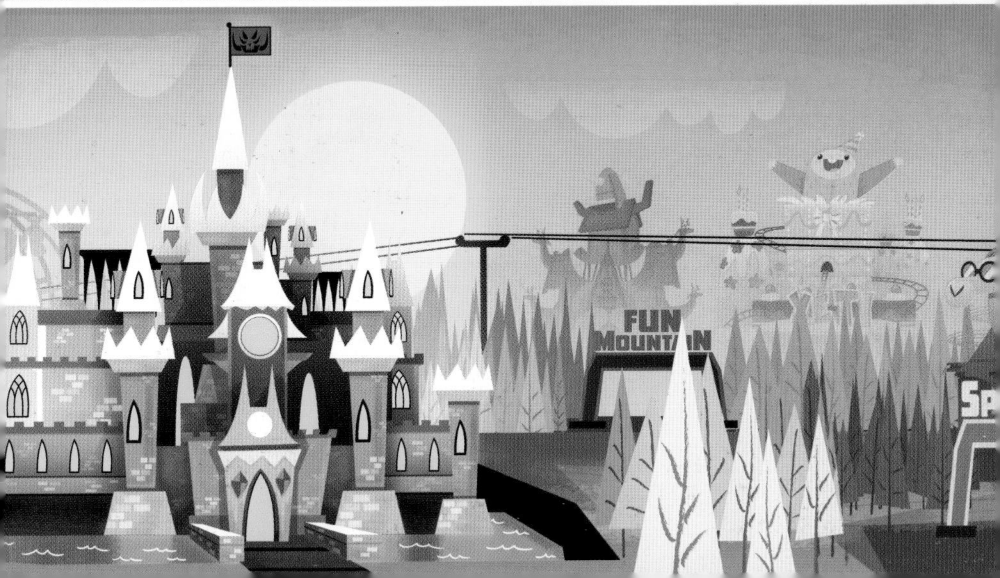
FUN

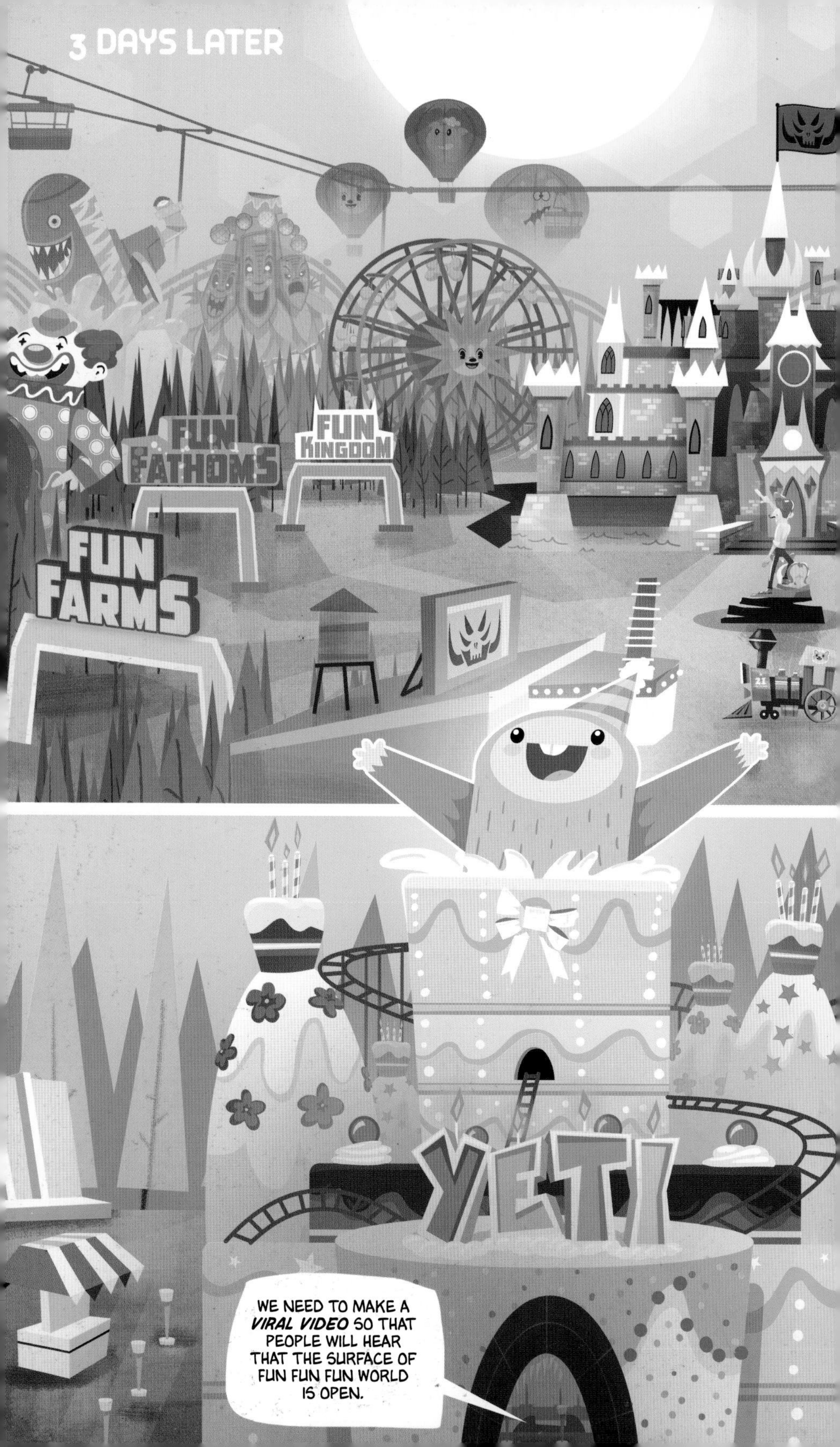

3 DAYS LATER
FUN FATHOMS
FUN KINGDOM
FUN FARMS
YETI
WE NEED TO MAKE A *VIRAL VIDEO* SO THAT PEOPLE WILL HEAR THAT THE SURFACE OF FUN FUN FUN WORLD IS OPEN.

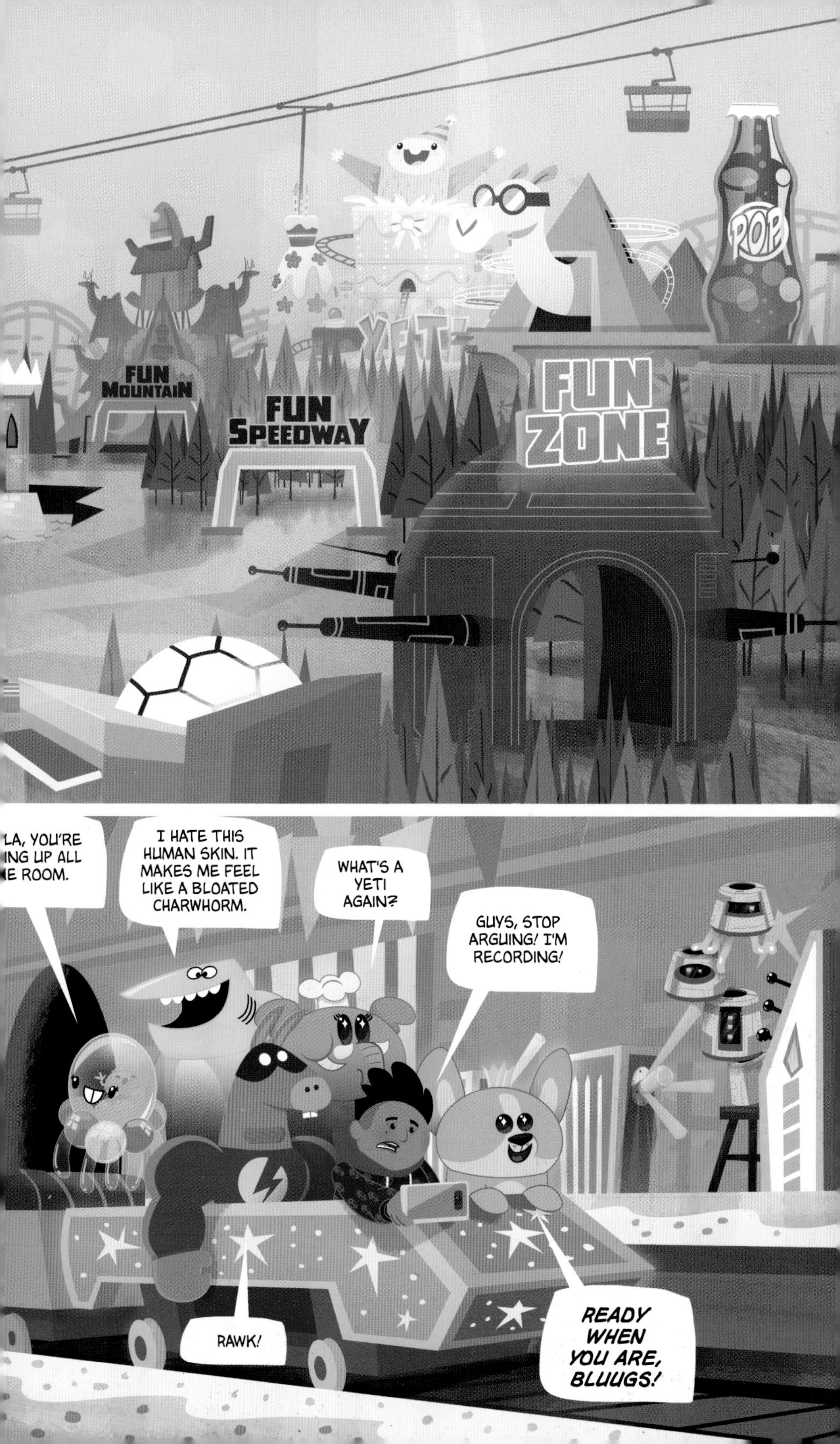

FUN MOUNTAIN
FUN SPEEDWAY
YETI
FUN ZONE
POP
LA, YOU'RE ING UP ALL E ROOM.
I HATE THIS HUMAN SKIN. IT MAKES ME FEEL LIKE A BLOATED CHARWHORM.
WHAT'S A YETI AGAIN?
GUYS, STOP ARGUING! I'M RECORDING!
RAWK!
READY WHEN YOU ARE, BLUUGS!

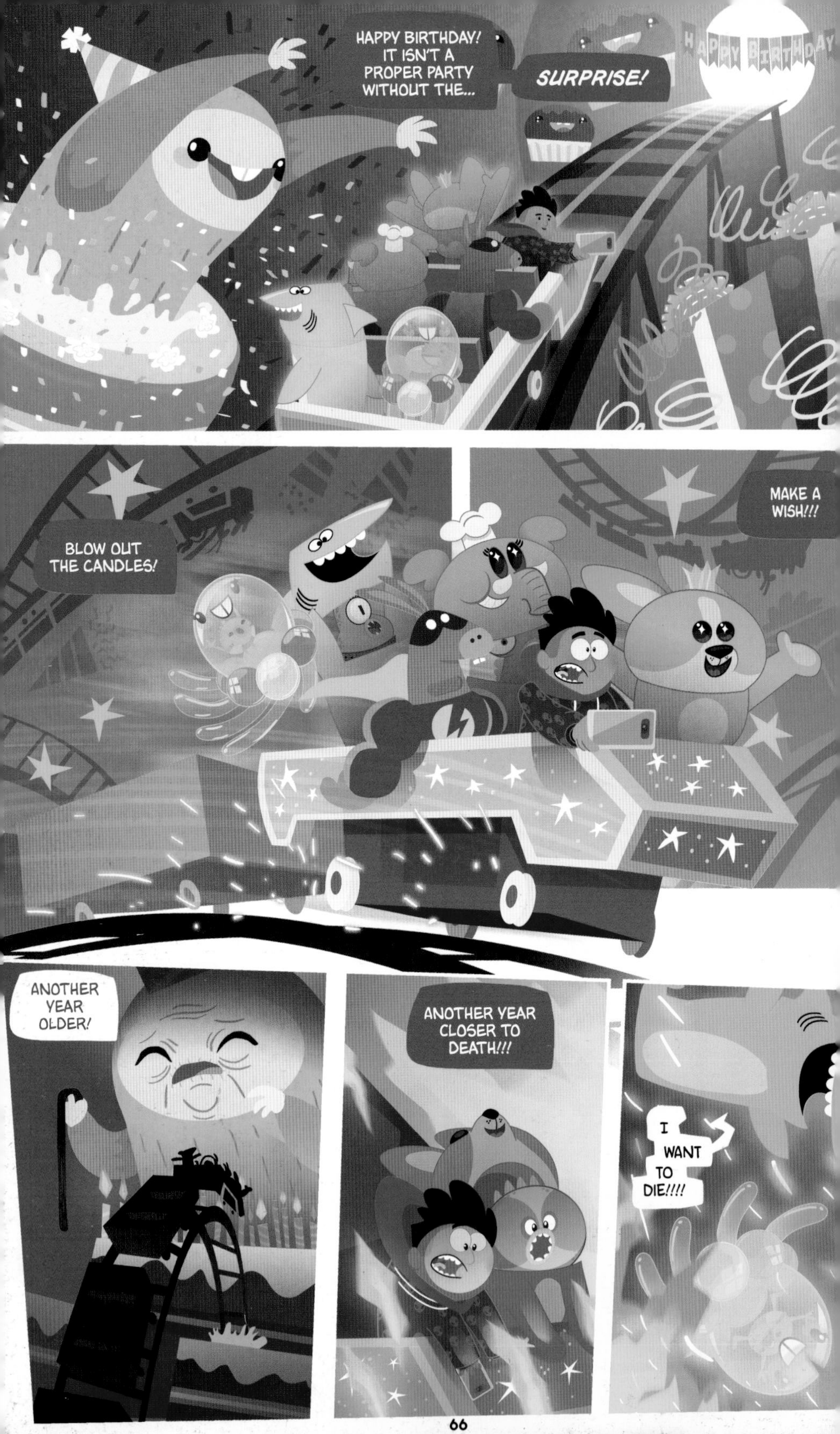
HAPPY BIRTHDAY! IT ISN'T A PROPER PARTY WITHOUT THE...
SURPRISE!
HAPPY BIRTHDAY
BLOW OUT THE CANDLES!
MAKE A WISH!!!
ANOTHER YEAR OLDER!
ANOTHER YEAR CLOSER TO DEATH!!!
I WANT TO DIE!!!!

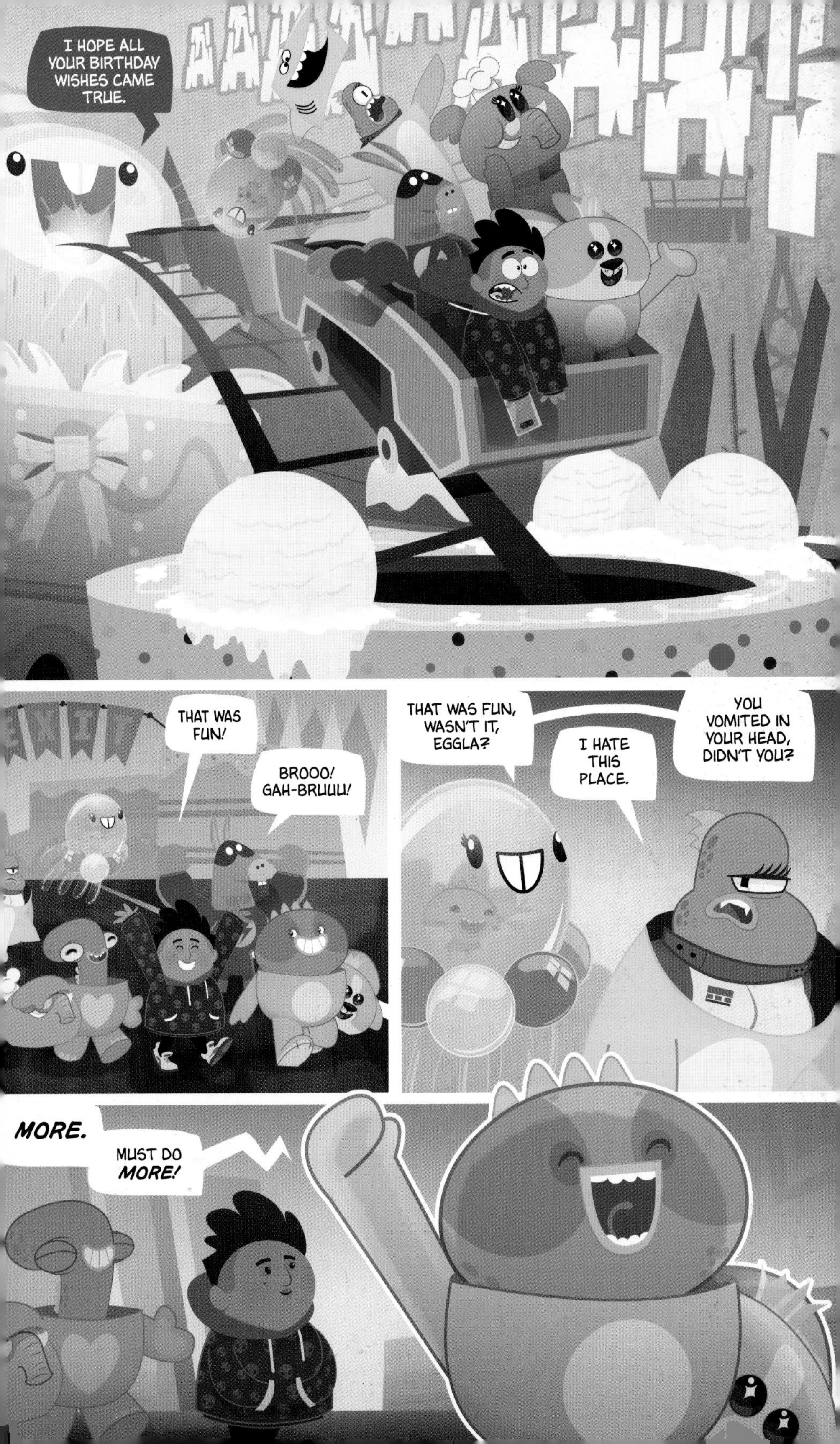

I HOPE ALL YOUR BIRTHDAY WISHES CAME TRUE.
THAT WAS FUN!
BROOO! GAH-BRUUU!
THAT WAS FUN, WASN'T IT, EGGLA?
I HATE THIS PLACE.
YOU VOMITED IN YOUR HEAD, DIDN'T YOU?
MORE.
MUST DO MORE!

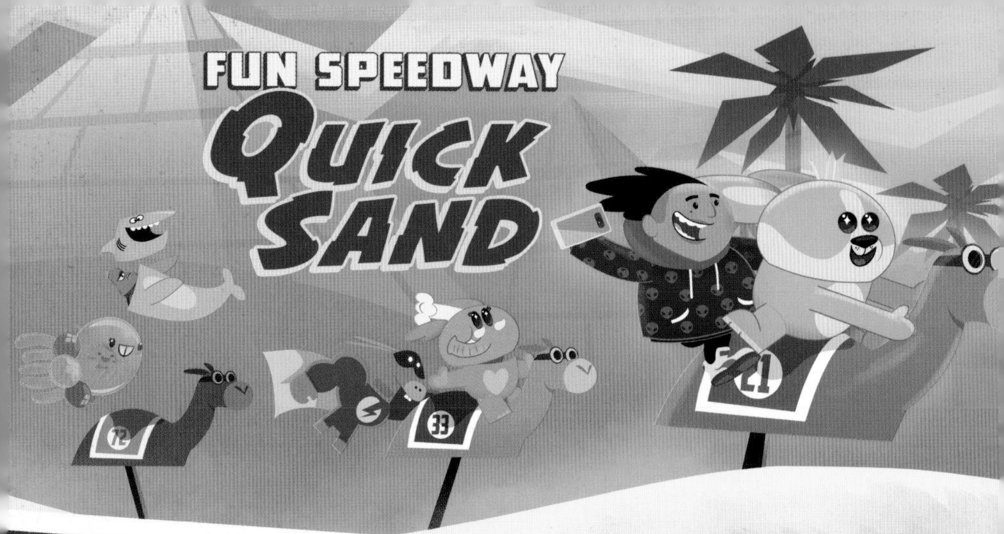
FUN SPEEDWAY
QUICK SAND
72
33
17

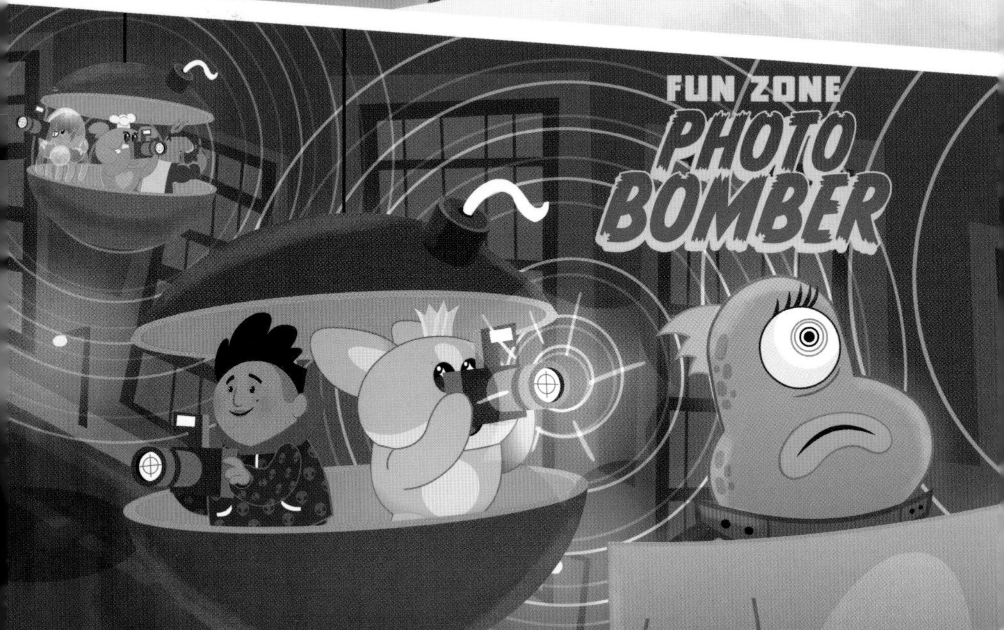
FUN ZONE
PHOTO BOMBER

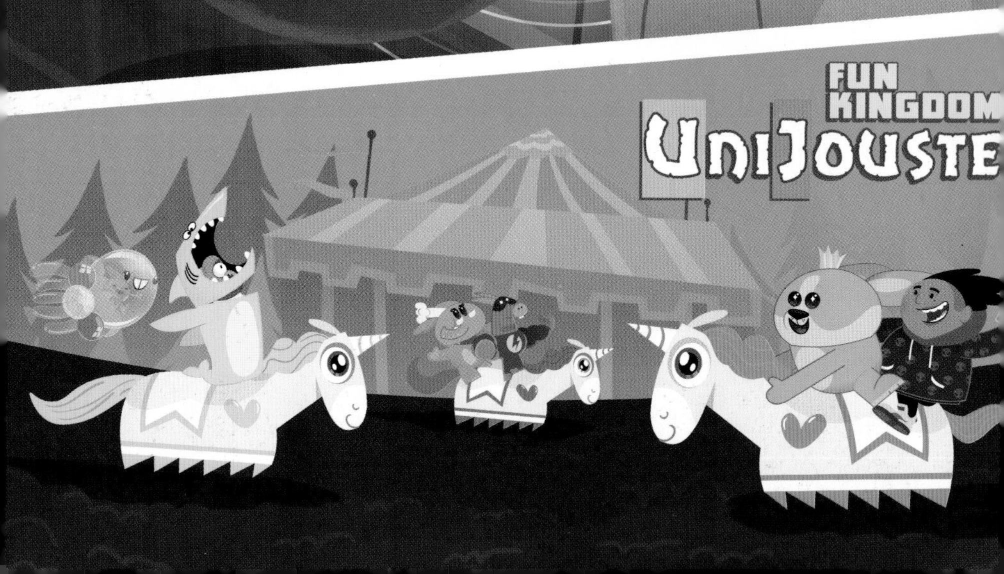
FUN KINGDOM
UniJouste

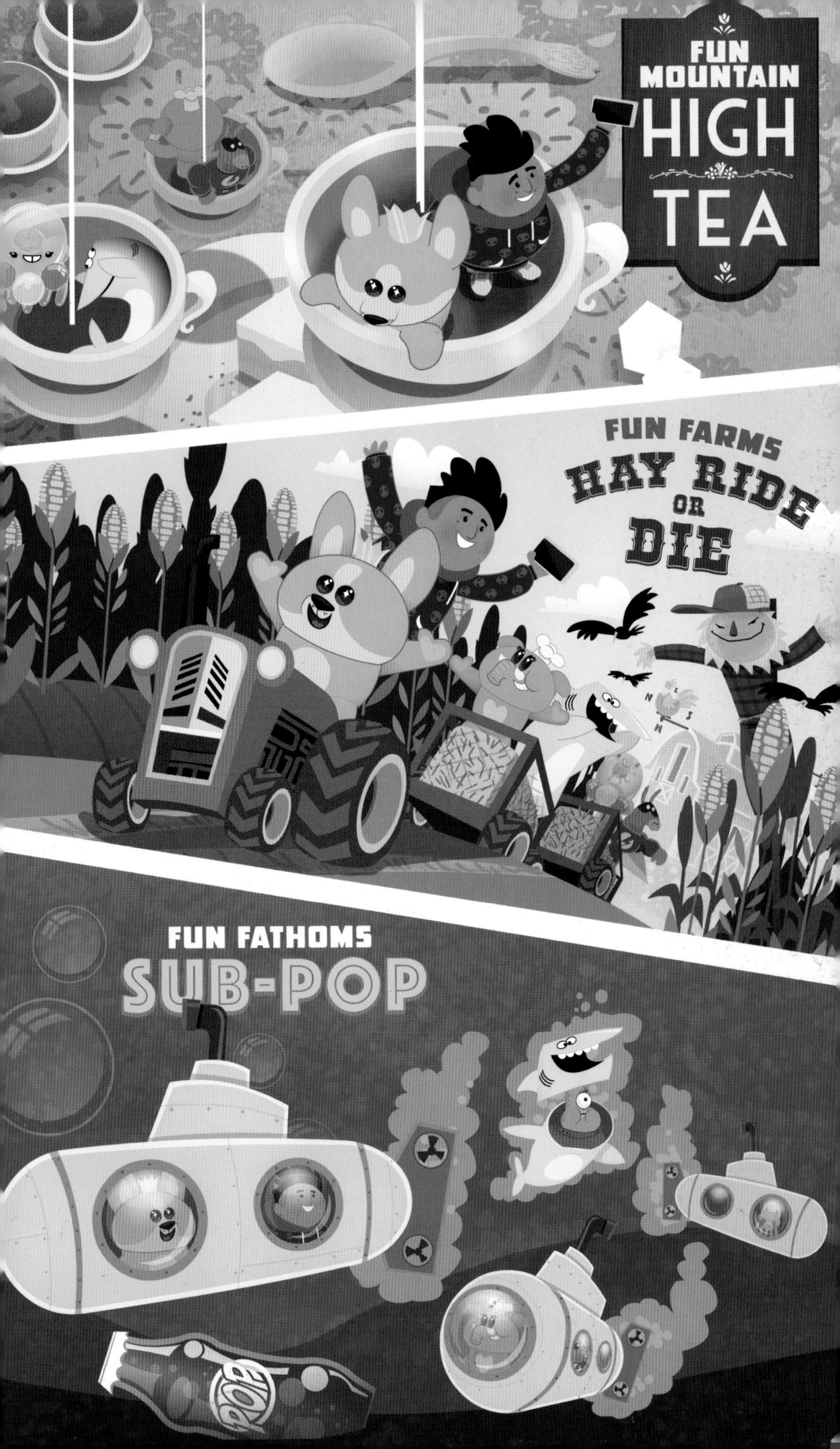
FUN MOUNTAIN
HIGH
TEA
FUN FARMS
HAY RIDE
OR
DIE
FUN FATHOMS
SUB-POP
POP

CAPTAIN, I THINK WE HAVE *THOROUGHLY* TESTED THE TRANSPORTATION. I WANT TO MAKE A PERIMETER SWEEP OF THE AREA BEYOND THE TREES—

WHY NOT?

NO!

DANGER SHARKS

CUZ WE HAVEN'T EVEN TOUCHED THE BIGGEST WATER TRANSPORTATION YET.

CAPTAIN, HOW CAN I KEEP YOU SAFE IF I'M NOT ALLOWED TO DO MY JOB?

I'M SOR THERE'S THREAT FOR TO NEUTRA EGGLA.

JAVI, IS THERE A REASON YOU DON'T WANT US GOING BEYOND THE TREE LINE?

YEAH. IT'S BORING. THERE'S NOTHING THERE.

YEAH, EGGLA. YOU'RE STARTING TO BE AS DUMB AS THE REAL SNARKY SHARK.

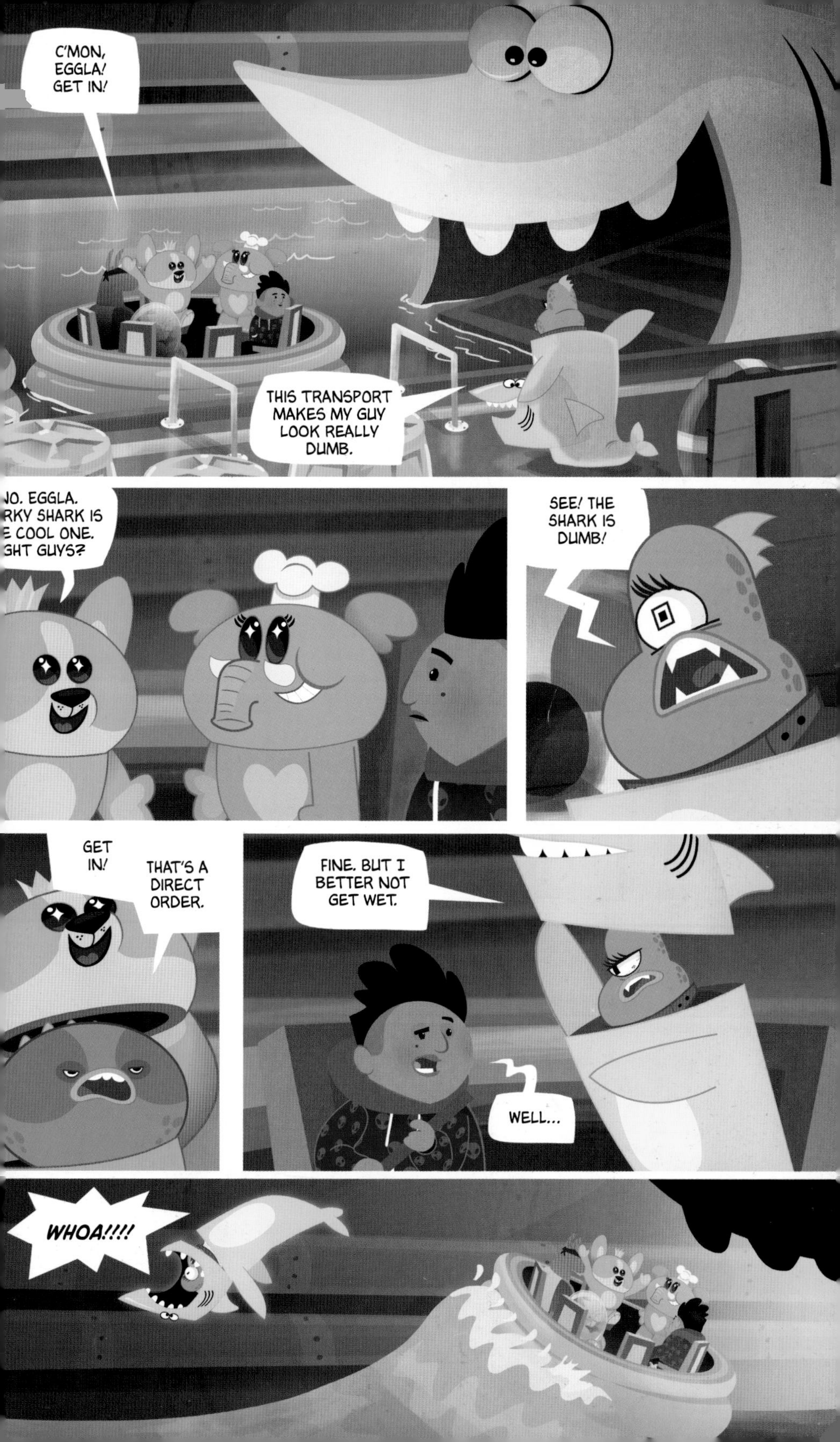
C'MON, EGGLA! GET IN!
THIS TRANSPORT MAKES MY GUY LOOK REALLY DUMB.
NO. EGGLA. RKY SHARK IS E COOL ONE. GHT GUYS?
SEE! THE SHARK IS DUMB!
GET IN!
THAT'S A DIRECT ORDER.
FINE. BUT I BETTER NOT GET WET.
WELL...
WHOA!!!!

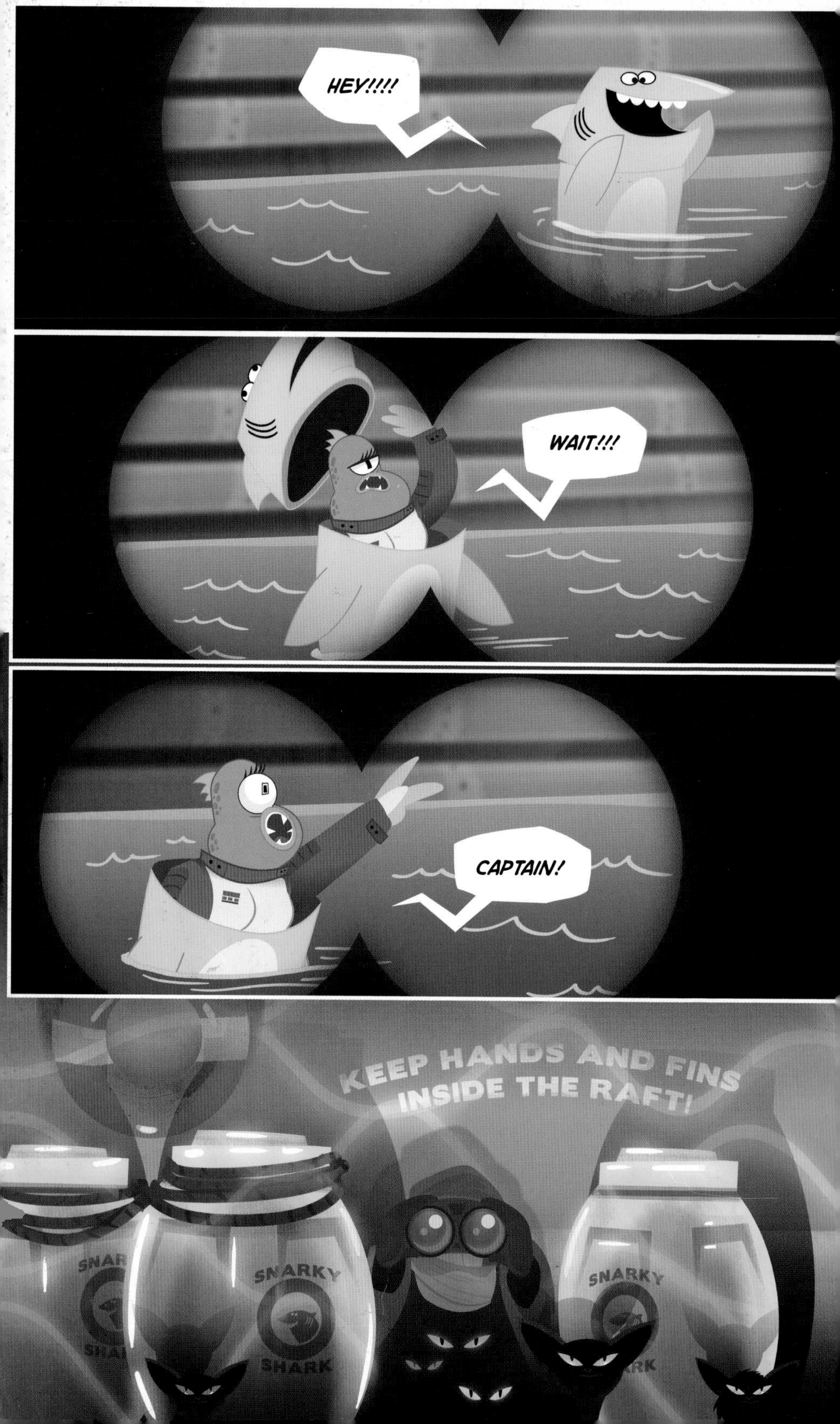
HEY!!!!
WAIT!!!
CAPTAIN!
KEEP HANDS AND FINS INSIDE THE RAFT!
SNARKY SHARK
SNARKY SHARK

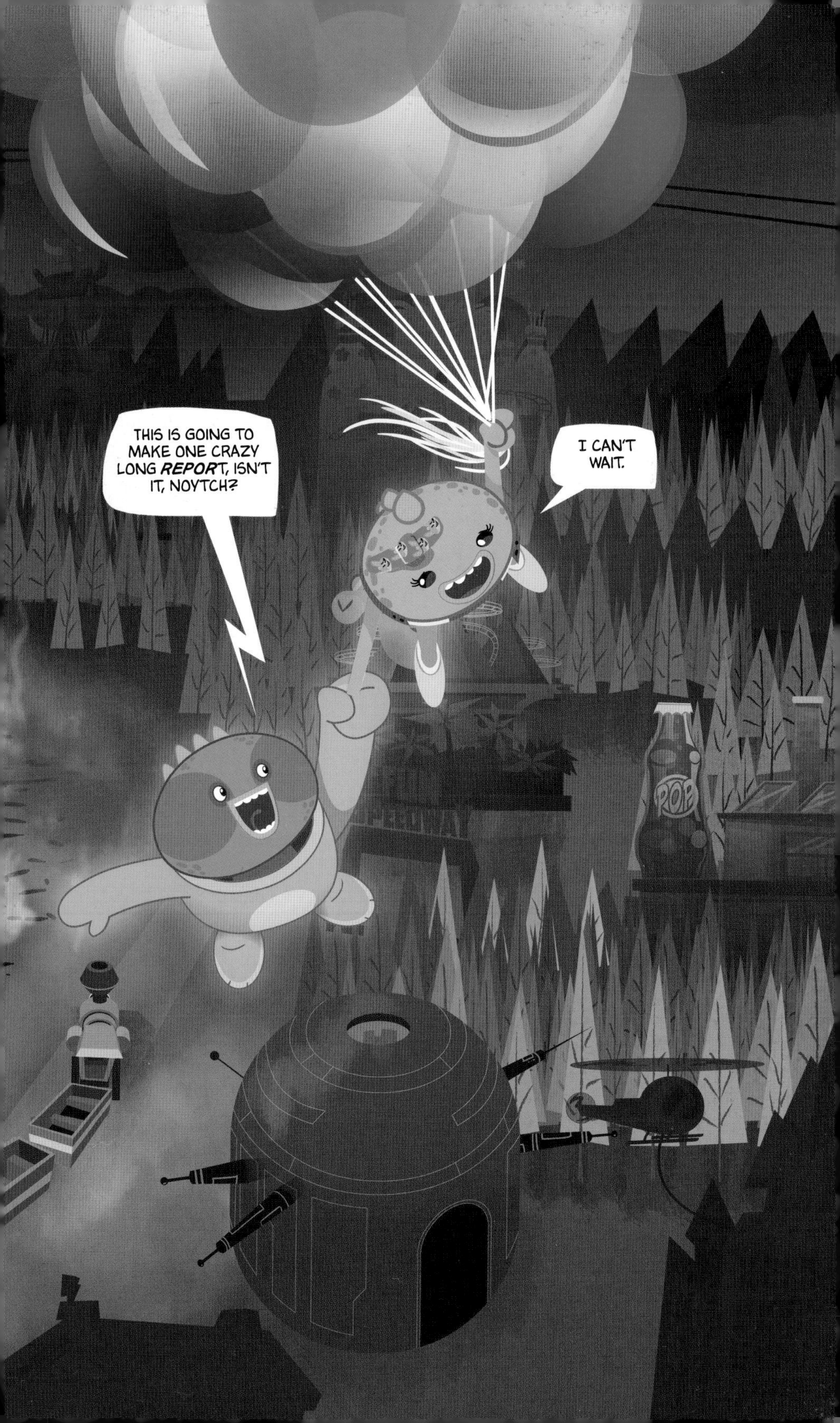
THIS IS GOING TO MAKE ONE CRAZY LONG *REPORT*, ISN'T IT, NOYTCH?
I CAN'T WAIT.
POP

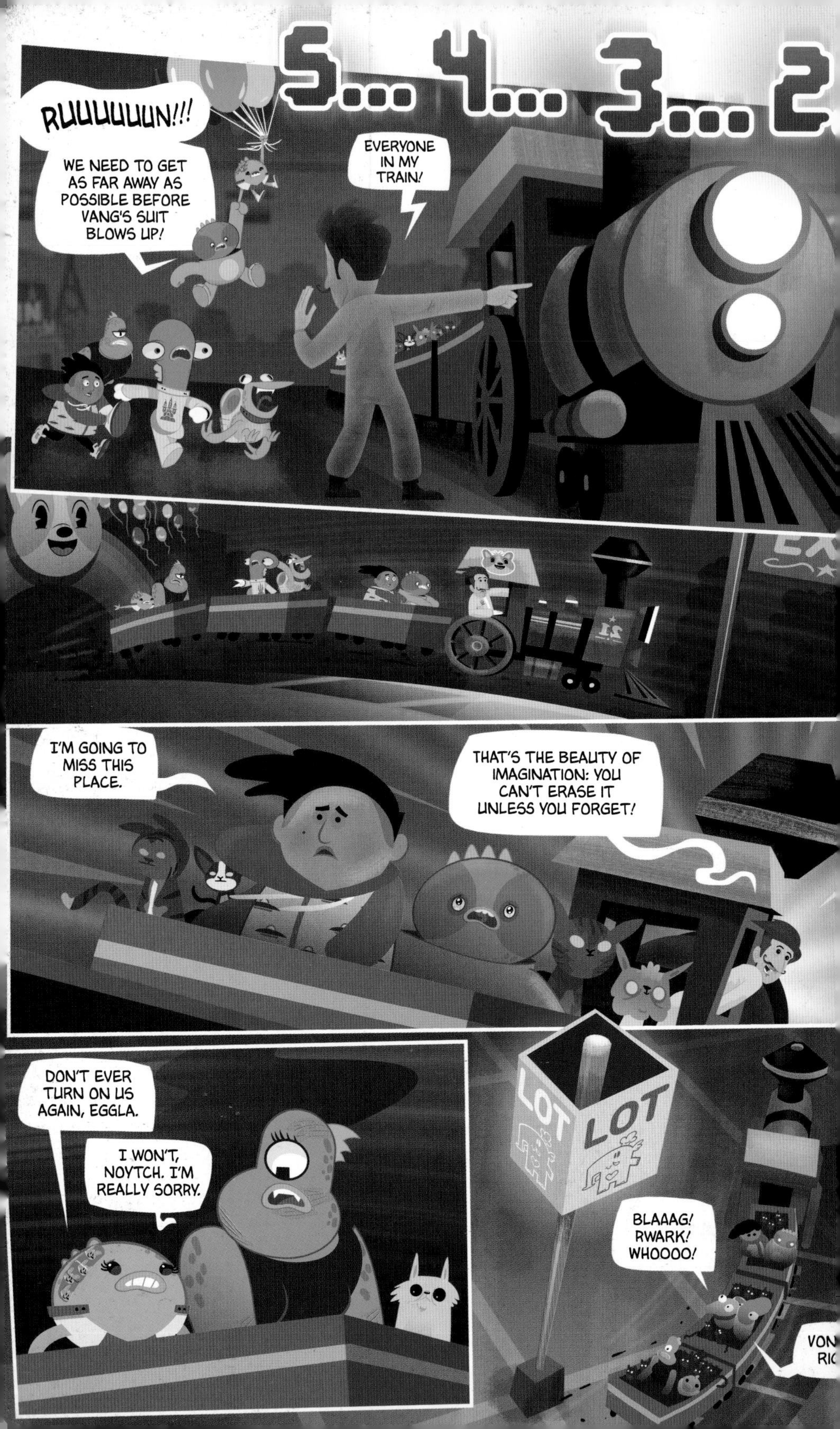
5... 4... 3... 2
RUUUUUUN!!!
WE NEED TO GET AS FAR AWAY AS POSSIBLE BEFORE VANG'S SUIT BLOWS UP!
EVERYONE IN MY TRAIN!
I'M GOING TO MISS THIS PLACE.
THAT'S THE BEAUTY OF IMAGINATION: YOU CAN'T ERASE IT UNLESS YOU FORGET!
DON'T EVER TURN ON US AGAIN, EGGLA.
I WON'T, NOYTCH. I'M REALLY SORRY.
LOT
LOT
BLAAAG! RWARK! WHOOOO!

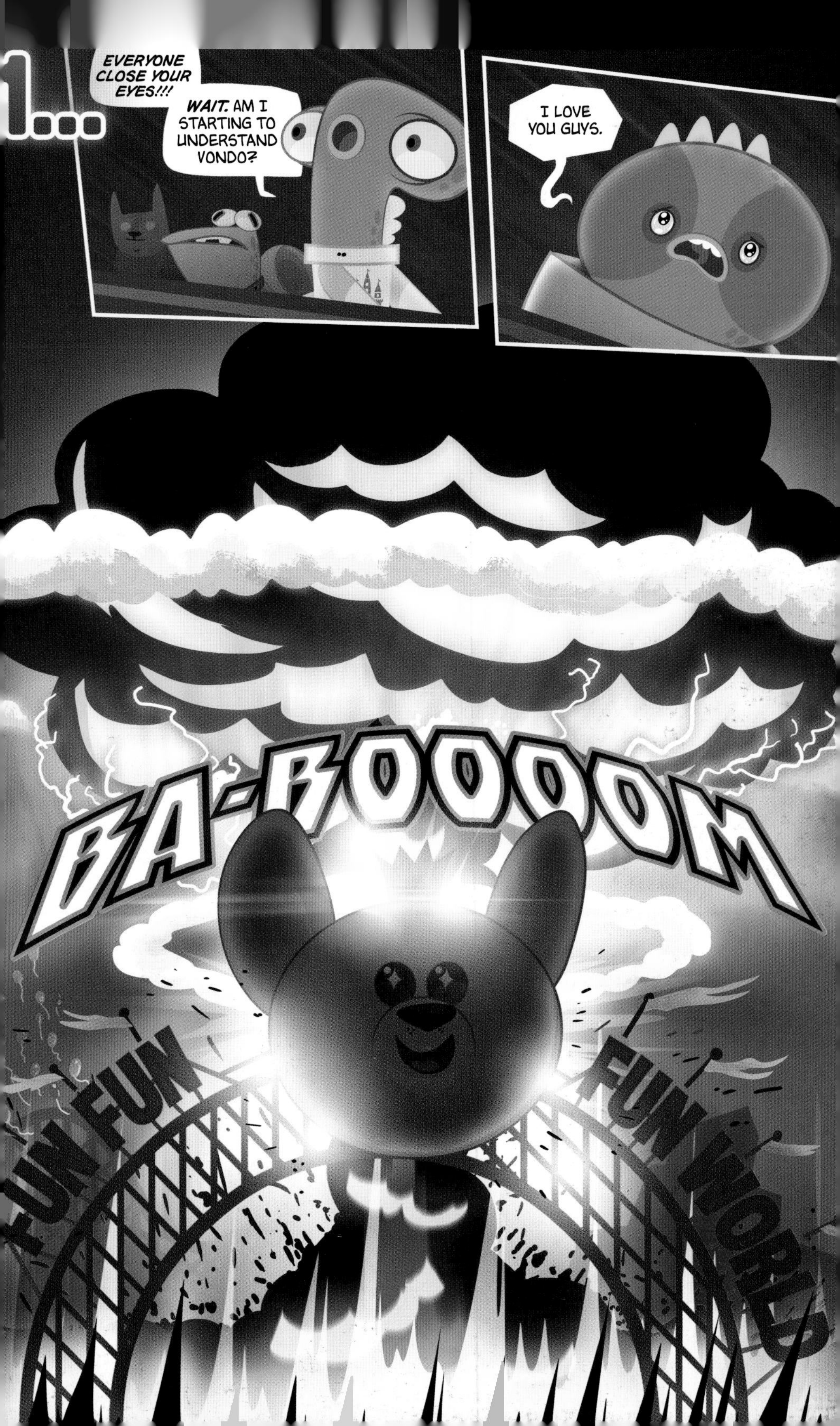
1...
EVERYONE CLOSE YOUR EYES!!!
WAIT. AM I STARTING TO UNDERSTAND VONDO?
I LOVE YOU GUYS.
BA-BOOOOM
FUN FUN
FUN WORLD

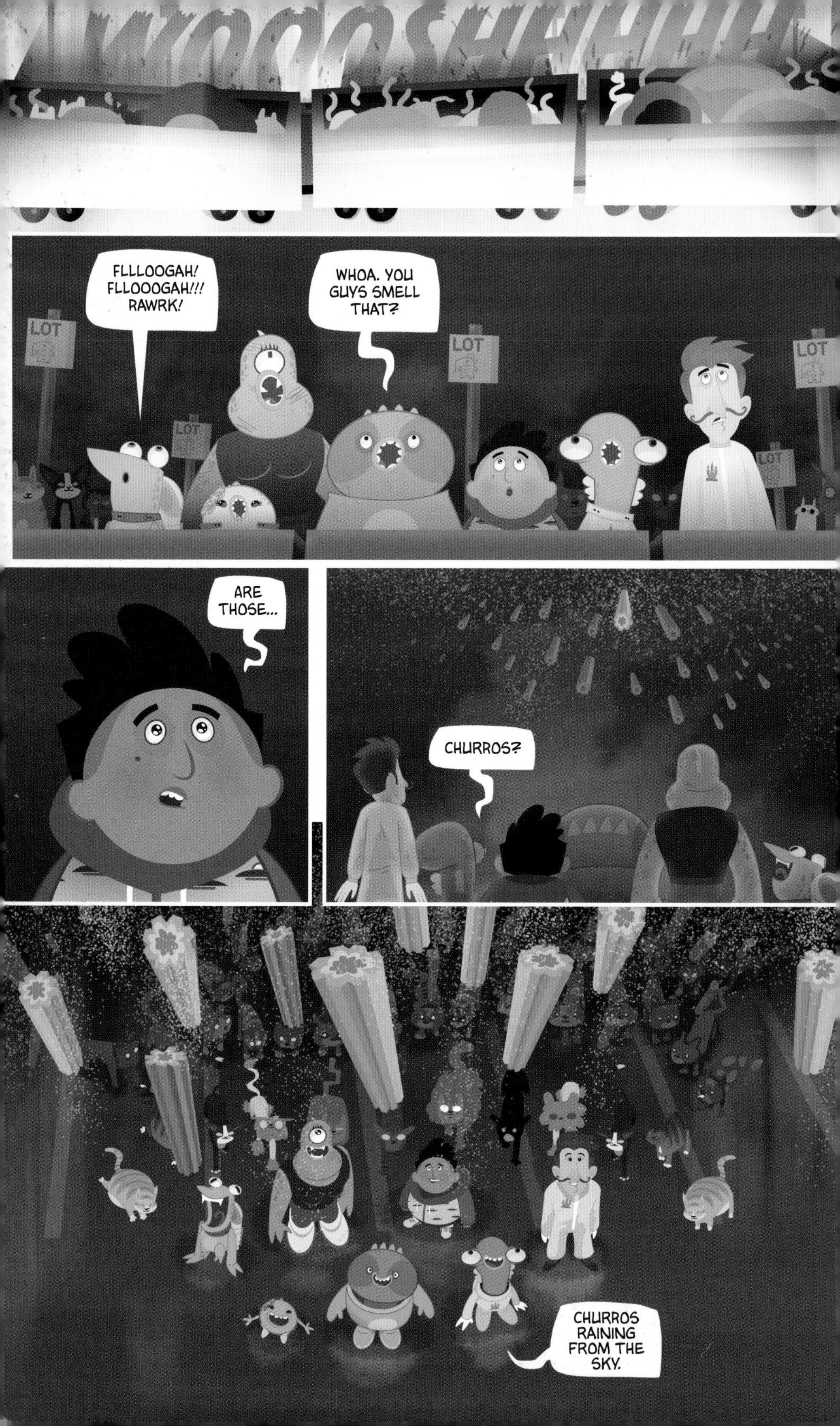
FLLLOOGAH! FLLOOOGAH!!! RAWRK!
WHOA. YOU GUYS SMELL THAT?
LOT
ARE THOSE...
CHURROS?
CHURROS RAINING FROM THE SKY.

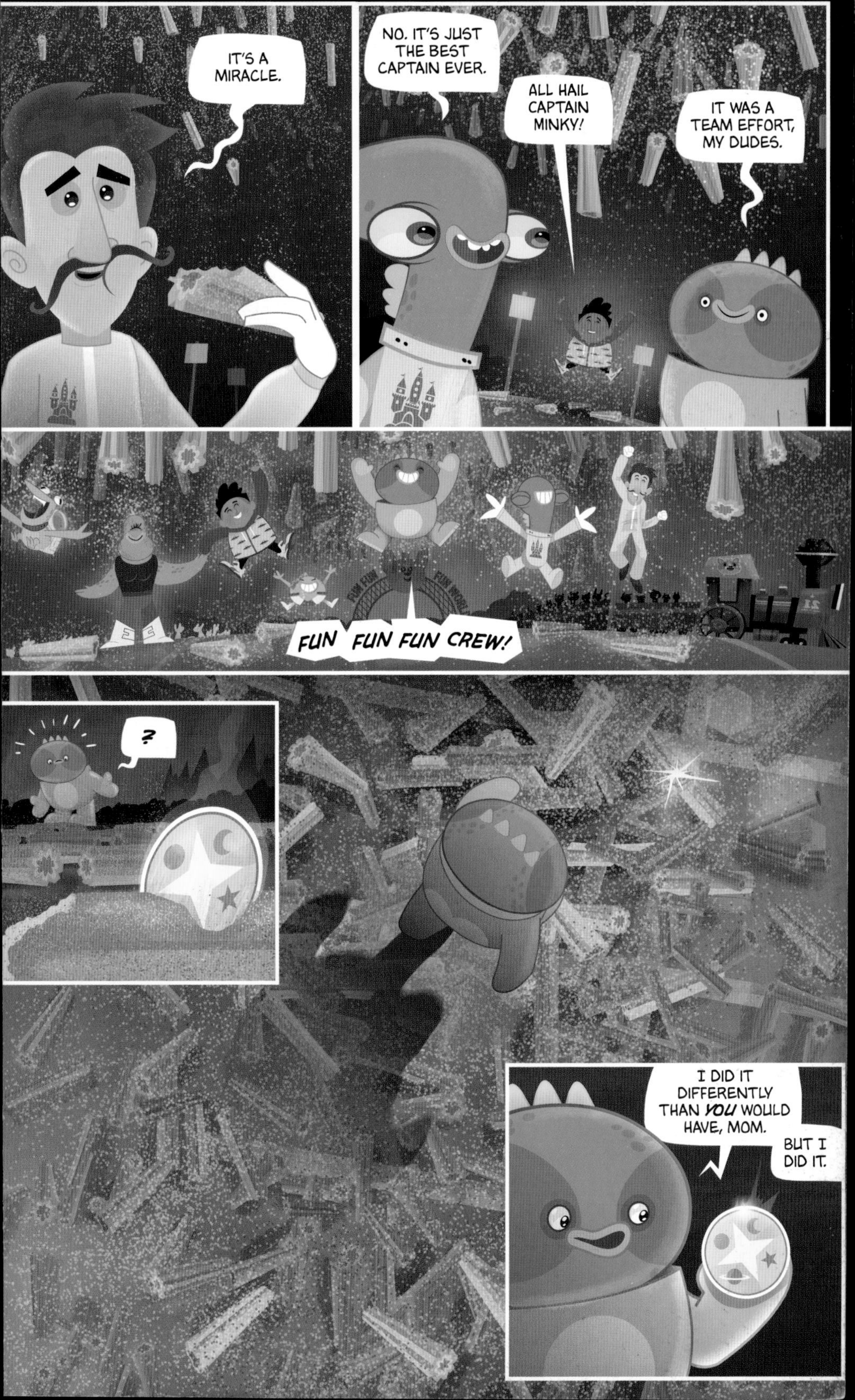
IT'S A MIRACLE.
NO. IT'S JUST THE BEST CAPTAIN EVER.
ALL HAIL CAPTAIN MINKY!
IT WAS A TEAM EFFORT, MY DUDES.
FUN FUN FUN CREW!
?
I DID IT DIFFERENTLY THAN *YOU* WOULD HAVE, MOM.
BUT I DID IT.

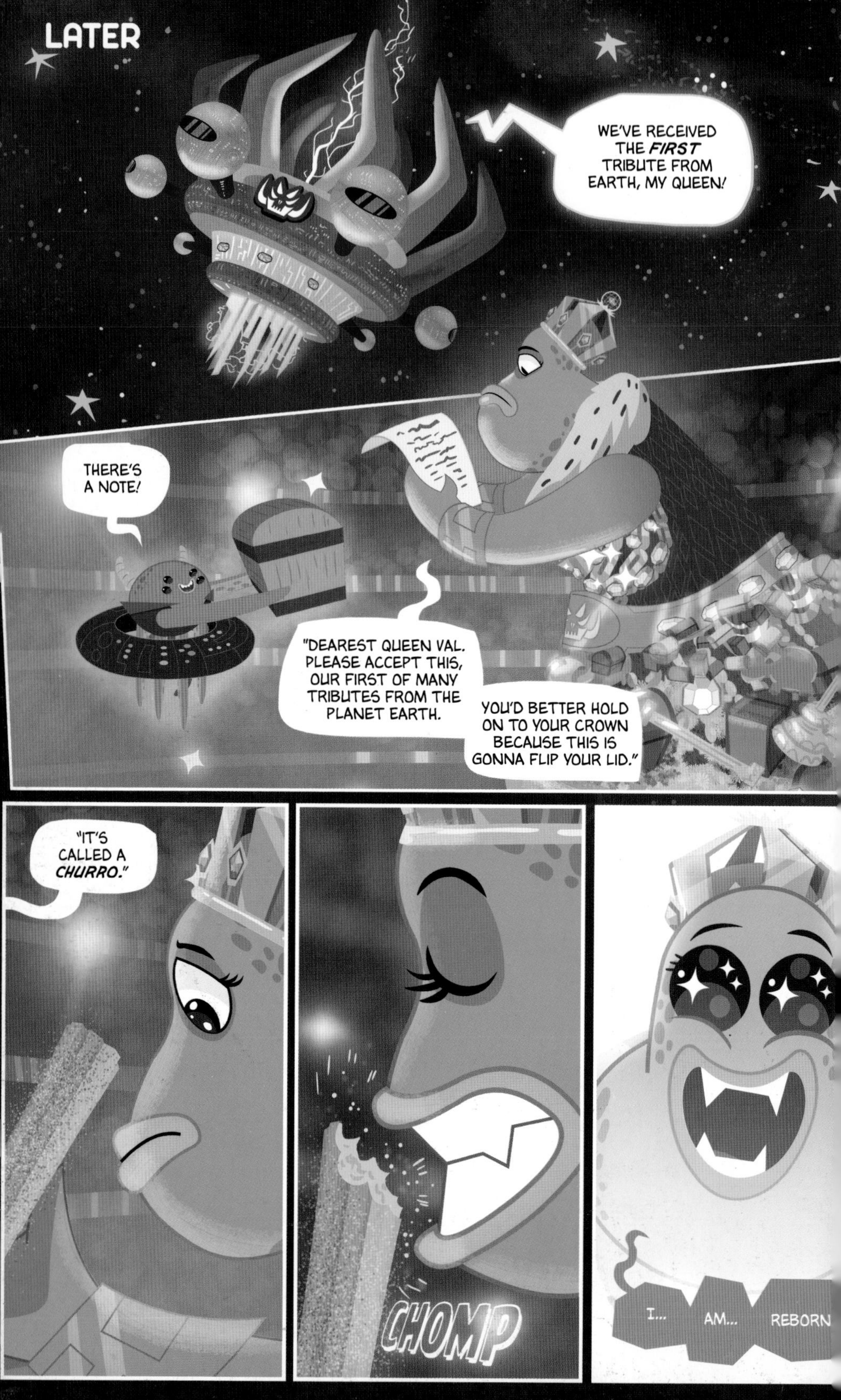
LATER
WE'VE RECEIVED THE FIRST TRIBUTE FROM EARTH, MY QUEEN!
THERE'S A NOTE!
"DEAREST QUEEN VAL. PLEASE ACCEPT THIS, OUR FIRST OF MANY TRIBUTES FROM THE PLANET EARTH.
YOU'D BETTER HOLD ON TO YOUR CROWN BECAUSE THIS IS GONNA FLIP YOUR LID."
"IT'S CALLED A CHURRO."
CHOMP
I... AM... REBORN

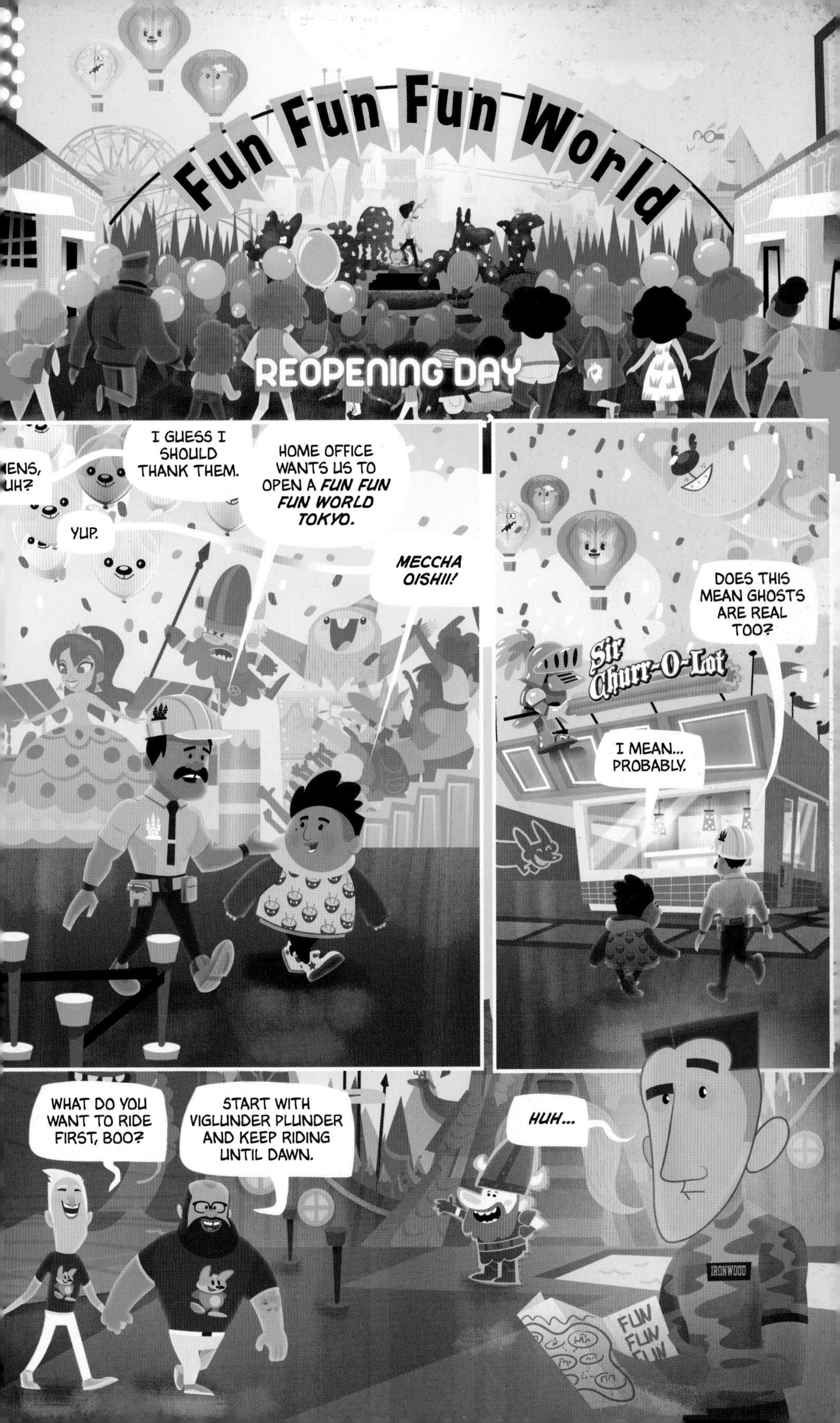
Fun Fun Fun World
REOPENING DAY
...ENS, ...UH?
I GUESS I SHOULD THANK THEM.
YUP.
HOME OFFICE WANTS US TO OPEN A *FUN FUN FUN WORLD TOKYO.*
MECCHA OISHII!
Sir Churr-O-Lot
DOES THIS MEAN GHOSTS ARE REAL TOO?
I MEAN... PROBABLY.
WHAT DO YOU WANT TO RIDE FIRST, BOO?
START WITH VIGLUNDER PLUNDER AND KEEP RIDING UNTIL DAWN.
HUH...
IRONWOOD
FUN FUN

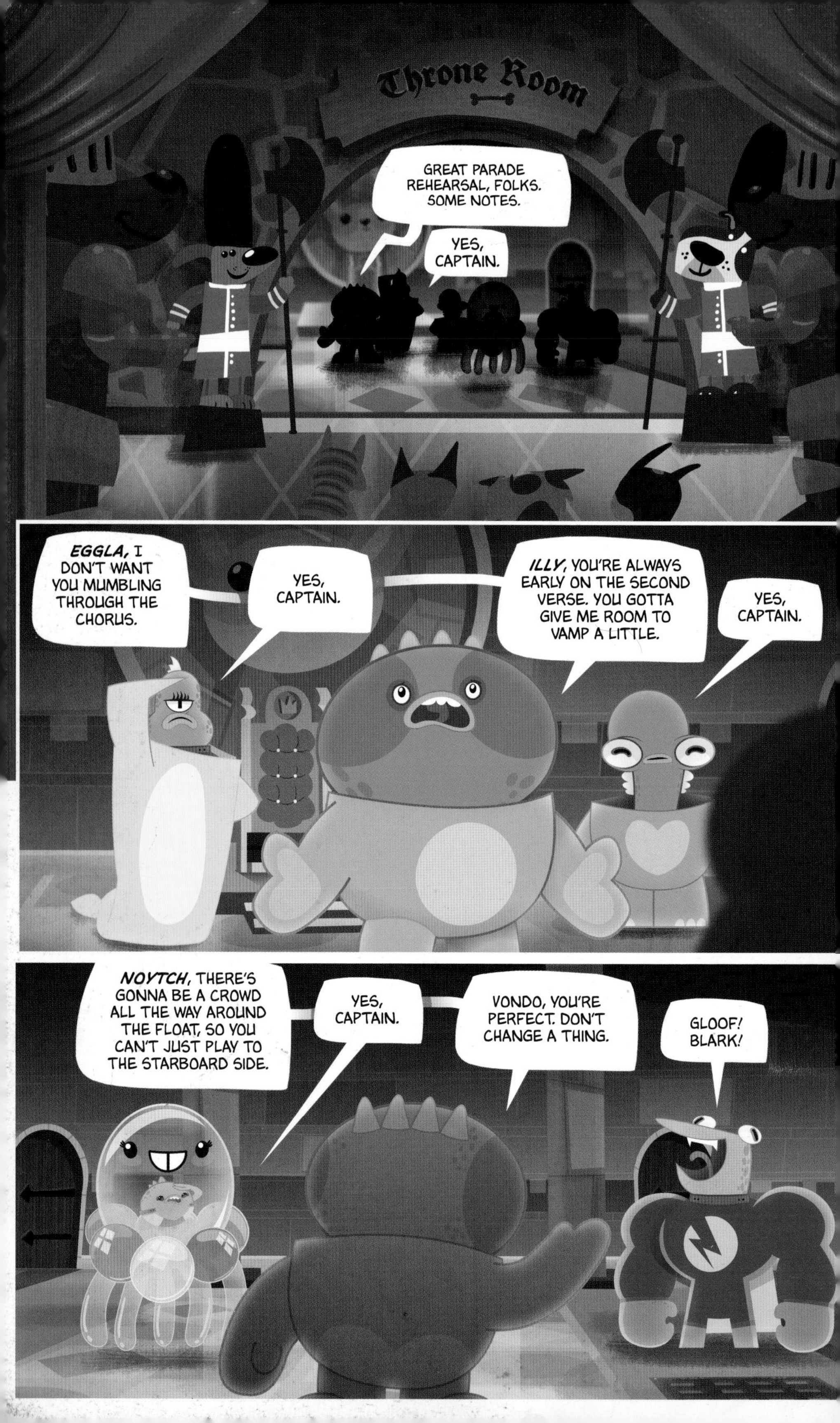
Throne Room
GREAT PARADE REHEARSAL, FOLKS. SOME NOTES.
YES, CAPTAIN.
EGGLA, I DON'T WANT YOU MUMBLING THROUGH THE CHORUS.
YES, CAPTAIN.
ILLY, YOU'RE ALWAYS EARLY ON THE SECOND VERSE. YOU GOTTA GIVE ME ROOM TO VAMP A LITTLE.
YES, CAPTAIN.
NOYTCH, THERE'S GONNA BE A CROWD ALL THE WAY AROUND THE FLOAT, SO YOU CAN'T JUST PLAY TO THE STARBOARD SIDE.
YES, CAPTAIN.
VONDO, YOU'RE PERFECT. DON'T CHANGE A THING.
GLOOF! BLARK!

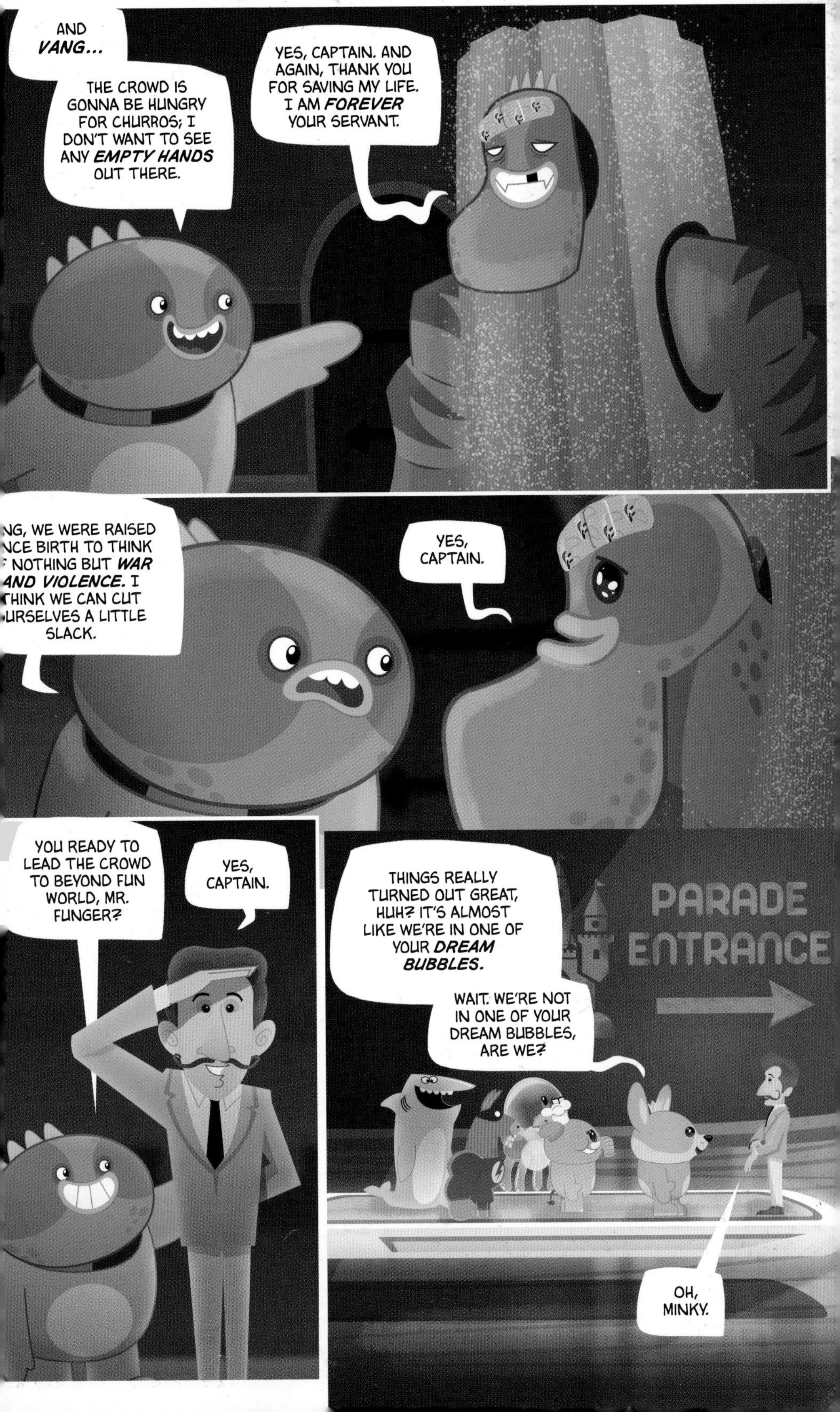
AND *VANG...*
THE CROWD IS GONNA BE HUNGRY FOR CHURROS; I DON'T WANT TO SEE ANY *EMPTY HANDS* OUT THERE.
YES, CAPTAIN. AND AGAIN, THANK YOU FOR SAVING MY LIFE. I AM *FOREVER* YOUR SERVANT.
NG, WE WERE RAISED NCE BIRTH TO THINK NOTHING BUT *WAR AND VIOLENCE.* I THINK WE CAN CUT URSELVES A LITTLE SLACK.
YES, CAPTAIN.
YOU READY TO LEAD THE CROWD TO BEYOND FUN WORLD, MR. FUNGER?
YES, CAPTAIN.
THINGS REALLY TURNED OUT GREAT, HUH? IT'S ALMOST LIKE WE'RE IN ONE OF YOUR *DREAM BUBBLES.*
PARADE ENTRANCE
WAIT. WE'RE NOT IN ONE OF YOUR DREAM BUBBLES, ARE WE?
OH, MINKY.

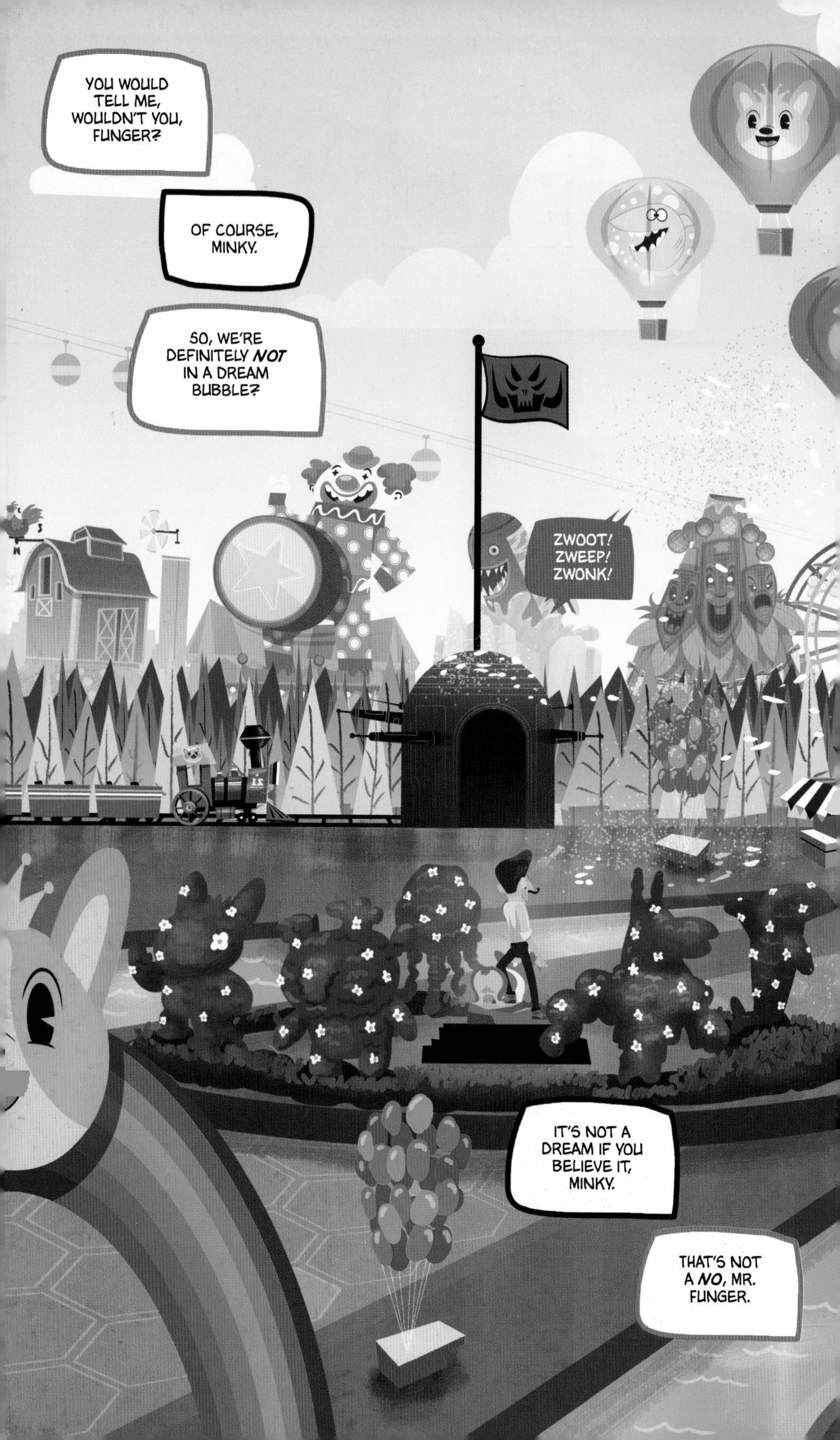
YOU WOULD TELL ME, WOULDN'T YOU, FUNGER?
OF COURSE, MINKY.
SO, WE'RE DEFINITELY *NOT* IN A DREAM BUBBLE?
ZWOOT! ZWEEP! ZWONK!
IT'S NOT A DREAM IF YOU BELIEVE IT, MINKY.
THAT'S NOT A *NO*, MR. FUNGER.

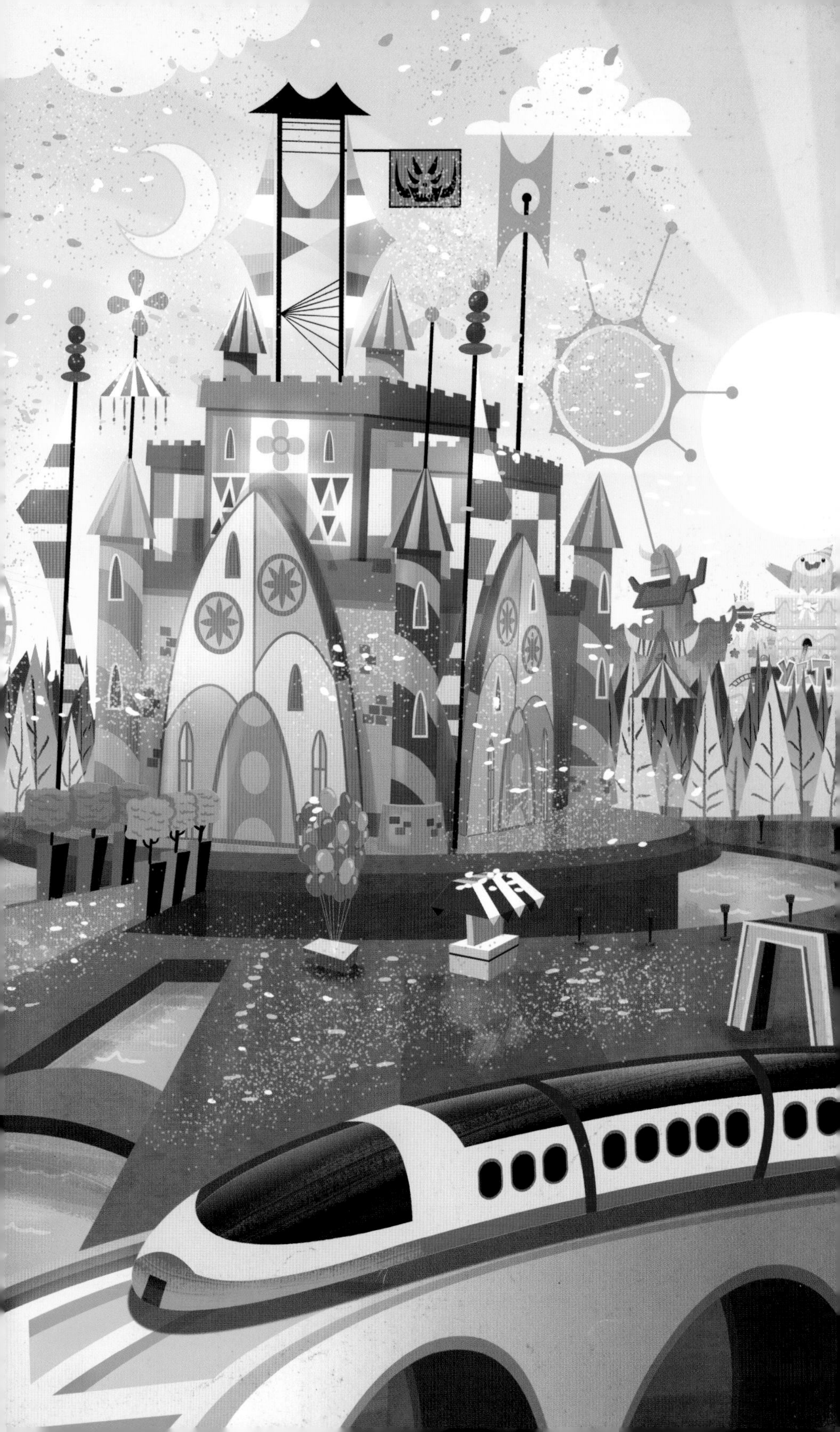

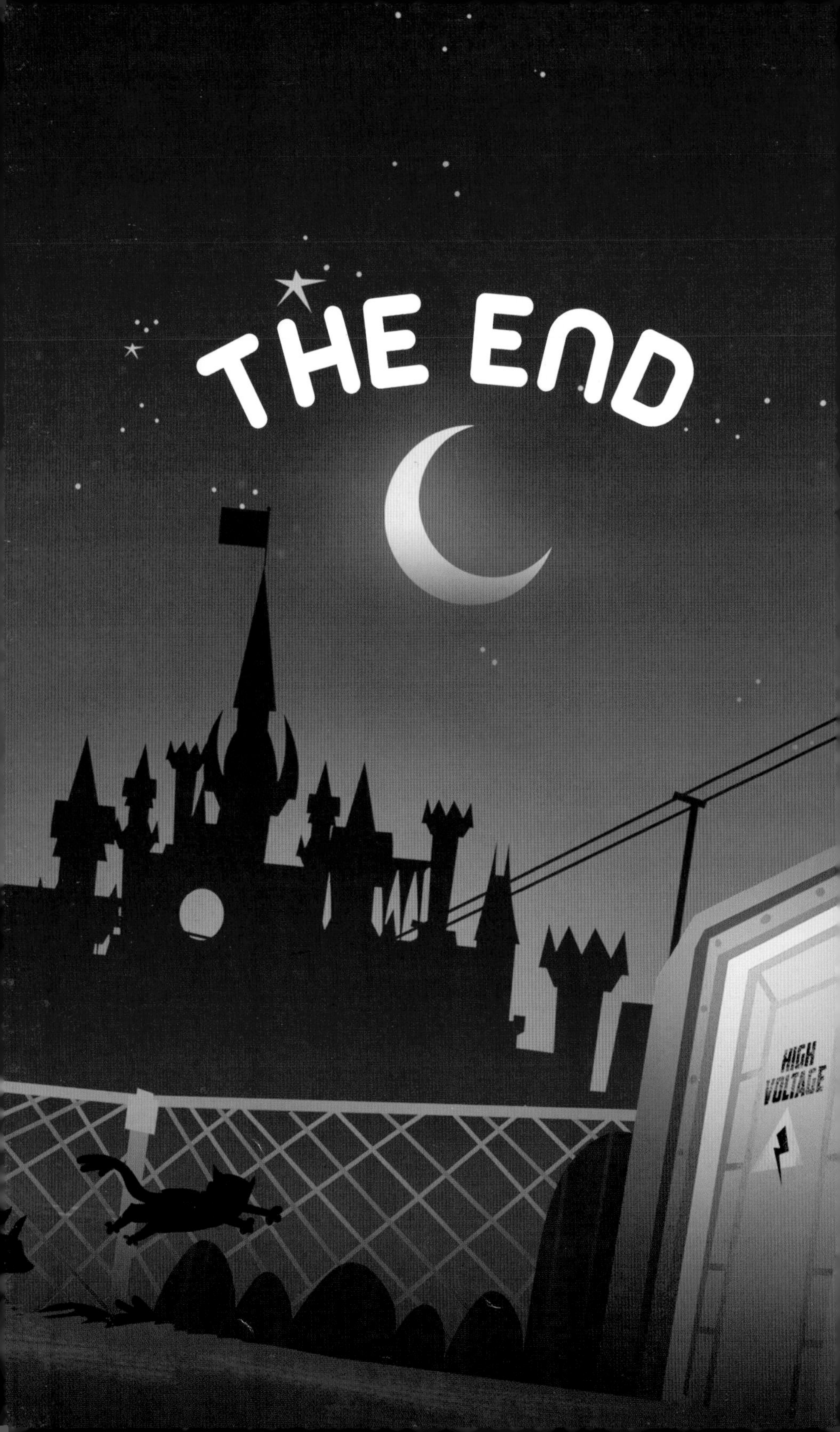
THE END
HIGH VOLTAGE

SCI-FU: KICK IT OFF
by Yehudi Mercado is available now from Oni Press!

SCI-FU: IT TAKES 2
coming soon!

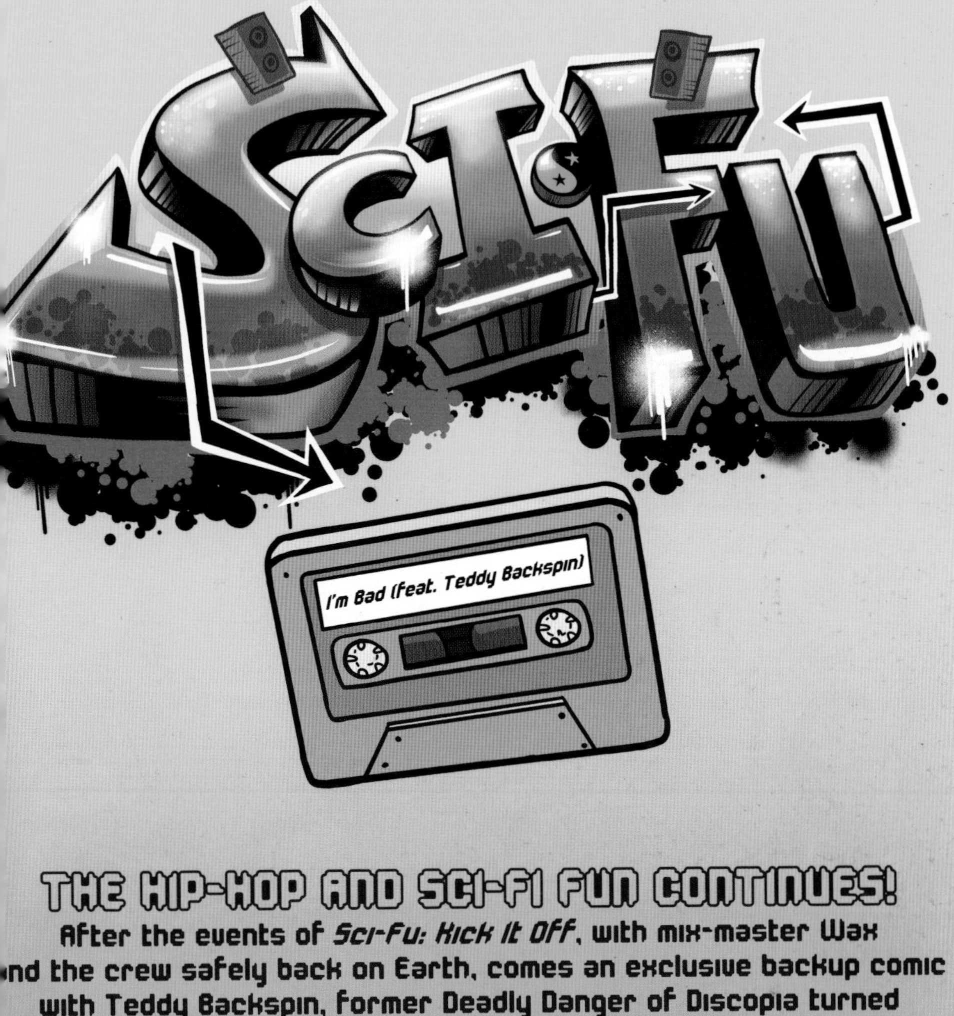
SCI-FU
I'm Bad (Feat. Teddy Backspin)

THE HIP-HOP AND SCI-FI FUN CONTINUES!

After the events of *Sci-Fu: Kick It Off*, with mix-master Wax and the crew safely back on Earth, comes an exclusive backup comic with Teddy Backspin, former Deadly Danger of Discopia turned Wax's loyal companion. The team thought the robot trouble was over, but Discopia's threats now have a cosmic bridge to Brooklyn.

Story and Art by Yehudi Mercado
Color Flatting by Dave Wheeler

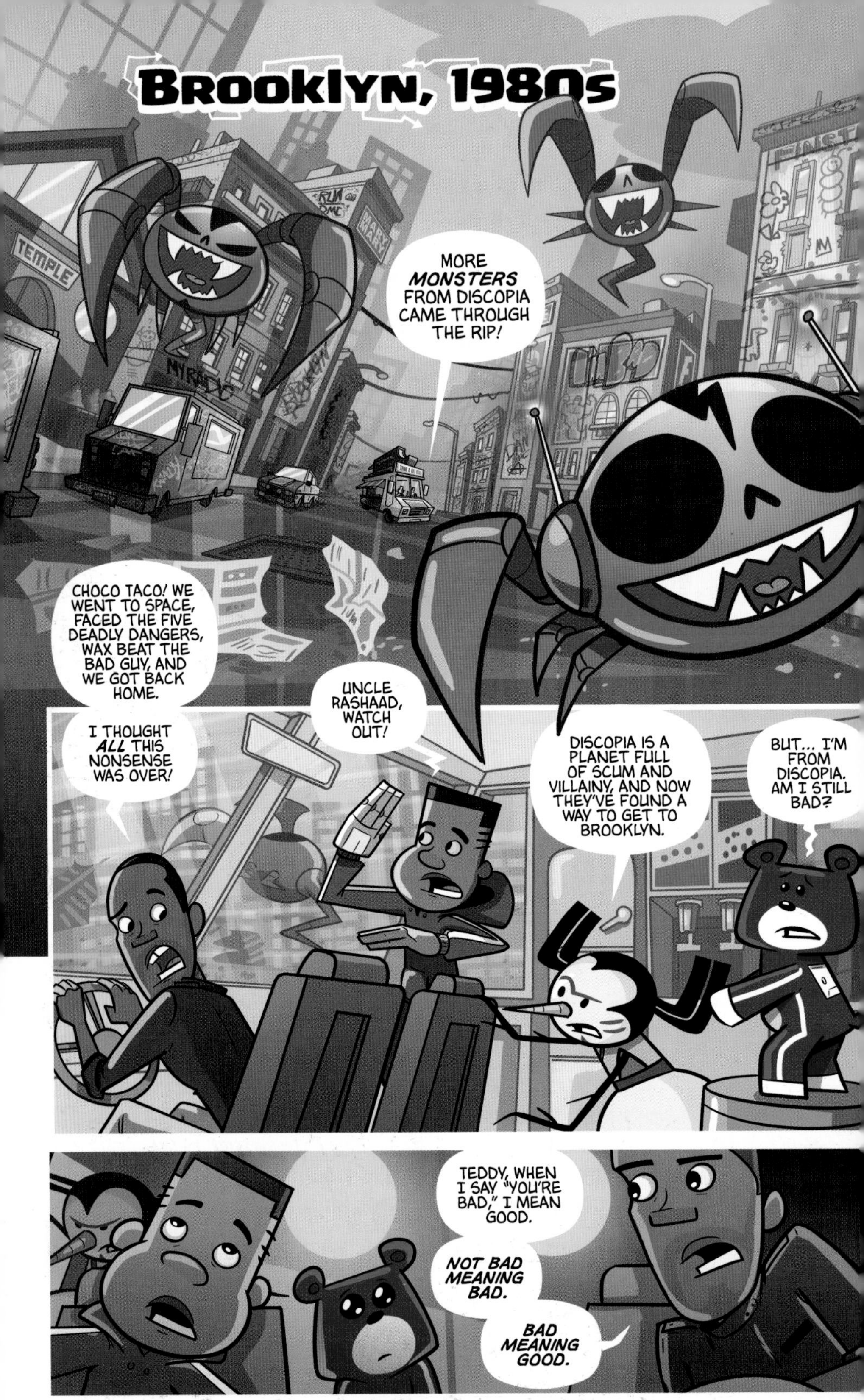

Brooklyn, 1980s
MORE MONSTERS FROM DISCOPIA CAME THROUGH THE RIP!
CHOCO TACO! WE WENT TO SPACE, FACED THE FIVE DEADLY DANGERS, WAX BEAT THE BAD GUY, AND WE GOT BACK HOME.
I THOUGHT ALL THIS NONSENSE WAS OVER!
UNCLE RASHAAD, WATCH OUT!
DISCOPIA IS A PLANET FULL OF SCUM AND VILLAINY, AND NOW THEY'VE FOUND A WAY TO GET TO BROOKLYN.
BUT... I'M FROM DISCOPIA. AM I STILL BAD?
TEDDY, WHEN I SAY "YOU'RE BAD," I MEAN GOOD.
NOT BAD MEANING BAD.
BAD MEANING GOOD.

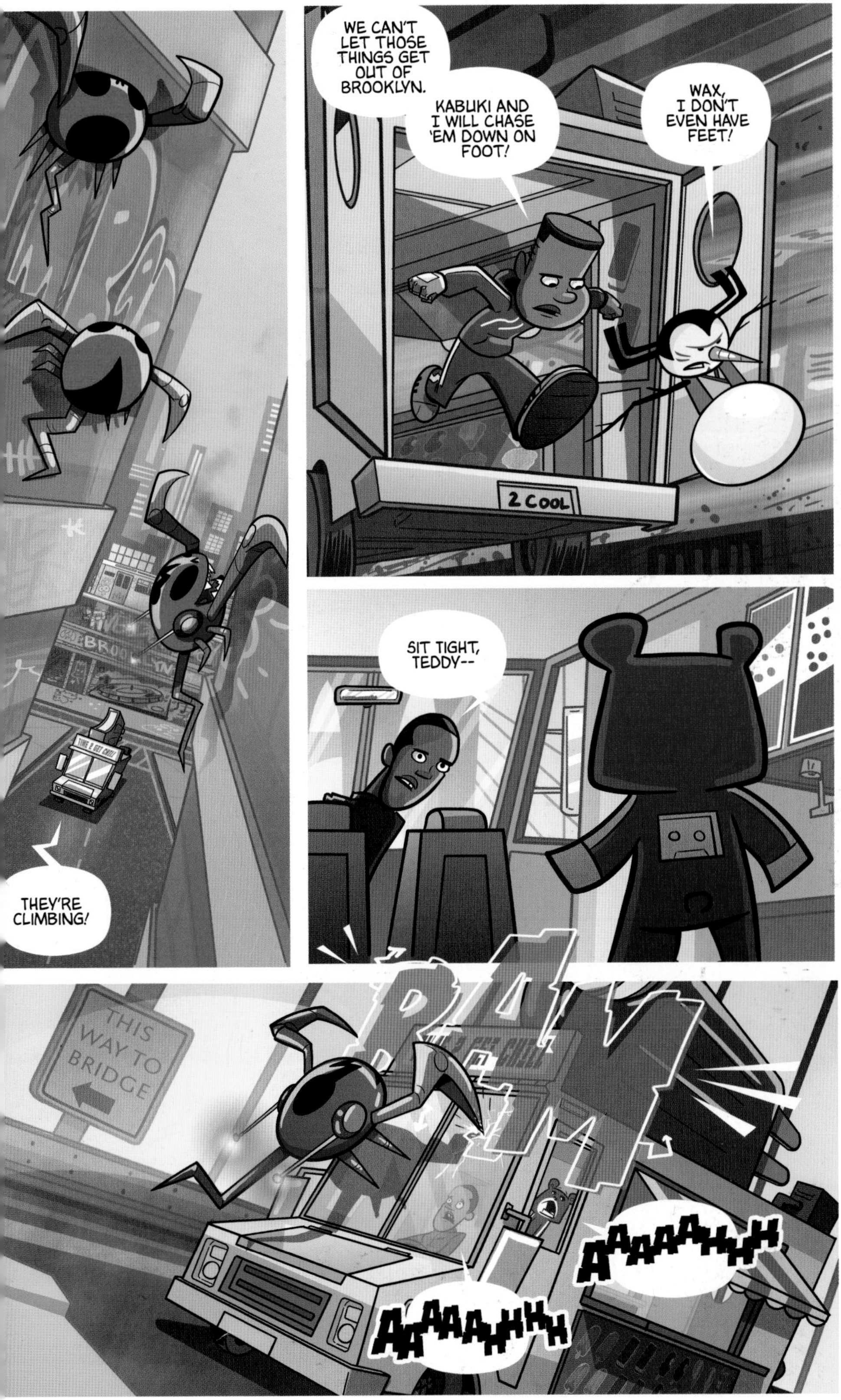
THEY'RE CLIMBING!
WE CAN'T LET THOSE THINGS GET OUT OF BROOKLYN.
KABUKI AND I WILL CHASE 'EM DOWN ON FOOT!
WAX, I DON'T EVEN HAVE FEET!
2 COOL
SIT TIGHT, TEDDY--
THIS WAY TO BRIDGE
RAM
AAAAAAHHHH
AAAAAAHHHH

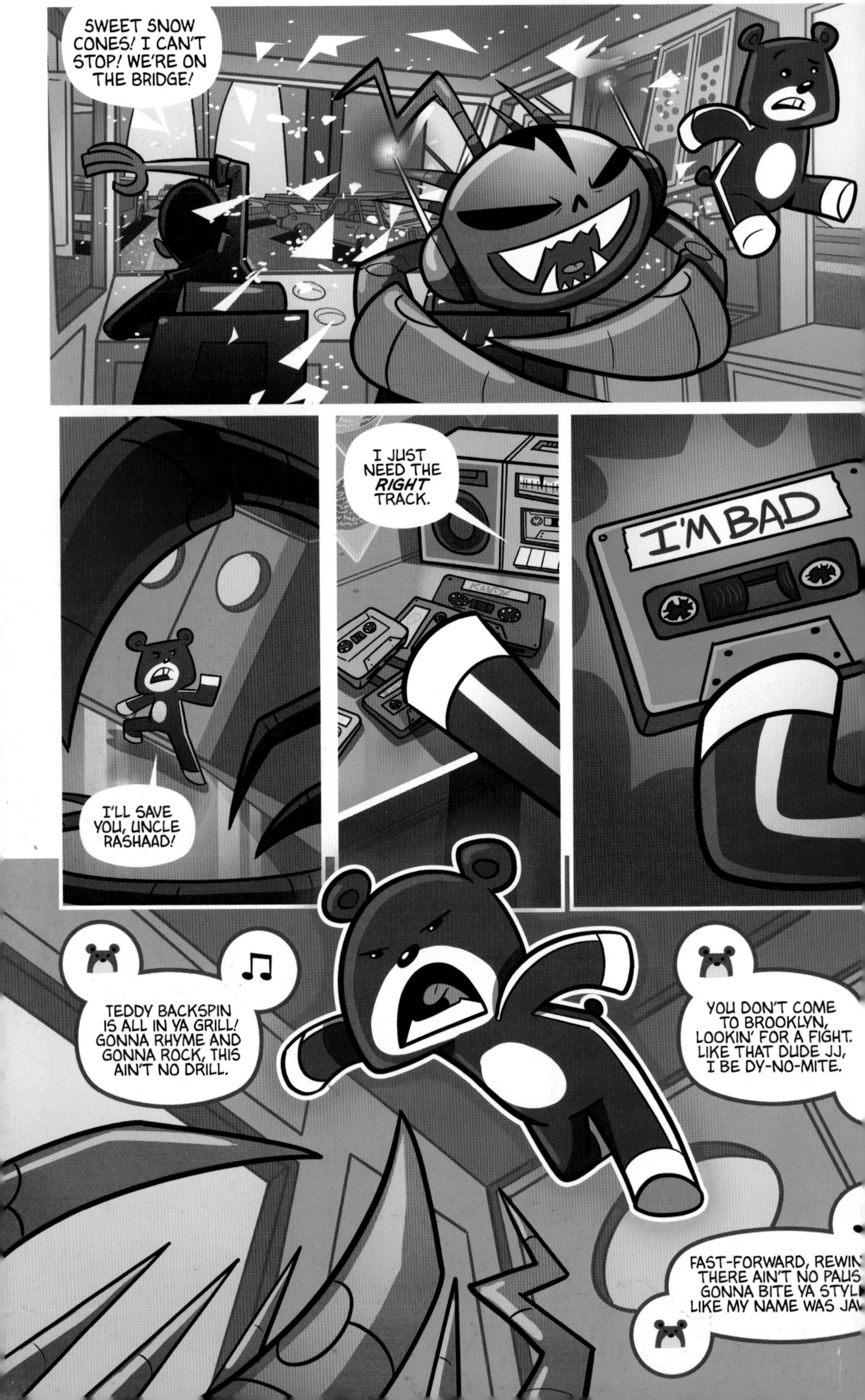

SWEET SNOW CONES! I CAN'T STOP! WE'RE ON THE BRIDGE!
I'LL SAVE YOU, UNCLE RASHAAD!
I JUST NEED THE *RIGHT* TRACK.
I'M BAD
TEDDY BACKSPIN IS ALL IN YA GRILL! GONNA RHYME AND GONNA ROCK, THIS AIN'T NO DRILL.
YOU DON'T COME TO BROOKLYN, LOOKIN' FOR A FIGHT. LIKE THAT DUDE JJ, I BE DY-NO-MITE.
FAST-FORWARD, REWIN
THERE AIN'T NO PAUS
GONNA BITE YA STYL
LIKE MY NAME WAS JA

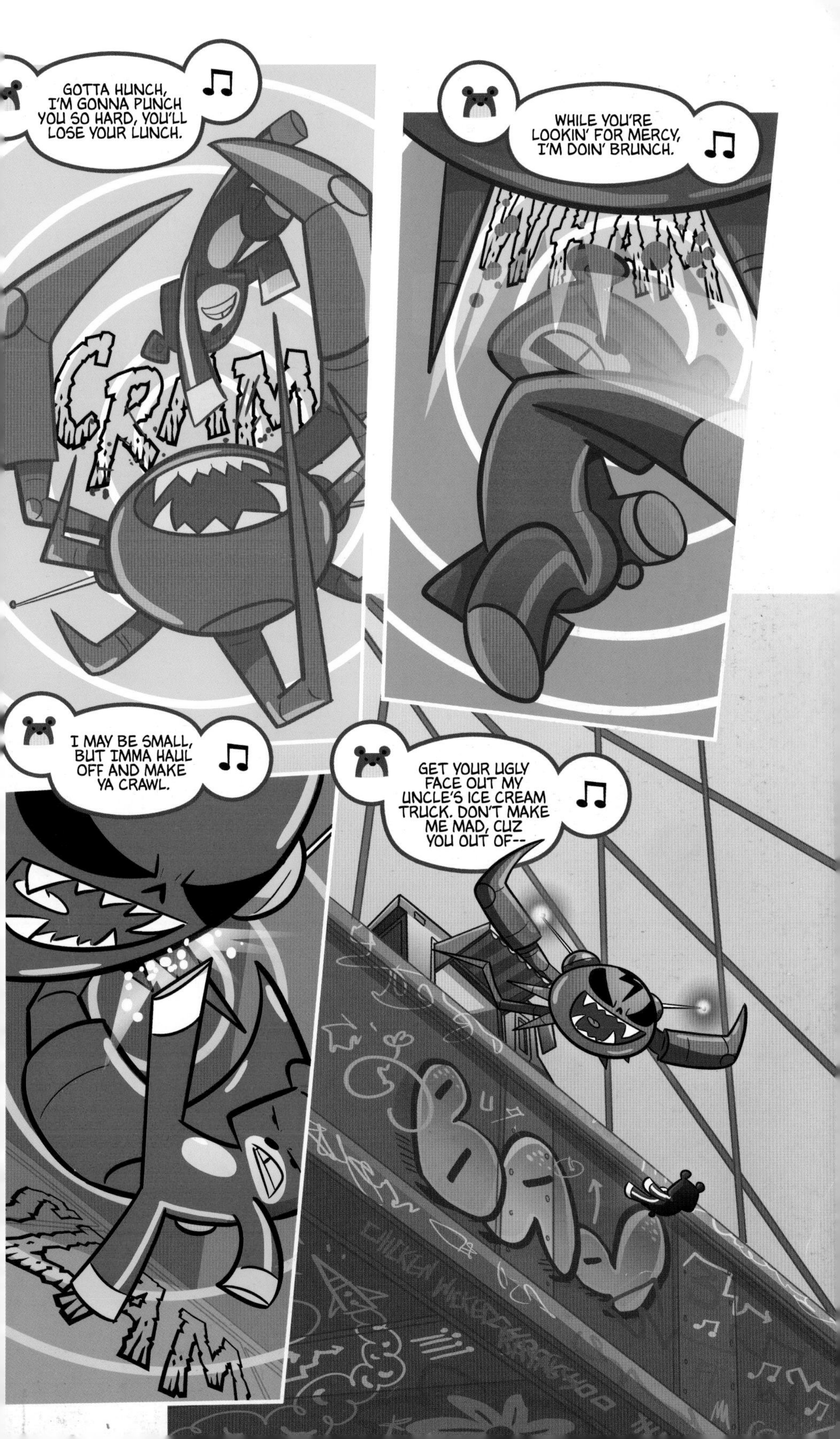
GOTTA HUNCH, I'M GONNA PUNCH YOU SO HARD, YOU'LL LOSE YOUR LUNCH. ♫
WHILE YOU'RE LOOKIN' FOR MERCY, I'M DOIN' BRUNCH. ♫
I MAY BE SMALL, BUT IMMA HAUL OFF AND MAKE YA CRAWL. ♫
GET YOUR UGLY FACE OUT MY UNCLE'S ICE CREAM TRUCK. DON'T MAKE ME MAD, CUZ YOU OUT OF-- ♫

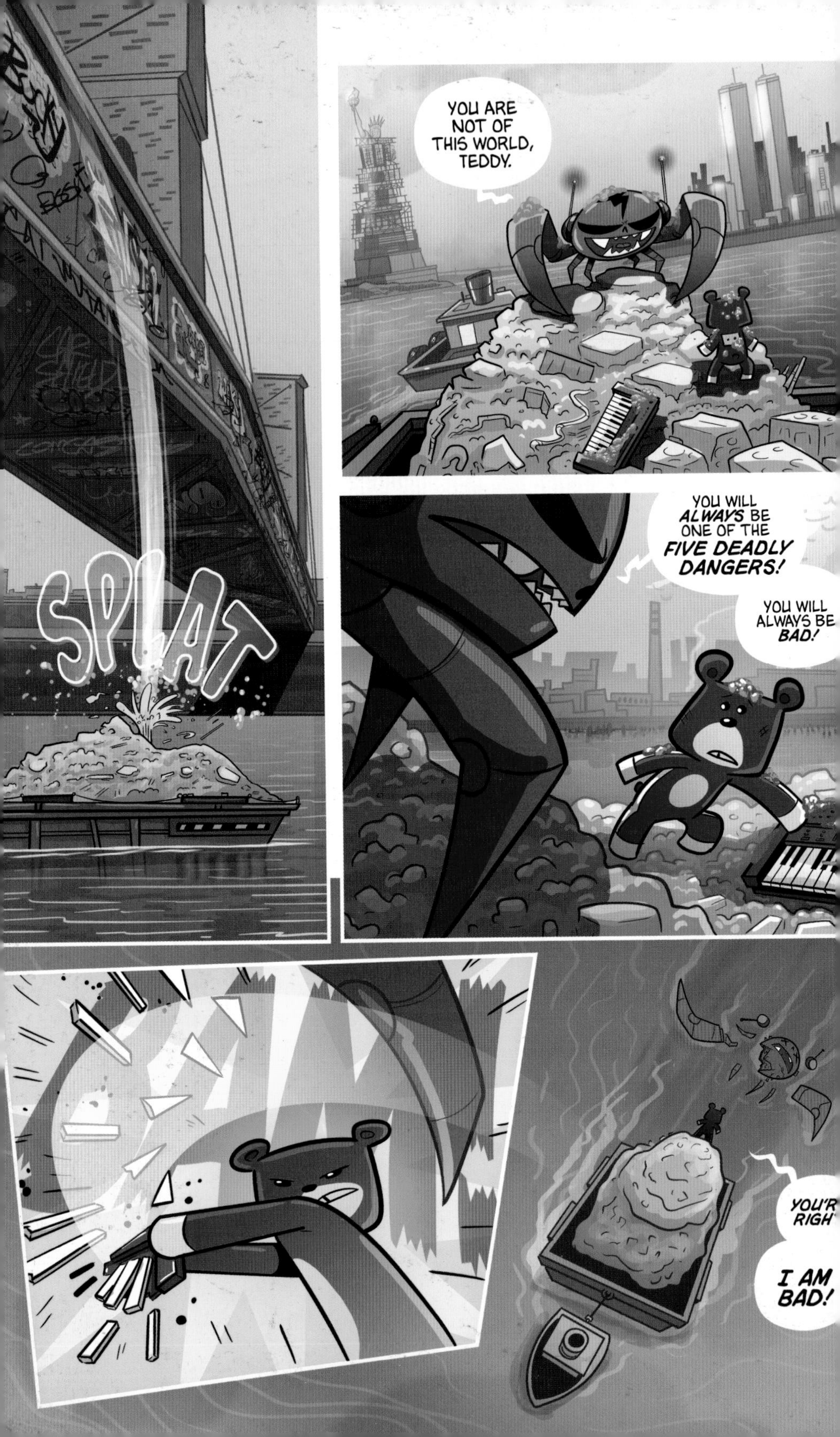
SPLAT
YOU ARE NOT OF THIS WORLD, TEDDY.
YOU WILL ALWAYS BE ONE OF THE FIVE DEADLY DANGERS!
YOU WILL ALWAYS BE BAD!
YOU'R RIGH
I AM BAD!

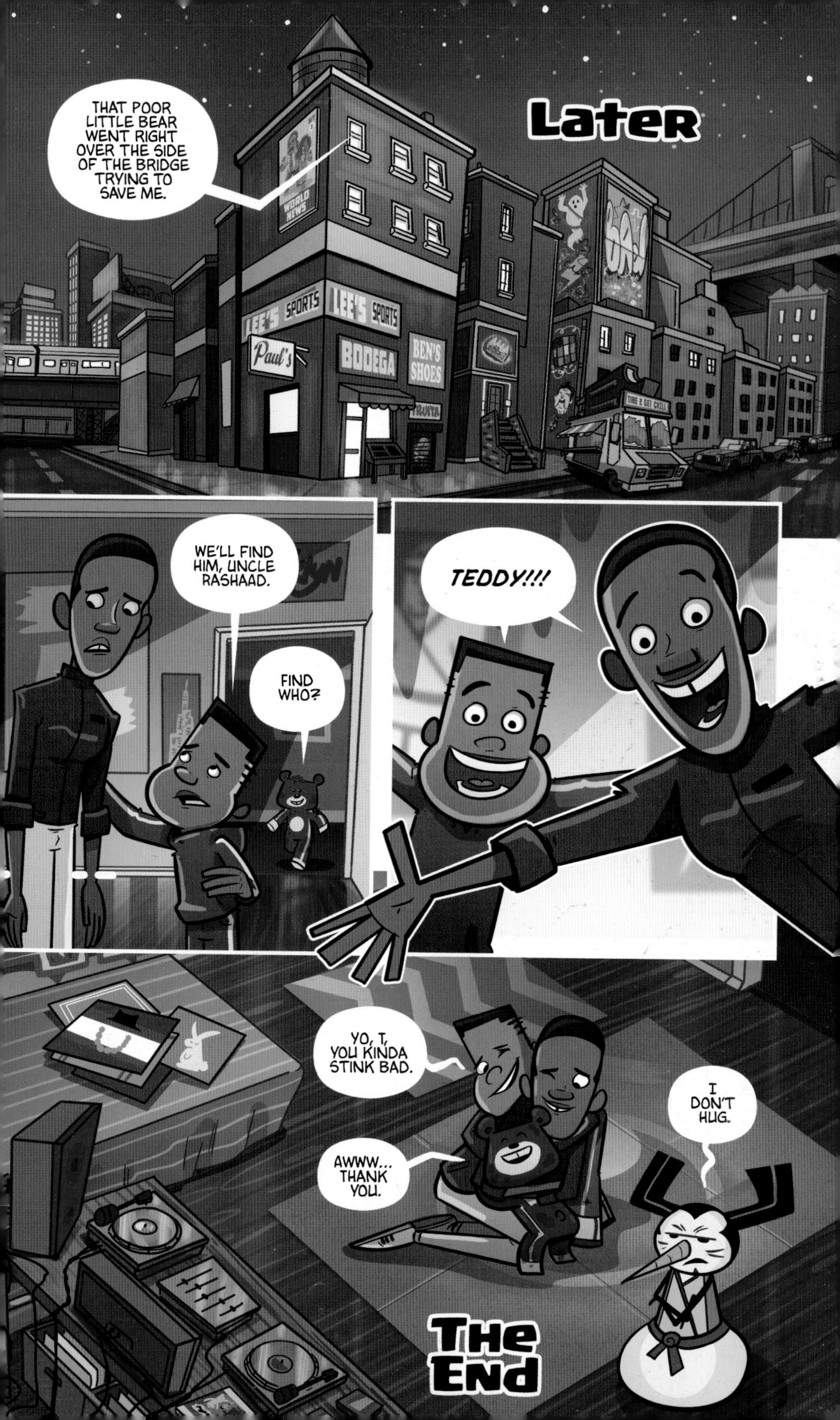
THAT POOR LITTLE BEAR WENT RIGHT OVER THE SIDE OF THE BRIDGE TRYING TO SAVE ME.
Later
LEE'S SPORTS
LEE'S SPORTS
Paul's
BODEGA
BEN'S SHOES
WORLD NEWS
TIME 2 GET CHILL
WE'LL FIND HIM, UNCLE RASHAAD.
FIND WHO?
TEDDY!!!
YO, T, YOU KINDA STINK BAD.
AWWW... THANK YOU.
I DON'T HUG.
THE END

CONCEPT ART

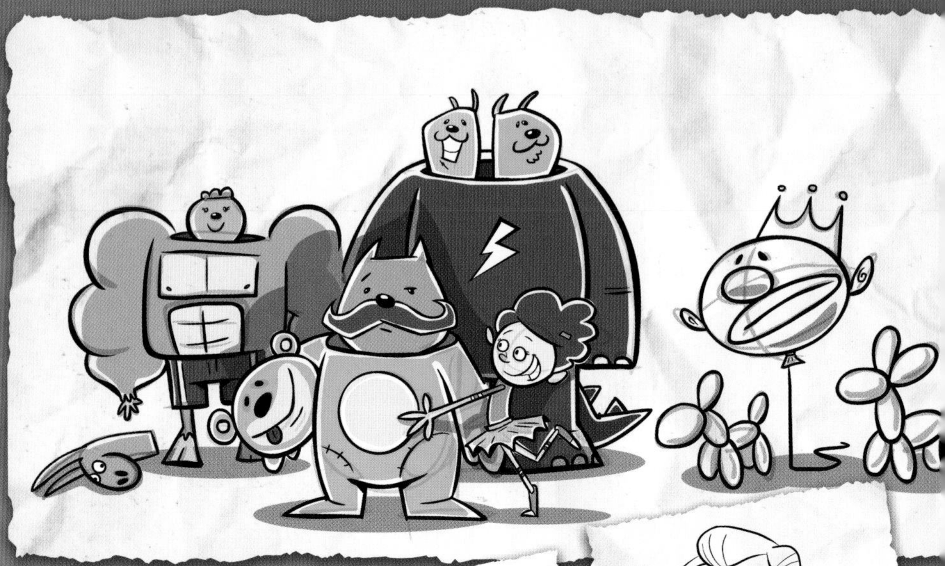

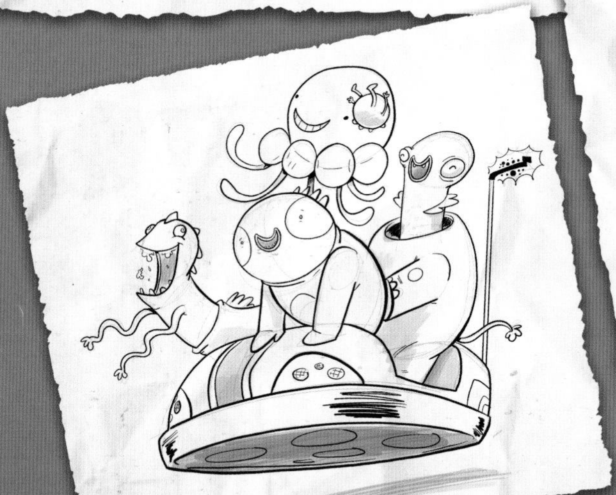

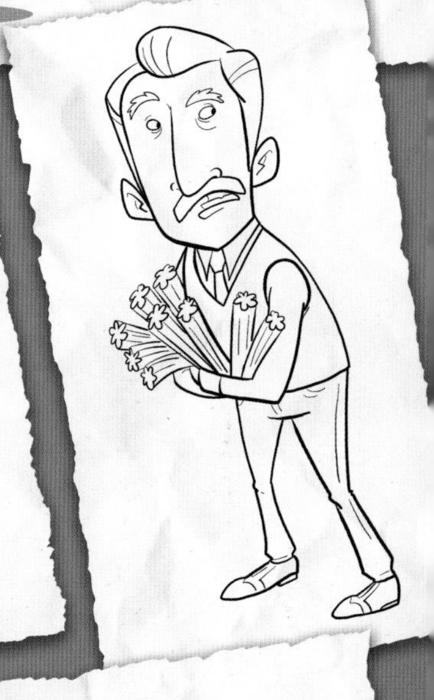

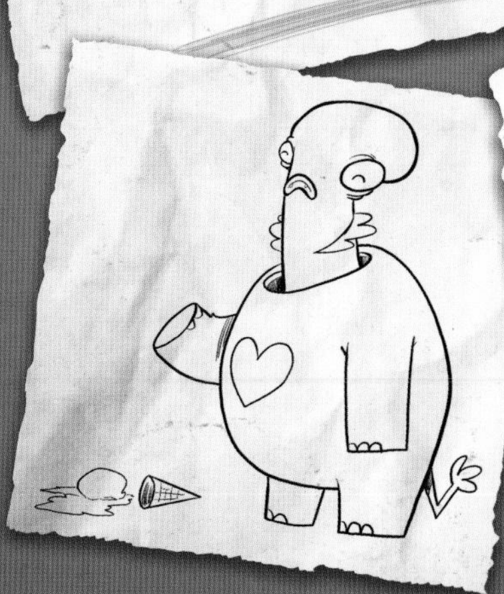

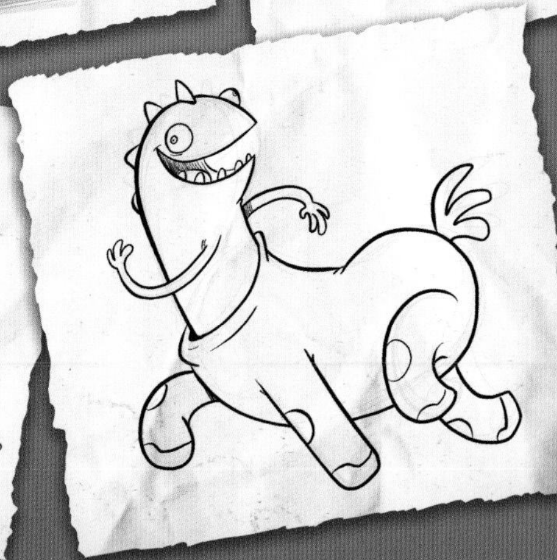

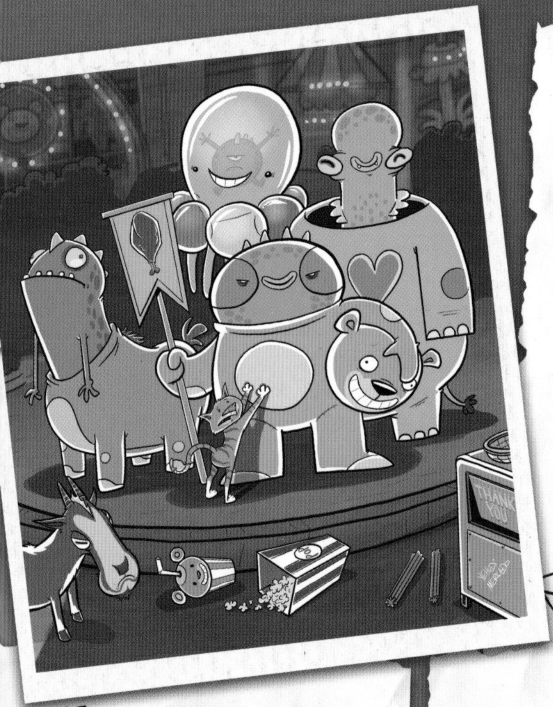
THANK YOU
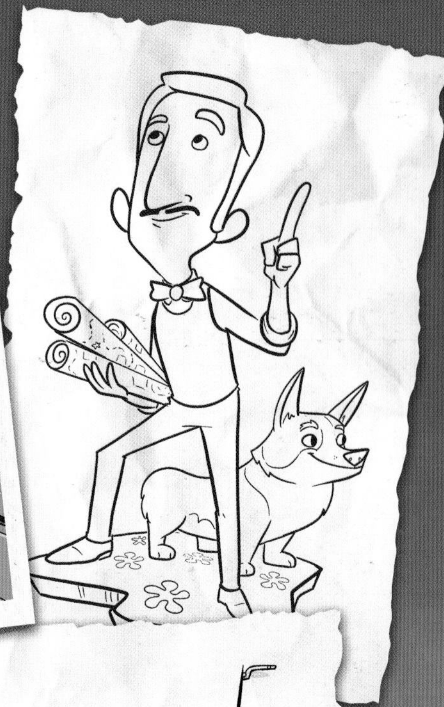
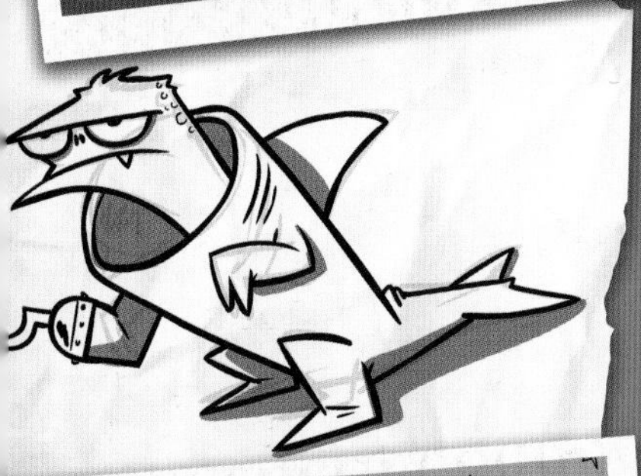
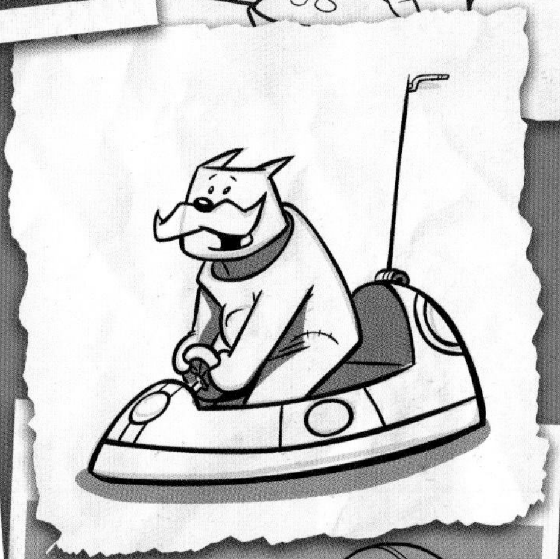
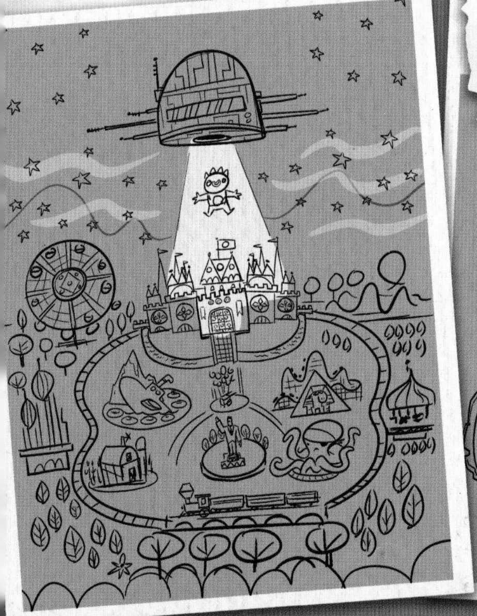
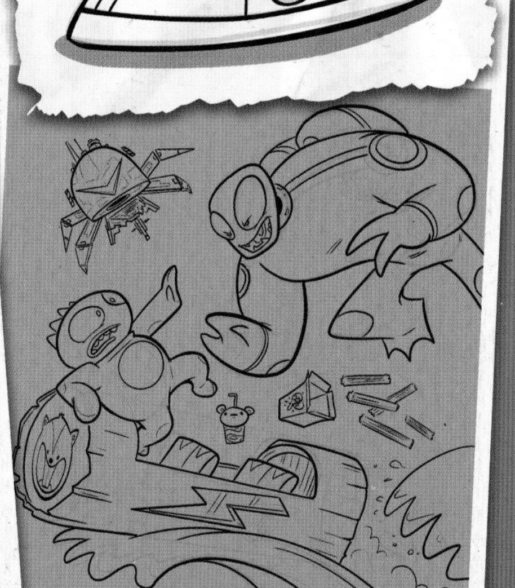

ROUGH PAGES

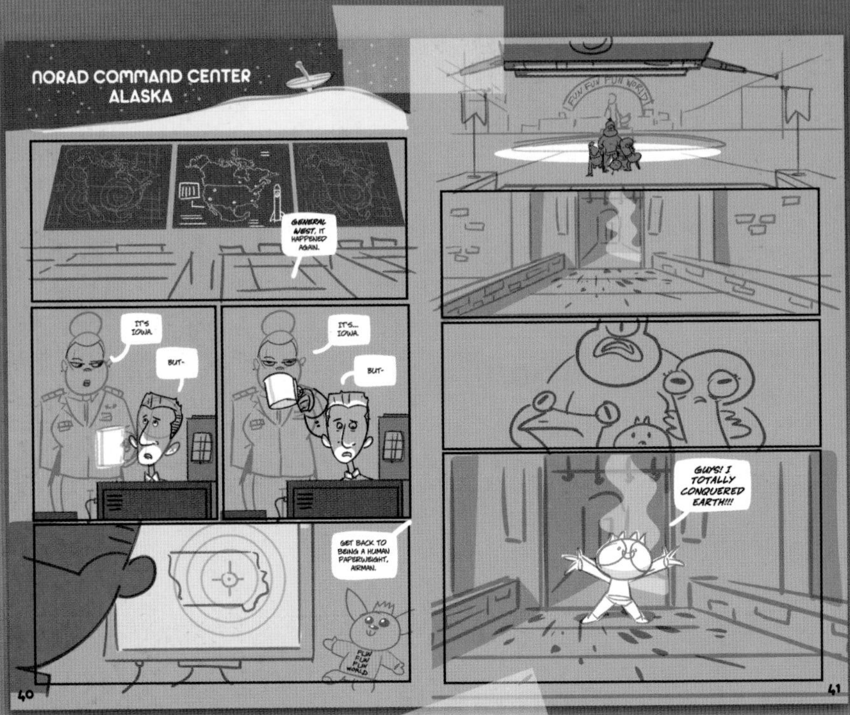
NORAD COMMAND CENTER
ALASKA
GENERAL WEST, IT HAPPENED AGAIN.
IT'S IOWA.
BUT-
IT'S... IOWA.
BUT-
GET BACK TO BEING A HUMAN PAPERWEIGHT, AIRMAN.
FUN FUN FUN WORLD
40
FUN FUN FUN WORLD
GUYS! I TOTALLY CONQUERED EARTH!!!
41

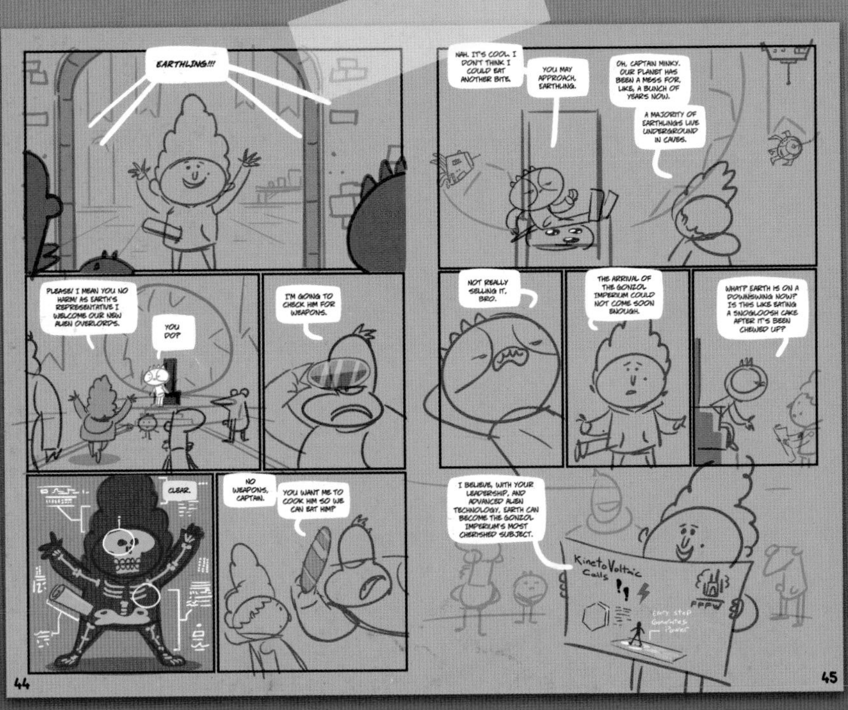
EARTHLING!!!
PLEASE! I MEAN YOU NO HARM! AS EARTH'S REPRESENTATIVE I WELCOME OUR NEW ALIEN OVERLORDS.
YOU DO?
I'M GOING TO CHECK HIM FOR WEAPONS.
CLEAR.
NO WEAPONS, CAPTAIN.
YOU WANT ME TO COOK HIM SO WE CAN EAT HIM?
44
NAH. IT'S COOL. I DON'T THINK I COULD EAT ANOTHER BITE.
YOU MAY APPROACH, EARTHLING.
OH, CAPTAIN MINKY. OUR PLANET HAS BEEN A MESS FOR, LIKE, A BUNCH OF YEARS NOW.
A MAJORITY OF EARTHLINGS LIVE UNDERGROUND IN CAVES.
NOT REALLY SELLING IT, BRO.
THE ARRIVAL OF THE GONZOL IMPERIUM COULD NOT COME SOON ENOUGH.
WHAT? EARTH IS ON A DOWNSWING NOW? IS THIS LIKE EATING A SNOGLOOSH CAKE AFTER IT'S BEEN CHEWED UP?
I BELIEVE, WITH YOUR LEADERSHIP, AND ADVANCED ALIEN TECHNOLOGY, EARTH CAN BECOME THE GONZOL IMPERIUM'S MOST CHERISHED SUBJECT.
KinetoVoltaic Calls
FFFW
45

S.C.R.A.W.L.

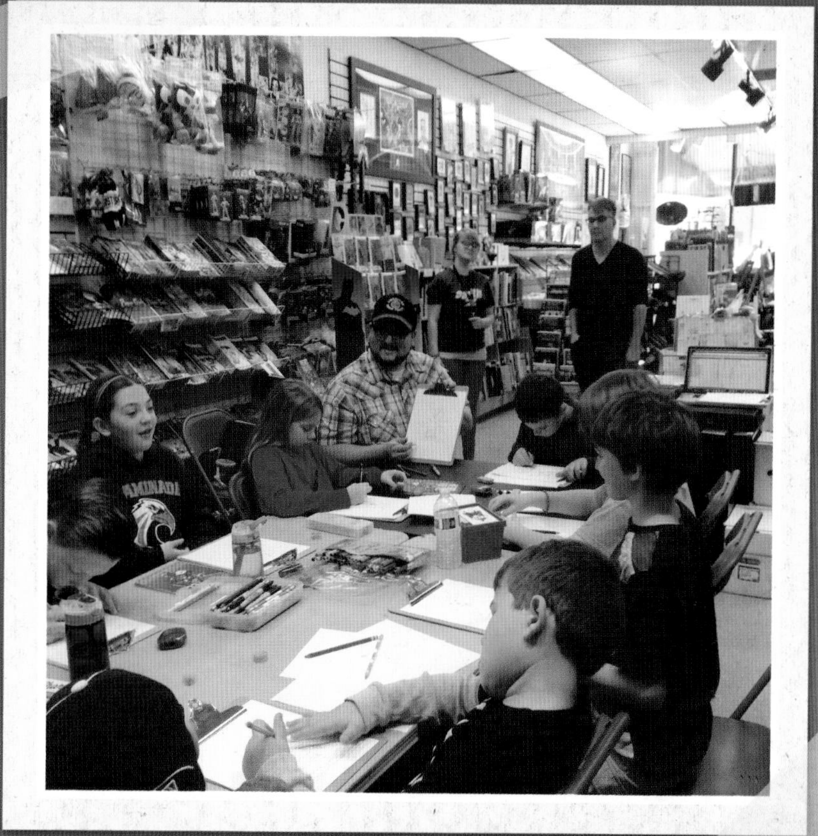

AMINADE

I want to say a special thanks to the kids from the S.C.R.A.W.L. class at EARTH-2 comics in Sherman Oaks. These budding artists helped me brainstorm various rides that appeared in the fictional amusement park in this book. We came up with lots of fun ideas including a Camel Racing Egyptian Pyramid ride called Quick Sand. Thanks, kids! And thanks to Susan Avallone and Carr D'Angelo for continuing to inspire the next generation of comic book artists.

ABOUT THE AUTHOR

Yehudi Mercado is a sci-fi fan and cartoonist living in Los Angeles by way of Austin, TX. His projects include *Buffalo Speedway, Pantalones, TX, Rocket Salvage, Guardians of the Galaxy: The Universal Weapon* (mobile game), *Hero Hotel,* and *Sci-Fu.* He was a storyboard artist on *DC Super Hero Girls.* He is the showrunner for the Hero Hotel narrative podcast for the Pinna Network. The only reason he wants to create cartoons is because he thinks that will get him his own amusement park.

SuperMercado.Pizza